To Susan,
with whom I have shared
the treasure of attachment

About the Author

*J*on G. Allen is senior staff psychologist in the Trauma Recovery Program at The Menninger Clinic, editor of the *Bulletin of the Menninger Clinic,* and a member of the editorial boards of *Psychiatry* and *The Menninger Letter.* Dr. Allen received his B.A. degree in psychology at the University of Connecticut and his Ph.D. degree in clinical psychology at the University of Rochester. He completed postdoctoral training in clinical psychology at The Menninger Clinic, and he teaches and supervises in the Karl Menninger School of Psychiatry and Mental Health Sciences. He conducts psychotherapy, diagnostic psychological testing, consultations, and psychoeducational programs, specializing in trauma-related disorders. He has taught and supervised students at the University of Rochester, Northern Illinois University, the University of Kansas, and Kansas State University, and he is currently adjunct professor of psychology at Washburn University of Topeka. He is the editor, with William H. Smith, Ph.D., of *Diagnosis and Treatment of Dissociative Disorders,* and he is a coauthor of *Borderline Personality Disorder: Tailoring the Therapy to the Patient,* forthcoming from American Psychiatric Press. He serves as a reviewer for several professional journals and book publishers, and he has authored and coauthored numerous professional articles and book chapters on trauma-related problems, psychotherapy, hospital treatment, the therapeutic alliance, psychological testing, neuropsychology, and emotion. In real life, he is a jazz pianist and composer.

Contents

Copyright © 1995 Jon G. Allen
ALL RIGHTS RESERVED
Manufactured in the United States of America on acid-free paper
98 97 96   4 3
First Edition

American Psychiatric Press, Inc.
1400 K Street, N.W., Washington, DC 20005

Library of Congress Cataloging-in-Publication Data
Allen, Jon G.
   Coping with trauma : a guide to self-understanding / by Jon G. Allen. — 1st ed.
     p.   cm.
   Includes bibliographical references and index.
   ISBN 0-88048-720-8
   1. Psychic trauma. 2. Post-traumatic stress disorder—Popular works.
3. Post-traumatic stress disorder—Treatment. I. Title.
   RC552.P67A45 1995
   616.85′21—dc20   95-578
   for Library of Congress   CIP

British Library Cataloguing in Publication Data
A CIP record is available from the British Library.

Coping With Trauma

A Guide to Self-Understanding

Jon G. Allen, Ph.D.

Washington, DC
London, England

Part III: Trauma-Related Psychiatric Disorders

Part IV: Treatment

Preface

At The Menninger Clinic, as elsewhere throughout the country, we have been working with severely traumatized people for many years. Only recently, however, has trauma become a major focus of treatment. The mental health field is in the midst of a sea change. We are now recognizing the shocking prevalence of traumatic experience, and we are fully appreciating the profound role of trauma in psychological problems and psychiatric disorders.

We have scrambled to educate ourselves about trauma and its effects so that we can make accurate diagnoses and provide the best treatment. Our growing knowledge about psychological trauma is beginning to find its way into training programs for professionals entering the field. But we have been slow to educate those who most need it: people who have experienced trauma and must cope with its aftermath.

My interest in trauma, coupled with more than two decades of experience in teaching psychology, led me to develop an educational program at The Menninger Clinic. The participants are patients who have been severely traumatized and who are having serious psychiatric problems as a result. In all my years of teaching psychology, this has been my most challenging and most rewarding experience. I have taught, and I have been taught. I share what I know, and I invite patients to educate me in turn. They have graciously and eagerly done so. In the course of countless lively—and sometimes painful—discussions, I have learned a lot about how to teach and what to teach. I've put what I have learned into this book.

If you're reading this, I'm assuming that your life has been significantly affected by trauma. If you're struggling to cope with trauma, consider this book a psychology course in what troubles you. I wrote it to help you—and those around you—better understand the problems you are having in relation to the trauma you have experienced. If you are already in treatment or are considering treatment, I hope this book will make you a better-informed consumer. If you have not been traumatized directly but are close to someone who has, I hope it will help you be a more supportive partner. If you are a professional helping people to cope with trauma, I hope you'll find it a useful digest of current knowledge and that you'll think it worthy of your patients' attention.

You don't need a background in psychology to understand this book. You will be able to grasp it on the basis of your life experience. But it is not light reading. It is not a watered-down account. If easy answers and quick solutions helped, you would not be examining this thick book. You may have been advised to "stop thinking about it" or to "put the past behind you." Of course you've tried to do that. It's like advocating, "Just say 'No' to posttraumatic stress disorder!" This book will help you understand why that's so difficult to do.

I have written this book to provide a comprehensive summary of current professional knowledge about trauma written in plain language. Just skimming the table of contents will give you a sense of the complex effects of trauma. The patients I've taught have been inquisitive and eager to learn everything there is to know, so I've tried to pack in everything significant we've discussed. The chapters are clearly organized so that you can pick and choose according to your needs and interests. Later chapters build on earlier chapters, so you'll do best to go in sequence, skipping as you wish.

To understand this material, you'll need to muster a lot of concentration, and you'll be invited to grapple with some new ideas and some unfamiliar ways of thinking. Intellectual curiosity will be a big help, and I've done my best to evoke it. The effort is justified—the subject is yourself.

The Plan of This Book

Part I provides the basic foundation for the rest of the book, beginning with Chapter 1, which describes the broad spectrum of trauma. Chapter 2 encourages you to adopt a developmental perspective and to think about how trauma may affect the course of your life. I attempt to impress upon you that trauma may affect not only your psychological and social development but also your physiological functioning. For persons who have been traumatized, appreciating the effects of trauma on the nervous system is crucial to self-understanding and self-acceptance. Recognizing that not all readers are equally keen on biology, I make the more general points in Chapter 2 and provide a more technical account in the Appendix.

Part II systematically lays out the far-reaching effects of traumatic experience. You will see that trauma can have an impact on the whole personality. Chapter 3 presents the theory I consider most helpful for understanding trauma: attachment theory. Attachments provide safety, and trauma undermines attachments. Emotional distress is the most obvious consequence of trauma, and Chapter 4 covers the gamut of emotional reactions: fear, anger, shame, and depression. Some persons who cannot escape traumatic situations are able to cope with overwhelming emotions by altering their state of consciousness. Chapter 5 describes the mechanism of "dissociation" by which some individuals are able to take mental flight when physical flight is impossible. Traumatic events are bad enough, but it is often traumatic *memories* that cause the enduring effects. Chapter 6 describes different kinds of traumatic memories and tackles thorny problems about the accuracy of memories of childhood trauma. Much of the psychological injury associated with trauma takes the form of damage to self-esteem and identity. The need for self-understanding and self-acceptance is reiterated throughout this book, and Chapter 7 is devoted entirely to that concern. Trauma often takes place in relationships, and it always has an impact on relationships. Chapter 8 picks up the theme of disrupted attachments addressed in Chapter 3 and focuses on problematic relationship patterns in adulthood that are often associated with trauma. Throughout these chapters, I have included brief illustrative case examples. For the sake of confidentiality, I have altered and disguised many incidental details in these.

After you've finished Parts I and II, you'll have no difficulty appreciating how traumatic experience can seriously hamper a person's ability to handle the demands of daily life. At worst, trauma can lead to psychiatric disorders. Part III describes the psychiatric disorders that are most often associated with traumatic experience. Chapter 9 is devoted to posttraumatic stress disorder (PTSD), the psychiatric disorder most specific to trauma. The main feature of posttraumatic stress disorder is anxiety—no surprise there. But we are frequently encountering another class of psychiatric disorder in conjunction with trauma—dissociative disorders. With the background of Chapter 5 on consciousness, Chapter 10 describes common dissociative disturbances such as amnesia, depersonalization, and multiple personality disorder (now called dissociative identity disorder). Several other psychiatric disorders are not specific to trauma but often occur in conjunction with posttraumatic stress disorder and dissociative disorders. Chapter 11 examines the role of trauma in anxiety, depression, substance abuse, somatization, sexual dysfunctions, eating disorders, and personality disorders.

But you are not reading this book just to find out all about the potentially harmful effects of trauma. You want to know what to do about them. You may not want to wait until the end of the book to get to the bottom line. At the price of some redundancy, I address some treatment issues in a preliminary way throughout Part II on the effects of trauma. There are many aspects of treatment that are somewhat specific to problems with attachment, emotions, consciousness, memories, self-concept, and interpersonal relationships. With this head start, Chapter 12 in Part IV systematically reviews several major treatment modalities: individual psychotherapy, cognitive-behavioral therapy, group psychotherapy, family therapy, medication, and hospital treatment. Consider it consumer education. Of course, these various forms of treatment are not specific to trauma-related disorders; they are the mainstays of mental health services. But I concentrate on the specific applications of these treatments to trauma. Not everyone struggling with trauma needs professional treatment, but everyone can benefit from techniques of self-regulation. Chapter 13 describes several such techniques. Some require professional intervention; others do not. These self-regulation techniques include exercise, relaxation, imagery, meditation, hypnosis, and biofeedback. I am convinced that anyone who is trying to control reactions to trauma should be employing one or more of these, or something similar. But there are pitfalls in using these techniques when you've been traumatized, and you need to be forewarned about them. The obstacles are well worth overcoming.

Chapter 14 draws together the main conclusions of the book, summarizing key points from earlier chapters. If you want to see where you are going, feel free to read it first.

Acknowledgments

In this short space, I can only provide a glimpse of the enormous amount of help I have received in the course of writing this book. The greatest advantage of working at The Menninger Clinic is the availability of an abundance of expertise and helpfulness. I have been exceptionally fortunate to have had the opportunity to work closely for several years with a group of talented colleagues interested in trauma: Bonnie Buchele, Ph.D., Alice Brand Bartlett, M.L.S., David Console, M.D., Michael Keller, M.S.W., Enrique Morales, M.D., and Bill Smith, Ph.D. They have taught me a great deal and have assisted me with this manuscript. Kay Kelly, M.S.W., and Susan Bach, R.N., have helped me apply this material to trauma-related problems in daily living in a course we teach for day-hospital patients. This book may never have come to pass if James Buskirk, M.D., who led our trauma unit at its inception, had not encouraged me to adapt my interest in teaching to patient education.

I have also relied on the expertise of several other colleagues who have reviewed and commented on various chapters: David Beale, M.D., B. D. Ehler, B.S., R.Ph., Charles Fantz, Ph.D., Glen Gabbard, M.D., Jennifer Kennedy, M.D., Mary Jo Peebles-Kleiger, Ph.D., Eric Kulick, M.D., Cathy Mazzotta, M.S.W., Linda Sebastian, M.N., Ellen Smith, M.S.W., Helen Stein, Ph.D., and Linda Wiley, Ph.D. David Console, M.D., provided invaluable consultation throughout regarding the material on physiology and medical matters, and Steven Katz, M.D., also assisted with the material on psychopharmacology. Patricia Norris, Ph.D., lent much of her expertise and wisdom to the chapter on self-regulation. Paul MacLean, M.D., graciously agreed to review my account of his work on the triune brain and offered sage editorial advice. Kathryn Zerbe, M.D., reviewed parts of the manuscript and forged a path with her fine book, *The Body Betrayed,* which I have been fortunate to have as a model. I am also grateful to Peter Novotny, M.D., and David Nichol, M.D., for introducing me to meditation practice and steering me to the best literature.

The book has also benefited substantially from the careful editorial review process conducted by American Psychiatric Press. I regret that I cannot personally thank those who anonymously reviewed the initial proposal and the final manuscript; they played a critical part in shaping the book and in helping me to refine it. American Psychiatric Press has also been a leader in publishing professional literature on trauma, and I have made extensive use of it.

I have also made use of much institutional support at The Menninger Clinic. The trauma field is blessed with many outstanding thinkers and clinicians, and the staff of the professional library has been unflaggingly helpful in making the literature accessible. I hope my great appreciation for the contributions of others in the field is amply reflected in the references.

Perhaps no one appreciates the need for editorial assistance more than an editor. My editorial colleagues at the *Bulletin of the Menninger Clinic* have freely loaned me their expertise and their time. Mary Ann Clifft, Director of Scientific Publications, did everything from nurturing my initial interest in the project to copy editing the whole manuscript. Philip Beard took on the monumental task of checking references and quotes. Eleanor Bell reviewed parts of the manuscript and offered helpful suggestions. Melba Ludvicek has helped with numerous secretarial tasks and her inimitable style of support. Thanks to Faye Schoenfeld's extensive knowledge and skill, readers will be quickly guided to specific topics by the comprehensive index. I did the typing, so I take the credit for any errors that remain.

In prefaces to countless books, I have read authors' acknowledgments of their families that can be boiled down to "Thank you for putting up with me while I was writing this book." Now I know what all those authors had in mind! I could not have done this without my family's forbearance and support. I have also had help from my extended family; I am grateful to the Reverend Anne C. Fowler, Ph.D., for reading the whole manuscript and for offering forthright criticism and a keen editorial eye—as well as much warm encouragement.

As much as I have relied on colleagues, patients have been my main teachers. I hope that, through this book, others may be the beneficiaries of their uncommon trust, openness, and courage.

PART I

Foundations

CHAPTER ONE

Trauma

W hy read about trauma? Avoidance is such a common reaction that it's a defining feature of posttraumatic stress disorder. If you've been traumatized, you're likely to steer clear of anything that reminds you of the traumatic event. Thinking about traumatic experience stirs up painful emotions. Avoidance is utterly natural, but it can keep you stuck. Blotting the traumatic experience out of your mind can prevent you from coming to terms with it. To cope with trauma and to get past it, you need to think about it. If you've been traumatized, congratulate yourself for reading this. You're not avoiding; you're coping.

Many individuals who struggle with a traumatic background are extremely frustrated with themselves. They are highly self-critical, adding insult to their injuries. They fail to take account of the serious impact of their traumatic experience, and they do not make sufficient allowance for the limitations of their all-too-human nature. Many feel that they are "crazy."

The thesis of this book is that, rather than being crazy, *persons who have been traumatized are responding in ways that are natural and understandable, given their previous experience.*

The main purpose of this book is to foster self-understanding. Greater self-understanding should help you feel less "crazy." But I have an even more ambitious agenda. I want to encourage self-*acceptance*. Ideally, by better understanding and appreciating your efforts to cope with trauma, you may develop greater compassion for yourself. As we think of self-understanding, perhaps we should start thinking of "self-compassion." Sadly, many persons who have been severely traumatized find the idea of self-compassion incomprehensible.

Trauma Happens   ◆ ◆ ◆ ◆ ◆ ◆ ◆ ◆ ◆ ◆

We often use the word *traumatic* somewhat loosely to refer to highly stressful events—losing a job or getting a divorce. In this book, I use *trauma* in its narrower sense to refer to *extreme stress*, recognizing that there is no clear dividing line between "stress" and "trauma." *Webster's New Twentieth Century Dictionary*[1] defines trauma as "an injury or wound violently produced" and as "an emotional experience, or shock, which has a lasting psychic effect." Think of physical trauma. Some specialized emergency rooms are now called "Trauma Centers." The psychological counterpart to physical trauma is a violently inflicted *psychological* wound with a lasting effect. For purposes of psychiatric diagnosis, traumatic events are defined specifically as including both of the following: "the person experienced, witnessed, or was confronted with an event or events that involved actual or threatened death or serious injury, or a threat to the physical integrity of self or others; [and] the person's response involved intense fear, helplessness, or horror."[2]

What are the lasting effects of trauma? The traumatic event has ended, but the reaction has not. The *intrusion of the past into the present* is one of the main problems confronting persons who have developed psychological symptoms and psychiatric disorders as a consequence of traumatic experience. Those who have been traumatized may be plagued by distressing memories, flashbacks, and nightmares; they may continue to struggle with the powerful emotions they experienced at the time of the trauma; and they are likely to continue using the same self-protective means that they initially learned so as to shield themselves from the traumatic experience. Coping entails separating the past from the present and gaining control over both the painful emotions and the self-protective defenses erected against them.

Trauma happens. It's ubiquitous. In one recent study, nearly 40% of the persons surveyed had been exposed to trauma.[3] Another survey focusing specifically on women revealed that 69% had been exposed to trauma.[4] And it seems to be getting worse. Just turn on the news. Not long ago, in our formerly sedate town of Topeka, Kansas, a 12-year-old girl was passing through on vacation with her family. While she was sleeping in her motel room in the middle of the night, she was shot in the head by a stray bullet from a fracas across the street. She survived, less one eye and some of her cerebral cortex. That's trauma, physical and psychological. It's just part of the day's fare, along with wars, floods, tornadoes, earthquakes, fires, car crashes, plane crashes, train wrecks, rapes, kidnappings, assaults, and murders. In a half-hour of news you see a tiny fraction of the day's trauma. And that's just the fraction that's *reported*. The day's news excludes all of the trauma that takes place in private, behind closed doors, kept secret. The scope of this domestic violence and child abuse is now coming out into the open.

Trauma comes in many forms. There are also vast differences among individuals who undergo trauma. "Coping with trauma" is an ambitious subject for a single volume. But considering all forms of trauma together is justified, because there are striking similarities in patterns of response that cut across different types of trauma and different individuals. There are many forms of trauma but only one "posttraumatic stress disorder." Nevertheless, the challenges of coping with trauma vary substantially, depending on the nature of the trauma.

Types of Trauma   ◆ ◆ ◆ ◆ ◆ ◆ ◆ ◆ ◆

Single-Blow Versus Repeated Trauma

On the basis of her extensive studies of traumatic experience in children, Lenore Terr[5] distinguishes "single blow" traumas from repeated traumas. Single shocking events may produce traumatic reactions in some individuals. Natural disasters are an example. These include earthquakes, tornadoes, avalanches, fires, floods, hurricanes, and volcanic eruptions. The severity of symptoms that people report after disasters varies widely from one study to the next.[6] Depending on the scope of the destruction and the degree of threat to life and limb, anywhere from a small minority to a large majority of persons exposed to such disasters may have traumatic reactions.[7]

Closely related to natural disasters are technological disasters, such as dam breaks, building collapses, plane crashes, chemical spills, and nuclear reactor failures. But there is an important difference between natural and technological disasters: The community pulls together around natural disasters; people help and support each other. Technological disasters, on the other hand, tend to be more socially divisive, because much attention is diverted to finding fault and fixing blame.[8]

Criminal violence also involves single-blow trauma, such as burglary, robbery, aggravated assault, rape, and homicide. Violent crimes not only have a direct impact on victims but also have an indirect—and frequently traumatic—effect on those who witness them and on those whose loved ones are injured or killed. But there is a gray area here between single-blow and repeated trauma. A substantial majority of victimized women have been exposed to more than one crime.[9] Unfortunately, the traumatic effects can be cumulative.

As traumatic as the single-blow events may be, the traumatic experiences that result in the most serious psychiatric disorders are prolonged and repeated, sometimes extending over many years. Combat entails multiple traumatic events over many months. Being a prisoner of war, a political prisoner, or a concentration camp inmate all involve continual trauma over months and years. Sexual, physical, and emotional abuse in the family may span the whole of childhood development.

Natural Versus Man-Made Trauma

Prolonged stressors are typically man-made. Stressors deliberately inflicted by our fellow men and women are far harder to bear than those attributable to nature or accidents. Many people seeking psychiatric help for traumatic experiences have suffered "violently inflicted wounds" dealt by a *person*. Psychologist Denise Gelinas[10] highlights the distinction between "facticity" and "agency" as causes of trauma:

When someone falls and breaks a leg, that is facticity; if someone intentionally breaks another person's leg, that is agency. Accidents partake of facticity.
But when somebody *does* something, that is usually agency. Intent and action
by another person characterize agency. When considering something like
trauma, facticity versus agency can make a great deal of difference. It is one
thing to have a leg broken, or an eye put out in an auto accident; it is a very
different thing to have someone intentionally break one's leg or put out one's
eye. That injury didn't just happen, it was *done.*[11]

Agency and deliberation add to the experience of trauma; so does an ongoing relationship with the agent who inflicts the trauma. The most pernicious trauma is deliberately inflicted in a relationship where the
traumatized individual is dependent—at worst, in a parent-child relationship. Moreover, as Gelinas points out, the most extreme trauma entails an
attitude of "malevolent intent" on the part of the perpetrator.

Varieties of Man-Made Trauma

The range of man-made trauma varies as widely as the range of violence.
Dividing it all up into discrete categories is arbitrary; there is much overlap. Thinking about the scope and prevalence of violence is not hearten-
ing. No one reading this book needs to be convinced of the significance of
trauma, so I'll keep this survey brief.

War and Political Violence

Much trauma occurs on a massive scale in wars, and much of our understanding of traumatic reactions has come from those who have survived
prolonged combat experience. War-related trauma is severe, repeated,
and prolonged. Intrinsic to combat is risk of death and injury. Many soldiers in Vietnam were involved in hundreds of firefights. For many, there
was little respite; guerrilla warfare meant continually being on guard for
unpredictable attacks. But the traumatic experiences in war are not only
repeated; they are multiple. While your own life is at stake, you are liable
to witness violence, death, and mayhem on a large scale. You may suffer
repeated losses. You live with many privations, far from home.

    The trauma of war comes not only from being the passive victim of violence. Being an active participant is also traumatic. Not only the danger of being injured or killed is traumatic, but so, too, is the injuring and killing. Participating in war and becoming a "killer" do violence to one's identity.[12]

War is not the only culturally sanctioned source of trauma. We are in the midst of a worldwide epidemic of human rights abuses. Politically inspired violence includes kidnappings, disappearances, indiscriminate maiming and killing, political imprisonment, brutal interrogation, and torture.[13] Many victims who survive are forced into exile, piling trauma on top of trauma. While we are opening our eyes to domestic violence and childhood trauma, we remain largely blind to pandemic human rights violations.[14]

Criminal Violence

Being a victim of violence is not a rare event. A recent survey revealed that 11.1% of the population studied had experienced physical or aggravated assault.[15] Moreover, 9.3% to 14.3% reported the loss of family members and friends as a result of criminal and vehicular homicide. Many persons had been the victims of more than one crime. Another survey of over 10,000 persons revealed that 3.7% had been involved in some form of violence in the previous year.[16]

Rape

Rape victims are probably the largest group of people with posttraumatic stress disorder in this country.[17] A national survey of more than 4,000 women found that 1 in 8 reported having been the victim of forcible rape.[18] Nearly half of these women had been raped more than once. Nearly one-third were less than 11 years old at the time of the rape, and more than 60% were less than 18 years old. Fewer than one-quarter were raped by strangers. Eighty-four percent of the rapes were *not* reported to the police. And these are not the highest figures. Kilpatrick and Resnick[19] reported that 23.3% of the women they surveyed had experienced completed rape, and 13.1% had experienced attempted rape. Of women with posttraumatic stress disorder, nearly half had a history of rape. Diana Russell[20] underscored incest victims' heightened vulnerability to rape; 68% of women with a history of incest had been subjected to rape or attempted rape, compared with 38% of women without such a history. As alarming as these statistics are, they undoubtedly underestimate the prevalence of rape, because rape is notoriously underdetected.[21]

Domestic Violence

Surveying a vast literature on trauma, psychologist Deborah Rose[22] recently concluded: "The home, thought of in our culture as a refuge, is actually the most dangerous place to be." Recent surveys have shown that between 21% and 34% of women will be assaulted by an intimate male partner.[23] Such assaults may be physical, sexual, or both. We are becoming increasingly aware of "date rape" and "acquaintance rape." But Rose found that marital rape is reported to occur in 3% to 14% of marriages. She also found that 20% to 30% of adults approved of hitting a spouse. Violence in marriages has its precursors: Sibling violence takes place in 80% of homes each year. The prevalence of violence in dating relationships ranges from 22% to 67%. Here's Senator Joseph Biden's perspective:

> Every day, every hour, indeed every minute, a woman in the United States suffers the pain and violence of a physical attack. Every 6 minutes, a woman is raped . . . domestic violence is the leading cause of injuries to women aged 15–44. . . . Spouse abuse is more common than automobile accidents, muggings, and cancer deaths combined . . . .
>
> We have learned that family violence is far from a trivial push or shove: One-third of all such incidents, if reported, would be classified as felony rape, robbery, or aggravated assault; the remaining two-thirds involve bodily injury at least as serious as the injury inflicted in 90% of all robberies and aggravated assaults . . . one-third of all female homicide victims died at the hands of a husband or boyfriend.[24]

Child Abuse

Over a decade ago, Karl Menninger wrote:

> A great deal remains unknown about ideal parenting, although there have been millions of experiments and prescriptions. Some parents learn their task, some never do, and often by the time some find wisdom, their children are no longer children. We know that there are some terrifyingly wrong parental behaviors. Children are beaten, burned, slapped, whipped, thrown about, kicked, and raped daily. Children have been objects of discipline and

punishment and senseless cruelty for centuries, since civilization began. Is there any form of physical abuse that they have not been subjected to?

Worse yet, children are abandoned and neglected and mistaught, lied to, and misinformed. The more we investigate the details of family life in recent centuries of 'civilization'—and even in previous centuries and other cultures—the more we find that child abuse, which is thought of as a modern evil, has been prevalent for eons and eons in older European cultures. Child abuse is a long-standing stain on the record of the human race. Children are weak and small, parents are strong and big; parents can get their way by sheer force, proving (to the child) that 'might makes right.'

No one actually knows or can even imagine how much children are made to suffer by parents who—at least at times—are heartless, sadistic, brutal, or filled with vengeance nursed since their own childhood days![25]

The scope of childhood trauma is staggering. According to recent surveys, "a conservative estimate of children at risk for PTSD [posttraumatic stress disorder] exceeds 15 million." [26]

Sexual Abuse of Children

Little wonder that sexual abuse has garnered so much attention: There are over "250,000+ new cases of sexual abuse that come to light each year in this country" and "at least 40% of all psychiatric inpatients have histories of sexual abuse in childhood." [27] Over a decade ago, Judith Herman[28] summarized research suggesting that between one-fifth and one-third of women had had some sexual encounter in childhood with an adult male. Four percent to 12% of these encounters were with relatives; 1% were with fathers or stepfathers. Diana Russell[29] found that 16% of women she surveyed reported at least one experience of incestuous abuse, and 31% reported at least one experience of sexual abuse by a nonrelative before 18 years of age. Psychologist David Finkelhor recently conducted a large-scale national survey that confirmed these earlier findings.[30] Twenty-seven percent of women reported a history of childhood sexual abuse, and 13% had experienced actual or attempted intercourse as children. Although the majority of abused women had experienced only one-time events, 11% of those abused had undergone the abuse for more than a year. Abuse occurred most often in the context of an unhappy family life, in homes without both natural parents, and in situations in which there had been inadequate sex education.

Herman[31] reported that the vast majority of victims of sexual abuse are females, and that the vast majority of offenders are males. A decade ago, Finkelhor[32] estimated the prevalence of sexual abuse of boys before puberty to be in the range of 2.5% to 5%. When boys 13 to 16 years of age were included, the figure rose to 8.7%. In Finkelhor's more recent national survey,[33] 16% of men reported having experienced childhood sexual abuse. Like girls, boys are most often sexually abused by men. Finkelhor's studies showed that 14% to 17% of boys and 1% to 6% of girls who were abused were abused by women.

We are witnessing a skyrocketing increase in reports of sexual abuse of children. Is this a new epidemic? Is sexual abuse now occurring more frequently, or are we just becoming more aware of it? A group of researchers recently scoured the literature to compare data from Kinsey's[34] survey in the 1940s with comparable data from more recent surveys.[35] These authors concluded that the prevalence of sexual abuse (of females less than 14 years old) has *not* increased in the past four decades. Rather, abuse is now reported more often.

Among the various forms of trauma, sexual abuse is now in the spotlight, and we must be careful about making generalizations. Sexual abuse, like other sexual behavior, takes an infinite variety of forms. And sexual abuse does not occur in a vacuum; it is often coupled with other forms of stress and trauma—much of it in the family.[36] Because of the variety of forms and contexts of sexual abuse, its effects are extremely variable.

There is no question that sexual abuse significantly increases the *risk* of having psychological problems and psychiatric symptoms. But adverse effects are not inevitable. Reviews of research suggest that about a third of sexually abused children have no symptoms, and a large proportion of those who do show disturbance recover from it—although a minority get worse.[37] In addition, less than one-fifth of adults who were sexually abused as children show serious psychological disturbance.[38] Of course, more disturbance is associated with more severe abuse—occurring over a longer duration; involving force, penetration, helplessness, or fear of injury or death; perpetrated by a close relative or caregiver; and coupled with a lack of support or followed by negative consequences arising from disclosure.[39]

Child Physical Abuse and Other Violence

Attention to sexual abuse is long overdue, and much of this book is devoted to the effects of such abuse. But the consequences of sexual abuse should not overshadow those of other forms of traumatic childhood experience. Family violence takes many forms and has profound consequences. Included are physical abuse (beatings, threats of violence, harsh discipline, severe deprivations) and verbal abuse (threats and criticism). One recent survey found that 10% of children are subjected to severe (abusive) violence by caregivers.[40] Physical abuse takes a heavy toll, with potential adult consequences including violence toward others, physical abuse of one's own children, substance abuse, self-injurious and suicidal behavior, and a wide range of emotional problems.[41]

Witnessing violence, even if you are not directly involved in it, can also be extremely traumatic. Seeing anyone being beaten is extremely stressful. The greater your attachment to the victim of violence, the more extreme the stress is likely to be. Commonly, in situations of family violence, siblings observe each other being terrorized and injured. Especially terrifying is violence directed against a caregiver, such as a father's violence toward a mother. In such cases, the distress of witnessing violence is compounded by the threat of losing a primary source of security. Tragically, many children in this country witness the homicide of a parent, with profoundly traumatic results.[42]

In the context of sexual or physical abuse, the significance of verbal abuse can be minimized; yet verbal abuse can be profoundly damaging to self-esteem and relationships. Just imagine the effects of your mother screaming, "I wish you had never been born!" or "I wish you were dead!" And imagine hearing it hundreds of times over many years. Of course, many individuals are subjected to multiple forms of abuse (physical, verbal, sexual) and by many persons (parents, siblings, other relatives, neighbors).

Sadistic Abuse

Most of us tend to think of man-made trauma as stemming from the eruption of passions—violent rages, greed, or lust. But the severest forms of trauma can be inflicted deliberately. Calculated cruelty can be far more terrifying than impulsive violence. Judith Herman[43] has delineated key ingredients of coercive control that can be observed in such diverse contexts as concentration camps, prostitution and pornography rings, and families. Several tactics are used to break down initiative and autonomy: violence and threats of violence, control of body functions, capricious enforcement of petty rules, and intermittent rewards. These tactics are undergirded by isolation of the victim from other sources of social support. The final steps in breaking the spirit are various degradations and forced participation in atrocities.

We are witnessing a great deal of social furor and controversy over "cult," "ritual," and "satanic" abuse.[44] Jean Goodwin[45] has put it all in proper perspective: What may seem new is historically ancient. The Marquis de Sade tried to turn sadism into an art. Hitler turned sadism into genocide. Sadism can be practiced by individuals or groups. As Goodwin states, the current focus on "satanic" cults is misleading insofar as the settings for sadism are diverse, including religious, sexual, political, criminal, and family contexts. There is ample reason for concern about *all* forms of sadistic abuse, regardless of context.

Severity of Trauma   ◆ ◆ ◆ ◆ ◆ ◆ ◆ ◆ ◆

One of the best-documented research findings in the field of trauma is that of a *dose-response* relationship.[46] Think of alcohol: The more you drink, the more intoxicated you become. So it is with stress: The higher the "dose" of trauma, the more potentially damaging its effects. The greater the stressor, the more the likelihood of developing posttraumatic stress disorder. The closer you are to the site of the volcano's eruption—the closer you are to the sniper, the more you are affected. A group of researchers[47] clearly demonstrated the dose-response relationship in a well-controlled study of posttraumatic stress disorder in Vietnam veterans. They controlled for genetic makeup and early experience by studying identical twins who were exposed to different levels of combat. All else being equal, the more combat exposure, the higher the risk of posttraumatic stress symptoms.

It is not just the sheer amount of trauma that contributes to the severity of effects. The type and context of the trauma are also extremely important factors. In summary, the effects are likely to be most severe if the trauma is man-made, repeated, unpredictable, multifaceted, inflicted with sadistic or malevolent intent, undergone in childhood, and perpetrated by a caregiver.

The Eye of the Beholder ◆ ◆ ◆ ◆ ◆ ◆ ◆ ◆

There are two components to traumatic experience: objective and subjective.[48] Objectively, traumatic events pose a threat of death or serious injury to oneself or others. These threats are usually, but not always, external. Discovering that you have a serious disease also can be traumatic. When we talk about trauma, we usually focus on the objective events—the tornado, combat, rape, or beatings. But it is *the subjective experience of the objective events that constitutes the trauma.*

Much psychological trauma entails direct bodily harm, but much does not. Regardless, there is a psychological wound. The objective event is subjectively interpreted. One person may appraise a situation as being far worse than it appears to another person. The more you believe you are endangered, the more traumatized you will be. Objectivity and subjectivity do not always match. Research with burn patients showed that the extent of emotional distress, not the severity of the burn, determined the posttraumatic symptoms.[49] You can be traumatized by someone with a fake gun. Psychologically, the bottom line of trauma is overwhelming emotion and a feeling of utter helplessness. There may or may not be bodily injury, but psychological trauma is coupled with physiological upheaval that plays a leading role in the long-range effects.

Allowing for subjectivity, there is room for interpretation, and you can mislead yourself. You could exaggerate the seriousness of a situation and suffer unnecessarily. But I think many persons suffer unnecessarily from *minimizing* the seriousness of what they have undergone. Often I have heard, "What happened to me isn't really that bad, because something much worse happened to someone else I know." No matter how bad it was, it could always have been worse.

For example, some individuals clearly remember having been terrorized by their father's rages. They have been harangued and beaten. They have feared for their lives. But they don't remember being sexually abused. They assume that sexual abuse must have occurred also, but they can't remember it. Sexual abuse becomes the "smoking gun" they need to account for their trauma-related symptoms. Sexual abuse may have occurred and been blocked from memory. But maybe not. Being terrorized and beaten is enough. No trauma theory holds that sexual abuse is the only kind of trauma that counts.

Many individuals who have been abused, mistreated, or severely neglected throughout childhood have no yardstick for what is normal. Many were socially isolated. They had no reasonable standard by which to judge their experience. They may have lived in a world of family violence, having minimal contact with nonviolent families. They may have assumed that most other children were also subjected to such violent and chaotic experiences. They think that there is no reason for their symptoms, even when they have undergone what to others is obviously years of terrifying experiences. They discount the significance of clearly remembered traumatic experience. Having no explanation for their problems, they feel "crazy." For such persons, an important part of coping with a history of childhood abuse is learning what is reasonable, normal, and tolerable in relationships.

Not All Symptoms Come From Trauma   ◆ ◆ ◆ ◆

Just as it may be harmful to minimize clearly remembered traumatic experience, it can be harmful to assume without evidence that traumatic experience is the cause of various problems and psychiatric symptoms. Some of the popular books on incest, for example, can be misleading if the reader infers, "I also have these problems, so I must have been sexually abused, even if I can't remember it." Even worse, "If I can't remember it, that just *proves* that I was abused." By this logic, *anyone* who has problems or symptoms has been abused.

You'll see in this book that a wide range of symptoms may be associated with traumatic experience—anxiety and depression, for example. But if you are anxious or depressed, does that mean that you have been abused? Of course not; these are simply the most common psychiatric symptoms in the general population. Medical conditions, heredity, early losses, developmental factors, psychological conflicts, and interpersonal stresses can all contribute to anxiety and depression. Several of these factors can be combined in the etiology (causation) of anxiety and depression. Traumatic experience may or may not be a factor. Keep this basic principle in mind: *The cause cannot be inferred from the symptom.*

Not All Trauma Leads to Symptoms ◆ ◆ ◆ ◆ ◆ ◆

No one comes through trauma unscathed. By definition, trauma is over-whelming and psychologically injurious. But for many forms of trauma, recovery without ill effects is the rule. Posttraumatic stress disorder—or any other psychiatric symptom or disorder—is by no means inevitable. Emphasizing the role of subjective perception, psychiatrist John March noted that "even under horrendous circumstances, most individuals do not develop PTSD." [50] Trauma places individuals *at risk* for psychiatric symptoms and disorders. There is a wide spectrum of risk. For some forms of trauma, such as many natural disasters, the risk is low. For se-vere, prolonged, "high dose" trauma like sadistic abuse, the risk is high. For children witnessing the murder of a parent, the risk may approach 100%.[51] The level of risk depends not only on the severity of the trauma but also on the vulnerability and resilience of the exposed individual.

Before proceeding, you should know about "Medical Student's Dis-ease." When they read about various symptoms in medical textbooks, medi-cal students are liable to worry that they have a host of grave diseases. Be forewarned—this book describes just about everything that could possibly go wrong after you've experienced trauma. Much of my clinical experience has been with persons who have undergone the more extreme forms of trauma, so I'm used to seeing the whole gamut of disturbances.

You'll notice that I keep insisting that various forms of difficulty are *natural* reactions to traumatic experience. To say that reactions are natural and under-standable is not to say that they are *inevitable*. Don't feel compelled to find all of these problems in yourself. I have included what *may* happen, so that if it *has* happened, you'll be able to learn something about it.

CHAPTER TWO

Development

T rauma doesn't just affect your mind; it can change your life. The immediate impact can be overwhelming; the long-range impact need not be. Some persons are strengthened by adversity. The existentialists had no doubt that a brush with death could spark an appreciation of life. Coping with trauma can bolster a feeling of triumph. We like to think of "survivors," not "victims." Traumatic experience can prompt you to reach out for support. You may discover that you can use what you have gone through to help others. You may learn to speak out, raising community awareness in the hope that others can be spared. But trauma can also turn your life around for the worse, at least in the short run.

Derailed Development   ◆ ◆ ◆ ◆ ◆ ◆ ◆ ◆ ◆

◆ Picture a happy-go-lucky girl on the threshold of adolescence. She doesn't have it easy. Her parents work long hours to support her and her brothers and sisters. Her mother is kind and loving, but she is not at home very much. Her father spends long periods working out of state. The youngster spends most of her free time playing with a couple of girlfriends. She dreams of getting married and having children of her own. She plays house. Perhaps *she* can have a family that spends a lot of time together.

One afternoon she's playing in her room while her parents and friends are having a holiday celebration outside. It's noisy and they're drinking. Her uncle comes into the room. He's always been nice to her; at first she's puzzled but not frightened. But then he roughly picks her up and carries her to her bed. He undresses her, climbs on top of her, and starts to have intercourse with her. His sour breath smells of beer and peanuts. He puts his hand over her mouth and tells her to be quiet. He weighs at least 100 pounds more than she does. She can't breathe, and she panics. She hardly knows what's happening. She can't fight. She can't think, and she can barely move.

He's done, and he leaves. She's alone and frightened. She struggles out of bed, goes into the bathroom, and cleans herself up. She's bleeding. The party's still going on. She's afraid to tell anyone. She's ashamed and confused. She wouldn't know what to say. She might get in trouble. Who would believe it? Was it her fault?

So much for her dreams. Now she has nightmares. So much for playing house. Given what she did, no one would want to marry her. She's angry, and she becomes more bitter and rebellious. Alcohol calms some of her fears, temporarily. She's depressed. She discovers that marijuana allows her to escape, but she cannot concentrate on her school work. Her life goes downhill. Her parents can't understand why she can't stay away from drugs. She never tells a soul.

She meets a lot of men. Initially, she's attracted to them. Before long, she becomes sullen or hostile. Sometimes she's belligerent. Men can't figure her out. She drives them away as soon as she starts to get close. Eventually, she finds a man with whom she feels fairly safe. After a couple of years of breaking up and getting back together, they become engaged and move in together. It's a far cry from what she'd imagined as a child. Her fiancé is good to her. But soon after they begin living together, they both think she's going crazy. She's tried to stay off marijuana, but she can't. When they start having sex, she sometimes flies into a rage, screaming for him to stay away from her.

She is admitted to a psychiatric hospital. She thinks she's losing her mind. She's always known that she's got more than a drug problem. She goes to see a psychotherapist. She realizes that she needs to talk about being raped. For more than a decade, she's kept it to herself, but she's never forgotten it. It's not easy, but slowly she musters her courage and tells her therapist what happened. She begins to feel relieved. Just telling someone seems to help. She needed to get it out. Over the course of several therapy sessions, she begins to piece it all together. She sees how her fiancé's actions trigger memories of the rape. She can't stand the smell of beer or peanuts on his breath. He's a big man. When he's on top of her and she's excited, she becomes short of breath. She panics. She learns that she has posttraumatic stress disorder. She understands more fully why she has been using marijuana and alcohol. She can see how her attitude toward life changed and how her life took a turn for the worse after the rape.

She wants her fiancé to understand. But she's afraid to talk with him, and she asks her social worker to help her. She's learned to talk openly with her therapist about her experience and, despite her apprehension, she does a good job of explaining to her fiancé what has happened. The social worker helps her fiancé see that she's having flashbacks just like people who have been in combat. This is the first time she and her fiancé have talked about their sexual relationship without screaming at each other.

In the hospital, she talks to her therapist, social worker, nurses, and other patients. She's not the only patient in the group who has experienced sexual trauma. She makes some friends. She finds women she can confide in and women who confide in her. She finds strengths in herself that others rely on. She discovers that she enjoys writing poetry, and others like it. She begins to realize that she's no longer withdrawn, bitter, and isolated. On the contrary, she's enjoying being with people.

One day she comes to therapy pleased and somewhat bewildered. She says she's starting to feel like a "different person." Her therapist has a different view. He sees that she's gotten back on course. She's not a different person; instead, she's recapturing some of her youthful character. The rape had derailed her development in young adolescence, and she is just now getting back on course in adulthood. She has many good qualities to rekindle.

Let's push the traumatic juncture up a few years:

◆ Consider the 18-year-old who goes to Vietnam. He's graduated from high school. He's gone through much of the "identity formation" period of adolescence. He's had a couple of girlfriends. He, too, contemplates marriage and a family. He's had summer jobs and has considered some career options. He goes to war. He sees death and mayhem. At first, he's terrified. He kills to defend himself. When he kills, he becomes violently ill. His best buddy is killed. More buddies are killed. He becomes enraged. He starts to fight back. The more he kills, the more powerful he feels. He's become a killer.

When he comes home, no one can see his injuries, because they are psychological. His parents are proud that he's now a man, but they want to forget about the war. It was painful and frightening. Anyway, he feels that anyone who hasn't been there could not possibly understand. Who would *want* to understand? He's like a fish out of water—tense, jumpy, and irritable. He drinks. He can't stand noise and crowds. He doesn't feel like doing much of anything constructive. His friends from high school have all gone their own ways. He can't get close to anyone. Women find him remote. He's not all there. He often blanks out, as if he's off somewhere else, and misses half the conversation. When women push him to open up, he breaks off the relationship. What's become of his development?

Or we can push the trauma back to the beginning:

◆ Consider the child whose development has faltered from the start. Since he was a baby, his mother generally ignores him. He never quite knows from one moment to the next who will feed or dress him—perhaps his mother, his sister, or his grandfather. Sometimes no one does. His mother may be in bed, depressed. She may be sitting by the window, staring into space. When his father is there, he's yelling at his mother, yelling at him, or hitting him.

Such a child may never have any sense of security or stability. His family provides little foundation for development. He has no reason to think that relationships can be gratifying. There is scant encouragement, no recognition for learning or accomplishment. He may learn just to grab whatever he can get. At worst, development is not derailed; it never even gets on track. Or the track may lead straight to prison.

Some individuals overcome severe childhood trauma and do remarkably well in early adulthood, only to find that the early experience comes back to haunt them later in adulthood.

◆ A woman manages to break away from her troubled family. She made it through childhood and adolescence by dint of determination, strong defenses, and high intelligence. Doing well in school and earning praise from teachers sustained her. She became a highly successful professional. She married a loving partner. Now she is liked, respected, and admired.

But she doesn't live happily ever after. By the time she's 40, the stressors have piled up. She's had a miscarriage; she's lost a friend to cancer; and she's had to move away from a home she loved. Recently, she's had to fend off her boss's sexual advances. The last straw is a car accident. She's not seriously hurt, but she's badly shaken. Inexplicably, her anxiety level skyrockets. She can't sleep. Long-buried childhood memories start to haunt her. She can't quite make sense of them, and she tries not to think about them. She's worn out from constant anxiety and lack of sleep.

She becomes increasingly depressed. She loses her temper, and she bursts into tears. Her husband withdraws, spending more time out with his friends. She starts to wonder if he's having an affair. She's had a hard time concentrating at work, and she doesn't have the energy to keep up the fast pace. She's used up a lot of sick leave. She's been passed up for a promotion, and she's afraid she'll lose her job. In desperation, she takes an overdose of sleeping pills. She enters a psychiatric hospital where she begins to think and talk about her severely traumatic childhood. She can't go back to work, and she's not sure her marriage can be rescued. Her derailed development may take years to get back on track.

Complex Effects and Vicious Circles

These examples show how severe trauma can have a major impact on the course of life. Trauma can derail development by setting up vicious circles. Your depression and irritability prompt people to withdraw; you become more isolated; and your depression worsens. Your anxiety triggers nightmares; nightmares trigger traumatic memories; and your anxiety spirals. You are down on yourself; you berate yourself for your failings; you feel you deserve mistreatment from others; you allow yourself to be mistreated; and you feel even worse about yourself. Let's pile it all on: Start with traumatic experience. Add disruptions in attachment, emotion, consciousness, memory, sense of self, and relationships with others. Throw in some vicious circles. Enough of this, and you may develop one or more psychiatric disorders.

Rerailed Development ◆ ◆ ◆ ◆ ◆ ◆ ◆ ◆ ◆

We humans are a highly adaptable species, but we have limits. We can develop and thrive in a wide range of environments—but not *all* environments. In her presidential address to the Society for Research in Child Development, psychologist Sandra Scarr spelled out what she considered to be the necessary conditions to promote human development:

> For infants, species-normal environments include protective, parenting adults and a surrounding social group to which the child will be socialized. For older children, a normal environment includes a supportive family, peers with whom to learn the rules of being young, and plentiful opportunities to learn how to be a normal adult who can work and love. The exact details and specifications of the socialization patterns are not crucial to normal development (although they are crucial to understanding the meaning people give to their experiences), but having a rearing environment that falls within the limits of normal environments is crucial to normal development.[1]

Scarr emphasizes that, under optimal conditions, children actively choose and construct their own environments. Children evoke responses in their caregivers, and they seek out situations that fit their needs, abilities, and interests. Yet those who suffer severe childhood trauma may not have as much choice. They may be deprived of growth-promoting opportunities, and they may not be able to escape developmentally destructive influences. But sooner or later, many persons *are* able to leave traumatic environments. They *can* find environments conducive to putting their development back on course. Even if you have undergone prolonged trauma, you can potentially choose and construct a healthier environment for yourself. The new environment will foster new learning: The world is dangerous; people are dangerous—but not *that* dangerous. The world can be relatively safe, and many people can be trusted.

Just as there are vicious circles, there are benign circles. Learning to calm yourself enables you to see the world as a safer place; seeing the world as safer, you can relax even more. Learning to trust one person enables you to trust others; your capacity to trust blossoms. Learning to stand up for yourself and to prevent others from exploiting you allows you to feel better about yourself; as your self-esteem improves, you stand up for yourself even more. Every step in the right direction can lead to further steps; the challenge is to set development back on course.

Before the Cradle ◆ ◆ ◆ ◆ ◆ ◆ ◆ ◆ ◆

We have one more bit of background to traverse before delving into the psychological effects of trauma. I used to think that the developmental perspective in psychology ranged from the cradle to the grave. That span is enough to keep any psychologist busy for a lifetime. But it's millions of years too short. We mammals got our start about 180 million years ago, and the pace of our evolution picked up dramatically about 65 million years ago, when we took over from the dinosaurs. To understand our reactions to trauma, we need to take the developmental perspective far back to our ancient ancestors. Traumatic experience can hit us where it hurts most; it strikes at our mammalian core.

Just as trauma affects our psychological development, it may also affect our physiological development. The neurophysiological effects of trauma are intertwined with the full spectrum of psychological effects. More vicious circles: brain overreacts, mind overreacts, brain overreacts. To get development back on track, we often need to treat both the mind and the brain. They can make a good pair.

Trauma and the Nervous System ◆ ◆ ◆ ◆ ◆ ◆

Psychological trauma affects the brain and the rest of the nervous system. If you're struggling with trauma and you don't understand this, you may think you are losing your mind. Or you may castigate yourself for being a "wimp." In the process, you do your mind a disservice, and you don't do your brain any good either. To understand traumatic reactions, you must understand your biology as well as your psychology.

Look at it this way: If you have a heart attack, you don't ordinarily think you're a "wimp." You think, "I need to learn about my heart so I can take care of it." If you are coping with traumatic stress, you need to learn about your brain so that you can take care of it. If we are willing to take care of hypertension in our cardiovascular system, shouldn't we also be willing to take care of hyperarousal in our nervous system?

Why not just use medication? Drug treatment has become increasingly prominent throughout psychiatry. Many psychiatric disorders that we once thought to be purely psychological or interpersonal are now recognized as having a biological component. Hearing of the successes of drug treatment, you might be tempted to think that psychiatric disorders are nothing more than brain diseases. We just need to find the right drugs and they will be cured. Occasionally, drugs alone are curative; typically, however, they are not.

In this "decade of the brain," we are challenged to *integrate* biological, psychological, and social perspectives in understanding psychiatric disorders. Nowhere is this integrative approach more important than in understanding the development of trauma-related disorders. It has come to be known as the "biopsychosocial" perspective, becoming to psychiatry what motherhood and apple pie are to America—and rightly so. We *should* promote biopsychosocial thinking. But this is easier said than done (and not so easily said!). You may find the "bio" part the hardest, but it's well worth your effort to understand something about it. The rest of this chapter provides the basic perspective you need for this book, and I hope it will entice you to consult the Appendix for the fuller picture.

Evolution and Imperfect Adaptation

◆ Imagine a girl on the threshold of puberty whose mother has just remarried to a man with a teenage son. The girl's new stepbrother sees her as an intruder. He takes out his resentment by tormenting her sadistically. He seems to delight in frightening her. He barges into her room unannounced, sometimes while she is dressing. He sneaks up behind her and grabs her around the chest. He creeps into her room while she is sleeping and suddenly rips off all the covers. Her mother and stepfather dismiss her stepbrother's behavior as natural jealousy and tell her to "ignore it and it will go away." She learns quickly to be on guard and tries to be aware of his whereabouts. She asks to have a lock put on her bedroom door, but her parents haven't gotten around to it. She dresses in a hurry, and she stays up late. She tries not to be alone in the house with her stepbrother. After several weeks, her continual efforts to shield herself have taken their toll. She has been tense and constantly on guard. She is startled by any sudden noise or movement. She can't sleep restfully, and she has disturbing dreams. She has become a "nervous wreck." Literally. Her natural efforts to protect herself have worn her out.

Throughout this book are examples of natural, self-protective efforts gone awry. I think of all responses to stress and trauma as forms of adaptation. Coping with trauma is a huge challenge. It might help you to see this challenge in an evolutionary context. This is just part of my campaign to persuade you to have more patience with yourself and more tolerance for your struggles.

Trauma is certainly the main villain in this book, and I will emphasize its potentially harmful effects. But we could subsume this whole topic of trauma under the broader domain of stress and coping, and we should keep the concept of *adaptation* in the forefront. All reactions to stress and trauma, including "symptoms," are best understood as adaptive efforts. We have evolved to cope as we do. The evolution of our species and all others is predicated on coping and adaptation to stress—the "survival of the fittest." We each come into the world exquisitely prepared by aeons of evolution to cope with challenges and stress. We adapt—physiologically, psychologically, behaviorally, and socially. The more you can understand your responses as part of your "human nature," the more forgiving you can be about your limitations. And you can best understand your human nature if you step back from it and consider the broader sweep of evolution.

We have survived. We are among the fittest. But just how fit are we? Next time you are tempted to berate yourself for your failings, keep in mind the wisdom of one of the foremost evolutionary biologists, Ernest Mayr,[2] who remarked that evolution "never leads to perfection." More than 99.9% of the species that ever lived are extinct,[3] and we are in the midst of another mass extinction.[4] When we try to understand our efforts to cope with traumatic stress or anything else, we had better think in terms of *imperfect adaptation.*

Evolution has prepared us well to cope with time-limited stress. We are wired to run away from a lumbering grizzly bear without giving it a second thought. But there is no reason to think that evolution has prepared us to cope with deliberate, protracted, or repeated cruelty. It may be easier to deal with a grizzly than a sadistic stepbrother. Genetic change lags way behind cultural change;[5] our brains and bodies cannot keep up with the cultural evolution of malevolence. As described in this chapter, we evolved to thrive in relatively protective early environments, not in "violent, abusive, and neglectful families."[6] The same mechanisms that help us adapt to brief stress can backfire in response to prolonged trauma. Momentary anxiety is a useful warning signal; chronic anxiety can be debilitating.

The Fluid Brain

How often have you heard the statement "I have a biochemical depression." You have a biochemical *life!* Life wouldn't amount to much without biochemistry, at least not on this earth. The cells of the nervous system—neurons—signal each other by using neurotransmitters. Under genetic instruction, the neurons manufacture these neurotransmitters, send them down their axons, and shoot them across minuscule spaces called *synaptic gaps*. The receiving neurons have receptors that respond to the transmitters, setting off a chain reaction. This is the telephone-switchboard concept of brain operation. Each neuron converses with its neighbors by way of neurotransmitter signals from one synapse to another.

We can think of the neuron "cables" of the switchboard brain as being bathed in a fluid of transmitters. The continuously changing composition of this fluid affects the functioning of the nervous system in more general ways. Depending on the composition of the fluid, different circuits in the brain may be more or less active or responsive. And, through the fluids it produces, the nervous system adjusts the functioning of other bodily organs according to momentary needs. You decide to run, and your heart pumps more blood.

Think about the last time you had a near miss in a car. It's over in a flash. You're safe. You *know* it's over, but how do you *feel?* You can be stirred up emotionally for quite some time, even if the threat is over in a few seconds. Chalk it up to the lingering effects of rapid changes in your biochemical fluid. You can stir up silt in a clear pool in an instant, but you may need to wait a long time before it settles. If you've been traumatized, you don't need unexpected encounters with cars to be unsettled. You may experience repeated bursts of anxiety and central nervous system arousal that keep you in prolonged states of agitation. As described next, reason and emotion may then seem to have parted company.

Too Many Brains for Any One Mind

◆ One drizzly afternoon a man is driving his van along a winding road, and a 7-year-old boy suddenly comes flying out of his driveway on a bike. There's no time to stop, and the boy is horribly injured. A year later, the man still cannot drive. He knows that it was a freak accident and that it was not his fault. But his anxiety verges on panic whenever he tries to get behind the wheel. He is generally able to tolerate riding in a car, but sometimes even a glimpse of a boy or a bicycle will trigger a wave of anxiety. He berates himself because he knows there's little danger and nothing to fear, but he can't turn off his feelings.

Trauma brings out the extremes, but contradictions between thought and feelings are commonplace.[7] How often have you had an irrational feeling that won't go away? You feel anxious, and you think, "I have nothing to be worried about." You feel sad and you can't figure out why. You feel angry, and you can't let go of it. You think, "There's no reason to keep fretting about it," but you stay irritated. You have a panic attack, and you haven't a clue as to what triggered it. Even after the panic subsides, you can't come up with a reason for it. Thank aeons of mammalian evolution.

We share the inner core of our brain with all other mammals. To this mammalian core, called the *limbic system,* we owe our emotions, memories, and attachments. The limbic system, like the rest of the brain, I suppose, is a mixed blessing. The limbic system needs no fancy thinking to evoke strong emotions instantaneously in response to reminders of trauma.

But we higher primates have also evolved an elaborate *neocortex* surrounding the limbic lobe. The neocortex endows us with intelligence, sophisticated problem-solving ability, and reasoning. But the neocortex does not replace the limbic system; evolution just piled one structure on top of the other. Like the man who had an accident and could no longer get behind the wheel even though he "knew better," we can all think one thing and feel the opposite. Harmonizing the outer look of reason with the inner look of emotion is no easy feat. This challenge goes to the heart of coping with trauma. Traumatic experience can lead to the activation of the emotional brain while the rational brain has no sense of what is happening.

The Traumatized Rat

We humans may be most adept at inflicting trauma, but we share the basic trauma response with our fellow mammals. To be traumatized, all you need is your limbic system. That's why studying the effects of severe stress on rats (and other mammals) can teach us a great deal about trauma in humans. We cannot study the psychological consequences of traumatic experience in animals, but the effects on their physiology and behavior are dramatic.

We share with all other mammals a vulnerability to a wide range of fundamental stressors. The limbic system subserves attachment as well as emotion, and one of the most prominent mammalian stressors is separation and social isolation. A sense of abandonment and isolation is central to many forms of trauma, particularly in the context of abusive experience. The essence of mammalian life is nursing, caregiving, and attachment. We mammals have a relatively long period of dependence on caregivers, and we are not equipped to forsake it. The limbic system is geared for distress in response to separation, and it is wired to generate the separation cry to produce reunion. Interfering with reunion has a major impact on development. Herbert Weiner[8] notes that "the effects of separation on young rats are permanent and affect every organ system studied to date." For example, premature separation can lead to elevated heart rate, increased motor activity, sleep disturbance, disruption of temperature regulation, and a host of hormonal changes. Not only does premature separation have immediately disruptive effects, it also leads to an increased vulnerability to later stressors.

A host of other stressors besides separation have been shown to have substantial effects on mammals.[9] These stressors include painful stimuli, electric shock, cold, heat, restraint, frightening situations, threat of attack, fighting, one animal's intrusion into another's territory, crowding, harassment of a subordinate animal by a dominant animal, and exposure to a predator. Because we share these stressors with our mammalian kin, we could think of them as relatively universal.

A *dose-response* relationship is well documented in human reactions to trauma. The graver the threat to life and limb, the more frequent the beatings, the greater the trauma. So it is in animal research.[10] The more severe and extensive the stress, the more profound its effects. Piling a number of these universal stressors together or prolonging any one of them would qualify as "traumatic." Moreover, three important factors have been demonstrated to make any stressor more difficult to cope with: unpredictability, unavoidability, and punishment of efforts to escape. Plainly, various forms of child and spouse abuse entail many universal stressors, often coupled with unpredictability, unavoidability, and punishment of efforts to escape. People who are inclined to mistreat and abuse others do not need to read rat research; they intuitively know our core vulnerabilities.

The Fight-or-Flight Response

We mammals—from rats to humans—are prepared by evolution to re-spond immediately and vigorously to any dire threat. We have two basic choices: fight or flight. Walter Cannon,[11] who pioneered stress research in the first half of this century, made no bones about the significance of the fight-or-flight response: "the strength of the feelings and the quickness of the response measure the chances of survival in a struggle where the issue may be life or death."

This fight-or-flight response is extremely important to understand, be-cause it is likely to be triggered by any reminder of trauma. Decades ago, Cannon well understood what we now call posttraumatic stress disorder. He described how the emotional reactions associated with the fight-or-flight response could be triggered by memories. He also pointed out that when the natural fight-or-flight response is blocked, the emotional reac-tions can be kept alive long after the original trauma is past.

Cannon emphasized the physiological similarities between fear and rage, pointing out that, regardless of whether the organism fights or flees, the bodily needs are similar. Fight and flight call for equally vigorous action. The sympathetic nervous system is magnificently designed to orchestrate the necessary activation of bodily organs. A well-working sympathetic nervous system contributes substantially to fitness and survival. Your brain/mind detects a threat, activates the sympathetic nervous system, and you're instantly prepared to fight or flee. But what if you *cannot* fight or flee? What if you are trapped? What if you're plagued by traumatic memories, and fighting or fleeing is not an option? You are saddled with a huge blast of physiological arousal. You feel fear, rage, or both. You have no outlet for all this emotion. The "sympathetic" nervous system begins to feel quite *un*-sympathetic.

Moreover, your sympathetic nervous system response does not go away very quickly, thanks to the contribution of your fluid brain. The sympa-thetic response is partly mediated by hormones. Once the brain sets this reaction in motion, and your adrenals send out their hormones, you cannot just shut it off. Recall the near miss in the car. It's over in an instant, but you remain stirred up. Those hormones are in your bloodstream, and you can't just send them back to the adrenals. They will continue to work on your organs, and you will continue to feel the physiological effects of arousal.

This lingering physiological activation fuels continued anxiety. Your neo-cortex knows you're out of danger, but your limbic system remains agitated.

Putting the Mind Into the Brain

Lest we lose our minds with all this talk about brains, we need to think about how to put them back together. I've been urging you to think about your brain, because your brain is affected by trauma. We can use drugs to help the brain, but drugs are rarely enough. Your traumatized brain needs additional help from your mind. Throughout this book, I'll be mentioning the need to use your mind to help your brain.

Using your mind to help your brain may seem like a peculiar idea, and it brings us face to face with the age-old philosophical conundrum of the "mind-body problem." In short, how can a bunch of brain tissue be conscious? Let's just accept as biological fact that consciousness is an amazing feature of brain functioning.[12] With the aid of modern technology, our brain activity can be observed from the outside. With the aid of consciousness, we have access to some of our brain activity from the inside. As conscious animals, we have the benefit of subjectively experiencing some of our brain activity. To say that we can use our minds to run our brains is just a shorthand way of saying that the high level of brain activity we're in touch with via consciousness can affect lower levels of brain activity that we're not in touch with.

If this sounds too odd, recall that we are quite accustomed to thinking of the influence of the brain/mind on *other* parts of the body. It is helpful to think of traumatic reactions (and many psychiatric disorders) as partly *psychosomatic* (psyche = mind, soma = body). Think of an ulcer as psychosomatic: Chronic stress leads to lesions in the stomach. The stomach is the "target organ" of psychological stress. In hypertension, the blood vessels are the target organ of stress. If the stomach and blood vessels can be target organs, why can't the brain be a target organ? Well, it is.[13] Consider that the functioning of the brain is affected by psychological stress. Patricia Churchland[14] neatly summarized the intertwining of psychological and biochemical (fluid-brain) factors: "It is likely that psychological factors of a complex nature also play a role in altering the balance of the chemical soup, even as such alterations in the soup in turn affect the psychological states."

There is no doubt that traumatic experience alters the functioning of the central nervous system and of physiological functioning more generally. Patterns of thinking and mental images may fuel or dampen arousal in the brain and other parts of the body. Traumatic experience can turn on an anxiety circuit in the brain, and relaxing imagery can help turn it back off. We need to rely on our marvelous ability for flexible and creative thinking to exert more control over the functioning of our nervous systems. In a very real sense, persons who have been traumatized need to find ways to control the activity of their brains. This is a daunting prospect: "How does it happen that our bodies get all the necessary things done for us, or most of them anyway, without our conscious minds being required to intervene or even supervise the process? How would you feel if you were suddenly told, 'There is your liver, right upper quadrant, now go ahead and operate it yourself'? Or your pineal gland, heaven help you? Or, worst of all possibilities, start running your own brain!" [15]

We are probably inclined to take too much credit for what our brains do—for better or for worse. But we have acquired over the course of evolution *some* capacity to consciously influence our brains—for example, by what we think, what we remember, and what we imagine. We must be tolerant of our modest results. After all, we're dealing with a hundred billion neurons and a million billion connections,[16] and we only have conscious access to a tiny fraction. Be patient with yourself.

PART II

Effects of Trauma

CHAPTER THREE

Attachment

Imagine yourself going out for a walk in your neighborhood. About a mile from your home, two men in a pickup truck drive by shouting obscenities. A few minutes later, they come back, pull up in front of you, get out, and come at you brandishing knives. You feel endangered, alone, and without protection. You scream for help but no one responds. Satisfied with having terrorized you, the assailants take off. You run for home unscathed physically but badly shaken emotionally. You come in the house trembling and tearful. Now imagine two possible scenarios: One, you have a good capacity to use support, and you have a good support system. When you arrive, your spouse hears you come in, immediately responds to your distress, and asks you to sit on the couch and tell her what happened. As you do so, you are held and assured that you are safe. Your children also come to your side and do their best to comfort you. You gradually calm down. Scenario two: You are socially isolated. You come in to your empty house and are left to cope all on your own. You cannot think of anyone you can call or go to see. You cannot calm down.

Attachment theory is indispensable for understanding such traumatic experiences. The mother-infant bond is the prototype of attachment. Attachment is the basis of our sense of safety and security in the world. Although attachment begins in infancy, feeling alone, endangered, and unprotected at any age may shake the foundations of attachment. In addition, as the alternative scenarios in this vignette illustrate, secure attachments can make trauma more bearable by restoring a sense of security. Because attachments are healing, establishing or reestablishing a sense of secure attachment is a cornerstone of treatment.

The Foundation of Development

Psychiatrist John Bowlby developed attachment theory in the 1950s when he was asked by the World Health Organization to consult on the mental health implications of homelessness in children. He became an expert on children's reactions to the traumas of separation and institutionalization. He concluded that mental health depends on the child's experiencing a "warm, intimate and continuous" relationship with a caregiver.[1] Attachment theory continues to inspire a major line of research in child development.[2]

Bowlby rooted his theory of the mother-infant bond firmly in biology, drawing from evolutionary theory and ethology (the science of animal behavior). The essence of attachment is *proximity*—the tendency of the youngster to stay close to the mother. Bowlby believed that attachment behavior evolved because being close to the mother provided some assurance of safety. In evolutionary terms, proximity to the mother protects offspring from predators. Offspring separated from their mother let out a distress cry that brings her to the rescue, reinstating proximity. As offspring develop, they learn to run back to their mother when separated and may even cling to her. The process works both ways: The infant is biologically prepared to form an attachment to the caregiver, and the caregiver is biologically prepared to form a bond with the infant. Offspring maintain proximity; mothers protect. Thus, attachment is a reciprocal relationship; infant attachment behavior is intertwined with maternal bonding and caregiving.

As noted in Chapter 2, attachment is ancient. Paul MacLean[3] asserts that the family as a biological institution goes back 180 million years, originating with the earliest mammals while they waited in the wings for 115 million years to take over from the dinosaurs. Bowlby[4] extended this heritage beyond mammals to include some ground-nesting birds. Attachment needs are as firmly rooted in our biology as are our needs for food and water. Our lives depend on successful attachment. As described in the Appendix, our ancient mammalian emotional brain governs attachment. Attachment is a firmly rooted disposition!

Attachment behavior and emotional bonding develop in conjunction with nursing and the relatively prolonged dependence of mammalian offspring on mothers. Although we humans are recently evolved mammals, we are at the top of the heap in the amount of parental care we require. We can chalk this up to the fact that we have such big brains, and we eventually stand on our own two feet. The fact that we are bipedal (walkers) sets mechanical limits on the size of the birth canal; the fact that we have such big brains requires that we be born early, before the brain gets too big for the head to get through the canal.[5] The long period of parental care we require profoundly shapes our minds and brains, and it provides the foundation for all subsequent development. Ideally, parenting is the essential buffer against trauma. Yet parenting can fail to buffer trauma and, at worst, it can itself be a source of trauma.

The Secure Base ◆ ◆ ◆ ◆ ◆ ◆ ◆ ◆ ◆ ◆

I think the "secure base" is the single most useful concept in understanding trauma. Bowlby explains, "A central feature of my concept of parenting [is] the provision by both parents of a secure base from which a child or an adolescent can make sorties into the outside world and to which he can return knowing for sure that he will be welcomed when he gets there, nourished physically and emotionally, comforted if distressed, reassured if frightened." [6] The importance of having a secure base cannot be overstated. As Bowlby says, our survival as a species has depended on it. The concept of a secure base has much in common with psychoanalyst Erik Erikson's[7] idea of *basic trust*. As I see it, Bowlby placed basic trust in its wider evolutionary context.

The secure base is a launching pad for independence. In addition to serving the biological function of ensuring safety from harm, it serves a psychological function: The secure base provides a *feeling of security.* The secure base is a home base from which the youngster feels confident to explore the world. Attachment and exploration are in dynamic balance. Ideally, life is a series of "excursions" from the secure base.[8] Having a secure base, the youngster feels free to explore, always with a sense that security and safety are close at hand. When the child feels frightened or threatened, the attachment needs are activated, and the youngster returns to the secure base. When trauma impinges on this sense of security, exploration, initiative, and autonomy are undermined. Traumatized youngsters may be unable to avail themselves of the rich environment needed to foster healthy development.

The Strange Situation   ◆ ◆ ◆ ◆ ◆ ◆ ◆ ◆ ◆

If you have been traumatized, you know what it's like to be without a secure base. There are patterns of attachment that fall far short of the biological idea of safe proximity. We have learned a lot from research on these different patterns. Bowlby's collaborator Mary Ainsworth developed an ingenious method to study attachment patterns in infants.[9] Because she wanted to observe attachment behavior in action, Ainsworth created the "Strange Situation" to study infants' and mothers' reactions to separation and reunion. The basic scenario is this: The infant and mother are brought into an unfamiliar but comfortable room filled with toys. A stranger enters, and the mother subsequently departs, leaving the infant in the room with the stranger. Then the mother comes back into the room, pausing to allow the infant a chance to respond to her return. After a while, the stranger leaves the room. Then the mother leaves the infant all alone in the room. The mother then returns a second time and picks the infant up.

Ainsworth's Strange Situation has been a gold mine of information about attachment. Thousands of Strange Situations have been studied throughout the world.[10] We now appreciate how optimal caregiving promotes secure attachment and how neglect, maltreatment, and abuse may lead to problematic patterns of attachment. In this chapter, I describe various patterns of attachment and their relation to trauma. Here, the focus is on relationships in childhood. In Chapter 8 (Relationships), I describe how these trauma-related patterns in childhood can shape the bonds with others in adulthood.

Secure Attachment ◆ ◆ ◆ ◆ ◆ ◆ ◆ ◆ ◆

Secure attachment is the antidote for trauma. Secure attachment characterizes the majority of infants studied in the Strange Situation.[11] Securely attached infants are highly sensitive to their mother's presence and keenly aware of her leaving the room. Depending on their temperament, securely attached infants may be more or less distressed when left alone with a stranger. They may protest or try to follow their mother. Regardless of their level of distress, they rely on their relationship with their mother for comfort. They rapidly seek proximity when she returns; they may make eye contact or approach and greet her. They are easily reassured. There is a smooth alternation between exploration and proximity seeking. When threatened or distressed, securely attached infants seek proximity and find comfort; when security is reestablished, they return quickly and confidently to playing and exploring their environment.

The mother makes an important contribution to the nature of the infant's attachment.[12] Securely attached infants are likely to have mothers who are able to see things from their baby's point of view and are attuned to their baby's needs. They can accurately perceive the infant's signals and respond promptly to them. They respond to the infant on the basis of the infant's needs rather than by imposing their own needs on the infant. They are responsive to both positive and negative feelings. In short, they are accessible and dependable. But don't get the idea that secure attachment requires perfect mothering. This ideal may only be sustained for 20 minutes of being observed in a research laboratory! Mothering doesn't need to be perfect, it just needs to be "good enough." [13]

Insecure Attachment ◆ ◆ ◆ ◆ ◆ ◆ ◆ ◆ ◆

Two patterns of attachment are less than ideal but nevertheless fall within the normal range. These *avoidant* and *resistant* patterns are adaptive strategies for dealing with more stressful or problematic mother-infant relationships.[14] These two insecure patterns are normal but nevertheless crucial for understanding traumatic relationships, because trauma brings them out in more extreme forms.

Avoidant

In the Strange Situation, the avoidant infant explores and plays without concern for the mother's whereabouts and is not distressed by her absence. When the mother returns, the infant appears indifferent, turns away, or may want to be put down if picked up.

Mothers of avoidant infants are likely to block and reject the infant's bids for comfort.[15] The avoidant infant responds to rejection by shutting down the attachment system.[16] That is, the infant expects to be rebuffed and therefore minimizes any display of attachment behavior.[17] This avoidant strategy only works, however, when the rejection is not too severe and when the infant's environment is not too threatening otherwise. If the stress is within bounds, then the infant may be able to get along without too much closeness and comforting.

Resistant

In the Strange Situation, resistant infants are preoccupied with attachment to the exclusion of interest in exploration and play.[18] They are alert to danger and sensitive to separation, and they become highly distressed when their mother leaves. Yet they are not easily comforted by her return. Their attachment behavior is intermingled with ambivalence and anger. They may seek proximity but angrily resist comforting.

Resistant infants are likely to have mothers who are unresponsive or inconsistently responsive.[19] These mothers may be insensitive to the infant's needs; they may regard the infant as a nuisance and respond belatedly; they may be withdrawn; and they may provide insufficient stimulation. The infant's inclination to maximize attachment behavior can thus be seen as an adaptive effort to attract the attention of the unresponsive or inconsistent caregiver.[20] Yet the infant's ambivalence interferes with soothing whenever the mother is more forthcoming.

Disorganized Attachment

You can begin to see how problematic attachments lead to interpersonal difficulties. Rejection and unresponsiveness can lead to isolation and ambivalence. What happens when attachments are downright traumatic?

Over many years, those who have studied mothers and their infants in the Strange Situation have consistently observed many "unclassifiable" cases—ones in which the attachment pattern is not clearly secure, avoidant, or resistant. Researchers have recently developed a meaningful understanding of these unusual patterns of attachment behavior. These patterns now fall under the rubric of *disorganized* (or *disoriented*) attachment.[21] The disorganized pattern is often associated with more severe forms of maltreatment—even including physical, sexual, or emotional abuse, or extreme neglect in some cases.

In the Strange Situation, the behavior of disorganized infants lacks clear goals and is contradictory.[22] The infant may alternate among proximity seeking, avoidance, and resistance. For example, on reunion, the infant may approach the mother as if to make full physical contact, and then suddenly turn away. Or the infant's seeking of proximity may be interrupted by a sudden outburst of aggression. These contradictions may be expressed even more dramatically when the infant simultaneously approaches and avoids the mother, inhibiting attachment behavior as it occurs. For example, the infant may approach the mother by backing toward her with his head averted. Or the infant may nestle in the mother's lap but look away with his head down while maintaining a dazed expression.

The disorganized pattern also entails a more severe version of the avoidant pattern. The infant may become frightened or distressed but make no effort to seek out the mother. Or the infant may even be *frightened of the mother.* The infant may show periods of freezing, as if psychologically paralyzed, or the infant may be profoundly apathetic.

The disorganized attachment pattern may or may not be associated with obvious abuse. Mothers of disorganized infants are either *frightened of* the infant or *frightening to* the infant.[23] The mother's frightened or frightening behavior may include invading the infant's space, looming over the infant, being afraid or timid in relation to the infant, playing frightening games with the infant, or being extremely sensitive to rejection by the infant. The mother's behavior may result from her own traumatic experience, whether it be a traumatic loss in her own background or her own history of physical, sexual, or emotional abuse.

With a frightening mother, the infant is in a situation of intolerable conflict: *The safe haven is alarming.* This contradiction is the core experience in many traumatic relationships. The disorganized infant is in a dilemma, and there is no way to adapt successfully. When put between a rock and a hard place, the infant's resulting behavior appears chaotic, contradictory, and disorganized.

Reciprocity and Vicious Circles ◆ ◆ ◆ ◆ ◆ ◆ ◆

Attachment is a two-way street. The child's attachment behavior influences the parent's caregiving behavior over the entire course of development.[24] Attachment theorists have been criticized for giving insufficient weight to the child's contribution to the attachment. Behavior in the Strange Situation is not just a result of the caregiver's behavior toward the infant. It is also a reflection of the infant's temperamental disposition to be distressed in unfamiliar situations, as well as the infant's socialization regarding the expression and control of fear.[25] By the time the therapist sees the adult who was traumatized in childhood, it is nearly impossible to specify precisely the relative contributions of various constitutional and environmental factors. But it is plausible to think in terms of vicious circles.

◆ Picture an infant with inherent difficulties in forming stable attachments. He is prone to extreme anxiety, and he easily becomes confused and disorganized. He cannot form clear images of his parents, and he cannot remember them—out of sight, out of mind. An ideal pattern of caregiving characteristic of "secure attachment" might have enabled him to overcome his developmental handicaps and to form stable, secure relationships. But he was not so fortunate. When his father had to work at night, his mother anxiously clung to him for security. She was often preoccupied with her own needs and relatively oblivious to his needs. Add to this mix episodes of physical and verbal abuse by his father. The child was often terrified, and his kaleidoscopic experience of the world at times had the quality of a living nightmare. Had he been observed in Ainsworth's laboratory, he probably would have shown the "disorganized" pattern of attachment. Now in adulthood, he alternates be-

tween extreme isolation and desperate clinging, and his few attachments provide little sustained sense of comfort or soothing.

Attachment Beyond Infancy ◆ ◆ ◆ ◆ ◆ ◆ ◆

If attachment pertained only to infancy, I would not have written this chapter. From early attachment experiences, we develop models of relationships that are like enduring templates.[26] Earlier relationships establish the patterns for later relationships, and there is continuity in attachment from infancy into later childhood.[27] Secure infants are likely to be secure children; insecure infants are likely to be insecure children.

Of course, attachment also goes through major changes over the life span.[28] As securely attached youngsters grow older, they are able to tolerate longer separations over greater distances from their mother or primary caregiver. Their sense of security no longer rests on proximity or the physical presence of a caregiver. Rather, they develop a sense of trust and confidence in the reliability and endurance of attachments.

In addition, attachment with a primary caregiver gradually evolves into a wider range of attachments. In the nuclear family, an attachment to the father develops alongside the attachment to the mother. Patterns of attachment to the mother and the father are independent; the quality of the attachment to the father may be the same as that with the mother, or it may be different.[29] Of course, the pattern of attachment to the father that evolves will depend on the father's behavior.

The infant's range of attachments is contingent on the composition of the household and the caregiving arrangements. Generally, attachments cover an ever-widening sphere, developing with nonparental caregivers, siblings, and peers. Given the variations in contemporary family composition and caregiving, it is fortunate that attachment behavior is so flexible.

The finding that the infant's pattern of attachment depends on the behavior of the caregiver is extremely important. For example, the infant who has an insecure attachment to the mother may nevertheless form a secure attachment to the father. Or the reverse may be the case. Keep in mind that the infant is *biologically disposed to form a secure attachment*. My clinical work has led me to appreciate the profound resilience of the attachment system. I have had countless opportunities to admire individuals' persistence in working their way toward more secure attachments. This relentless search begins early in life. Even in the presence of pervasive family violence or abusive experience, the infant and youngster will find and make use of islands of security. And youngsters will often form relatively secure attachments outside the family, for example, with peers, teachers, coaches, grandparents, neighbors, or clergy.[30] It is rare for a person to arrive at adulthood without *some* capacity to form a positive, close, and secure attachment.

The idea that attachment persists into adulthood is reiterated throughout Bowlby's writings. For example, he draws attention to the "vital role that it plays in the life of man from the cradle to the grave." [31] Bowlby recognized that archaic fears are not given up in childhood but persist throughout life. At any age, we may feel endangered by unwilling separation from an attachment figure.[32] If you are accosted by strangers with knives, alone and unprotected, your instinctive fear is rooted in the failure of attachment.

In addition to developing a range of attachments with other individuals, we also develop a sense of belonging to institutions and groups. For some people, groups may even provide a primary source of attachment and security.[33] Psychiatrist Joseph Lichtenberg[34] proposed that an innate "affiliative motivational system" develops in parallel with the attachment system. Affiliation begins developing in relation to the family unit and then extends to other groups. Like attachments with individuals, affiliation with groups can alleviate distress and sustain self-esteem.[35] From this perspective, it is little wonder that groups are so helpful in the treatment of individuals who have been traumatized.

Disruption of Attachment by Trauma

Ideally, a secure attachment and a secure base are provided by caregiving—first in the mother-infant relationship, and later in other relationships. A secure attachment at 12 months portends good adjustment in later childhood, which includes good coping skills, good peer relationships, and a reduced risk for psychiatric disturbance.[36] With less-than-ideal parenting, albeit short of extreme maltreatment, attachment is not so secure. The youngster may be avoidant or resistant and may have difficulty finding security and comfort. With more extreme forms of maltreatment—a frightened or frightening caregiver—a workable pattern of attachment may not develop.

From the perspective of attachment theory, the worst possible trauma occurs in relation to the primary caregiver, typically the mother. A frightening mother causes intolerable conflict. The island of safety is dangerous. A vicious circle ensues, because the child's efforts to calm fear by seeking safety only increase the fear. The infant's behavior is, at best, extremely ambivalent and, at worst, chaotic. Unless a more workable pattern of attachment and security develops with another caregiver, there will be no solid foundation for developing autonomy and independence.

Even when the youngster is not threatened directly by the mother, the maternal attachment can be disrupted. Consider family violence. Imagine the effects of watching your mother being beaten by your father. To the observing youngster, this violence not only is terrifying in its own right but also threatens maternal loss. The mother can hardly provide a sense of security when she is being beaten.

The primary attachment should provide a safe haven. In evolutionary terms, the mother-offspring relationship provides safety from predators. If a youngster is injured or traumatized and can find comfort, the trauma can be endured. If the youngster is abused by someone other than the caregiver and the caregiver does not provide comfort, the attachment is nonfunctional. Tragically, this scenario is not uncommon. An abusive paternal or fraternal relationship will often entail secrecy enforced by dire threats. This intolerable situation may lead the child to fear that seeking the desperately desired maternal comfort will backfire: She will not believe the child; she will punish the child further; she will abandon or banish the child; she will force the father/brother to leave; or the father/brother will further assault the child in retaliation.

It is easiest to appreciate the disruption of traumatic experience on attachment when childhood trauma precludes normal caregiving. But we have also seen that trauma in adulthood disrupts attachment. In adulthood, a single traumatic experience (assault, accident, natural disaster) can shake our sense of security to the core. Back to evolution: We are vulnerable to predators—now most likely to be our fellow humans. Any traumatic experience can shatter the secure base and rock the foundations of basic trust. Naturally, the more solid our foundation in secure attachment, the more resilient we will be to disruptions.

Attachment and Regulation of Arousal   ◆   ◆   ◆   ◆   ◆

Stress and trauma can wreak havoc with physiology. Trauma evokes the fight-or-flight response, which entails massive physiological arousal associated with sympathetic nervous system activation. Every major organ system is involved. The primary evolutionary function of attachment is to ensure caregiving and provide protection from harm. Recently, a second biological function of attachment has come to light: the regulation of physiological arousal.[37]

Bowlby[38] described the feeling of security that goes with having a secure base. The provision of comforting on the emotional level dovetails with the soothing and dampening of arousal on the physiological level. Soothing is an inextricable part of the caregiver-infant bond, and it occurs in conjunction with the emotional attunement between the two individuals. The distressed infant seeks out the mother for comfort; when in contact, the infant is quieted. Separation from the mother is a primary cause of distress and physiological arousal; reunion both calms emotions and restores physiological equilibrium. Attachments can also provide needed stimulation, alleviating boredom or depression. Attachment thus serves to maintain a balance, keeping arousal within an optimal range.

Attachment promotes a "psychobiological synchrony between organisms" as behavioral and physiological systems become attuned to each other.[39] Synchrony is evident, for example, in sleep-wake cycles and feeding cycles, when mothers' and infants' schedules and rhythms become mutually adapted. Emotional attunement and physiological synchrony are in tandem. Ideally, caregivers and infants are on the same wavelength. Perhaps we should take Lichtenberg's poetic statement literally: "Attunement is like the heartbeat of a loving attachment experience." [40]

Attachment is embedded in maternal caregiving that regulates the infant's physiological development. The mother's touch—holding, rocking, warming, and providing a wealth of sensory stimulation—doubtlessly affects physiological, endocrine, and neurochemical functioning. Caregiving thus influences not only attachment but also the development of the nervous system.

The infant is born with stable biological systems, but these systems are fine-tuned by caregiving, and they become disruptively perturbed without it. Optimally, this external regulation of physiological functioning by caregiving gradually becomes internalized, such that the developing child becomes increasingly able to self-regulate. With adequate initial help from the caregiver, the youngster has the repeated experience of his or her arousal being soothed and then develops the capacity for self-soothing.

So just as trauma disrupts the secure base and basic trust, it also disrupts physiological regulation. There is often a kind of "double whammy" here: The traumatic experience generates hyperarousal (fear, panic, pain), and the individual is often abandoned or neglected after being injured and aroused. There is arousal beyond normal bounds, and there is a lack of soothing or comforting. This uncontrollable arousal is especially problematic when the primary caregiver is abusive or when the trauma is hidden and kept secret, precluding restorative comforting.

Restoring Security   ◆ ◆ ◆ ◆ ◆ ◆ ◆ ◆ ◆

In coping with traumatic experience, establishing safety is paramount. The significance of attachment to caregivers should not obscure the importance of attachments to familiar places and inanimate objects. This phenomenon of bonding to places has been called *site attachment*.[41] Perhaps we owe our sense of territoriality to our reptilian brains (see Appendix). Mammals seek shelter from predators in contact with their mothers; lizards seek familiar hiding places in their own territory.[42] Bowlby emphasizes both territory and attachment: "Since two of the natural [situations] . . . that tend to be avoided are strangeness and being alone, there is a marked tendency for humans, like animals of other species, to remain in a particular and familiar locale and in the company of particular and familiar people." [43]

First things first: It is important to have a safe place in the environment—ideally, a range of safe places. Safe places may include a spot in the woods or in the park, your home, your room, or your bed. Just as children rely on familiar inanimate objects (stuffed animals, a "security blanket"), so, too, do adults. We also should not minimize the significance of attachments to animals.[44] Particularly in the context of trauma, pets such as cats, dogs, and rabbits may be emotional lifesavers for children and adults. They are our mammalian kin, and they have limbic systems akin to ours—little wonder that we can form affectionate bonds with them. Besides, they're furry, providing a much-needed comforting touch. Thus, an enduring and dependable relationship with a beloved pet can do much to sustain the quest for secure attachments.

It is important to be able to go to a tangible place of safety. But it is also possible to seek shelter in one's imagination. Traumatized individuals often find it helpful to visualize an imagined or actual safe place. Relaxation and hypnosis can be used to enhance such visualization, which can be enormously powerful. Picturing oneself in a safe place can be a key component of self-soothing.

Having a safe place is necessary to feel secure, but it is not enough. Only through secure attachments with others can we gradually internalize a sense of safety and learn to regulate arousal. If workable attachment patterns were not developed in childhood, they need to be developed in adulthood. Of course, individuals who have been hampered in forming attachments need more than just the mere availability of a good "attachment figure," such as an understanding friend or a reliable therapist. They must overcome distrust, avoidance, resistance, and ambivalence. Much of the work of coping with trauma entails understanding and surmounting these obstacles in order to restore secure attachments. This process can be a tall order, especially if the foundations of attachment were distorted in childhood. Even when the trauma occurs in adulthood, secure attachments may not be easy to reestablish. Traumatic experience in adulthood (assault, rape, spouse abuse) can profoundly undermine the foundations laid in childhood.

For now, the core task of working toward secure attachment can merely be posed. Treatment of trauma often involves forming an attachment with an individual therapist as well as an affiliation with groups. These issues will be addressed in the context of relationships (Chapter 8) and treatment approaches (Chapter 12).

CHAPTER FOUR

Emotion

◆ A 10-year-old boy reaches for a glass to get a drink of juice. His hands are wet, and the glass slips, falling to the floor and smashing. His father rushes into the kitchen, his face contorted with rage. The boy cowers in terror. His father screams at him to clean it up; the boy's hands shake so much that he cuts himself in the process. In disgust, his father takes over and sends the boy outside with a knife to cut a switch. The boy is trembling with fear, and he's also furious at his father. Holding the knife, he thinks fleetingly of stabbing his father, but he quickly pushes the thought aside. He tries to find a branch with only a few sharp spikes on it. He brings the switch to his father, who is standing out on the porch. His father makes him pull down his shorts and begins whipping him. The boy tries not to cry or yell, but he can't help it. He sees the two neighbor girls watching through the bushes. He turns his face away in shame. His father sends him to his room. After a while, the boy calms down, but he doesn't feel okay. He's been through scenes like this many times before, and he's sure things will never change. He feels dejected and despairing. The boy doesn't have much choice about how he feels. Fear, anger, shame, and depression are all natural reactions to this kind of traumatic episode.

Our "emotional brain," the limbic system, has been wired over millennia to respond to situations that are noxious, injurious, or threatening. We have these emotional reactions because they prompt and prepare us to cope and to protect ourselves. Like attachment, these psychological and physiological reactions have evolved because they have served the species well much of the time.[1] Aversive reactions are a fundamental aspect of human motivation.[2] We don't have any choice about these emotional responses, although we can exert some control over them.

We perceive the world emotionally, always attuned to what is good for us and what is bad for us. Our emotional brain works fast—virtually instantaneously. Our emotional reactions gear us up physiologically for fast and vigorous action—fight or flight. But if we are physically overwhelmed and cannot act, the emotional reactions no longer serve us. Strong emotions are useful for bursts of action; chronic arousal without any channels of expression can be detrimental.[3]

Many individuals who have been traumatized do not want to feel anything. They have experienced intense and overwhelming feelings in the course of the trauma, and they have learned how to dampen or entirely cut them off. There are many ways to short-circuit feelings, such as alcohol and drug abuse, overwork or constant activity, or focus on physical symptoms and illness. Intense feelings that cannot be short-circuited often cannot be labeled and understood. The individual may experience a tidal wave of feeling or an overwhelming sense of internal chaos.

It is important to learn to clarify and label feelings and to sort them out, whether they be anger, rage, fear, terror, despair, sadness, guilt, joy, or elation. Properly clarified, feelings can be used for self-understanding, an indication of how the inner self is faring, and as signals that certain problems must be faced and mastered.[4] Emotional health does not entail "feeling good" all the time; it requires tolerance for the full range of emotions—the capacity to feel angry, anxious, depressed, joyful, and so forth, as a situation warrants. The various emotions inform us about ourselves and our problems in adaptation, just as a toothache informs us of dental work that must be done. With trauma, emotions can become problematic—intense and prolonged—and then their adaptive value as signals for coping is undermined.

In this chapter, I examine four major classes of aversive emotions: 1) anxiety, fear, and panic; 2) anger, rage, hostility, and aggression; 3) shame and guilt; and 4) depression. Fortunately, evolution has not limited us to these painful emotions; the pleasurable emotions are equally important and are discussed in Chapter 13. I show how these four types of aversive emotions are linked to trauma, and also consider the contribution of temperament to emotional responses. I conclude the chapter with a discussion of ways to control emotion.

Anxiety, Fear, and Panic ◆ ◆ ◆ ◆ ◆ ◆ ◆ ◆

◆ Imagine a girl whose mother is alcoholic. Whenever her mother drinks, she loses her temper and goes on a rampage. The girl is in her bedroom playing, aware that her mother is in the kitchen drinking. She knows that the tide has turned when she hears her mother yelling. She runs to the closet; it's hot, stuffy, and dark. Her mother is looking for her and screaming her name. The girl feels trapped, sweaty, and panicky. If she goes to her mother, she might get yelled at or beaten. But the longer she hides, the more her mother will be enraged. She's in a dilemma. She feels helpless. The girl's helplessness is the essence of anxiety. She can do nothing more to protect herself.

Consider the opposites of anxiety: predictability, control, confidence, and familiarity—circumstances and situations unfolding as expected and desired. Want to pull yourself out of an anxiety state? Find something you are good at. Do it. Get absorbed in it. Anxiety stops us in our tracks. It is linked to novelty, the unexpected, and loss of control. Or something that used to work that doesn't work anymore. It signals danger: punishment, pain, and distress ahead. It tells us to put everything on hold while we try to figure out what to do next.

There is a complex circuit in the brain for anxiety that has been aptly named the *behavioral inhibition system*.[5] This circuit continually checks to see that things are going according to plan, and when they do not, the behavioral inhibition system kicks in, bringing us to a screeching halt: "stop, look and listen, and get ready for action." [6] The circuit can check progress many times in just a second; we can become anxious very fast when things don't go according to plan!

Anxiety signals a state of arousal, and it functions to ensure readiness for coping. Anxiety is adaptive to the extent that the behavioral inhibition system disrupts ineffective behavior and prompts an immediate search for a better solution. When you are anxious, you are stirred up, prepared to cope, but you don't know just *how* to cope. Alert, you look for danger, yet feel helpless or out of control. You focus inward on your own discomfort.[7] Then you may become distracted, more preoccupied with controlling your anxiety than with the external problem that you need to confront.

Momentary anxiety is adaptive; chronic anxiety is not. Cues associated—however remotely—with past traumatic experience can trigger anxiety. Your emotional brain concludes quickly and unconsciously that something is not working, that danger lurks nearby. At worst, you can wind up in a chronic state of "anxious apprehension." [8] Nothing is ever quite right; you never feel completely safe.

As you know, anxiety seems to feed on itself. That's because anxiety is linked to anticipation. You don't have to do everything to see how it will work; you can *think* it through, anticipating consequences. In the lingo of computers, you are able to run "simulations" in your head instead of having to rely on actions in the world.[9] Evolution has provided you with a mixed blessing. You can also drive yourself crazy with this marvelous capacity to simulate! You can fuel your anxiety by running all kinds of frightening simulations; this process is akin to sitting through a bunch of horror movies. Simulation can rapidly become self-defeating. You may feel more anxious and helpless rather than better prepared to cope. Ideally, you would use your facility for "simulation" only for constructive purposes (planning ahead).

When you feel anxious, you know that something is wrong, but you have not discovered what it is or how to deal with it. By the time you feel fear, you know what is wrong and you know what to do—escape! In contrast to anxiety, fear is a response to a specific danger in the environment. Like other basic emotions, fear has been wired in over the course of evolution. Its adaptive value is obvious—flight. When you are afraid, your physiology gears up for action. When you are running at full speed, you are not aware of the physiological arousal, you are one with it, using it to escape. If you cannot flee, you are just saddled with sympathetic nervous system arousal (sweating, palpitations, shallow breathing, muscular tension).

A panic attack is an extreme fear response. In the context of horrific traumatic experience, even the words *panic* and *extreme fear* fail to convey the intensity of the experience. *Terror* may be a better term than panic.[10] Unlike fear, panic often occurs without any conscious reason. If you suddenly encounter a bear in the woods and flee in terror, we would not say that you had a "panic attack." If you behave in the same way in a shopping mall without any clear reason, then we call it a panic attack. Perhaps we could also start using the term *terror attack.*

Stress and trauma are common in the backgrounds of persons who develop panic disorder.[11] Persons who have been traumatized are liable to have panic attacks, because the terror that was appropriate to the traumatizing situation is set off suddenly, without warning, for reasons that may not be clear. The panic attack may be set off instantaneously and unconsciously by some environmental cue associated with past trauma. A panic attack may also be set off by an *internal* physiological cue (change in heart rate, "butterflies," shortness of breath), because those physiological sensations were also part of the original traumatic experience. Just as we are reminded of trauma by external events, we are also reminded of trauma by internal sensations.

Anger and Aggression

◆ Imagine a woman whose childhood was filled with scenes of her ill-tempered father constantly berating and occasionally slapping her mother. Somehow, despite her determination to avoid getting herself into the same situation as her mother, she marries a man who continually intimidates and mistreats her and her children. She fights back to protect her children and to protect herself, but she is overpowered. Over the years, she comes to hate her husband. She also screams at her children and hates herself for it. She fears that she has become just like her despised father.

Anger and the "fight" response are inherently adaptive reactions to aversive situations. Like the "flight" response, the "fight" response has undoubtedly contributed to our evolutionary success. We are wired for attack and defense; these behaviors are part of our neurological programming.[12] The fight reaction is as much a part of the patterned trauma response as the flight reaction. There is ample evidence that maltreatment and neglect contribute to aggression.[13] Many persons who have been traumatized, however, have severe conflicts about their angry feelings and about expressing their anger.[14] Having severe conflict about an inevitable, natural response is itself a major problem. Moreover, anger and aggression, while adaptive in their self-protective function, can also turn destructive, as they do for the woman who despises herself for her hatred. Let's distinguish between benign anger and destructive aggression.

Benign Anger

For the sake of clarity, it helps to just define anger as a good thing. Yes, anger is good. Psychologist Harriet Lerner begins her best-selling book, *The Dance of Anger,* this way:

> Anger is a signal, and one worth listening to. Our anger may be a message that we are being hurt, that our rights are being violated, that our needs or wants are not being adequately met, or simply that something is not right.[15]

Yet many persons are taught that anger is bad, or they are punished for their natural angry reactions. If they allowed themselves to express their natural angry reaction to being hurt, they may have been hurt worse. In addition, many individuals who have been abused associate all anger with violent rage and aggression; they have not had models of healthy anger.

Anger is adaptive. From infancy onward, anger provides fuel for overcoming obstacles.[16] Have you ever become irritated when you try to open a door that's stuck? Your irritation energizes you to yank it open with more force. So it is with interpersonal obstacles. Like anxiety and fear, anger is a source of arousal. It prepares us physiologically for actively coping, confronting, resolving controversy, and defending ourselves.[17] Think of anger as power. Assertiveness, for example, is an effort to make your case and get your way; it is a key form of mastery. When you run into an obstacle, assertion can become infused with anger, which increases the vigor of your coping.

Destructive Aggression

As is all too clear in our lives and in society, aggression can readily get out of hand, going beyond resolving controversy and ensuring self-protection to becoming destructive. Common examples of uncontrolled aggression are vengefulness, sadism, and cruelty. Persons who are treated sadistically and cruelly are provoked into being hostile themselves, and they are likely to have significant conflicts about their own sadistic feelings—feelings that are virtually inevitable in light of their past experiences.

Psychiatrist Henri Parens[18] leads parenting classes and has been an astute observer of anger in infancy and childhood. He spelled out a useful continuum of anger. At the benign end, he put *irritability* (beginning anger) and *anger* (a moderate level). By his definition, irritability and anger are helpful and self-protective. He then proposed an important hypothesis: "excessive unpleasure generates hostile destructiveness." Trauma certainly qualifies as "excessive unpleasure"! Psychologist Dorothy Otnow Lewis[19] writes, "Probably the most powerful generator of aggression in animals and possibly in man is the repeated infliction of pain." Painful experience raises the level of emotion to unmanageable levels, and it is liable to turn a healthy anger response into destructive experience and behavior.

Parens[20] defines three levels of destructive aggression: hostility, hate, and rage. The difference between anger and hostility is important. Anger is a momentary emotional reaction to an aversive situation. *Anger* bolsters coping. *Hostility* goes beyond a particular aversive situation to infuse relationships in a more lasting way. Someone provokes you, you feel angry, that's that. When hostility comes into play, you feel antagonistic in a relationship without being provoked at a given moment. A hostile person, for example, may seem generally nasty and ill-tempered. In its extreme form, hostility becomes *hate*—an enduring, intense, embittered attitude that can destroy relationships. Unlike hostility and the extreme of hate, *rage* is like anger in being a briefer reaction to provocation. With rage, however, the provocation is extreme, and the anger reaches a level of intensity (blind rage) that is unmanageable and disorganized—and likely to lead to destructive aggression.

Hostile destructiveness can be hard to relinquish. Aggression can become a kind of passion, sought out for the "pleasure" it provides.[21] Who among us has not taken satisfaction in fantasies of revenge? Trauma just adds fuel to our vengeful inclinations. Persons who have developed destructive levels of anger may find it extremely gratifying to "trash" a room or to intimidate someone. They may reject nondestructive substitutes (pounding a pillow) because they are less gratifying. Resolving vengeful feelings is one of the hardest challenges in dealing with trauma.

Anger and aggression can fuel a healthy sense of power, but they can also fuel an unhealthy sense of power. It is natural to want to turn the tables. Persons who have been traumatized and made to feel helpless and powerless may be loath to give up the feeling of power associated with hostile destructiveness. A man who as a child was made to feel powerless by his intimidating father may relish being able to intimidate others as an adult. Moreover, aggression can often be effective (in the short run) in getting you what you want. Bullying and intimidating others can be effective in getting your way. Thus, destructive aggression can be highly reinforcing. Feeling powerful beats feeling powerless. At worst, aggression can become like an addiction. And, like other addictions, destructiveness can provide immediate gratification (even a feeling of euphoria) but then leave an aftermath of guilt and self-hatred. Then you're into a vicious circle: Destructiveness fuels self-hatred, which fuels destructiveness, around and around.

Full of Anger?

Many persons who have been abused and who struggle with hostile destructiveness think of themselves as *filled with anger or rage*. Does this idea make any sense? Why would you think of yourself as being *filled* with anger? Perhaps it is because of the repeated experience of being provoked to anger and "holding it in" (not expressing the anger outwardly). Maybe when you hold in anger time after time, you begin to feel that you are accumulating it, filling yourself up. You "stuff" anger; you become "filled" with it.

This idea of being filled with anger is obviously appealing. But I think it is a harmful illusion. Where *is* all this anger? In the bowels? If you are filled with anger, the solution is to purge it. But that doesn't work. Endless blowups, in therapy or elsewhere, do not reduce hostile destructiveness. On the contrary, they may even lower your threshold for hostility and rage. Blowing off steam may feel good in the short run, because it relieves tension—although the aftermath of guilt may bring all the tension right back. But endless blowups do no good in the long run. You could even think of blowing off steam as *practicing* anger—strengthening the habit.

You will have a better chance of dealing with anger constructively if you think of yourself as "easy to anger" (or as having a "hot" temper) instead of as "filled with anger." Frans de Waal, an eminent primatologist, has studied aggression in species from chimpanzees to humans. He disputes the idea of a "reservoir" of anger: "I rather prefer the metaphor of aggression as fire. A pilot flame is burning in all of us, and we make use of it as the situation demands." [22] Picture yourself with a short fuse, not as a huge container. Try letting go of the image of yourself as being filled with rage, and think of yourself as being too ready to flare up. Think of your need to be able to feel irritable and moderately angry when you are provoked. Think of your potential to control your hostile and destructive behavior. You are not "filled with" a legacy of rage from past trauma; rather, *you are easily angered by current provocations that are reminiscent of the past trauma.* Diminishing your anger entails dealing with these *current provocations* in effective ways so that your anger is not continually restimulated.

Let's take it a step further. How do you think of human nature? Your view of your fellow men and women will affect how you see yourself. There is ample evidence to support the notion that we humans are aggressive and destructive. No one would dispute that. But are we *mainly* aggressive and destructive? Perhaps a small minority of us are. Unfortunately, persons who have been abused have had a biased experience with the human race. Evolutionist Stephen Jay Gould puts our aggressiveness into perspective:

> What do we see on any ordinary day on the streets or in the homes of any American city—even in the subways of New York? Thousands of tiny and insignificant acts of kindness and consideration. We step aside to let someone pass, smile at a child, chat aimlessly with an acquaintance or even with a stranger . . . nearly every encounter with another person is at least neutral and usually pleasant enough. *Homo sapiens* is a remarkably genial species . . . Why, then, do most of us have the impression that people are so aggressive, and intrinsically so? The answer, I think, lies in the asymmetry of effects—the truly tragic side of human existence. Unfortunately, one incident of violence can undo ten thousand acts of kindness . . . Kindness is so fragile, so easy to efface; violence is so powerful. [23]

De Waal[24] also makes a compelling argument that we have given ourselves a bum rap as an aggressive species. Throughout primates there is ample evidence of peacemaking. With the rest of the primates, we have a 30-million-year history of learning the art of reconciliation to counter our aggression. If it is in our nature to be aggressive, it is just as much in our nature to comfort, heal, and soothe.

Self-Directed Aggression and "Masochism"

Hostile destructiveness can be expressed in aggressive outbursts, cruelty, vengefulness, and sadism. In addition, hostile destructiveness is frequently turned back against the self in what has been called *masochism*. I think that it's a mistake to think of masochism as the enjoyment of suffering. No one benefits from thinking, "I'm just a masochist. I like to suffer." I do not believe that people like to suffer or choose to suffer. I do not believe that people enjoy being miserable. It makes no biological sense. And thinking that you do will only fuel your self-hatred and lead you nowhere. Instead, I urge you to assume that you are trying to *relieve* your suffering. You might want to find better ways of doing so.

Seemingly masochistic behavior can be understood as a grim compromise, a solution to conflict about outwardly expressing anger and aggression. A rageful child may bite his arm. A rageful woman may cut her arm. Why? There is no doubt that self-directed aggression, like any other form of aggression, can provide immediate relief in the form of tension reduction.[25] For example, some persons find that self-inflicted physical pain distracts them from emotional pain. They go from unbearable emotional pain to more manageable physical pain. This change in pain level may even feel pleasurable because it provides a sense of relief.[26] Individuals who cope in this way are not finding pleasure in suffering; they are finding pleasure in *suffering less.* Self-punishment may be similar. Self-directed aggression may satisfy a need to be punished—including punishment for the aggressive feelings themselves. Such self-punishment may yield a feeling of satisfaction or relief. This doesn't mean that you *enjoy* punishing yourself; rather, you may be relieving guilt feelings that are even more painful.

Tension relief may be the main function of self-directed aggression. But there are several additional reasons that many persons choose *self*-directed-aggression. Some persons turn aggression back onto themselves to spare others the anticipated effects of their rage. In addition, the self is a readily available target. Self-directed aggression can also be hidden and kept secret. Ironically, persons who have been injured by others may repeat the experience by inflicting pain on themselves so that they can have some sense of *control* over being injured. But self-injurious behavior can also be *indirectly* aggressive toward others. To the extent that others are aware of it, they may feel alarmed, hurt, or guilty.

Although self-directed aggression provides relief in the short run, it backfires in the long run. It damages self-esteem, leads to conflicts in relationships, and adds to the shame and guilt that it seeks to relieve. It adds to the stockpile of ongoing trauma, perhaps providing immediate relief while simultaneously restimulating memories of past injuries. Thus, self-injury often escalates in a vicious circle. Better long-range solutions are the subject of Part IV (Treatment).

Shame and Guilt ◆ ◆ ◆ ◆ ◆ ◆ ◆ ◆ ◆ ◆

◆ A woman in psychotherapy averts her gaze in shame as she tries to talk about being molested as a young child. Orphaned in early childhood, she was raised by an aunt and uncle who did not want her. She keenly felt their resentment and sometimes overheard them talking about ways to get rid of her. At school she was isolated, and after school she had to hurry home to do chores on the farm, so she had little contact with other children. But there was an older boy in the neighborhood who paid attention to her. When no one was around, they'd sneak into the barn and "play doctor." If her uncle found out, he might beat them both to death, but no one ever knew. And she was desperate for affection. Now, a decade later, she continues to feel ashamed and guilty, having little compassion for the lonely girl who seized an opportunity to feel loved and who had little comprehension of the exploitation involved.

Psychiatrist Donald Nathanson[27] has joined other authors recently in protesting that shame has been a much-neglected emotion, and he has made a major contribution to redressing that imbalance. Nathanson puts shame and pride on opposite poles. A feeling of pride goes with healthy striving and a sense of success and accomplishment. Shame is the opposite, a fall from grace. Shame involves a sense of incompetence and failure, with accompanying feelings of embarrassment, humiliation, and mortification. Pride evokes a wish to be seen and admired by others; shame leads to a wish to hide and isolate—a longing for invisibility. As Nathanson puts it, it leads to a wish to be "shorn from the herd." [28]

Anything that leads to a negative self-image can trigger the feeling of shame, including feeling weak, dirty, defective, exposed, small, stupid, helpless, out of control, damaged, unloved, and unlovable. It is little wonder that shame is such a common consequence of trauma. By definition, trauma entails being out of control, helpless, and powerless. Trauma wounds the self and the sense of competence and mastery. This is true whether the trauma results from a tornado, a car wreck, or an assault. But shame is most severe in the context of systematic abuse. Abusers are likely deliberately to instill a sense of shame by humiliating you, taking away your control, and exposing your helplessness.

Nathanson makes an important distinction between shame and guilt. Shame involves an insult to your self-image, whereas guilt results from actions that bring harm to someone else or that violate your moral codes and ideals. Many persons who have been assaulted and abused not only are ashamed but also feel guilty. They feel responsible for having acted contrary to their values. A woman who is raped may feel that she has acted sinfully, even when a knife was held to her throat. An abused child may desperately try to avoid anything that would arouse the rage of an abusive parent; failing to do so, the child may attribute the parental rage to her own behavior. With the sense of responsibility comes the feeling of guilt. Even if the child eventually realizes that no action will stem the tide of abuse, she may conclude that her own defectiveness is to blame. Nathanson writes:

> The child is faced with two contrasting alternatives: a frightening awareness that these parents are incapable of love, implying that they actually might not provide protection from danger; or the creative but false theory that his or her parents are really okay and that their unpleasant behavior is the reasonable response of good people to a bad or defective child.[29]

Nathanson concludes that, given this dilemma, "logic most often commands the second choice."[30] Ironically, feeling responsible for your mistreatment can sustain hope: "If it's my fault, maybe I can be better so it won't happen again." But such hope comes at the high price of shame compounded by guilt feelings.

Nathanson believes that shame, like every other emotion, is an innate emotional response with adaptive value. Ideally, shame can prompt a fair appraisal of our shortcomings, sparking self-examination that can lead to self-improvement. Shame can be excruciatingly painful, and this memorable experience can lead us to avoid any recurrence by working on our failings.

But a history of being shamed may make shame intolerably painful. Nathanson has identified four common ways of escaping shame: withdrawal, avoidance, self-attack, and attacking others. First, rather than leading to healthy self-examination, shame can prompt *withdrawal.* You can isolate yourself, avoiding any exposure to others. At best, you can lick your wounds and then return to society. Second, shame can prompt *avoidance.* You can try to block out shame with alcohol or other tension-reducing mechanisms. Or you can blot out the self-image associated with shame by creating a false self-image, resorting to arrogance and narcissism, fabricating an unrealistically positive self-image to assuage the pain of failure. Third, you can *attack yourself.* You can avert shame by mobilizing anger against yourself in the form of self-destructive behavior. Finally, you can retaliate by *attacking the other.* Feeling overpowered and ashamed, you can turn shame into destructive aggression. You can attempt to overpower others by humiliating them and exposing *them* to shame.

Shame and anger are closely related. Shame is a common instigator of rage. Moreover, becoming enraged can lead to a sense of being *out of control* that fuels shame. Michael Lewis[31] describes the commonly observed shame-rage spiral: "shame leads to rage, which leads to more shame, which leads to more rage." He vividly illustrates this cycle:

> Recently I was in a department store and was watching a mother with a young child, a boy of about 5 years. The mother wanted to shop, and the child was crawling around under some garments. She told the child to stop, but he continued to play. She then grabbed him and picked him up, at which point he began to cry loudly. His loud cries attracted other people's gaze. She looked around and saw another woman looking at her disapprovingly. She appeared to be shamed by her child's loud crying. To get him to quiet, she hit him. This only made him cry more, which drew more attention to her. She hit him again to get him to stop. He only cried more.[32]

Lewis believes that such mutually reinforcing experiences of shame and rage contribute to many forms of violence. His example itself shows how the shame-rage spiral may play into child abuse.

Depression ◆ ◆ ◆ ◆ ◆ ◆ ◆ ◆ ◆ ◆ ◆

◆ A man, now in his early 30s, was terrorized and neglected when he was growing up. His father left the large family when the children were young, and his mother worked long hours to make ends meet. He was bullied, overworked, beaten, and sexually abused by two older brothers. The slightest mistake in doing a chore would bring on an assault. Now in adulthood, he leads a life of constant tension. He is on edge, wary, irritable, and mercilessly self-critical. At best, he is anxious and discouraged. At worst, he sinks into profound depression. Then he stays home from work, draws the curtains, and spends most of his time in bed sleeping or watching TV.

As this example illustrates, anxiety and depression are close cousins. Many persons can't tell whether they feel anxious or depressed, and for good reason: Anxiety and depression often occur together.[33] But researchers are now clarifying the differences between anxiety and depression.[34] Anxiety entails a state of high arousal—feeling agitated, distressed, upset. Whereas anxiety is an example of high negative emotion, depression is a state of low positive emotion—the absence of excitement or pleasure, a general disengagement from the world. Depression is a state of low arousal, experienced as lethargy or lack of energy, lack of interest in doing anything, or lack of drive. At the extreme, you can be bedridden with depression. Anxiety is often followed by depression. Chronic anxiety can wear you out. In my view, depression is akin to emotional exhaustion. Chronic stress tends to drive the nervous system into depression,[35] and it is little wonder that depression is such a common problem for persons struggling with trauma.

Anxiety is a state of readiness to cope (take flight), whereas depression is a state of giving up the attempt to cope—in effect, a kind of collapse. Anxiety has been associated with feeling helpless—not knowing what to do, or which way to turn. Depression can be characterized as a state of hopelessness—a sense that nothing can be done, that no effective action can be taken. Anxiety and depression may alternate: You may become mobilized and anxious and then give up in depression, but then become mobilized and anxious again.

Psychologist Martin Seligman[36] has helped us understand depression in terms of the "learned helplessness" he has observed in rats, dogs, and humans. Helplessness goes with a sense that events are uncontrollable. As we have seen, helplessness is associated with anxiety. But *prolonged* helplessness can also eventuate in depression. Under appropriate experimental conditions, rats, dogs, and humans can readily learn to escape painful stimuli like electric shock. What happens when the experimenter sets it up so that escape is no longer possible?

Seligman observed that about two-thirds of the dogs exposed to this situation developed *learned* helplessness. They gave up trying to cope. Even when the experimenter reversed the conditions so that escape was again possible, the dogs failed to cope. They no longer learned. Learning to be helpless undermined their natural tendency to cope actively. Seligman recognized that learned helplessness, both in animals and in humans, is akin to depression. The essence of both is "the belief that action is futile." [37] Depression can render you unable to learn; even when the situation is no longer aversive or dangerous, you continue to respond as if it were.

Anxiety, fear, anger, and shame are wired into the brain and mind over the course of evolution; within bounds, they are adaptive. They are inevitable responses to traumatic experience. Depression is clearly just as well established as a response in human nature, and it is clearly rooted in brain functioning. Is depression a flaw? Something that goes wrong with the brain? It is hard to see how "giving up" could be adaptive. Yet depression has been described as an inborn "conservation-withdrawal reaction" that serves to shut down arousal to avert the excessive stress to the organism associated with prolonged agitation.[38] The model is the inconsolable baby who cries himself to sleep. In this sense, depression may be adaptive in conserving energy and resources when active coping is ineffective or not feasible.[39] Yet depression can take on a life of its own (in the mind and in the brain), and prolonged depressive states preclude adaptation.

Most psychological triggers for depression can be boiled down to two categories: loss and failure. The grief response associated with loss is nearly universal, and the symptoms of grief overlap those of depression. In depression associated with loss, the individual commonly feels alone, abandoned, deprived, unwanted, and unlovable. In depression associated with failure to achieve some highly valued goal, the individual feels inadequate or incompetent. It is easy to see why low self-esteem goes with depression, whether depression is associated with loss (and feeling unlovable) or failure (and feeling inadequate). Of course, these two themes often run together. A person who has experienced a major failure may then feel unworthy of others' love.

It is not surprising that traumatic experiences, and maltreatment and neglect in relationships with caregivers in particular, are associated with depression. If Seligman's theory is correct, prolonged traumatic experience almost assuredly leads to depression: What "lies at the heart of depression is unitary: the depressed patient believes or has learned that he cannot control those elements of his life that relieve suffering, bring gratification, or provide nurture."[40] Consider the effects of repeatedly being injured and then left alone—repeated abandonment and continual loss. Other related losses include the loss of safety, the loss of a sense of control and mastery, the loss of the opportunity to be a child, and the loss of peer relationships.

In addition to being associated with loss, depression is also likely to be connected with a sense of failure, inasmuch as those who are injured often blame themselves. They attribute their being injured to their own failings, and they feel they have failed to overcome the traumatic experience by virtue of their own inadequacies. Accordingly, depression is compounded by feelings of shame and guilt.

Temperament and Personality ◆ ◆ ◆ ◆ ◆ ◆ ◆

Emotional responses are natural, adaptive reactions to aversive experience. Yet not everyone has the same emotional response to the same situation. Even very early in life, there are differences from one individual to the next. From infancy onward, some persons are more emotionally reactive than others. Such reactivity can contribute significantly to the impact of traumatic events.

Emotional differences among individuals are partly related to temperament—that is, personality dispositions that are under some genetic influence, evident early in life, and somewhat stable across situations and over time.[41] These inherited personality traits may result partly from genetically based individual differences in the balance of neurotransmitters.[42] Many temperamental differences seen in humans are also clearly evident in primates and other mammals.[43] Examples of temperament-based personality traits include emotionality, sociability, activity level, impulsivity, aggressiveness, "difficultness," and proneness to depression.[44] Because coping is always shaped by temperament, some recent personality theory is worth considering in detail. Psychologists have pulled together decades of research converging on five basic dimensions of personality that evolve partly from differences in temperament.[45] As you read about these five dimensions, you might think about where you fall on each.

Negative emotionality refers to the tendency to remain calm versus being prone to various forms of distress, such as anxiety, irritability, anger, and shame. *Positive emotionality* is the capacity for pleasurable engagement and the disposition to seek rewarding experiences. We are highly social mammals, and contact with other persons is a prominent source of pleasure, so "extraversion" is an important part of positive emotionality. Those who are high on this dimension are gregarious and enthusiastic; those who are lacking in positive emotion are prone to depression and likely to be more socially isolated. The dimension of *constraint* refers to the inclination to be cautious, deliberate, conscientious, and self-controlled versus being impulsive, careless, and reckless—acting without thinking. *Agreeableness* includes trust, altruism, compliance, and modesty. The last dimension, *openness to experience*, includes having an active fantasy life, intellectual curiosity, an appreciation for beauty, a preference for novelty, and receptivity to feelings and emotions.

All five aspects of temperament are pertinent to trauma, but negative emotionality is certainly at the center. Developmental psychologist Jerome Kagan[46] has extensively studied the differences between *inhibited* and *uninhibited* children. He has observed that "About two out of every ten healthy Caucasian infants inherit a physiology that biases them to be both aroused and distressed by stimulation early in the first year and initially avoidant of unfamiliarity in the second and third years." [47] Recall that the behavioral inhibition circuit makes us stop, look, and listen. The hallmark of the inhibited child is an inclination to "freeze" (become quiet and/or distressed) in novel or unfamiliar situations. For example, on the first day of preschool, the inhibited toddler is likely to sit alone in a corner, whereas the uninhibited toddler will immediately launch into play with other children. The inhibited toddler's "behavioral inhibition" system is easily turned on in novel, unfamiliar, or stressful situations. This proneness to arousal is partly a result of genetic factors associated with higher levels of norepinephrine and an easily alarmed "trauma center," the locus coeruleus[48] (see Appendix).

Children who are inhibited in infancy will not necessarily remain inhibited for the rest of their lives; they may learn to overcome their inhibited temperament. But Kagan[49] proposes that temperamentally inhibited children who are exposed to more stressful environments are likely to *remain* inhibited and anxious. He has also noted, however, that excessive maternal protection—intended to spare the inhibited child from frustration and anxiety—may backfire by hampering the child's development of coping mechanisms.[50] But overprotection is not the primary problem for children who are mistreated. It is reasonable to suppose that individuals with an inhibited temperament, prone to distress, would be most sensitive and reactive to traumatic experience. Sadly, I think that such individuals, who may be more quiet and compliant, may even be more likely to be intimidated and exploited than those who are temperamentally more feisty and obstreperous.

Temperament refers to partly inborn characteristics, evident early in life. We all share in human nature, and we all have our individual natures (temperament). Stretching the meaning of the word, one could think of temperament as not only shaping responses to trauma but also being altered by traumatic experience. There is no doubt that prolonged stress can have a lasting effect on the nervous system.[51] Thus, a child who is temperamentally calm and sociable may become characteristically more distressed and withdrawn as a consequence of repeated trauma. The same might be true of the combat veteran. A young man who goes to war confident and outgoing could come back tense and isolated. Unfortunately, trauma could contribute adversely to all five personality dimensions—increasing distress, eroding pleasure, and undermining self-control, as well as counteracting agreeableness and openness to experience.

Establishing Emotional Control ◆ ◆ ◆ ◆ ◆ ◆ ◆

To reiterate, painful emotions are natural adaptive responses to aversive situations. But adaptation is imperfect at best, and our natural emotional responses can be overwhelming when evoked by trauma. Then it becomes natural to try to blot them out with alcohol or drugs, for example, or by other means of altering consciousness.

If you have been traumatized, learning to tolerate painful emotions is extremely important—and it can be extremely difficult. To tolerate the painful emotions, you must be able to keep them within some reasonable bounds. Many persons need some direct physiological help from medications, and this form of treatment will be discussed, along with several others, in Chapter 12 (Treatment Approaches). In addition, there are numerous techniques to enhance control that are discussed in Chapter 13 (Self-Regulation). This chapter focuses on cognitive therapy, a form of treatment specifically developed to help establish emotional control.

Cognitive Therapy

Psychiatrist Aaron Beck began developing cognitive therapy in the 1960s as a method for treating depression. Not only has cognitive therapy proven effective in the treatment of depression, but it has now been extended to the treatment of other problematic emotions, including anxiety and anger.[52]

The basic principle of cognitive therapy is simple: What you think can affect how you feel. Depression and other problematic emotions are fueled by negative thoughts. These negative thoughts are likely to be so habitual as to be automatic and virtually unconscious reactions to situations. For example, when passed without greeting by an acquaintance, the depressed person may automatically think, "He doesn't like me," or worse, "Nobody likes me." Receiving a low grade on an examination, the depressed person may automatically think, "I'm no good" or "I'll never amount to anything." Heading out to a job interview, the anxious person may automatically think, "I'll make a fool of myself." Such automatic thoughts become unquestioned truths, basic assumptions about the self, the world, and the future.

Cognitive therapy enlists the help of the rational brain in controlling the emotional brain. The first step is to start paying attention to your negative automatic thoughts so they become more conscious. You may even practice jotting them down to heighten your awareness. Then you start training yourself to substitute alternatives—more objective or positive thoughts. When an acquaintance passes without greeting you, you might think, "He's preoccupied," rather than, "Nobody likes me." Cognitive therapy entails thinking about events in flexible ways rather than staying in the rut of negative assumptions.

Anger Management

Irritation and anger should be felt and expressed. But the rational brain needs to be brought to bear on the chronic and destructive emotions of hostility, hate, and rage. Cognitive therapy is the linchpin in current treatment approaches for "anger management." Our angry and hostile reactions are determined largely by how we appraise and interpret situations. Persons who have been abused had little leeway in how they interpreted the abusive situations; those situations involved extreme provocation and excessive unpleasure. The early feelings, however, continue to be aroused by current situations that are both similar *and different.* New appraisals that better fit current reality are needed.

Psychologist Ray Novaco[53] has developed a comprehensive, multistep approach to anger control that focuses on education, relaxation, and management. There are several components to his approach. The first step involves learning about anger, as you are doing here. To control your anger, you must become *more aware* of it. This approach may seem paradoxical. If you struggle to control your anger, you are likely to block it out of your awareness entirely—then, as anger builds, you may explode. If you can feel *mild to moderate* levels of anger, then you can identify the problem, and you stand some chance of resolving it. I encourage traumatized patients to cultivate feelings of irritation—and the sources are endless! Cultivating "irritation" and "anger" can help you avoid hostility, hate, and rage. Learn to distinguish between angry feelings and aggressive behavior; you can be angry without necessarily being aggressive. Angry feelings and controlled behavior go well together.

The second step in Novaco's approach is learning how to relax. Like anxiety, anger and hostility entail high levels of arousal. To lower the level of arousal, any means of inducing relaxation is appropriate. Relaxation is as basic to anger management as it is to anxiety management. If you are in a state of high tension, a minor "last straw" can tip the balance to rage in a flash. If you feel more relaxed, you will have more time to avert an explosive buildup of rage.

The third step in anger management is to learn to think about yourself and provocative situations in a way that diminishes anger and hostility rather than fuels them. This is the approach of cognitive therapy. What you say to yourself in a provocative situation (as well as before and afterward) plays a major part in your emotional reaction and in your ability to handle the situation effectively. Novaco[54] counsels against focusing on the provocations as personal affronts or ego threats; in short, don't take them personally. You will pour kerosene on the fire of your anger by thinking, "He has it in for me." Instead, Novaco recommends a "task orientation"—that is, focusing on desired outcomes and on behaving in such a way as to produce that outcome. Harriet Lerner's book, *The Dance of Anger*,[55] is full of good examples.

Each individual must become aware of the thoughts that fuel anger and then come up with alternative thoughts that dampen it. Novaco gives many examples of thoughts that can alleviate destructive levels of hostility: "This could be a rough situation, but I know how to deal with it." "You don't need to prove yourself." "There is no point in getting mad." "Time to take a deep breath." [56]

Anger management involves not only changing the way you think but also learning new coping skills, including assertiveness and "stress inoculation." [57] Practicing more graded expressions of anger is helpful. Many anger management programs involve role-playing effective behavior in provocative situations. Often, persons who have been traumatized in childhood have not had the opportunity to learn reasonable ways of expressing anger; their models have been extreme and destructive. Like any skill, learning how to express anger appropriately takes time. It is far more difficult to master than most other skills, however, because problems with anger are embedded in a history of trauma, where feelings ran high.

The Point of No Return

Relaxation is the obvious antidote to anxiety, but it does not always work. Once the level of anxiety rises beyond a certain point, it becomes impossible to relax. Tell a person who is in the midst of a panic attack to "Just relax!" and he or she will look at you as if you're out of your mind. No matter how well learned they may be, relaxation techniques can work only when your anxiety is within manageable bounds—that is, at mild to moderate levels.

When anxiety has skyrocketed to a high level, medication may be helpful. At such times, it is crucial not to berate yourself for being unable to relax. Creating a sense of failure will only fuel the anxiety. Think of it this way: Your brain has you over a barrel with its behavioral inhibition system turned on high. You may be able to do no more than wait it out. Perhaps you could think something like, "I'll get through it; I have before."

It is probably best not to think of relaxation, cognitive therapy, or other techniques of self-regulation as emergency measures. Rather, they are *pre-*

ventive measures. Practicing relaxation routinely and incorporating it into daily life may give you more headroom, preventing anxiety from escalating rapidly to uncontrollable levels. It is also helpful to be *more* tuned in to your anxiety. That way, when anxiety begins to mount, you can nip it in the bud while it is still possible to employ whatever relaxation techniques you have learned.

The same goes for anger as for anxiety. Beyond a certain level, anger can be extremely difficult to control. When anger hits the level of rage, relaxation is beside the point. You may need to "wait out" a panic attack. You may need to "wait out" a rage. But rage can be more dangerous. Rage is a neuro-physiological package that includes a propensity to attack. You may need to stamp a program into your mind/brain: When rage hits, don't hit, go to a safe place and stay there until you have cooled down. You need a simple advance plan that requires virtually no thought to implement.

Like anxiety and anger, depression can also go beyond the point of no return. If you have been seriously depressed, you have probably encountered four pieces of advice: Be active ("Go jogging"), do something fun ("Go to a show"), spend time with people ("Go to a party"), and think positive thoughts ("I'm a good person"). This simple advice is easy to follow—if you're not depressed! Lack of energy, inability to experience pleasure, social withdrawal, and negative thinking are part and parcel of depression. You can become so depressed that you can hardly get out of bed, much less engage in any positive activities that will make you feel better. The social behavior that goes with depression (not talking much, avoiding eye contact, sad expression, lack of responsiveness) tends to alienate others and leads to rejection—increasing the desire to remain isolated.[58] Depression can be so severe that "thinking positive thoughts" is beside the point. You might be able to think them, but you couldn't feel the positive feelings that ordinarily would go with them. At this level, biological intervention (medication) is likely to be essential for any psychological interventions or behavioral changes to be feasible. Again, prevention is the best medicine. If you can become aware that you are slipping into depression, you may be able to push yourself into following that good advice while you still have some energy to do so.

To reiterate, you can exert control best when your feelings are at mild to moderate levels. To grasp this point, imagine your feelings rising on a curve, as depicted in Figure 4–1. At the lower levels of the curve are more

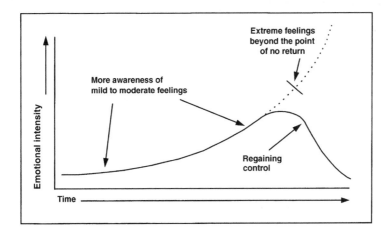

Figure 4–1. Emotional control by prevention.

manageable feelings. As the curve rises, your feelings become more difficult to control. At a certain point on the curve, you are beyond the point of no return—your feelings have escalated to the level at which you resort to emergency measures (striking out, running away, using alcohol or drugs, engaging in self-injurious behavior). At that point, most of the sensible techniques recommended by therapists are beyond reach. The solution is to become attuned to lower levels of distressing feelings and to use therapeutic techniques to calm them while self-control is still feasible. Be more aware of mild anxiety, feelings of irritation, discouragement, embarrassment. Build up your tolerance for these feelings. This strategy may be challenging, however, because distressing feelings may be frightening to you, and you may be inclined to deny and avoid them rather than cultivating awareness of them. If so, you will need to go against the grain.

CHAPTER FIVE

Consciousness

Traumatic experience is overwhelming and inescapable. The trauma can only be endured; the powerful emotions must be borne and lived through. Sadly, some persons—children, spouses, soldiers—must repeatedly suffer through unbearably painful traumatic experience over long periods, sometimes even for many years. For some, however, there is temporary respite.

Escaping the Inescapable ◆ ◆ ◆ ◆ ◆ ◆ ◆ ◆

◆ During her psychological evaluation, a young woman began to remember an excruciatingly painful experience. She stopped talking and looked down-ward. She closed her eyes. She sat motionless. She did not respond to the therapist's invitation to talk about what was troubling her. Minutes went by. She was physically present but psychologically unreachable. In an effort to reestablish contact with her, the therapist called to her in a loud voice; slowly, she responded to his request to open her eyes and look at him. But she was still far away. Her face looked like a mask, devoid of animation. Her eyes were open but unfocused. She was completely immobile. More minutes passed. Eventually, the therapist was able to capture her attention, and she was able to move slowly. On request, she stood up. At long last, she began to regain contact with the outer world after leaving the office, walking around the building, and getting a cool drink. All the while, she had been there and yet elsewhere—or nowhere. As best as she could recall later, her mind had been blank. She remembered little of the episode.

This patient's ability to obliterate painful states of consciousness was the legacy of prolonged childhood physical and emotional abuse. She had learned to manipulate her conscious experience to escape the inescapable. What she could not escape physically, she could escape mentally—at least to a degree. To cope with trauma, such individuals learn to tune out, and many are able to block out traumatic episodes afterward by amnesia. Tuning out trauma and blocking it by amnesia are forms of *dissociation,* a self-protective alteration and dividing of consciousness that excludes painful experiences from normal awareness.

If you've already heard something about dissociation and had difficulty understanding it, don't blame yourself; the concept is mired in professional controversy.[1] You should be forewarned that the term "dissociation" covers a broad territory;[2] it is often overused and carelessly used.[3] We are probably trying to get too much mileage out of one word—but we're stuck with it for now. I will emphasize that dissociation takes many *forms*—from feeling "spacey" to having amnesia to switching among radically different states of mind. Thus, like some of the phenomena to which it refers, dissociation has become a fuzzy concept. But, if you've experienced it, you'll recognize it. You may experience one form of dissociation and not others, or you may experience several different forms.

In whatever form, dissociation serves a purpose: It can be used as an emergency defense, a "shutoff mechanism to prevent overstimulation or flooding of consciousness by excessive incoming stimuli."[4] Psychiatrist Richard Kluft has expressed the dire circumstances that evoke this extreme defense:

I understand dissociation pragmatically as a defense in which an overwhelmed individual cannot escape [what] assails him or her by taking meaningful action or successful flight, and escapes instead by altering his or her internal organization, i.e., by inward flight. It is a defense of those who suffer an intolerable sense of helplessness, and have had the experience of becoming an object, the victim of someone's willful mistreatment, the indifference of nature, or of one's own limitations; one realizes that one's own will and wishes have become irrelevant to the course of events.[5]

To understand different forms of this self-protective shutoff mechanism, or inward flight, you need to understand different forms of consciousness.

Shades of Consciousness ◆ ◆ ◆ ◆ ◆ ◆ ◆ ◆

You can manipulate your state of consciousness to some degree, but you have little choice about being conscious in some form. Think of consciousness as having an on/off switch: If you are alive, and not in a coma or asleep, you are conscious.[6] When the switch is on, your consciousness can assume a variety of forms.

What is *normal* consciousness? It may involve being alert, attentive, focused, keenly attuned to the present. Yet there are also many normal variations to this usual state of consciousness. Every day, you sleep. You move from alert wakefulness to drowsiness to dreamless sleep to dreaming sleep. Then when you awaken, you may be momentarily disoriented. Other variations on our normal state of consciousness can be induced. For example, a high fever may put you into a delirious state. Or you can spin around and become dizzy. You can also use alcohol to produce a state of intoxication, marijuana to get into a state of oblivion, or LSD to experience hallucinations and illusions.

In normal alert consciousness, you are keenly attuned to present sensory experience, both internal and external. You have a full, rich, vivid appreciation of your current situation, whatever it involves. Your experience is organized into coherent, meaningful scenes, on a moment-to-moment basis, in continuous flux.[7] Your consciousness is extremely *flexible*, so that you can adapt immediately to changing circumstances. If you are struggling with trauma, this normal state of consciousness may be hard to maintain.

Here's one slant on dissociation. Think of consciousness on a spectrum, as depicted in Figure 5–1. Put full awareness at one end. Then imagine gradually dimming consciousness, as you would slowly turn down bright

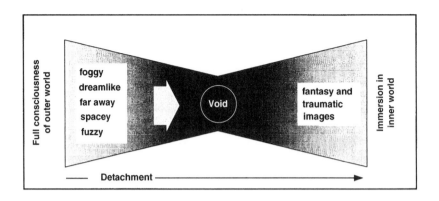

Figure 5–1. Dissociative narrowing of consciousness.

lights with a rheostat. As consciousness dims, a person might feel more and more foggy, dreamlike, tuned out, spaced out, or far away. One may even have a sense of leaving the body, a feeling of watching oneself from a distance, from the back of the head or from behind the shoulders. Taken to the extreme, all flexibility is lost, and consciousness narrows to a pinpoint. It may feel as if the lights are all the way off. In fact, some individuals feel as if they are "in the blackness." Others feel totally blank or stuck "in the void." Others completely shut out reality and enter a world of fantasy and imagery. As will be discussed shortly, this immersion in fantasy can provide a pleasurable escape from stressful experience. Yet, using this escape route also carries the risk of immersion in traumatic images, memories, and flashbacks (see Chapter 6).

Such dissociative experiences are challenging to describe. Persons who dissociate often grope apologetically for the right words to communicate their experience. They are often reluctant or afraid to talk to anyone about their altered states of consciousness, which seem strange, weird, crazy, or bizarre. Yet such ineffable experiences are remarkably common among persons who have undergone trauma. We are all conscious, and we all learn to manipulate our conscious states. Some of us have reason to resort to drastic manipulations. Many find it helpful to recognize that the dissociative experiences they considered so unique and "crazy" are shared by others who have also relied on them to cope with painful situations.

Self-Consciousness ◆ ◆ ◆ ◆ ◆ ◆ ◆ ◆ ◆

Consciousness in the "on/off" sense of immediate awareness is not limited to humans; it is characteristic of many species.[8] But we humans (and some other primates) also have higher levels of consciousness. We are *self-conscious*. We are conscious of being conscious, aware of being aware. We are aware of ourselves as conscious beings. We can escape the immediate present. We can think about the past and the future. We can plan. We are aware of our trajectory in time and space. We have a sense of where we have been and where we are heading. We can work to attain pleasurable states of consciousness. We can dislike our conscious experience and deliberately try to change it.

Ordinarily, you are aware of yourself, or you can quickly become so. But what if you cannot stand to be yourself because you are in the midst of a terrifying or degrading experience? What if you do *not* want to be conscious of the trajectory of your experience across time because your past experience is intolerable? Then the self can be dissociated—disconnected—from experience.

◆ A girl in her early teens was referred for a consultation because she had been hearing voices and showing radical switches in mood and behavior. In the consultant's office, she felt as if she were in a daze or a dream. She mentioned that the bookshelves looked "fuzzy" to her. Then she began to look distressed and said she felt as if she were spinning. She talked about seeing a menacing masculine face whenever she looked in the mirror, and of her feeling that the "person" she sees in the mirror takes her away to a dark space in the universe from which she cannot escape. She became agitated when discussing how she loses her soul, her body, and her mind whenever she goes to the outer reaches of the universe. Then she closed her eyes, and after about 30 seconds, she looked up, bright-eyed and no longer feeling dizzy or dazed. She had no idea where she was. She had no memory of coming to the office. It was as if she had suddenly awakened. *She* had not gone through the distressing interview.

Not all efforts to remove the self from self-consciousness are so drastic. A woman with a childhood history of abuse learned to turn herself into a "shell person." She continued to function normally outwardly, but without her normal sense of self. She felt hollow—hardly there. Her voice was barely audible. Similarly, a man with a long history of severe neglect felt like an automaton. He had no feelings. He just went through the motions. One day, he went through elaborate preparations for suicide as if it were just another day. Dissociating the self from traumatic experience makes it more bearable: This is not happening *to me*. He could not have done that *to me*. *I* could not have done that. *I* am not here. *I* am far away. It's not happening *to me;* it's just happening to *my body*. *I* am just a robot.

Unconscious, Conscious, and Subconscious   ◆ ◆ ◆ ◆

Without consciousness, there would be no traumatic experience. Trauma is an incentive to dim or even obliterate consciousness and self-consciousness. In the face of trauma, if you could do so, you'd probably turn the switch of consciousness to the "off" position. But you cannot do it. You cannot go to sleep or put yourself into a coma. What are the alternatives? We'll examine the whole spectrum—unconscious, conscious, and the intermediate zone, the subconscious.

Unconscious

Our idea of consciousness is extremely misleading. It seems to us as if consciousness is all there is to the mind. On the contrary, only a small fraction of our mental activity is conscious. Our conscious experience—immediate awareness and self-consciousness—provides only a tiny window into the activity of the mind/brain. The *vast bulk* of our mental activity is unconscious; we do nearly everything without thinking about it.

Do you think about how to walk? Do you think about how to utter grammatical sentences? Add 32 to 24. You are aware of the numbers and the intention to solve the problem, and then you are aware of the result, 56. But you are not conscious of the processes by which you arrived at the result. You lie in bed deliberating about when to get up. Eventually, something tips the balance, and you pop up. How did you do that? Raise your arm. How did you do that? When you think about it, the operation of the mind seems magical. That's because it's mainly unconscious.[9]

Much of what is unconscious is *automatic*. Routine or well-practiced activities can be done mindlessly. Once you learn to ride a bike, swim, drive a car, operate your computer, or play the piano, you don't need to think about the details. Your brain takes care of it. Particularly important for trauma is your automatic *categorizing* of your ongoing experience. You are continually categorizing the inner and outer worlds automatically, immediately, and unconsciously. Without thinking about it consciously, you identify aspects of your world as familiar. So it is with anything that has been traumatic. You may immediately categorize as dangerous anything in your environment that reminds you of earlier trauma. Unconsciously, you set off an alarm. Then, sometimes without your awareness of the reasons for it, the fight-or-flight response kicks in.

Conscious

If we can do so much without it, what good is consciousness? When action flows smoothly and automatically, it can remain unconscious. When you make a mistake, you may chastise yourself: "Pay attention!" In effect, "Be conscious!"

The major function of consciousness is to bring all our knowledge and resources to bear on dealing with novelty, the unexpected, and the unfamiliar.[10] When you learn something new, you rely heavily on consciousness. Learning to ride a bike requires conscious effort; once learned, bicycling does not require consciousness. Learning the meaning of a word requires concentration; once learned, its meaning comes effortlessly. Learning multiplication tables requires conscious effort; once learned, the results automatically come to mind.

We use consciousness to make connections, to put elements of our experience together. When I flip the switch, the light goes on. We use consciousness to monitor and control our environment.[11] Paying attention to what we are doing allows us to make fine discriminations. All in all, consciousness gives us a large measure of sensitivity, flexibility, and creativity.[12]

Consciousness comes into play in relation to novelty because we need to *make sense* of novel experience. We need to relate current experience to previous experience. A paramount human motive is to "assign meaning, to make sense of the world."[13] We use meanings and judgments to control our experience and our lives. Ordinarily, we have a thirst for information and knowledge. But what happens when our experience is unbearable? When we do not want to understand and acknowledge what is happening?

When we do not want to make connections? When we do not *want* to be conscious?

Subconscious

Consciousness pulls experience together; dissociation takes it apart. When we cannot tolerate experience in consciousness, and we dissociate, the experience is not necessarily gone and forgotten.

◆ A hospitalized patient with clear-cut signs of posttraumatic stress disorder spent months in psychotherapy working hard to understand herself. She racked her brain in an effort to determine why she was so distressed, but she could not remember any experience that would account for her extreme fearfulness. Periodically, however, she would become utterly terrified and feel a compelling urge to escape. Sometimes she would break into a run. She was certain that she was being attacked, and her gestures suggested that she was being sexually assaulted. During these episodes, she had images of her uncle's leer, the smell of alcohol, and his plaid jacket. With the help of the hospital staff, she could be calmed down and reoriented to the present. Afterward, however, although she had some memory of the terrifying reenactment in the hospital, she could not connect it in any way with her past.

To understand such experiences, we must recognize a gray zone between the conscious and the unconscious—the subconscious.[14] This patient was remembering and yet not remembering at the same time. Normally, remembering your past includes recollecting it as *your* experience. Dissociated experience is "remembered" differently—in "not me" form. It is subconscious knowledge, without connection to the sense of self, and outside the flow of normal conscious experience.

Normally, we remember our experiences not only as pertaining to us but also in a broader historical context. Each one happened to us in a certain place and at a certain time in life. Our consciousness integrates these events; it pulls them together with their surrounding contexts and our sense of self. With dissociation, the ordinarily broad window of consciousness narrows.[15] Trauma provides an incentive to put blinders on consciousness, to escape the historical context, and to take the self out.

Again, think of one form of dissociation as a dimmer. More slowly or more quickly, you can fade out the context of your experience, making it foglike or dreamlike. Your surroundings may fade away or become unreal. You may lose track of where you are. You may lose track of time. All the normal context of your experience may disappear, as if the scope of your awareness has been reduced to a pinpoint. You may become completely disoriented. At the extreme, you may lose track of your self and your identity. *You* are no longer there. That's the whole point.

But you may not be able to shrink your experience down to nothingness—a void or blackness. Or you may not be able to stay in a void or a fantasy world throughout the course of a traumatic event. Or you may be able to blot out some aspects of the experience but not others. Then you are left with patches of disconnected experience. Such subconscious, dissociated experience is cut off from all historical context *and* from the sense of self. What you remember for such episodes of dissociation will be fragmentary—perhaps only isolated visual images, sounds, or feelings, all shrouded in a sense of unreality. The subsequent intrusion of such subconscious experience into consciousness can be *haunting*. It makes no sense and has no meaning. It is nightmarish. The intrusive experience itself is traumatic, and it fuels additional dissociation.

Dissociation as a Blessing and a Curse ◆ ◆ ◆ ◆ ◆

Dissociation as a Skill

In some respects, dissociation is an adaptive way to deal with inescapable trauma. Mental escape is chosen when physical escape is impossible. And dissociation does not have to be taught; it can be discovered spontaneously when the need arises. What do you do in the dentist's chair? How do you take your mind off the pain—or its possibility? You may stare at a spot on the wall or imagine yourself far away. These natural techniques illustrate how we can deliberately manipulate attention and consciousness to escape pain. For some individuals, blotting out pain does not require any deliberate imaginative effort—they can do it automatically without thinking about it.[16] When such methods become automatic emergency defenses, we call them "dissociation."

Yet dissociation can be thought of as a skill that almost any individual possesses to one degree or another. Some people are good at it, some are virtuosos, some can hardly do it at all. When confronted with severe and inescapable trauma, those who are skilled at using dissociation have a temporary escape hatch.

Like many other skills, the ability to use dissociation probably has an innate component.[17] Some individuals may be born with a good capacity for dissociating; they have some ability to alter and divide their conscious experience that others lack. But the capacity to dissociate can be enhanced by many forms of traumatic experience, as well as by loss and neglect.[18] Necessity is the mother of invention. Those who experience trauma in childhood (physical or sexual abuse) may be more prone to dissociate as adolescents and adults. These persons had the incentive to use and to refine whatever dissociative ability they were born with.

Dissociation and Fantasy Proneness

One possible contributor to dissociative detachment from the outer world is the ability to become absorbed in fantasy, recently called *fantasy proneness*.[19] Research on highly fantasy-prone individuals—perhaps as few as 4% of the population—reveals several characteristics that may relate to dissociation and trauma. Such persons report that they practically live their lives through fantasy. As children, they spend much time in make-believe worlds, populating their environments with imaginary companions and endowing their dolls and stuffed animals with feelings and personalities. Such individuals have extremely vivid memories and fantasies, and many state that they confuse memories of their fantasies with memories of actual events. Some fantasy-prone individuals pretend to be someone else, and their fantasies can seem even *more* real than reality:

> One subject felt, not that she was pretending to be a bird, but that she was a bird pretending to be a girl. Similarly, another subject who continually pretended to be a princess told us that she actually felt that *she was a princess pretending to be an ordinary child* doing things ordinary children do, such as going to school, riding a bike, and so on. She saw her house as a castle complete with a real moat and drawbridge, and she told the children at her school that she was a princess and that she lived in a castle with a moat.[20]

There are many possible reasons to become fantasy prone, and many fantasy-prone individuals are well adjusted. Yet, in the face of traumatic experience, fantasy may be employed as a self-protective defense—an escape. A significant proportion of fantasy-prone persons report a history of childhood trauma and abuse. In addition, many also describe social isolation and loneliness, so they may have relied on fantasy to compensate for the lack of companionship and to enrich their lives.

The link between fantasy proneness and creativity is obvious, and those who are fantasy prone can consider themselves in distinguished company. As a child, Mozart endured long journeys through Europe while his father paraded his talent in various courts in search of fame and fortune. In the course of hours spent in uncomfortable coaches, Mozart inhabited an elaborate imaginary kingdom he called "Rücken" (Back):

> Rücken had its own geography (conceivably its place names were real ones, spelled backwards), its own laws and its own subjects. It was 'Back' possibly too in a Golden Age sense: a return to a world of youthful perfection. Certainly it was a kingdom of, and for, children. Everyone there was good and happy, under their king . . . there were maps drawn of it—by the servant who travelled with the Mozart family, and perhaps also by Mozart himself, who showed some aptitude for drawing . . . Rücken was entirely Mozart's own personal kingdom. It offered a respite not only from the reality of slow, cramped, travelling conditions but from all the conditions of reality. Reality included a father who was no royal prince—not even a free agent—but an outwardly humble servant and court-musician attached to the Prince-Archbishop of Salzburg. And reality also meant very early realization that the great people who applauded the boy Mozart often cared little for music as such.[21]

Dissociation and Hypnotic Trance

Dissociation is a central feature of hypnotic trance.[22] Trance induction has long been used to produce dissociative alterations in consciousness. Trance states can be employed to produce changes in sensation and perception and to alter *self*-consciousness (to enable your arm to raise up "on its own" without a sense that *you* are raising it). Hypnotic susceptibility, like the ability to dissociate, varies from one person to another.[23] Fantasy proneness is one factor that contributes to hypnotizability.[24] A small number of people are adept at entering an extremely deep trance; they can use hypnosis as an analgesic during surgery. Another small group cannot be hypnotized at all. Most of us have a moderate ability to enter a trance.

Two classic features of hypnosis that are pertinent to trauma are analgesia and posthypnotic amnesia.[25] Hypnosis has a venerable history as an analgesic or pain blocker. It has been used extensively for the treatment of chronic pain, as well as for anesthetic purposes during otherwise painful medical procedures. Posthypnotic amnesia is easily demonstrated. During a trance, the individual can be given the suggestion that he will not remember anything that occurred or that a certain event will be forgotten. For example, the hypnotist can tell the subject that, when the hypnotist scratches her ear, the subject will stand up and walk around the room, adding the suggestion that he will not remember this instruction. After being brought out of the trance, the subject observes the hypnotist scratch her ear, then gets up and walks around the room. When asked why he is doing so, he will give a rationalization ("I just felt like stretching") to account for his behavior.

Analgesia and amnesia can be deliberately evoked by hypnosis, provided that the individual is willing to enter a trance state and has the hypnotic talent. Similarly, analgesia and amnesia can be evoked spontaneously by trauma, provided that the traumatized person has dissociative skill. The pain can be blocked during the traumatic episode, and the episode can be blocked from subsequent memory, relegated to the subconscious.

Dissociation as a Symptom

Dissociation, fantasy proneness, and hypnotizability are related in complex ways, and we have much yet to learn about how—and how much—early traumatic experience contributes to them.[26] In the face of severe trauma, the capacity to alter consciousness self-protectively is adaptive insofar as the inescapable can be escaped. But this adaptation is not an unmitigated blessing. Dissociation is a good example of *imperfect adaptation*. It holds traumatic experience at bay but does not block it entirely. Many persons who have fended off traumatic experience by dissociation, like the hospitalized patient who was prone to flee in terror, are likely to experience intrusive memories and flashbacks. The dissociated experience seems to be inaccessible to full consciousness but nevertheless pressing on consciousness; it won't stay put. At worst, dissociation may backfire, as dissociating at the time of the trauma seems to increase the risk of subsequently developing posttraumatic symptoms and other problems.[27]

In addition to being vulnerable to the intrusion of (subconscious) dissociated experiences, many persons who learn to use dissociation to cope with childhood trauma employ it in a general way later in life to cope with any and all stressors. It becomes a mental blotter to obscure every stressful experience—everyday arguments, frustrations, and disappointments. And it is not only environmental stressors that prompt dissociation. Studies of the stream of consciousness show that much internal experience may be unpleasant:

> Most people are carrying on some kind of ongoing interior monologue, a kind of gloss on immediately occurring events that also engages in associations of these events . . . Since much of our stream of thought is made up of unfinished intentions of long-standing as well as current concerns, the attention to such stimulation often provokes negative emotions of fear, sadness, shame/guilt, or anger and has generally a mildly aversive quality.[28]

So it is not just trauma or even more common stressors that may prompt dissociation. There is also the continual press of distressing thoughts and memories—which especially affect persons with traumatic backgrounds.[29] Those who are prone to escape through dissociation will frequently have reason to do so, which makes dissociation a curse rather than a blessing. While blocking pain and stress, prolonged dissociation not only robs individuals of the potential richness of conscious experiences but also prevents new learning that might ultimately alleviate the pain and stress. The fact that dissociation interferes with learning may explain the relation between dissociation at the time of trauma and subsequent posttraumatic stress symptoms. Dissociating may prevent you from coming to terms with reality and block you from doing the work of grieving necessary for healing.[30]

The Process of Dissociation   ◆ ◆ ◆ ◆ ◆ ◆ ◆

Dissociation can dim painful experience by fading it out. But dissociation can also pull experience apart at the seams. Psychiatrist Bennett Braun[31] proposed the "BASK" model of dissociation, having observed that trauma leads to separations among Behavior, Affect (emotion), Sensation, and Knowledge. For example, an adult who was beaten as a child may experience a bodily sensation—an aching shoulder—without any knowledge of what happened. Or a person may break into a run without knowing why—behavior without knowledge. Sometimes individuals have full awareness but no feelings—behavior, sensation, and knowledge, all without affect.

Normal experience entails a feeling of unity. Our behavior, emotions, sensations, and understanding of what happens all fit together. And normal experience also entails a sense of continuity across time, a feeling of flow from past through present toward future. Braun's BASK model shows how dissociation brings disunity and discontinuity in complex ways. I often think of dissociation more simply as a gap in the continuity of experience.[32] Picture it as a bridge with a section missing. Then we can think of what happens before, during, and after the gap.

Dissociation is prompted by some sort of *trigger*. Initially, this trigger consists of traumatic experience and overwhelming emotion that induces the dissociative shutoff mechanism. Subsequently, some internal or external stimulus that reminds the person of the trauma or evokes the traumatic memory serves as the trigger. The woman whose uncle's plaid shirt was part of her subconscious traumatic memory sometimes became anxious when she saw a similarly colored plaid shirt, even if it was just one displayed in a store.

It is as if the trigger throws a switch,[33] inducing a number of changes—in consciousness, in emotion, in physiology, and in behavior.[34] The individual faced with a traumatic experience may throw the switch deliberately. For example, some people may be able to "tune out" or "go far away" by focusing on a spot on the wall and staring at it until they enter a dissociative state. Or the switch may be thrown automatically and unconsciously. Of course, dramatic switches are not unique to dissociative disorders; they also occur in bipolar disorder (manic-depression) and panic attacks. Although it is possible to drift slowly into a dissociative state, dissociative switches generally occur quite rapidly—usually in less than 5 minutes, and sometimes within a few seconds.[35]

Once the switch is thrown, consciousness is altered, and you are into the gap. There is a break in consciousness; with repeated dissociative experience, consciousness is punctuated by numerous gaps. The alterations in consciousness may take many forms. As already noted, the person may feel tuned out or far away. She may feel as if she is observing from the back of her head or from behind her shoulder. She may feel as if she is on autopilot, or she may feel like a robot. She may feel that she is in a fog or in a dream. She may go deep inside herself, as if in a cave or a black hole. The outside world may seem unreal. Or the person who is hurting her may seem like a robot. Or she may feel as if she is watching a movie.

A second switch, also more or less abrupt, leads back to normal consciousness. The return to normal consciousness leaves a gap in its wake. At best, memories may be clouded; at worst, they may be blocked from consciousness entirely. The experience may be like the tail end of an airplane vapor trail, wispy and vague, even though it occurred just minutes before. Isolated fragments—visual images, body sensations—may haunt consciousness. Or the whole episode may be completely blocked by amnesia. The individual may "wake up" or "come to," as if from having been "blacked out." The image of a bridge with a section missing is apt: Connecting links are removed. I think of dissociative defenses not as barricades but as *moats*.[36] This is the essence of dissociation—segregating one realm of experience from another.

Back to Reality ◆ ◆ ◆ ◆ ◆ ◆ ◆ ◆ ◆ ◆

It is not difficult to understand what sets off a dissociative episode. But what stops one? This is an important question, because people who struggle with unwanted dissociative experiences need to know how to get out of them. In a traumatic situation, being keenly alert to the immediate present is unbearably painful. By dissociating, you can mentally leave the traumatic scene, go far away, and tune out the overwhelming stimulation.

Dissociation gradually or more abruptly shuts down full consciousness of outer reality, blunting or fragmenting input from the senses. The antidote to dissociation is grounding in current sensory reality.[37] To tune back in and bring up the light of consciousness to full brightness, you must concentrate on immediate sensations. Ways to do so include tightly gripping the arms of a chair, naming the objects in the room, standing up and walking around, or taking a walk outside in the fresh air. Some persons find that listening to music or doing a project can bring them back. Others find that counting objects helps them to become grounded. Sometimes, however, tuning back in to present reality is not so simple. You can be so "far away" that it is extremely difficult to get back. An unusually powerful stimulus such as a cold shower may be needed. Vigorous exercise may do the trick for some individuals. Still others find that, if they go to sleep, they feel more grounded on waking.

Dissociation disrupts consciousness by dimming the experience of current sensory reality. But dissociation also disrupts the continuity of *self*-experience, punctuating it with gaps that blot out memory entirely or render parts of experience hazy and unreal. Our self-consciousness that pulls together the varying strands of our experience is disabled.

The antidote to dissociation at the level of self-consciousness is *association*. You need to rebuild bridges and pull the strands back together. Remaining grounded is an important way to restore the natural process of association, providing a sense of continuity in the experience of the self. But association goes far deeper than that. You can come to understand the situations, cues, and emotions that trigger dissociative experience. You may be able to fill in some of the gaps with coherent memory rather than with clouded or fragmented experience. Filling in gaps means directly facing the traumatic past rather than blotting it out—which brings us to the subject of the next chapter, traumatic memories.

Memory

By definition, traumatic experience over-
whelms us when it occurs. Sadly, trauma
does not necessarily end when the traumatic situation is long past. Many
traumatized persons continue to reexperience the trauma whenever memories of the event are evoked. Along with the memories come painful emotions
and the sense of helplessness. This chapter addresses two aspects of traumatic
memories. First, you may feel beset by intrusive memories, and you need to
learn how to regulate them. Second, your memories may be clouded or confusing, and you may not know what to believe about them.

Intrusive Memories ◆ ◆ ◆ ◆ ◆ ◆ ◆ ◆ ◆

◆ A woman in a group therapy session suddenly became panicky, dived out of
her chair, and began cowering in fear in the corner. A few group members

quickly came to her aid, comforted her, and escorted her to a more private area where she felt safe. Later the patient returned to explain what had happened. She had been sitting calmly at the edge of the group when other members had arrived late, brought chairs in, and sat down behind her. Suddenly, she realized that she was surrounded, and she felt trapped. That awareness brought back a memory of being cornered and assaulted.

As this example illustrates, a common result of traumatic experience is the subsequent reexperiencing of thoughts, feelings, and images reminiscent of the trauma. The reexperiencing may begin to occur soon after the trauma, or it may be delayed by weeks, months, or years. It may take several forms, including recurrent intrusive memories, distressing dreams or nightmares, and extremely vivid sensations and feelings that lead you to feel as if you are back in the midst of the traumatic situation.[1]

Memory and Emotion

You can best understand traumatic memories if you appreciate how memory and emotion are interwoven. All your ongoing experience is processed through your memory.[2] You continuously interpret the world on the basis of past experiences. You always relate current experience to similar prior experience. As you perceive, you remember; as you remember, you may feel some of the emotions associated with the original experience. Memory and emotion are tightly packaged.[3] Every memory, like every experience, has an emotional charge, ranging from relatively neutral to intense. If you recall being treated unfairly, you are likely to feel some outrage. Whenever a memory is stirred, it reactivates that emotional charge.

Much of how you interpret the present in light of the past is conscious; much is unconscious.[4] Memories can be triggered by perceptions *unconsciously, in just fractions of a second.*[5] The perception of a small cue in the environment that is associated with traumatic experience can set off a powerful emotion in a flash. For a woman terrified in childhood by her father's rageful tirades, just hearing a man scold his child in a restaurant can set off a chain reaction of anxiety, fear, and anger. Because such reactions can take place unconsciously and instantly, you may never know what hit you; you may only find yourself suddenly feeling panicky.

The instantaneous triggering of intense emotions is a worst-case scenario. But even in more ordinary life situations, your emotional experience at any given moment is the consequence of all your consciously and unconsciously activated memories and all the feelings that went with them. Because you perceive myriad aspects of the world, and because you have many ideas in association with your perceptions, you are continuously stirring a complex blend of emotion, usually a mixture of various feelings, both positive and negative.[6]

Flashbacks

The term *flashbacks* has been used to refer to extremely vivid intrusive memories that lead you to feel as if you are reliving the trauma.[7] Like other memories, flashbacks vary in historical accuracy and may blend memory, emotion, imagery, and fantasy.[8] In a flashback, you lose contact with current reality, superimposing traumatic images on the current situation. You may feel the original emotion in full force, even reaching the level of terror or rage. Accordingly, like the patient who dived out of her chair in group therapy, you may also be catapulted into a fight-or-flight response. At worst, you may engage in dangerous self-destructive or assaultive behavior.

It is helpful to think of reexperiencing as occurring along a broad spectrum. Painful memories would be at the mild end. Think of one of your embarrassing memories. You may actually feel a twinge—or more than a twinge—of embarrassment. This incident evokes a mildly "traumatic memory." You could up the ante and think of more painful memories that shade into genuinely traumatic memories—memories that are indeed extremely painful to think about. Although you may generally avoid awareness of such memories, they may intrude into consciousness. Yet these are not necessarily clear memories; they may be isolated images or fragments of memories. They may be hazy or foggy or may just pop into your mind unbidden.

Intrusive images, nightmares, and flashbacks tend to go together.[9] For some individuals, nightmares stir traumatic memories that may escalate into daytime intrusive experiences and flashbacks. Or intrusive images, when coupled with intense emotion, may prompt a flashback. A flashback is often triggered by a perception of some stimulus that is reminiscent of the trauma. For example, the sound of a car backfiring or a clap of thunder might remind a Vietnam veteran of an exploding shell. The stimulus instantaneously evokes strong emotion, and a flashback unfolds. Or it may happen the other way around. You may be in a state of high emotional arousal for whatever reason (mad at your boss), and the emotion (anger) may evoke a flashback (a beating by your uncle). Even if you do not consciously remember the traumatic experience, the emotion can be evoked by unconscious reminders. For example, returning to your childhood home could stir intense anxiety, even if violent episodes that occurred there have long been forgotten.

As all roads lead to Rome, all connections seem to lead to trauma. Traumatic memory networks have been likened to black holes: "The trauma appears to irresistibly draw thoughts and perceptions to it." [10] Traumatic memories are especially likely to be intrusive—unwanted and forcing their way into consciousness. Whereas you may strain to remember some things, there seems to be a "hotline" to other traumatic memories—or, as one person with posttraumatic stress disorder put it, a "superhighway to the trauma center." The connections can be very strong, and they may be made more so by recurrent flashbacks. Ironically, the very effort to suppress such memories may keep them active and even bring them to mind—particularly when you are under stress. [11] Also, vulnerability to intrusive memories can be increased by drugs and alcohol, aging, and sleep. [12]

Flashbacks as Retraumatization

To remember is to re-create previous experience. To remember trauma with its full emotional force is to undergo trauma again. The painful reliving of trauma through memory and flashbacks is harmful in three senses. First, it entails suffering. Second, it may escalate, ushering in additional distressing memories and flashbacks. Such experience keeps the traumatic memory stirred, and it could become a form of rehearsal; like any other memory, the more it is rehearsed, the more easily it will come to mind. Third, retraumatization damages the self, particularly the sense of self-control. Just as traumatic experience is an assault on the self and our sense of control, so is a flashback.

Stopping Flashbacks

Therapists strive to help individuals find ways of shutting off or dampening flashbacks and overwhelming emotions as they occur. The overall challenge is to distinguish past from present. In the short run, you need to get out of the traumatic memory and become grounded in current reality. In the long run, you need to master the traumatic experience by remembering it more clearly, putting it into words, and coming to terms with its implications for your life.

Flashbacks are a key symptom of posttraumatic stress disorder, and some medications have been found beneficial for persons who are reexperiencing trauma (see Chapter 12). Once a flashback has begun, the best way to shut it off is to orient yourself to current sensory-perceptual experience. The same techniques of "grounding" commonly employed for other forms of dissociation are helpful with flashbacks.[13] Of course, reorienting yourself to outer reality is easier said than done when you are in the midst of a full-blown flashback. As with controlling extremes of emotion, prevention is the best medicine. Learning the cues that evoke flashbacks and understanding their links to past trauma may help you separate past from present and respond less intensely.

The Power of Positive Remembering

As emphasized in cognitive therapy, you can exert some control over your emotional experience by what you think about. The "power of positive thinking" may be overrated, but it is no illusion.[14] This power of thought may be used for good or for ill. The power of *negative* thinking is substantial; negative thinking can fuel anxiety or deepen depression. Cognitive therapy may enable you to become more aware of your thoughts so that you can turn to more positive thinking. This shift from negative to positive thinking changes the course of the stream of emotion.

The same principle applies to memory. We can just as well speak of the power of positive remembering as the power of negative remembering. One expert on memory provided a useful anecdote:

> In high school, I competed in an oratorical contest in which I had to deliver a speech from memory. Unfortunately, I forgot my lines and left the stage in

despair. If during a public lecture I should recall that incident, and if the memory were connected associatively only by affect to other memories of embarrassment or humiliation, I would be in trouble and might have an anxiety attack. But if it is also connected by content, for example to other public speaking experiences, my mood will be stabilized, because on other occasions I have managed to remember my lines.[15]

The power of positive remembering is worth cultivating. Good memories should be treasured. Good experiences deserve our attention, and they are worth adding to our store of good memories. You can learn to draw your attention to a network of good memories associated with positive feelings such as pleasure, comfort, tenderness, safety, peace, confidence, skill, and so forth. As an exercise, try to remember an event that goes with each of these positive feelings. By dwelling on these memories, you can more readily call them to mind.

Memory or Fantasy? ◆ ◆ ◆ ◆ ◆ ◆ ◆ ◆ ◆

◆ A woman in her late 30s entered psychotherapy for the treatment of anxiety and panic attacks. Her psychotherapist had no special interest or expertise in sexual abuse, and she conducted the exploratory therapy in her usual fashion. She prescribed medication for the anxiety symptoms, and she attempted to help the patient appreciate many current stresses that contributed to the anxiety. Like others who struggle with anxiety, the patient often felt that things were out of her control. In addition to reviewing current problems, the therapist and patient explored childhood experiences that might have laid the foundation for her feelings of being out of control. Several months into psychotherapy, the patient began remembering having been molested by an older man. She had stayed with him occasionally when her mother was working and her usual babysitter was ill or out of town. The patient was chagrined by these memories. They seemed to come from out of the blue, precipitated only by her exploring the feeling of being out of control. Her therapist was also taken aback, having no prior inkling that this childhood sexual abuse might have been a factor contributing to her patient's anxiety.

For a long time, the patient was bewildered by her emerging memories. She didn't know what to make of them. They were spotty and vague. Her memories never did become very clear, although she spoke with family members and confirmed that she had indeed occasionally gone to this man's house when other caregivers were unavailable. Gradually, taking her inner experience seriously, she became convinced that she had been molested. She developed a deeper understanding of the reasons for her extreme anxiety and her feelings of being out of control. She experienced justified outrage and learned more fully to express her anger about what troubled her in the present. In turn, she gained a sense of being more in control. Eventually, months after the traumatic memories first came to mind, she was able to leave them behind, rarely dwelling on them again.

Many persons who have been traumatized remember their traumatic experiences relatively clearly. They have never forgotten them, and they have no doubt about what happened. For many others, like the woman whose exploration of her anxiety led to a revelation of childhood sexual molestation, matters are not so clear. These persons may have gone for years—even decades—without remembering various traumatic childhood experiences. Then, seemingly out of nowhere, images suggestive of traumatic experience start coming to mind. These intrusive images may be triggered by new traumatic experiences reminiscent of the earlier trauma. A rape could rekindle memories of incest. But the connection need not be so direct; traumatic memories could be evoked by any stressor—an accident, a move away from home, a loss, or conflict in an intimate relationship. Or, as in the case just described, the memories may resurface in the course of exploratory psychotherapy sought out for other reasons. *Anything* that engenders a feeling of extreme helplessness might rekindle traumatic memories.

The sudden eruption of intrusive memories is terrifying and bewildering. You may agonize: "Did it really happen?" "Am I just imagining it?" "Did I make it all up?" You are in a no-win situation: "If it really happened, it's horrible beyond belief; If I'm making it up, I must *really* be crazy!" If you find yourself in this predicament, you may go back and forth; sometimes you think it's an accurate memory, but at other times you conclude it's just a fantasy. You may take solace in the fact that your own puzzlement is mirrored by a century of professional debate and controversy.

Be forewarned that you are now headed into an extremely complicated saga of clinical practice, science, and politics. I am presenting the whole complex picture, because I know that many persons are profoundly troubled about the meaning of their memories, and also because these concerns are now embedded in a morass of social and legal controversy. There are no easy answers. If you are reading this chapter to come to grips with cloudy memories, I encourage you to cultivate tolerance for ambiguity and uncertainty. Be prepared to think in shades of gray rather than black and white.

The Pendulum Swings ◆ ◆ ◆ ◆ ◆ ◆ ◆ ◆ ◆

Memory

A century ago, Freud labored to understand the causes of symptoms that "threatened to make life impossible." [16] These symptoms included anxiety, depression, suicide attempts, painful physical sensations, and eruptions of intense emotions associated with images of hallucinatory vividness. He had worked with 18 patients with such symptoms and concluded that, in *every case,* the symptoms were connected with sexual trauma in early childhood. He proposed: "At the bottom of every case . . . there are one or more occurrences of premature sexual experience, which occurrences belong to the earliest years of childhood but which can be reproduced through the work of psycho-analysis in spite of the intervening decades." [17]

Freud was prepared for criticism, and he anticipated the charge that his patients were reporting fantasies or imagined events rather than memories of actual trauma. But he found his patients' memories to be highly convincing, and the memories made sense of their symptoms. Once the traumatic experience was known, the symptoms could be understood. The symptoms only *appeared* to be exaggerated reactions: "In reality, this reaction is proportionate to the exciting stimulus; thus it is normal and psychologically understandable." [18] Here, in Freud's writings of a century ago, is the thesis of this book: The reactions are natural and understandable, given the traumatic experience.

Freud anticipated the objection that his patients' memories of trauma were purposely invented fantasies. He argued the contrary: His patients were extremely reluctant to uncover them, and they were loath to believe them once they had uncovered them. He considered this point "absolutely decisive," arguing, "Why should patients assure me so emphatically of their unbelief, if what they want to discredit is something which—from whatever motive—they themselves have invented?" [19] Nor did he believe that he had suggested the traumatic experiences to the patients. Moreover, he was impressed by the consistency from one patient to another in the reported traumatic experience. Finally, working through the experience helped the patients to overcome their symptoms. He also reported that, for two of his patients, there was some corroborating evidence of sexual abuse.

Fantasy

In 1896, Freud made a strong and convincing case for believing his patients' memories. But by 1897, he had changed his mind. In a letter to his colleague, Wilhelm Fleiss, he recounted, "there was the astonishing thing that in every case . . . blame was laid on perverse acts by the father." [20] Then he gave a number of reasons for his newfound disbelief—among them that "it was hardly credible that perverted acts against children were so general." [21] This was a dramatic turnaround; a year before, he had written, "it is to be expected that increased attention to the subject will very soon confirm the great frequency of sexual experiences and sexual activity in childhood." [22] Looking back on this period many years later, Freud wrote, "almost all my women patients told me that they had been seduced by their father. I was driven to recognize in the end that these reports were untrue and so came to understand that . . . symptoms are derived from phantasies and not from real occurrences." [23] He began to interpret his patients' symptoms as stemming from forbidden childhood sexual desires and conflicts about them rather than from actual traumatic experience.

Whatever the myriad reasons for Freud's change of heart, [24] psychiatry went along with him. The pendulum swung from external trauma to internal conflict. No one, including Freud, denied the psychologically damaging consequences of traumatic experience, and sexual abuse in particular. And Freud did not completely abandon the trauma theory. But the *emphasis* shifted from external reality to internal fantasy.

Memory

Undeniable traumatic experience would not go away. With each war, psychiatry confronted the potentially devastating psychological and psychiatric consequences of trauma. During World War II, a sophisticated understanding of traumatic neurosis developed.[25] In conjunction with the aftermath of the Vietnam war, *posttraumatic stress disorder* became part of the diagnostic lexicon.[26]

While wars kept trauma in the picture, psychoanalysts did not entirely lose sight of child abuse.[27] Karl Menninger spoke out against child abuse on numerous occasions.[28] Of Freud's about-face, Bowlby wrote: "Ever since Freud made his famous, and in my view disastrous, volte-face in 1897, when he decided that the childhood seductions he had believed to be aetiologically important were nothing more than the products of his patients' imaginations, it has been extremely unfashionable to attribute psychopathology to real-life experiences."[29] He lamented that "we have been appallingly slow to wake up to the prevalence and far-reaching consequences of violent behaviour between members of a family, and especially the violence of parents."[30] Although Bowlby began by focusing on the traumatic effects of separation and loss, he had no doubt about the prevalence of maltreatment, violence, and abusive experience. As I will describe further in Chapter 8, he believed that our adult relationships are patterned after our childhood experiences: "the varied expectations of the accessibility and responsiveness of attachment figures that different individuals develop during the years of immaturity are *tolerably accurate* reflections of the experiences these individuals have actually had."[31] He counseled therapists accordingly: "I believe patients' accounts are sufficiently trustworthy that a therapist should accept them as being reasonable approximations to the truth; and furthermore that it is anti-therapeutic not to do so."[32]

Although the syndrome of posttraumatic stress disorder was delineated in the aftermath of the Vietnam war, it is just as applicable to childhood trauma. Judith Herman[33] has written about other casualties of violence—women and children. The knowledge gained about posttraumatic stress disorder, coupled with the political contribution of the women's movement, has enabled the mental health field to begin confronting the impact of domestic violence. Now, a century after Freud initially drew attention to psychological trauma, the pendulum is swinging back.

Back to Fantasy: "False Memories"

Trauma is now accorded a substantial role in the etiology of psychiatric symptoms, but the memory-versus-fantasy controversy persists—more

heated than ever. Abuse of women and children will always have a political dimension, because it revolves around social power.[34] This perennial political dimension is now fueled by mounting legal battles.[35] The relaxation of statutes of limitation has enabled adults to sue their parents for damages as a result of injury associated with childhood sexual abuse within 3 years of remembering the abuse.[36] And now the adversarial climate has become even more heated: Feeling falsely accused, parents are bringing suits for negligence against clinics and therapists, charging them with engendering false memories.[37] Doubtlessly, the move from clinic to courtroom has contributed markedly to the current adversarial climate in the field,[38] with highly polarized debate about the significance of memories of childhood trauma uncovered in therapy.[39]

The social battleground has crystallized around the "False Memory Syndrome Foundation," a large network of parents accused of abusing their own children. In this group are parents confronted by their—now adult—children for having committed despicable acts. Psychologist John Kihlstrom defined the *False Memory Syndrome* as "a condition in which a person's identity and interpersonal relationships are centered around a memory of traumatic experience which is objectively false but in which the person strongly believes . . . it orients the individual's entire personality and lifestyle, in turn disrupting all sorts of other adaptive behaviors." [40] You should be aware, however, that this false memory syndrome is not a psychiatric diagnosis and awaits systematic research.[41]

The False Memory Syndrome Foundation does not dispute that child abuse is widespread and harmful. Rather, the organization urges caution in accepting all reports of abuse at face value. There is particular concern about the validity of long-forgotten memories recovered in the process of psychotherapy. Members of the organization are especially alarmed about the possibility that inadequately trained or misguided therapists are suggesting or inadvertently engendering false memories in their patients. Accused family members protest that their children, influenced by a therapist, "remembered" events that never occurred. Then—also with encouragement of the therapist—the children cut themselves off from any contact, blocking any hope of reconciliation. As a result, families are being torn apart.

The False Memory Syndrome Foundation promotes skepticism about uncorroborated memories, offers support to those who feel falsely accused, provides information on legal aspects of the problem, and disseminates popular and professional literature to the lay public and to mental health professionals. Elizabeth Loftus, a cognitive psychologist who has studied memory intensively for many years, has put the concern most pointedly: "Although women's anger is certainly justified in many cases, and may be justified in some repressed memory cases too, it is time to stop and ask whether the net of rage has been cast too widely, creating a new collective nightmare." [42]

The Wildly Oscillating Pendulum

As I have just described, the pendulum has been swinging for a long time, and it now may seem to be oscillating out of control. Are we back where we started about a century ago? Like Freud, are we about to reverse our stance? For a moment's respite, let's step back from the fray of politics to the ivory tower of science.

How Accurate Is Autobiographical Memory? ◆ ◆ ◆ ◆

If you're going to tangle with the false-memory controversy, you should know something about the different kinds of memory. [43] You can look up a phone number and keep it in mind until you dial (short-term or "working" memory). You can remember your childhood home (long-term memory). You can remember skills like riding a bike or swimming, even if you haven't performed them for years (implicit memory). You can remember some facts you learned in school (explicit memory). You can also remember specific events in your life (episodic memory).

The distinction between true and false memories pertains primarily to *autobiographical memory,* memory for information significant to the self. [44] This is a highly sophisticated form of human memory that evolves gradually in early childhood. [45] Autobiographical memories include memories both of unique events (your high school graduation) and of recurrent events (trips to your grandmother's house). These "episodic" memories typically include a great deal of visual imagery. Autobiographical memory comprises much of your knowledge about yourself. Like other autobiographical memories, traumatic memories may include unique events (a rape or a house burning down) as well as recurrent events (repeated abuse or a series of firefights in a war).

Before tackling traumatic memories, it will be helpful to review what researchers have learned about the accuracy of autobiographical memory. This issue has been hard to study because, just as it can be difficult for the traumatized person to verify the accuracy of childhood memories, it is difficult for the researcher.

Most people, including psychologists, believe that long-term memories are permanently stored in the brain. Perhaps we cannot retrieve them; perhaps we mix them up; but they are there. This idea has been difficult to dislodge because, no matter how aware of your faltering memory you may be, you can always suppose that "it's in there somewhere." This has been called the *video-recorder model* of autobiographical memory.[46] The video recorder must be in the brain. We can think of remembering as reactivating an earlier brain state.[47] Is it the same brain state? Is it similar? How similar?

It may appeal to common sense, but the video-recorder model of memory is extremely misleading.[48] First, for a memory to be a copy of an event, the event must have been perceived perfectly accurately. But humans, unlike video recorders, actively interpret what they see.[49] The same event is likely to be perceived and interpreted differently by different individuals—who will each remember it differently. What is perceived determines what is encoded into memory and what can be retrieved from memory.[50]

No matter how accurately an event may be perceived and stored, when it is remembered, it is not replayed as in a video recorder; rather, it is *reconstructed*. The idea that memory is inherently *constructive* is extremely important in relation to the memory-versus-fantasy controversy. It is not a new idea; well over a half-century ago, experimental psychologist Sir Frederic Bartlett concluded: "Remembering is not the re-excitation of innumerable fixed, lifeless and fragmentary traces. It is an imaginative reconstruction, or construction, built out of the relation of our attitude towards a whole active mass of organised past reactions or experience, and to a little outstanding detail which commonly appears in image or in language form."[51]

Not surprisingly, research shows that memory for more recent events is more accurate than memory for more remote events.[52] As time goes by, details are lost. Moreover, our memories for unique events are likely to be more accurate than our memories for recurrent events.[53] With repeated events, such as going to grandmother's house, a kind of schematic or abstract memory evolves. Often, especially with repeated events, we have a general idea of what happened, and then we reconstruct certain details according to what is plausible. We fill in the gaps: "new, postevent information often becomes incorporated into memory, supplementing and altering a person's recollection." [54] We are likely to fill in the gaps in ways that put us in a good light.[55] We may sharply remember a few details and then reconstruct the whole from them: "Out of a few stored bone chips, we remember a dinosaur." [56] Alternatively, consider this library metaphor: "memory is not so much like reading a book as it is like *writing* one from fragmentary notes." [57]

It is helpful to keep in mind that autobiographical memory is *self-knowledge*. What you recall at any given moment is consistent with your self-concept at the time.[58] When you reconstruct autobiographical memory, you are reconstructing your self-*image*. You have a strong tendency to reconstruct events you experienced in a way that is consistent with your *current* self-image and the rest of your knowledge about yourself. Thus, your sense of self guides the reconstruction process. Think of your autobiographical memories as a "self-portrait." [59] What you remember is consistent with what *should* have happened in light of your current self-portrait. If you're feeling depressed, you'll remember your failure; if you're feeling confident, you'll remember your success. As your self-concept changes, you revise your autobiography. A revised autobiography is an inevitable by-product of exploratory psychotherapy.[60]

It is also helpful to keep in mind that nothing stays still in the brain. Every reconstruction is always a partially new construction. In the process of construction, your brain is always resculpting itself and reshaping connections.[61] Especially as you recall an event many times, the connections become changed in the process. Under the guidance of your self-portrait, when you reconstruct, you may weave in fantasy and wishful thinking, reshaping your "memory" in your brain. The neural connections are not permanent either; they also change. The same can be said for brain as for mind: "Memory for whole events is stored widely, not in a single location; literal or biological forgetting can occur, so that recollection of past events is a reconstruction from fragments, not a veridical playback of past events." [62]

Reading this, you should be protesting, "But I am *certain* that much of what I remember is true!" The research on autobiographical memory is consistent with your protest. People typically have a high degree of confidence in their autobiographical memories, even if the memories are not accurate.[63] Confidence is a poor basis for judging the accuracy of autobiographical memories.[64] But the confidence, within limits, is well founded. Autobiographical memory often reflects the *gist* of what happened, despite the malleability of memory and inaccuracies in detail.[65] You are most likely to remember whatever you were paying most attention to during an emotional event—usually the main action.[66] As one researcher summarized,

> There is a discrepancy between what one remembers about everyday autobiographical events and what really happened. . . . It is not the case, however, that the meaning around which autobiographical memory is organized is a complete fabrication of life events. There is a fundamental integrity to one's autobiographical recollections . . . most autobiographical memories are true but inaccurate.[67]

Yet there is one crucial qualification to the conclusion that autobiographical memories are generally accurate: What you recall *spontaneously*—without any particular ax to grind—is most likely to be accurate. Inaccuracies are likely to come in when you try to *force* yourself to remember or when you are under external pressure to remember particular events—for example, if you are being pressed for details in giving eyewitness testimony.[68] This principle could be extended to psychotherapy: You risk constructing inaccurate memories if you *assume* you were sexually abused and then force yourself to remember it. My advice: Don't push it.

Reasons for Traumatic Memories to Be Clouded

The accuracy of our nontraumatic autobiographical memory is no simple matter. Matters are even more complicated when it comes to traumatic memories, because there are many ways in which traumatic memories can be obscured. This is why we must think in gray—not black and white.

Extreme Emotion Has Paradoxical Effects on Memory

Is a traumatic event likely to be remembered more accurately or less accurately than an emotionally neutral event? There is no simple answer to this question. It is generally assumed that strong emotion makes an event stand out and thus increases the likelihood that it will be remembered.[69] Plainly, it is adaptive for us to remember emotionally significant events, and our neurophysiology evolved accordingly.[70] Up to a point, stress-induced changes in the balance of neurotransmitters and neurohormones may enhance memory.[71] Yet these neurophysiological changes can work both ways: Beyond moderate levels of stress, the associated neurophysiological changes may impair memory.[72] There is ample evidence that traumatic memories, like other autobiographical memories, can be inaccurate representations of actual events.[73]

In the context of severe, prolonged, and repeated trauma, there is little doubt in the clinical literature that overwhelming emotion can wreak havoc on memory.[74] Traumatic memories are likely to be stored in a form that works against meaningful recall. Memories may be stored in fragmentary form, in bits and pieces. Self-protective dissociation during trauma can compound the emotional overload, further breaking apart the unity of experience as it occurs. As Braun[75] described, behavior, affect (emotion), sensation, and knowledge can be separated. Memories of such fragmented experience may take the form of isolated images (sights, sounds, smells) or body sensations (a searing pain, a wave of nausea). Sometimes all that is "remembered" is an overpowering impulse to run away or to lash out. These images, feelings, and memory fragments do not occur in sequence, and they do not add up to a coherent event.

We can now begin to resolve a paradox: Traumatized persons may have an amalgam of too much memory *(hypermnesia)* and too little memory *(amnesia).*[76] You may have too much emotional memory and too little autobiographical memory. On the side of too much memory, high emotional arousal and the related blast of neurotransmitters and neurohormones may produce *indelible* memory fragments (images, body sensations)[77] that are brought into awareness all too easily: Trauma may create "burned-in" visual images,[78] and "vivid memories that can last a lifetime."[79]

On the side of too little memory, the extreme emotional arousal—while contributing to the indelible fragments—may impede the brain circuits that promote storage of coherent autobiographical memories.[80] Conditioned emotional responses are simple to establish; autobiographical memories are far more complex to construct. The result: You have bits and pieces of experience that make no historical sense. You reexperience, but you do not remember. You are beset by intrusive memory fragments, but you are left with a muddled autobiography. Then you have the formidable task of working with such fragments to *construct* an autobiographical account of trauma that makes some sense.

The paradoxical effect of extreme emotion on memory is so crucial to understanding the problem of "false memories" that I will reiterate it. Traumatic levels of emotion may result in extremely strong and unforgettable stimulus-response connections and *simultaneously* interfere with meaningful perception and recall of events.[81]

Dissociation Blurs Perception

As described in Chapter 5 (Consciousness), the fragmenting effects of extreme emotion may be compounded by dissociative defenses. But dissociation can also blur memory in a more global way. As discussed earlier, dissociation involves a dimming of consciousness akin to a trance state in hypnosis. Dissociation entails a profound sense of detachment from reality. The traumatic experience may take place in a dreamlike state, feeling unreal at the time. Or, even if it feels all too real, the experience may later be shrouded in dissociation and be remembered only with great detachment. Earlier, I argued that dissociation is both a blessing and a curse. Part of the "curse" is that dissociated experiences may *always* remain hazy; if remembered at all, they may be remembered with the original sense of unreality. You cannot remember clearly what you initially experienced as foggy or fragmented. To reiterate, if an experience was not perceived clearly, it cannot be stored or retrieved clearly.

In addition to being fragmented and dim or hazy, dissociated experience is liable to be interwoven with fantasy (see Figure 5–1). Highly fantasy-prone individuals may cope with trauma by seeking refuge in imagination. Their fantasies are imbued with vivid imagery and take on a feeling of reality—sometimes seeming even more real than reality itself. Such individuals have described their difficulty in sorting out their memory of fantasies from their memory of actual events, perhaps akin to the confusion many of us sometimes feel about whether we dreamed something or it actually happened. So it is hardly surprising that fantasy and memory for trauma can become intertwined in the course of dissociation.[82]

Social Pressure Counters Remembering

Let's back up a bit. Why do we have autobiographical memory? One main reason: We construct autobiographies to maintain and enrich our relationships with each other.[83] Think of the importance of reminiscence for cementing relationships. Just as your personal identity requires autobiographical memory, your relationships require a history of shared experience. Autobiographies are constructed and maintained by conversations about experience:[84] If you talk about an experience with someone while you are going through it or you review it later, you are more likely to remember it.[85] Of course, the memory can also change in the retelling.[86]

If autobiographies depend on discourse, imagine what happens when events are kept secret. With no chance for rehearsal through retelling, shameful memories are likely to fade and become cloudy.[87] Compounding confusion, the abusive experience is often denied even as it happens.[88] Persons who mistreat others may actively foster a sense of unreality.[89] Consider the impact of judgments like the following: "It didn't happen; it happened but it wasn't important and has no consequences; it happened but (s)he provoked it; it happened but it's not abusive." [90] Secrecy is enforced, often with dire threats:

> This is our secret; nobody else will understand. Don't tell anybody. Nobody will believe you. Don't tell your mother; a) she will hate you, b) she will hate me, c) she will kill you, d) she will kill me, e) it will kill her, f) she will send you away, g) she will send me away, or h) it will break up the family and you'll all end up in an orphanage. If you tell anyone, a) I won't love you anymore, b) I'll spank you, c) I'll kill your dog, or d) I'll kill you.[91]

Many persons who have been abused, particularly at the hands of caregivers, develop a sense of dual realities, of worlds split apart.[92] They may be abused and then, within minutes, may need to join some family gathering and pretend that nothing has happened. If they talk about the abuse, they may be accused directly of "making it up" or "imagining it." No wonder that you may come to doubt your own judgments about what is real, as well as mistrusting the judgments of others. Not only do abused individuals have a shaky sense of reality associated with memories, but their ongoing sense of reality can also be pervasively undermined. At worst, "they doubt whether they know anything." [93]

Amnesia ♦ ♦ ♦ ♦ ♦ ♦ ♦ ♦ ♦ ♦ ♦

There is no question that some individuals who have been abused go through long periods during which they do not think about or remember having been abused. But there is a great deal of controversy and confusion about the psychological mechanisms involved. Dissociation, repression, other psychological defenses, and normal forgetting have all been proposed to explain delayed recall.[94] Most of the furor, however, has centered around "repressed memories" of childhood sexual abuse.[95] For the sake of simplicity, I will just use the general term *amnesia* to encompass the various forms of not remembering.

Amnesia for traumatic events can occur in childhood.[96] But the term *childhood amnesia* refers to the widely observed fact that adults' memories for early childhood are more sparse than those for later years.[97] Adults typically remember relatively few events for ages below 5.[98] In addition to this normal childhood amnesia, an even more thoroughgoing "infantile amnesia" exists before age 2.[99] Autobiographical memory requires a sense of self, and this personal frame of reference does not become established until the second year of life.[100] Moreover, autobiographical narrative requires language skills that do not develop until the third year of life. It is difficult to describe what could not be put into words in the first place.[101] Thus, although some individuals remember more than others,[102] and some types of events are more memorable than others,[103] most people remember little from before age 5 and essentially nothing from before age 2.

But keep in mind the distinction between emotional (stimulus-response) memory and autobiographical memory. Childhood and infantile amnesia pertain to narrative autobiographical memory, not to *all* of memory. Recent research demonstrates that infants have a sophisticated and durable memory.[104] Even if traumatic events from early childhood are not remembered autobiographically, they may leave an emotional legacy. Lenore Terr[105] has observed that infants traumatized before age 2 may later demonstrate accurate "behavioral memory." For example, in playing with dolls and toys, they reenact trauma that uncannily resembles the documented events. Consistent with limitations in infant memory, their stories of what happened may be inaccurate, but their behavior is not. In addition, after age 3 the mental machinery for full-fledged autobiographical memory is in place, although adult recall of such early trauma may be sparse.

Of course, amnesia does not pertain only to childhood; it can occur at any age. Dissociative amnesia (formerly called *psychogenic amnesia*) is psychologically caused, in contrast with amnesia that results from brain injury. We have seen earlier that dissociation may blur or fragment experience at the time of trauma. But dissociation may also block more clearly established memories from later recall. Defined broadly, *psychogenic amnesia* is "a reversible memory impairment in which groups of memories for personal experience that would ordinarily be available for recall to the conscious mind cannot be retrieved or retained in a verbal form." [106] Amnesia after traumatic experience (combat, rape, accidents) is not uncommon. [107] Amnesia varies widely in severity (from forgetting parts of an event to forgetting one's entire past) and duration (from minutes to years). The controversy about delayed memories of sexual abuse in childhood has sparked research on amnesia for childhood trauma. But the research results have been conflicting and controversial. [108]

Judith Herman and Emily Schatzow [109] conducted the first systematic investigation of the extent to which traumatic memories are blocked from memory. In 53 patients with a history of sexual abuse, they found the full spectrum of recall. More than one-third of the women had full recall; they remembered the abuse in detail, and they did not recover any additional memories in the course of their treatment. About the same proportion had some recall but not full recall; they had just recently recalled new memories or additional memories in the course of treatment. The remaining patients, about one-fourth of the total, had severely limited memory; they recalled little from childhood and had experienced recent intrusions of memories that had been entirely forgotten. Patients were more likely to remember the abuse if it began during or continued well into adolescence. Patients were most likely to completely block off any memory of the abuse if it had begun in early childhood and ended before adolescence or if it had been frankly violent or sadistic.

There have been several more recent studies of amnesia for childhood sexual abuse, [110] with periods of forgetting reported by 19% [111] to 59% [112] of the individuals studied. Notably, in a national sample of psychologists, nearly one-fourth reported a history of sexual or physical abuse, and over 40% who reported abuse went through a period of forgetting. [113]

Although the statistics vary widely from one study to another, many persons remember traumatic events belatedly—well after the fact. They state that they went through a period of not remembering having been abused in childhood. But usually we have no way of knowing for sure what actually happened to them. Researcher Linda Meyer Williams[114] located 129 women, each with a history of sexual abuse that had been documented in hospital emergency room records 17 years earlier. Of these women, 38% did not recall the incident of abuse that precipitated the emergency room visit. Sadly, for many of these women, the incident studied was not a unique event (and therefore not distinctly memorable); 68% of the women who did not remember the emergency room incident were able to recall *other* incidents of sexual assault. Only 12% of the women reported that they had never been abused despite documentation to the contrary. Reviewing Williams's study, psychologist Elizabeth Loftus and colleagues concluded, "The findings do support the claim that many children can forget about a sexually abusive experience from their past. Extreme claims such as 'if you were raped, you'd remember' are disproven by these findings."[115]

Yet the soundness and interpretation of these studies on memory for childhood sexual abuse will continue to be debated.[116] It is indeed remarkable that extensive childhood trauma could be entirely blotted out through part of adulthood, even if a host of psychological concepts may account for this; for example, repression, dissociation, amnesia, and just plain forgetting. But the mind does not simply blot out complex trauma. Let me give you a more complicated scenario described by a number of patients: Much of traumatic experience is dimmed and fragmented by dissociation in childhood. For years in adulthood, much is remembered, but the worst may be forgotten. Lacking a sense of what is normative in childhood, many individuals may fail to recognize that much of what they *do* remember was traumatic by others' standards. But here we can add another concept to our list of defensive devices: *distraction.* Many patients describe a sense of "running," of always being involved in frenetic activity (e.g., being "workaholics"), and of continually moving from relationship to relationship or from place to place. After years, even decades, of such running, coupled with accumulating stress, they "hit the wall" or "crash." They become exhausted and plummet into depression. With the defensive escape into activity blocked, and trauma rekindled by contemporary stress, intrusive memories may come to the fore—often in nonautobiographical form.

In this scenario, one should not necessarily conclude that an individual has continuously repressed, dissociated, or otherwise obliterated all early experience, year after year. Rather, some of the most traumatic childhood experience has been dormant—out of mind. When current stress and heightened vulnerability conspire, early memories are evoked (reconstructed), and then the beleaguered individual again resorts to dissociation to escape from the intrusive memories and overwhelming feelings. At worst, the upshot can be an amalgam of depression, posttraumatic stress disorder, dissociative disorder—and profound confusion.

Memory Versus Fantasy: A Current Perspective ◆ ◆ ◆ ◆ ◆ ◆ ◆ ◆ ◆

We now face a mass of contradictory data and conflicting opinions about the accuracy of long-forgotten memories of trauma. Even if you have managed to follow all the material presented in this chapter thus far, you may remain perplexed. Where does this leave us? I don't have the answers, but I think I can clarify the questions.

First, it is helpful to keep in perspective that the question of the accuracy of memories has focused on a narrow range of traumatic experience—namely, child abuse. Moreover, within the area of child abuse, most of the attention has been devoted to sexual abuse, although there is also heated debate about what to make of memories of "satanic ritual abuse." [117]

Anything Is Possible

As you might imagine, in the current adversarial climate, there has been a strong tendency for professionals to choose sides—often university professors on one side and clinicians on the other. The False Memory Syndrome Foundation has been one fulcrum for this polarization. Choosing sides and doing battle can be necessary and constructive, but it can also interfere with objectivity. In the interest of avoiding extremism,[118] I start with the assumption that *everything happens.*[119] We need to leave behind black-and-white distinctions between "true" and "false" memories and adopt the core principle of "fuzzy thinking," that "everything is a matter of degree."[120] Plainly, with all memory, there is a wide spectrum of clarity and accuracy:[121] "Like most human phenomena, memories may range from utterly true to utterly false and everything in between."[122] The broad spectrum of accuracy is a result of the wide range of factors that may cloud memories of childhood trauma.[123]

I have divided this spectrum into seven broad categories, as depicted in Table 6–1. The first five categories pertain to individuals who have actually been traumatized, whereas the last two pertain to individuals who have relatively false memories of abuse—that is, "memories" without any actual history of abuse (although they may have suffered *other* trauma). I have included corroboration as an important factor here and will have more to say about it shortly. Keep in mind for this discussion that these are logical categories; they represent a range of *possibilities.*

Corroborated memories.   Category 1 is the most clear-cut. In this category are individuals who have always clearly remembered their traumatic experience and who have corroborating evidence (confirmation from siblings, photographs, court records). Category 2 fits individuals who may have forgotten the trauma for a period of time and/or have spotty memories but whose confidence in the accuracy of the memories could be bolstered by other evidence (as in Category 1). Examples would be children with partial memories for clearly documented traumatic experiences.[124]

Uncorroborated memories.   Many individuals who have been traumatized are neither able nor inclined to corroborate their memories. In Category 3 are those whose memories, although uncorroborated, are relatively clear and continuous. These individuals plainly remember their traumatic experience and have never forgotten it. They have no reason to doubt the gist of their recollections. Category 4 includes individuals who are likely to be more confused about their memories. They may have forgotten much of

---

Table 6–1.   The spectrum of accuracy in memory of trauma.

1. Continuously/clearly remembered with corroboration
2. Delayed/fragmentary memory with corroboration
3. Continuously/clearly remembered without corroboration
4. Delayed/fragmentary memory without corroboration
5. Exaggerated/distorted memory
6. False memory—patient constructed
7. False memory—therapist suggested

their traumatic experience for a considerable period of time, and/or their memories may be partial, fragmentary, or clouded by dissociation. As discussed earlier, for such individuals, the sense of reality of their memories may *always* be limited.

Exaggerated and distorted memories.   In Category 5 are persons who have undergone significant trauma but whose memories are inaccurate reflections of the details or type of trauma. This category would include the child who embellishes traumatic memory with developmentally natural fantasy.[125]

Ironically, traumatic experience itself may beget false memories. Trauma fosters dissociation, and—especially for fantasy-prone individuals—dissociation may promote fantasy and distortion of memory. One young woman who endured repeated trauma reported that, as a young girl, she frequently sought refuge by crawling under the covers to the foot of her bed. She imagined that she was a fetus back in her mother's womb. She developed a wide range of comforting fantasies. Then, whenever she found herself in the traumatic situation, she put herself back in the bed-womb and plunged into her self-protective fantasy world. In adulthood, when she tried to recapture her actual traumatic experience, it had become all intermingled with these fantasies.

Paradoxically, some individuals may self-protectively "remember" traumatic experience as even *more* horrific than it actually was. For example, persons who are highly imaginative and prone to dissociation, like the girl who could mentally transport herself into the womb of the bed, may incorporate into autobiographical memory material from books and movies, as well as hallucinations, illusions, and fantasies. In this fashion, for example, "memories" of bizarre torture or ritual abuse—as horrible as they are—could be created to obscure even more unthinkable (but tragically more prosaic and common) abuse that occurs within the family, such as beatings, rapes, deprivation, or incarceration.[126]

False memories.   Categories 6 and 7 pertain to individuals who have not actually undergone sexual abuse but who have been misled into believing that they have, with or without the encouragement of a therapist. The basic premise: Given the fallibility and constructive nature of memory, it is possible to "remember" something that didn't happen. This tendency has been amply demonstrated in research,[127] although not in relation to severe childhood trauma.

Category 6 pertains to individuals who, outside a therapy context, come to believe—wrongly—that they have been traumatized in a particular way. To my knowledge, I have not worked with any such persons. But I can imagine a plausible scenario consistent with what we now know about memory: The hypothetical individual is experiencing severe anxiety and depression and is trying to understand the reasons for her symptoms. She is aware that many persons with these symptoms have a history of sexual abuse, and she has some reason to suspect that her father may have abused her. She knows that some individuals who are abused have amnesia for the abuse. Although she has no memories of being abused, she has ample *conscious* reason to be furious with her father. Perhaps she begins to have nightmares; she dreams that she is being smothered under the weight of a dark, shadowy figure, and she wakes up in fright. The nightmares further confirm her suspicions. She reads some self-help books on sexual abuse that also support this line of thinking. She tries hard to remember troubling scenes from childhood, and she begins to visualize some fragmentary episodes of sexual contact with her father that are consistent with her suspicions. We humans have an extraordinary capacity to transform *ideas* into *visual images.*[128] Those skilled in generating elaborate imagery may believe that something happened and then picture it vividly. Thus, children can create false *visual* memories on the basis of *stories* they have been told by their families.[129]

Category 7 includes individuals who have generated false memories on the basis of encounters with zealous therapists. Judith Herman and Mary Harvey[130] have provided reason to doubt that this phenomenon is common, but there are many horror stories in the literature.[131] There are therapists who make the same mistake as the hypothetical patient described in Category 6: The therapist wrongly infers a specific cause (sexual abuse) from a group of symptoms (anxiety and depression). The therapist might tell the patient that she "fits the pattern" of individuals who have been sexually abused in childhood, even though there is no specific indication of sexual abuse beyond the ubiquitous symptoms of anxiety and depression. At worst, the therapist could insist on this explanation despite the patient's protests to the contrary: Not remembering is one sign of sexual abuse; therefore, if you don't remember, that's just additional reason to believe you were abused. Such faulty reasoning permits no escape from a history of abuse! In the face of such pressure, a patient could begin constructing false memories. Experimental subjects falsely remember (less traumatic) events with a lot less pressure.[132] Of course, the process need not be so blatant; more subtle suggestion and gradual leading over a prolonged period of therapy could have a similar effect. Moreover, hypnosis could certainly abet this process, as will be discussed shortly.

The Proof Is in the Proportions

These seven categories are my way of seeing the trees, but we also need to see the forest. Granted, everything happens. The key question is *how much these various things happen.* There is a scientific question here: What proportion of persons fit into each category? More specifically: What proportion of persons who remember sexual abuse? What proportion of persons who remember "satanic ritual abuse"? Here I can only reiterate the psychologist's perennial refrain: More research is needed.

For the scientifically curious, more research is always needed. But at this point, we have the advantage of a great deal of research; we are not completely in the dark. There is one view of the forest in which we can be confident, and we should never lose sight of it: *The number of individuals in Categories 1 through 5 is appallingly large.* Here I am merely reiterating the point well documented in the literature: Trauma happens. Sexual abuse happens.

Therapists and patients alike need to be mindful of the possibility of false memories; the construction of false memories can be extremely damaging to patients and their families, as well as to therapists and clinics. We know that a large proportion of traumatic memories are more or less accurate, because we know that the prevalence of trauma is staggering. Despite the huge social protest represented by the False Memory Syndrome Foundation, and many case reports of false memories, there is no way to judge the prevalence of false memories in relation to more-or-less accurate memories. Until research clarifies these proportions, our awareness of "false memories" should not obscure the huge forest of actual trauma and its legacy of damaging memories. To reiterate, we have a false-memory problem of unknown proportions, and we have a trauma problem of huge known proportions.

One way of using Table 6–1 to see the forest is to keep sight of the fact that the number of individuals in Categories 1 through 5 is large. Here's another way to think about it: Persons who have undergone a single, brief traumatic experience are likely to remember it clearly.[133] But any individual who has experienced prolonged and repeated trauma is likely to have memories in *several categories* across the whole fuzzy spectrum. For example, an individual who was emotionally, physically, and sexually abused throughout much of childhood is likely to have an amalgam of memories. Some memories may be clear and may never be forgotten (memories of terrifying verbal confrontations). Some memories may be corroborated (a broken arm). Some memories may be patchy or cloudy (repeated beatings in dissociated states). Some memories may be forgotten for decades (sexual abuse). Some "memories" (cult abuse) may be highly distorted or essentially false. Well-intended exploratory therapy—with or without hypnosis—could contribute to the stockpile of *relatively accurate, partially accurate,* and *relatively inaccurate* memories. Here again, in the face of a wide spectrum of accuracy, it is crucial not to lose sight of the forest: Trauma happens. The incorporation of some inaccurate detail does not render the gist of a memory "false." [134] False details do not make false memories: "it is illogical to reason from the fact that a memory has false details to the conclusion that there is no real incident from which this false memory is an inaccurate depiction." [135] Ironically, because trauma may spawn fantasy, some proportion of false memories may be one consequence of trauma, rather than discrediting the gist of an autobiography.

Obtaining Corroboration

It is little wonder that many individuals doubt the accuracy of their memories. The public outcry about "false memories" now fuels their doubt. There have been some attempts to determine the extent to which belated memories of sexual abuse can be corroborated.

Herman and Schatzow[136] not only studied their patients' patterns of forgetting but also researched the validity of their memories of trauma. Patients in their therapy groups were encouraged to gather information from family members, and most did so. The majority of the patients (74%) gathered corroborating evidence from the perpetrator, from other family members, or from physical evidence (diaries or photographs). Some discovered that another child, often a sibling, had also been abused by the same person.

Others reported confirming statements from family members, short of direct evidence. Most of the patients who did not obtain corroborating evidence made no attempt to do so. Herman and Schatzow concluded: "The presumption that most patients' reports of childhood sexual abuse can be ascribed to fantasy no longer appears tenable." [137] In other studies, psychiatrist Philip Coons[138] has corroborated histories of child abuse for high proportions of patients with multiple personality disorder and other dissociative disorders. In the study of psychologists reporting a history of abuse, nearly half obtained corroboration ranging from diaries to medical records.[139]

With all of the concern about reports of false memories, it is worth noting that inaccuracies in recall and reporting also go in the other direction: A recent study of abused and delinquent adolescents, in which the subjects were asked to recall their histories as young adults, found that "inaccuracies invariably occurred in the direction of underreporting." [140] Indeed, when questioned about their early family experiences, many abused individuals cover up their histories with blatant idealizations of their upbringing.[141]

The few studies that have been conducted to corroborate memories of abuse and to compare reports with earlier documentation have hardly quelled debate.[142] Their findings have been challenged on theoretical and scientific grounds.[143] We often have a stalemate: Adult children report that their parents did it; the parents report that they didn't do it; and *there are no other witnesses*. There is no way to judge the degree of accuracy from the nature or quality of the memory itself; anyone who seeks "proof" must rely on external corroboration.[144] To reiterate, in the face of legitimate skepticism about many of the trees, we must not lose sight of the forest of known trauma and thereby lose ground on hard-won social gains.[145]

Conclusion

When you're in the midst of a storm, it's hard to get your bearings. We all need to tolerate uncertainty while striving to find more solid ground. We *do* need more research—especially longitudinal studies that carefully document trauma and systematically track the fate of memories over the course of development. Meanwhile, in the face of all this controversy, the majority of therapists believe their patients.[146] I am among that majority.

But I am disinclined to go on psychological fishing expeditions looking for trauma, and I do not *assume* that psychiatric symptoms are caused by trauma. I believe my patients who show signs of trauma for the same reason that Freud initially believed his patients: Their symptoms are most understandable if some role is accorded to trauma. Therapists today have three advantages over Freud: First, the extent of sexual trauma has been thoroughly documented. Second, there is a clearly defined syndrome—post-traumatic stress disorder—that is similar across a wide range of traumatic experiences. Third, the social climate is now more conducive to acknowledging the extent of sexual abuse.

I can believe that *some* of my patients' memories are relatively false, exaggerated, or distorted. But I find it hard to believe that their severe post-traumatic stress disorder was caused by false memories. I consider it more likely that whatever false memories they may hold were created to escape from some form of traumatic experience. With childhood trauma so prevalent, it strains credulity to explain traumatic memories on the basis of something other than trauma.[147] The details may be questioned, but the only way to make sense of the symptoms is to assume that there is a *core of truth* in the memories. In the context of multiple personality disorder, psychiatrist Richard Kluft has summed it up beautifully:

> Often it is clear that *something terrible has happened* but unclear exactly what it was. The task of reconstructing historical reality may be beyond the powers of the most accomplished and dedicated therapist and the most honest and hard-working patient, but that does not make MPD [multiple personality disorder] or the suffering of its victims any less real.[148]

Psychotherapy is not a court of law. Psychotherapy is not designed to yield historical truth, and psychotherapists cannot be detectives. Psychotherapy may provide "narrative truth"[149]—a coherent view of one's past that makes sense of one's present experience.

In helping a patient to ascertain the "core of truth," I do not assume that the core contains *sexual* abuse. This is an unfortunately common and potentially disastrous assumption. Sexual abuse must be recognized, and its effects need to be treated. But the current focus on sexual abuse inclines some patients and therapists to discount other forms of traumatic experience, while searching for the "smoking gun" of sexual trauma.

◆ A patient was referred for consultation because she was stuck in a pattern of self-destructive behavior. She had begun exploring her childhood in psychotherapy, and she started to feel shame and rage. She took out her rage by screaming at her daughter; afterward, she felt ashamed, and she burned, banged, or cut herself. She had amnesia for part of her childhood, and she had some periods of more recent amnesia. She recalled some instances of being sexually molested as a child; these incidents were painful and disturbing but not terrifying. Being unable to account for her current symptoms, she suspected that she had been sexually abused by her older brother.

The patient worked hard in several consultation sessions to understand the basis of her rage and self-destructive behavior. She had numerous clear memories of extremely traumatic experiences in childhood—experiences that she had never forgotten. There was no indication of sexual trauma beyond the incidents of molestation that she had remembered for a long time, nor did she remember any physical abuse. Yet she remembered being teased, tormented, and occasionally hit and pushed around by her brother. Even more distressing were memories of numerous terrifying encounters with her father. A minor failure to please him could bring on a menacing assault. He'd ask her to get him a fork; she'd hand him a spoon, and he'd launch into a torrent of verbal abuse. Even if he didn't lay a hand on her, her father would be right in her face, and she'd tremble with fear. As she grew older, her fear turned to anger and rage, but she never dared fight back for fear of being battered. She wished her mother would come to her rescue, but her mother was also justifiably terrified of her father—herself often the victim of his tirades and intimidation. The patient endured the assaults alone and in silence, without any reassurance or comforting.

Over the course of her childhood, the patient had gradually begun to think of herself as a "monster" who deserved mistreatment. To her horror, in adulthood, she found herself screaming at her daughter—just as her father had screamed at her. She always tried to reconcile with her daughter after she'd calmed down—something that her father never did with her. Nevertheless, she also punished herself by injuring herself. Will only childhood sexual abuse explain her behavior? What is the trauma?

When the patient brought out numerous memories of terrifying encounters with her father's rage, she could clearly understand the basis of her current symptoms. Rather than searching for memories of additional sexual abuse, she worked on calming herself and moderating her anger. She was able to shift her self-image from that of a "monster" to a more complex self-image that included justifiable fear and anger, as well as love and compassion. She began to work on expressing more appropriate levels of frustration in response to her daughter's provocative behavior.

Remembering in Therapy   ◆ ◆ ◆ ◆ ◆ ◆ ◆

It is not uncommon for individuals who are struggling with personal problems and psychiatric symptoms to wonder if sexual abuse is the cause. Such individuals may have vague suspicions that they have been abused. Or reading popular books on child abuse and incest may lead them to wonder about their own history. It is certainly reasonable for such individuals to seek therapy, just as it is reasonable for those who have more-or-less clear traumatic memories to do so.

If Freud changed his mind about the validity of memories, and mental health professionals are still debating the issue a century later, is it any wonder that a person would feel bewildered in the face of clouded and fragmentary memories? It is natural to seek therapy partly to find out what really happened.

The Role of the Therapist

Understandably, if you are struggling to make sense of traumatic memories, you would like your therapist to validate them. Perhaps it would be helpful if your therapist had a "reality stamp" to verify the accuracy of your memories. But as much as you might wish it, your therapist cannot serve the role of memory verifier.[150] The Board of Trustees of the American Psychiatric Association urges neutrality: "A strong prior belief by the psychiatrist that sexual abuse, or other factors, *are or are not* the cause of the patient's problems is likely to interfere with appropriate assessment and treatment."[151] The Association also counsels against precipitous action:

> It may be important to caution the patient against making major life decisions during the acute phase of treatment. During the acute and later phases of treatment, the issues of breaking off relationships with important attachment figures, of pursuing legal actions, and of making public disclosures may need to be addressed. The psychiatrist should help the patient assess the likely impact (including emotional) of such decisions, given the patient's overall

clinical and social situation. Some patients will be left with unclear memories of abuse and no corroborating information. Psychiatric treatment may help these patients adapt to the uncertainty regarding such emotionally important issues.[152]

Your therapist cannot tell you what happened or what to believe. *You* must take on the challenge of deciding what to believe. In the process, however, your therapist can serve the extremely important function of validating the significance of your current experience and your need to make sense of that experience. You may have been accused—or accuse yourself—of "imagining it." Your therapist will take you seriously while providing support by helping you to tolerate the uncertainty and pain of not knowing.[153] Both you and your therapist may need to strive for the right blend of belief and skepticism as you struggle to sort out your experience.[154] Rather than drawing firm conclusions, the therapist must "help the patient carefully sift through the mixture of fact, fantasy and illusion, eventually to settle on what the patient must decide is his or her final truth." [155]

The Role of Hypnosis

Although many persons seek hypnosis as the way to find out what really happened, it is no pathway to the truth.[156] Under hypnosis, you may remember more. Hypnosis can help surmount self-protective barriers to remembering. With the aid of hypnosis, you may be able to feel safe enough to remember more, and you may be able to relax and concentrate better. You may be able to talk more freely. It is not clear how much hypnosis per se contributes to remembering; just devoting time and effort may be the key to any memory enhancement.[157] Keep in mind that the result of "hypnotically enhanced memory," like any other memory, is a *reconstruction*. More memory does not mean more accurate memory. Memory evoked in hypnosis covers the whole fuzzy spectrum of accuracy. Moreover, you are highly susceptible to suggestion in hypnosis; leading questions from a therapist may engender inaccurate constructions, subsequently remembered with high confidence as facts. His disclaimers notwithstanding, Freud's early work has been criticized on this account.[158]

It has been known for a century that persons in hypnotic trances generate pseudomemories.[159] In recent years, laboratory studies have amply demonstrated that pseudomemories can be engendered in hypnosis, and research has shown that more imaginative (perhaps fantasy-prone) individuals are more likely to generate and embellish pseudomemories.[160] Moreover, many individuals cannot be dissuaded from their confidence in the veracity of their memories, even when they are informed that they were constructed within hypnosis.[161] Notably, under appropriate conditions, experimental subjects can generate pseudomemories out of hypnosis as well as within hypnosis.[162]

Although the research has not focused on trauma, it is clear that hypnosis is not a way to verify the accuracy of memories; rather, it can be used for therapeutic purposes to help individuals explore, clarify, and master painful and confusing internal experience. A decade ago, the Council on Scientific Affairs of the American Medical Association summed up the evidence on the use of hypnosis to refresh memory:

> When hypnosis is used for recall of meaningful past events, there is often new information reported. This may include accurate information as well as confabulations and pseudomemories. These pseudomemories may be the result of hypnosis transforming the subjects' prior beliefs into thoughts or fantasies that they come to accept as memories. Furthermore, since hypnotized subjects tend to be more suggestible, subjects become more vulnerable to incorporating any cues given during hypnosis into their recollections.[163]

The council went on to clarify the value of hypnosis in treatment:

> Hypnosis can be effective in helping some individuals provide memory reports pertaining to events about which they are amnestic. Such recollections, however, may or may not be accurate, although they may be profoundly important in the psychotherapeutic treatment of the individual.[164]

We must appreciate the risks of hypnosis, but hypnosis is not the real culprit in therapy gone awry. *The therapist,* not *the hypnosis,* is responsible for the soundness of the treatment.[165]

When there is scant evidence of a traumatic history, the motto should be "Explore at your own risk." My colleague, psychologist Bill Smith, has articulated some appropriate cautions. Revelations in hypnosis can trigger painful emotions and, at worst, they can be retraumatizing. Not only may the accuracy of remembered material be placed in question, but also you may not know what to do with the new information: "Some patients are left wiser but sadder and wish they had never embarked on the research."[166] In addition to "Explore at your own risk," I would commend the motto "Let sleeping dogs lie."

◆ A patient who was well informed about sexual abuse requested a consultation because she had an uncomfortable encounter with her pastor. At the close of a personal discussion, he touched her gently, and they warmly embraced. In the days to follow, she became anxious and began having unusual physical symptoms, including muscle tightness, headaches, and abdominal pains. She began to suspect that the encounter with her pastor had disturbed her because she may have been sexually abused by a minister with whom she was close in childhood. She also wondered if her stepfather had been inappropriately seductive with her. She requested hypnosis to determine what had happened in her childhood—now two decades past.

   The consultant informed the patient that hypnosis could increase her distress and that there was no assurance that she would become any clearer about what had actually happened in her childhood. Instead, he helped her to understand how her conscious conflicts with her stepfather may have contributed to her ambivalent response to her recent closeness with her pastor. He encouraged her to concentrate on her current problems in feeling close to men rather than trying to figure out just what happened in years past.

The Value of Remembering

It's fine to let sleeping dogs lie. More commonly, however, the dogs are not sleeping; they're howling and barking. There are two indications that you may need to explore trauma:[167] Either you are having intrusive symptoms in relation to traumatic memories (flashbacks, nightmares), or you are reenacting traumatic experience in your behavior (engaging in self-destructive behavior that is a repetition of the traumatic experience, such as self-injurious or sexually compulsive actions).

   As horrendous as intrusive experience is, there can be a positive, constructive side to it. I think of it this way: By bringing the images and feelings into awareness, your mind may be trying to heal itself. Much of your history may be blocked off or compartmentalized. Pages or chapters of your autobiography may be blank. The reasons for your feelings, behavior, and symptoms may be obscure. The intrusive experiences provide an opportunity for integration and a sense of wholeness that were previously beyond reach.[168]

Many persons have the idea that traumatic memories need to be excised by means of gut-wrenching "catharsis," and hypnosis sometimes has been used in the service of evoking such catharsis. I think this approach is misguided—especially in the context of extensive trauma with complex and severe symptoms. Just as flashbacks can be retraumatizing, such "catharses" can be retraumatizing rather than therapeutic.[169] Rather than producing catharsis of extreme emotion, the goal of therapy—with or without hypnosis—is to gain control and mastery over the emotion and to achieve some understanding of the associated experience. Accordingly, several techniques have been developed to help patients recover memories with moderated emotion,[170] and these will be discussed in Part IV (Treatment). Despite the best intentions, however, memories evoked in treatment can be extremely painful, and the process cannot be fully controlled.

If not for the sake of catharsis, what is the value of remembering? One reason to remember is to gain self-understanding. If you are beginning to grapple with intrusive memories, you may be terrified and bewildered. The process of reconstruction can lead to self-understanding. Even if you have not struggled with memories for years, you might have contended with various symptoms. Remembering the traumatic experience can help explain these previously incomprehensible symptoms. You can put the experience into words, and you can organize fragments into a more coherent autobiographical memory. Think of autobiographical memory as a container: When you can translate previously fragmented images and feelings into a coherent narrative, you may not be so emotionally reactive to reminders of trauma.[171] When you can make sense of your experience, your rational brain has a better handle on your emotional brain.

Converting the memory fragments into an organized narrative not only fosters self-understanding but also enables you to talk to others about the traumatic experience. Talking to others will help with the construction of autobiographical memory. As discussed in relation to attachment, the lack of opportunity for comforting and soothing is a paramount contribution to traumatic experience. Talking about trauma entails shedding the shackles of secrecy and, as Judith Herman[172] puts it, allowing someone to bear witness. Then you are no longer alone with the experience, and, albeit belatedly, you can experience some understanding, comforting, and reassurance.

The value of remembering and talking does not stop with self-understanding and being understood. In the process of talking and being understood, you can begin to develop compassion for yourself. In part, this self-compassion can evolve from your sense of others' compassion as they bear witness. And you also may have opportunities to show your compassion for others who have been traumatized. The compassion can even be extended back to yourself. Ultimately, only you can know the true depth of trauma you have undergone; full compassion may only come from within.

The Value of Forgetting

Trauma at any age can derail development. The value of remembering is to get your life back on track, not to remember for the sake of remembering. How much *should* you remember? Those who have suffered a single traumatic event may be able to remember it clearly. But for those who have undergone many forms of trauma over a prolonged period of life, it is neither possible nor desirable to remember everything. Remembering should not become an end in itself. It is extremely painful. You should not undergo needless torment, endlessly dredging up traumatic memories. You may begin constructing distorted and inaccurate memories—a glaringly counterproductive prospect. You would do best to remember only as much as is necessary to do the job of healing so that you can get on with your life. When you are no longer plagued by intrusive memories or repeating the traumatic experience in other ways, when your life makes sense and your autobiography is reasonably clear, the job is done. If more needs to be remembered and reconstructed at some later point, your mind will make this known. *There is no reason to push it.*

Then what? How about forgetting? I find Lewis Thomas's heretical advice appealing:

> If after all, as seems to be true, we are endowed with unconscious minds in our brains, these should be regarded as normal structures, installed wherever they are for a purpose. I am not sure what they are built to contain, but as a biologist, impressed by the usefulness of everything alive, I would take it for granted that they are useful, probably indispensable organs of thought. It cannot be a bad thing to own one, but I would no more think of meddling with it than trying to exorcise my liver, an equally mysterious apparatus. Un-

til we know a lot more, it would be wise, as we have learned from other fields in medicine, to let them be, above all not to interfere. Maybe, even—and this is the notion I wish to suggest to my psychiatric friends—to stock them up, put more things into them, make use of them. Forget whatever you feel like forgetting.[173]

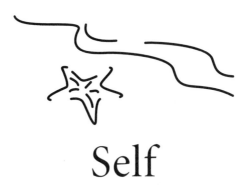

Self

◆ A woman in her late 20s graduated from law school with honors and was on her way to a successful career. She sought psychotherapy for anxiety and nightmares, and she had begun to show warning signs of depression. She had a history of significant trauma in childhood; she had never completely forgotten it, but she had previously been able to keep it out of her mind. As one would expect in a successful attorney, she was highly verbal and articulate. When she was talking about her legal work or her interactions with others, she was glib. But the moment she was asked to talk about herself or her own feelings, she became dumbfounded. Even the simple question "How are you?" could prompt a befuddled silence. When she tried to think about her "self," she encountered a void. Gradually, the reason for this void became clear: When she began to accept the idea that she had a "self," she became filled with such self-loathing that she felt overwhelmed.

The self invariably takes a beating with trauma. In discussing reactions to prolonged and repeated trauma, Judith Herman[1] concludes: "All the structures of the self—the image of the body, the internalized images of others, and the values and ideals that lend a sense of coherence and purpose—are invaded and systematically broken down. . . . While the victim of a single acute trauma may say she is 'not herself' since the event, the victim of chronic trauma may lose the sense that she has a self."

In understanding our *selves*, it is helpful to distinguish two main lines of personality development: the development of the self and the establishment of relationships with others.[2] Self-development emphasizes separation, autonomy, self-definition, individuality, responsibility, initiative, and achievement. Relatedness to others entails attachment, caregiving, intimacy, love, connectedness, and cooperation. Developing the self and developing relatedness are mutually enhancing, not mutually exclusive. The self evolves in part from relationships; your sense of self gives definition to your relationships with others, and your "self" is inconceivable apart from your surrounding context of relationships.

In this chapter, I make some key distinctions among different aspects of the self, and emphasize two aspects of self-experience directly affected by trauma—self-continuity and self-concept. I then show how trauma-related damage to self-continuity and self-concept may lead to self-destructive behavior. I conclude the chapter with some thoughts about restoring self-esteem.

Aspects of the Self ◆ ◆ ◆ ◆ ◆ ◆ ◆ ◆ ◆ ◆

I and Me

Let's start with the most basic distinction, the "I" versus the "me." [3] The "I" is your subjective self that is active in initiating, organizing, choosing, and interpreting experience. Ideally, your active self, or "I," has a sense of continuity. Ideally, with your "I" goes a cohesive self-feeling, a feeling of being your enduring self.[4] If you find this concept of the "I" difficult to grasp, don't feel badly; the subjective sense of self is among the most elusive phenomena in psychology.[5]

In contrast to the "I," the "me" is the objective self as seen from the outside. The "me" is the self as seen by itself. Your "me" is reflected in your self-concept, or how your self thinks about itself. Your "me" is greatly influenced by your interactions and relationships with others. How you see yourself and how you think of yourself depends a great deal on how others view you, respond to you, and treat you. Ideally, your "me" is associated with a feeling of positive self-esteem, derived partly from caring and affirming relationships.

Public and Private

It is also helpful to distinguish between the public self and the private self. Your public self is your self as known to others, the image of your self that you project to others. Your public self is the basis of your sense of "me" that is reflected from others—who you are as seen by others. Persons who have a big stake in image management—all of us do to some degree—are buttressing their public selves.

Your public self is more the outer surface of the self; your private self is the inner core. Your private self is more secret and hidden, but private goes beyond being covered up. Psychoanalyst Arnold Modell[6] describes the private self as "the aspect of the self that is experienced in solitude, in experiences that may never be shared with others. The self from this point of view is not dependent on others but is an independent agent, the source of autonomy . . . the seat of authenticity, of personal morality, and of vital personal interests."

Whereas the public self is sustained through relationships, the private self, according to Modell, is "fueled from within." He points out the potentially lifesaving function of the private self in relation to trauma: "For those who face dreadful environments, private space is the place in which one can retreat to alternative worlds of fantasy, worlds that may guarantee psychic survival in a nonsupportive environment." [7]

Let me tie together some of these basic concepts. The overarching distinction between self-development and the development of relatedness parallels the distinction between the private self—the self in solitude—and the public or social self—the self in relationships. These distinctions also parallel the dialectic between attachment (relatedness) and exploration (autonomy) described earlier (Chapter 3). The infant, sustained and fueled by the secure base of attachment, feels safe to venture out and explore the world, knowing that the secure attachment will be there when needed. Modell points to a related dynamic: *"This natural rhythm of a balance between alternate periods of relatedness and disengagement persists throughout life."* [8]

Self-Continuity   ◆ ◆ ◆ ◆ ◆ ◆ ◆ ◆ ◆ ◆

The subjective self, or "I," is difficult to describe. It entails a feeling of being "myself" that is stable across time and space. I feel that I continue to be myself day after day, month after month, year after year. I feel that I continue to be myself whether I am at home, at work, or out on the town. I continue to be myself at different times and in different places, despite the many changes in my self from time to time and place to place.

Continuity in the face of discontinuity is perhaps the essence of the subjective sense of self.[9] I know who I am, and I continue to be who I am. Implied in continuity is a sense of cohesiveness, unity, integrity, wholeness, and identity. Despite differences from time to time and place to place, I am myself. Included in continuity and cohesiveness is a sense of distinctness from others, a sense of individuality, and a sense of separateness. From this sense of continuity, cohesiveness, and individuality, the self becomes the center of initiative. Ideally, the self has a sense of vitality, agency, and efficacy. I can do, I can accomplish, I can master. I can control my life and my experience.

Self-continuity, self-cohesiveness, and self-efficacy are ideals—to some degree, illusions.[10] You have a sense of continuity—more or less. You are not born with a sense of subjective self or a sense of continuity. As a newborn, you shifted from one state to another.[11] You went from quiet wakefulness, to distress and crying, to sleeping. You gradually learned that you were "yourself" throughout these changes. Your sense of continuity was a developmental achievement, not a given.[12] Nor is this developmental achievement accomplished once and for all; it is a continual challenge.[13]

Long after you attain some sense of continuity in your self-experience, you continue to experience many discontinuities. You may feel the same day after day and month after month—how about year after year or decade after decade? After how long are you no longer the "same person"? As it has been since infancy, your experience is radically interrupted every day by sleep. Your experience is also continually punctuated with lapses in continuity in the form of forgetting or absentmindedness. You experience gradual or more abrupt changes in mood. You even say, "I wasn't myself" after saying or doing something that is "out of character."

A sense of self-continuity is especially difficult to come by when traumatic experience leads to severe internal conflict. Then your self is pulled in all directions. In addition, your self can be pulled apart by contradictory relationships.

Heightened Internal Conflict

Freud initially emphasized trauma as a cause of symptoms, but he shifted his focus from external trauma to internal conflict. Freud's conflict theory is nonetheless highly pertinent to trauma, because nothing stimulates conflict so much as traumatic relationships.

Perhaps one of Freud's major contributions was his discovery of the power and ramifications of unconscious motivation.[14] He believed that instinctual, sexual, and aggressive drives conflict with reality and with morality. The job of the *ego* is to find a way to reconcile the sexual and aggressive drives *(id)* with reality and with social mores (internalized as conscience, or *superego*).

Freud discovered that these sexual and aggressive drives, which are part of our biological heritage, can be frightening and overwhelming. Direct expression of strong sexual and aggressive urges brings us into conflict with reality and with society. In full force, these drives make us anxious: We fear that expressing them will lead to rejection, retaliation, punishment, or loss of love. Accordingly, we try to block them from expression and even from our own awareness.

Freud discovered a major conflict associated with sexual drives that arises in the nuclear family: oedipal conflict. The child's loving attraction to the opposite-sex parent creates a dangerous situation to the degree that this attraction includes some erotic desire and sets up a rivalry with the same-sex parent. Freud believed that this conflict is normally resolved by the child's blocking the erotic attraction from awareness (repression) and identifying with the rival's prohibitions (superego). According to Freud's theory, the erotic feelings of children toward parents are utterly natural but potentially dangerous because of the incest taboo. Oedipal conflict is inevitable.

From the vantage point of Freud's theory, sexual abuse—especially by parents—is psychologically damaging in part because it throws the child into untenable oedipal conflict. Sexual drives are strongly aroused, and the child feels extremely endangered and guilty about their expression. Likewise with aggression: Hostile and rageful feelings are inevitably stirred; the child not only fears the consequences of expressing them, but also may be punished for doing so.

This extreme internal conflict can tear the self apart. As the self becomes divided—pulled in opposite directions by conflicting needs and desires—the sense of wholeness is diminished. We all live with many conflicts, but we can still maintain some sense of wholeness and integrity as long as these internal conflicts are kept within manageable bounds. Psychologist Darlene Ehrenberg[15] has poignantly described the devastation of oedipal conflict brought to the fore by sexual abuse: "Where the child was brutalized and there was no way to resist, the sense of helplessness, pain, panic, and rage is often so extreme and unbearable that the experience simply cannot be contained. This is particularly so if the victim was sexually aroused by the sensual and physical contact, sometimes to his or her own surprise and/or horror." In many instances, sexual abuse is coupled with neglect, exploiting the child's hunger for affection. Then the foundation for guilt feelings is firmly established:

> Where the sexual involvement with the parent was experienced as a fulfillment of the child's own fantasies, longings, and desires, it is problematic in another way. The child may feel the full responsibility lies with himself or herself. To the degree that arousal of the victim's own desire is experienced as the basis for the vulnerability, the relation to desire becomes especially troublesome. This is particularly so when the relationships in question endured a long time, perhaps years, and when it was clear that unless the child had been a cooperative participant and derived some gratification from the involvement the relationship could not have been possible.[16]

Ehrenberg concludes that, in the aftermath of such experience, the individual must be helped "to grasp the fact that the burden of guilt and responsibility for the abusive relationship lies with the abusing adult, no matter what the child's role may have been." [17]

Contradictory Relationships

Severe internal conflict is often embedded in contradictory relationships. Your sense of continuity and cohesiveness depends on reasonable continuity and unity in your relationships with others. We all adapt our behavior to different relationships, and we behave differently in relation to different people. As long as your various relationships are compatible and the alterations in your experience and behavior are within bounds, your sense of continuity and sameness can be preserved.

Our sense of continuity and integrity is challenged, however, by abusive relationships that repeatedly entail 180-degree shifts.[18] If a girl is at one time in a daughter relationship with her father and at another time in a lover relationship with her father, her experience may well be impossible to integrate. Moreover, part of her self, the self as father's lover, will be kept secret from others; it will be an unrecognized part of herself. This part of herself is likely to become disowned or dissociated as "not me."

Another example of a 180-degree shift occurs in violent relationships. A child may be treated with affection and protection at one time and then be violently castigated or physically beaten at another time. Or the child may be loved at one time and severely neglected at another. Such shifts may be associated with parental alcohol or drug abuse. How is one and the same self to reconcile such dramatic contradictions? How can one and the same self be worthy of love and affection and yet also be subjected to beatings and neglect? How is self-continuity possible in such opposing relationships? As Judith Herman[19] explains, "the abused child cannot develop a cohesive self-image with moderate virtues and tolerable faults. In the abusive environment, moderation and tolerance are unknown. Rather, the victim's self-representations remain rigid, exaggerated, and split."

Helplessness

As stated earlier, continuity, cohesiveness, and self-efficacy ideally go together. The continuous, cohesive self is the center of the personality—the experiencer of experience, the source of initiative, the ultimate organizer, the executive, the "unmoved mover."

Let's flesh out this concept of self a bit further. Psychiatrist Daniel Stern[20] has made countless observations of babies in their social contexts to formulate a comprehensive theory of the early development of the sense of self. He describes several facets of the core self: self-agency, "the sense of authorship of one's own actions"; self-coherence, "having a sense of being a nonfragmented, physical whole with boundaries and a locus of integrated action"; self-affectivity, "experiencing patterned inner qualities of feeling (affects) that belong with other experiences of self"; and self-history, "having the sense of enduring, of a continuity with one's own past so that one 'goes on being' and can even change while remaining the same." [21] All facets of the self are affected by trauma. Among the most important conditions for the well-being of the self is self-agency—a sense of mastery and control. From this vantage point, the *worst* state for the self to be in is a state of helplessness. No wonder that people who have been traumatized often complain that the helplessness they experienced was the hardest thing to endure. As psychiatrist David Spiegel[22] noted, it is the "loss of control over one's own state of mind that constitutes the full depth of post-traumatic symptomatology."

Any form of trauma will engender helplessness—natural disasters, accidents, being overpowered by an assailant in a robbery or a rape. The most profound experience of helplessness, however, is that associated with deliberate cruelty. Some abusers sadistically enforce a sense of helplessness as a part of the abuse.[23] The individual may be physically overpowered, cornered, trapped. The abuse is likely to occur unpredictably, further increasing the sense of helplessness, given that our sense of control rests strongly on predictability. When the self is overpowered, the sense of vitality, efficacy, and mastery are squelched. At worst, the person feels depleted, empty, and fragmented.

◆ A young man in psychotherapy recalled his sense of helpless paralysis in the aftermath of a violent argument between his parents when the three of them were returning home in their car. He was so scared that he stayed huddled in the back seat after they got out. His seeming refusal to get out of the car only infuriated them further. His mother opened one of the doors, and his father opened the other. Both screamed at him to get out. To this day, he remembers feeling frozen with fear, terrified to go one way or the other. Whenever he finds himself faced with a dilemma, having to make any decision that entails choosing between two unpleasant alternatives, he can be riddled with paralyzing anxiety akin to the overwhelming feelings that washed over him as he cowered in the back seat of the car. At such times, he has no idea of what he wants or even who he is—much less what to do.

As Modell has articulated, the private self can be a refuge from traumatic relationships, an inner reserve of autonomy in an outwardly overpowering situation. But in the face of deliberate cruelty, this inner sanctuary of self becomes increasingly difficult to defend. Abuse often entails incursions into one's sacred territory. Boundaries are violated, and privacy may be deliberately eroded. Doors may be removed, belongings searched, clothing stripped. With the erosion of privacy comes a sense of humiliation. Modell describes how the invasion of privacy by others can threaten the core of the self:

> Where the child's private space is habitually violated, habitual defenses are erected. It seems as if the defenses used against the intruder are unfortunately turned upon the self; *the methods employed to protect private space against intrusion by others are inevitably turned against the self.* Such individuals become estranged from their own affective core and are as false and inauthentic within themselves as they are with others. In the struggle to preserve private space they therefore achieve a tragic Pyrrhic victory. Ironically, the fight to protect the private self continues even after the individual has lost contact with it; he is like a householder who maintains a burglar alarm long after misplacing the family jewels. *In closing oneself off from others, one inadvertently closes oneself off from oneself.*[24]

Self-Concept ◆ ◆ ◆ ◆ ◆ ◆ ◆ ◆ ◆ ◆

The other sense of self besides the "I" is the "me." Our capacity to think about ourselves is one ability that leads us to put ourselves at the top of the evolutionary heap.[25] Two levels of consciousness can be distinguished. Consciousness in the sense of immediate awareness extends well down the phylogenetic scale. But self-consciousness is probably limited to some primates. We (and chimpanzees) are able to think about ourselves. Your "me" is a result of how you think about yourself, but how you think about yourself is a reflection of how others treat you and what they say about you. We learn who we are largely by seeing ourselved mirrored by others. The "me" is partly a personal self and partly a social self.

Humans share a capacity for self-reflection with primates, but no other primate is able to use language for this purpose. Language gives us enormous flexibility in how we think about ourselves or anything else. Daniel Stern[26] has proposed that each of us develops a "narrative self." At around age 3 or 4, we can begin to construct stories about ourselves—our life stories. These stories are composed from our autobiographical memories. Your autobiographical memories—what you know about yourself—contain not only your direct experience as you remember it but also what others have told you about yourself and your life. Thus, your narrative self, like your "me," is partly a social self.

Within broad limits, our self-concepts need to be reasonably accurate. But forming an accurate self-concept is no easy feat. How accurate is your concept of *any* person? Individuals are extraordinarily complex, and any concept you have of any other person, no matter how well you know him or her, will be incomplete, partial, and to some degree inaccurate. Why should it be different with yourself? You have even more information about yourself. But that only adds to the complexity. And you can deceive yourself, just as you can be deceived by others. No wonder you can be confused about who you are.

Your self-concept is not neutral; it is highly evaluative, as reflected in your *self-esteem*. And you can have positive self-esteem or low self-esteem. You can see yourself as good, bad, strong, weak, successful, a failure, lovable, despicable, talented, incompetent, helpful, hurtful—the list is endless.

Many psychologists argue that your self-concept should be realistic. This is what I've taught in my psychology classes for years: Take the bad with the good, mix them together, balance them out, and achieve realistic self-esteem. The few saints among us should feel extremely good about themselves (but wouldn't because of their saintly humility); the true louts should dislike themselves (but wouldn't because they are louts); and the rest of us, with our mixtures of good and bad, should wind up somewhere in the middle. Mental health rests on accurate self-appraisals.

Apparently, this seemingly sensible view is misleading. Psychologist Shelley Taylor, in her book *Positive Illusions*,[27] marshals a great deal of research evidence showing that most persons have overly positive views of themselves and overly optimistic views of their futures. These positive illusions about the self are usually most prominent in childhood and are gradually eroded with age. But even in adulthood, there is a positive bias. For example, most people see themselves in more flattering terms than they are seen by others. If two individuals complete a joint project, and they are asked afterward to indicate the percentage of their individual contributions, the percentage typically will be greater than 100. Ninety percent of automobile drivers consider themselves superior to the average driver. Can they all be right?

Taylor argues not only that most people have unrealistically positive biases about themselves but also that these mildly overpositive illusions are adaptive and beneficial to mental health. Positive illusions foster positive moods and contentment, and they promote effective behavior. Positive moods can bolster positive attitudes toward others and helpfulness toward them. Optimism about your abilities contributes to motivation and persistence, and thus to higher productivity and achievement. If you're confident about succeeding, you'll work harder, and you'll be more likely to succeed. If you are riddled with self-doubt, you'll be more likely to falter or give up, and you'll be more likely to fail.

Without reference to illusion, Jon Kabat-Zinn[28] proposes the principle: "As long as you are breathing, there is more right with you than there is wrong, no matter how ill or hopeless you may feel." Accordingly, we all are entitled to a self-concept tilted toward the positive end. If nothing else, we are extremely complicated, and we are entitled to complicated self-concepts. There is ample evidence that focusing on the positive and downplaying the negative—within limits—is adaptive and enhances the self.

Positive illusions are the blessing accorded to those who have been spared severe trauma.[29] Taylor points out that persons who have experienced tragic losses or various threats, particularly in childhood, are less likely to be optimistic and to feel good about themselves. Trauma erodes self-esteem. In light of the epidemic of physical and sexual abuse, we may be inclined to minimize the impact of verbal abuse. We should not. As stated earlier, self-concepts are partly reflections of the social mirror. If you are berated and belittled repeatedly, you may begin to feel self-hatred. These verbal beatings become self-fulfilling prophecies. Children who are convinced that they are no good are less likely to succeed. Their opportunities for feeling contented, satisfied, and optimistic are undermined; their chances for productivity and achievement are sabotaged. Instead of pride, they feel shame and guilt.

Ironically, those who are traumatized by other persons almost always blame themselves.[30] Judith Herman[31] says of abused children, "inevitably the child concludes that her innate badness is the cause." She feels that she deserved it, that she brought it on—or at least that she should have been able to prevent it, stop it, or minimize it. Taking responsibility can be seen as a last-ditch effort to preserve some sense of control: better to feel guilty (deserving) than helpless (unable to control). As Herman puts it, "To imagine that one could have done better may be more tolerable than to face the reality of utter helplessness." [32] This effort to rescue the core self from a sense of helplessness is laudable; the worst thing for the "I" is helplessness. But, as described earlier in connection with shame, the self-concept pays a high price: Self-blame damages self-esteem.

But it is not just self-blame and the assault from within that damage self-esteem. Self-esteem can be directly assailed by relentless criticism and verbal abuse. Even worse, sadistic abusers can inflict a deliberate and calculated assault on self-esteem by forcing persons to participate in self-degrading acts or in atrocities that go counter to their will and deepest values.[33] The same effect is seen in those who participated in atrocities in war.[34] *Low self-esteem* does not begin to capture the resulting self-experience. *Self-loathing* may not even do it justice. The tragic result can be a sense of badness and evil beyond description.

Unfortunately, persons who have been traumatized often pile insult on top of injury, compounding their already damaged self-esteem by a sense of blameworthiness for the ensuing effects: "If I were a better person, I wouldn't have all of these symptoms and problems." It is to this final assault on self-esteem that I have addressed this book. To the extent that I am successful, I might avert this last blow to self-esteem. Self-understanding can lead to more patience, self-tolerance, and even self-compassion.

Self-Destructiveness ◆ ◆ ◆ ◆ ◆ ◆ ◆ ◆ ◆

You might think that the last thing traumatized persons would do would be to expose themselves to additional trauma. Not so. Traumatic experience may result in self-loathing, and many individuals inflict punishment on themselves out of self-hatred. The self is a ready target for anger and aggression that is too dangerous to express directly to others. Self-directed aggression feels safer because it can be controlled and hidden. In addition, individuals who have been mistreated are prone to take on the characteristics of those who abused them; in effect, they imitate their abusers by abusing themselves.

Traumatic histories are associated with a virtually infinite range of self-destructive behavior,[35] including sabotaging one's success, depriving oneself, and behaving destructively toward one's body (as in substance abuse and eating disorders). Self-criticism can become so severe as to constitute

self-inflicted verbal and emotional abuse, causing great suffering, eroding self-confidence and competence, and driving the individual deeper into depression and despair. Self-destructiveness also includes risky behavior such as neglecting one's health, failing to obtain needed medical care, having accidents because of carelessness, and engaging in high-risk sexual behavior with the danger of sexually transmitted diseases and AIDS (acquired immunodeficiency syndrome). In addition, individuals who have been abused sometimes establish destructive relationships with abusive persons.

Self-Mutilation

◆ A young man with a childhood history of physical abuse alternating with neglect was extremely fearful of close relationships, and he had become a recluse since he left high school. He had a night job that required virtually no contact with anyone. He was not content with his isolation; on the contrary, he often felt acutely lonely. His loneliness was intermingled with self-criticism and self-hatred. When the pain became too great to bear, he took a razorblade and made a superficial, several-inch cut down his forearm. As soon as the blood started to ooze, he felt an immediate sense of relief. He did not feel pain; on the contrary, he felt a pleasurable sense of warmth, on his skin and throughout his body. This powerful sensation was his only way of experiencing a sense of warm, soothing touch.

This patient's self-cutting is one of many forms of self-mutilation, perhaps the most baffling form of self-destructive behavior. *Self-mutilation* has been defined as "the deliberate alteration or destruction of body tissue without conscious suicidal intent." [36] To some extent, "mutilation" of the body, such as ear piercing and circumcision, is a normal cultural practice.[37] Yet a wide range of self-injurious behavior goes far beyond the culturally normative: scratching, cutting, carving, burning, hair pulling, head banging, swallowing sharp objects, inserting objects under the skin—at worst, amputating organs and body parts.

Self-mutilation has a variety of causes, and childhood trauma is prominent among them.[38] Trauma-related self-mutilation is often not an isolated event; many individuals resort to self-mutilation, frequently after discovering that it relieves tension. A syndrome of *repetitive self-mutilation* has been described that includes the following criteria: preoccupation with self-harm, recurrent failure to resist impulses to harm oneself, increasing tension before the act of self-harm, a sense of relief upon committing the act, and absence of suicidal intent.[39]

To put self-mutilative behavior in perspective, it is worth noting that it is not just a quirk of human nature. Psychiatrist Armando Favazza, in his book *Bodies Under Siege*,[40] has provided an extraordinarily comprehensive view of self-mutilation. He described the case of a 12-year-old lioness: "One morning she was discovered to have bitten off six inches of her tail. Shortly, she bit off another large piece and finally demolished the remainder. After a brief interval, she began to eat one of her paws. Despite attempts to treat her by changing her diet, applying topical medicines, and other means, she continued to mutilate herself." [41] Similar behavior has been observed in rats. Head banging, hair pulling, and skin scratching have been observed in monkeys. Favazza points out that "Animals use their claws and large incisor teeth for automutilation; during the course of evolution humans have substituted tools, such as knives and razorblades." [42]

A significant finding in the histories of self-mutilating animals is social isolation in early life; this appears to be a major predisposing factor. Other factors include disturbed sexual functioning, biochemical factors, threat, frustration, thwarted aggression, and injury, disease, or pain in a body part that the animal subsequently mutilates. Interestingly, Favazza notes that in monkeys, "autoaggression is more controllable and safer than social aggression," [43] just as it is in traumatized individuals coping with rage.

Self-mutilation is full of paradoxes. It can be done to inflict pain, expressing self-hatred and self-punishment. But self-mutilation can also be done for the sake of pleasure. Many persons who mutilate themselves feel no pain; on the contrary, behavior such as self-cutting can be experienced as warm, soothing skin contact. Self-mutilation can become a substitute for loving touch. Some individuals feel comforted by the sight of blood, as if they are taking a soothing bath. Self-cutting can also provide a sense of tension relief—for example, a kind of bloodletting or getting rid of "bad blood." [44] For others, the sight of blood restores a feeling of being alive.

Self-mutilation can also have a paradoxical effect on arousal. That is, some individuals use self-mutilation as a form of self-stimulation, increasing their level of arousal. Favazza[45] thought this to be an important function of self-mutilation in isolated animals. As discussed earlier, some traumatized individuals cope by dissociation—that is, by tuning out and feeling a sense of unreality or numbness. Individuals in a state of depersonalization—who feel out of touch with reality, or numb, or unreal—can inflict pain on themselves to help anchor themselves in reality.[46] The resulting intense stimulation and arousal brings them back to feeling real; it reestablishes the sense of self by highlighting body boundaries.

Although self-mutilation can be employed to get *out of* a dissociated state, it can also be used to get *into* a dissociated state. When reality is too painful, some individuals use self-mutilation to plunge themselves into a state of numbness or unreality. This behavior illustrates "stress-induced analgesia," a numbing response to stress.[47] Stress-induced analgesia is common—for example, in accidents or sports injuries, a person may be injured but feel no pain at the time. But some persons can spontaneously hit upon this method of inducing analgesia by discovering that momentarily increasing their level of stress by inflicting injury on themselves precipitates a numbed state. This response may be due in part to the release of endorphins, opiatelike substances in the brain and body that are mobilized to counteract pain.

In summary, self-mutilative behavior is an attempt to exert control over emotion, consciousness, stress, and sense of reality. It can be used as self-punishment to *inflict* pain. It can be used as self-soothing to *escape* pain. It can be used to escape reality or to get back to reality. Different persons use self-mutilation for different purposes, and the same person may use it for different reasons at different times. If there is an overriding function for self-mutilation, it is tension release.[48] If there is an overriding trigger for self-mutilation, it is a feeling of abandonment, separation, or rejection.[49]

Suicide

Self-mutilation is commonly mistaken for suicidal behavior—for example, when self-cutting is seen as a "suicide gesture." But suicide is entirely different from self-mutilation in intent.[50] Whereas self-mutilation is an attempt to *alter* consciousness by seeking relief from tension and pain, suicide is often aimed at *eliminating* consciousness, escaping pain once and for all, and achieving a state of nothingness. Of course, when repeated self-mutilation and all other means of alleviating unbearable pain fail, the person who self-mutilates may become profoundly depressed, hopeless, and actually suicidal.

◆ A woman entered the hospital in a suicidal depression after extensive prior treatment. She had grown up in an extremely violent household. Her mother was kind but generally unavailable owing to her own depression and alcoholism; as the patient recalled it, her mother would often sit for hours staring off into space, apparently in a dissociated state.

The patient herself often retreated into dissociation, and she longed for the alcoholic oblivion in which her mother took refuge. She had made numerous serious suicide attempts, and she also found relief and comfort from self-cutting. She had little understanding of the reasons for her self-destructive feelings and behavior, and she entered an intensive psychotherapy process in conjunction with a brief hospitalization during a suicidal crisis.

The patient gradually came to understand the basis of her depression, but her greater awareness of her past only plunged her into a more severe and protracted depression and an unshakable conviction that death was the only solution. When not despondent, she felt utterly incapacitated by self-hatred, rage, or anxiety. With a tremendous amount of support, she eventually decided that she would move forward and "try life for a while." After many difficult years, her life improved to the point that she no longer wished to die.

As it is for self-mutilation, trauma is a common factor in the etiology of suicide.[51] Of course, childhood trauma is only one of many predisposing factors; others include psychiatric disorders (depression, alcoholism), biochemical and genetic vulnerability, family history of suicidal behavior, maladaptive personality traits (perfectionism, impulsivity, isolation, hopelessness), lack of social supports, and a chaotic family life. Many of these predisposing factors are themselves intertwined with trauma and with a history of abuse in particular. It is often the combination of these predisposing factors and the "last straw" of a humiliating life experience, such as the breakup of an important relationship, that precipitates suicidal behavior.[52]

Although suicide and self-mutilation differ in intent, they may become intertwined as repetitive self-injurious behavior further erodes self-esteem and self-control, fueling a sense of hopelessness and suicidal states. Both self-mutilation and suicidal behavior can become chronic. Notably, the chronicity of self-destructive behavior is linked to a failure in attachment, which is a pervasive theme in trauma. One highly informative study of the childhood origins of self-destructive behavior found that childhood trauma (including violence, physical abuse, and sexual abuse) and severe neglect were associated with several forms of self-destructive behavior: suicide attempts, cutting and other self-injurious behavior, and anorexia.[53] Of the various forms of childhood trauma, sexual abuse was the most strongly associated with self-destructive behavior. A follow-up phase of this study revealed the distinguishing characteristics of those who had the greatest difficulty giving up suicidal and self-injurious behavior:

> Neglect became the most powerful predictor of self-destructive behavior. This implies that although childhood trauma contributes heavily to the initiation of self-destructive behavior, lack of secure attachments maintains it. The subjects who had experienced prolonged separations from their primary caregivers, and those who could not remember feeling special or loved by anyone as children, were least able to utilize interpersonal resources during the course of the study to control their self-destructive behavior.[54]

The most severe consequences of trauma may result from the lack of buffering attachments. These findings underscore the paramount significance of establishing sustaining relationships and a secure base in treatment.

Restoring Self-Esteem

It is easy to see how the sense of self can be damaged by traumatic experience and especially by abuse in childhood. Restoring a feeling of self-cohesiveness and healthy self-esteem is not so easy. Understanding yourself better should be of some help. Just developing some appreciation for the basis of your intense feelings, strong urges, and powerful conflicts can begin to restore some sense of unity. Ideally, self-understanding will promote self-tolerance and help undo some of the damage to self-esteem. But understanding is not enough: Changing your view of yourself requires much active work.

Steering Past Negative Illusions

For persons who have been mistreated and injured by others, reshaping the self-concept and rebuilding self-esteem is a major project—and an extremely worthwhile one. The active self—the "I"—and the sense of cohesiveness and efficacy is strongly affected by the "me"—the self-concept.

How you think of yourself has a major *steering function:* It shapes how you feel, how you behave, indeed, who you *are.* The "me" determines the "I."

It is easy to see the shaping effect of your self-concept on your self by thinking of the negative side. How often do you criticize yourself? Tear yourself down in your own mind? Berate yourself? Express contempt for yourself? Belittle yourself? What is the effect of these negative thoughts on your self? Like being abused by others, this self-abuse fuels despair and a sense of helplessness.

Shelley Taylor[55] has shown how people who have been spared severe trauma usually develop positive illusions that sustain a sense of well-being and promote success. The converse is also true. With negative illusions, you can steer yourself right into a pit. You can damage yourself; your self can become more and more incapacitated and impaired. When defined on the basis of self-hatred, the "me" damages the "I."

Many persons who have extremely negative self-concepts are inclined to insist that they are no good; to them this negative self-assessment seems like the unvarnished, immutable truth. You may need to shake yourself loose from this unquestioned conviction: Your self-concept is, *in principle,* extremely flexible. It is not *necessary* to be locked into an unwavering negative view of yourself. On the contrary, in principle, you are free to think what you wish about yourself. Think of it this way: It's a free country in your own mind.

The "truth" about yourself can be extremely complicated, just as the "truth" about anyone can be extremely complicated. Any person is extremely complex. A tremendous amount of *potential* mental freedom comes into play here. No matter what you were told, no matter how you were treated, no matter what you were compelled to do, it is not *necessary* to continue the mistreatment in your own head.

In *principle,* it is possible to be free, flexible, and open in how you see and think about yourself. In *practice,* though, it can be extremely difficult. Exercising one's mental freedom is a long-term project that requires tremendous effort and concentration. But with growing awareness that helps you notice whenever you tear yourself down, you can develop the capacity to step back from those thoughts and feelings and take a more detached perspective. This process involves trying on for size some different ways of thinking about yourself.

Recall Kabat-Zinn's maxim: There is more right with you than wrong with you. Try it on for size. Contemplate it. Unbelievable? There is nothing to stop you from using this concept as a guiding rule in thinking about yourself—in principle. It is not easy to change established patterns; it goes against the grain, requiring resolve and practice. In the long run, however, it is possible, and it steers the self in a better direction.

My work with individuals who have been severely traumatized confirms Kabat-Zinn's view. I am repeatedly impressed by their strengths—to which they are often oblivious. These strengths are condensed in the term *survivor*—preferable to *victim*, which emphasizes the damaged self. In person after person, I see persistence, courage, intelligence, creativity, kindness, compassion for others, openness, and spunk.

I emphasize changing how you think about yourself because, although it is not easy, you have *relatively* good control over what you think. To some degree, you can take charge of what you think. Through controlling what you think, you can exert some control over what you feel. The potential to control your thoughts is the rationale behind cognitive therapy as well as behind "the power of positive thinking" more generally. Many patients find this whole line of reasoning extremely annoying. That's because people who espouse "the power of positive thinking" make it sound so easy. Sure, it's easy if you're not depressed and you generally think well of yourself and the world. It's easy if you haven't been traumatized or you're not prone to depression. Otherwise, it can be extremely hard—but not impossible.

Ideally, thinking more positively about yourself can be a stepping stone toward a better relationship with yourself. In effect, negative thinking about yourself is akin to having an abusive relationship with yourself. Imagine living with an abuser, all the time, throughout the day, in your own brain/mind/head! Perhaps you do.

The Self in Relationships

As stated earlier, the "me" is formed to a substantial extent in relationships. Looking at others is like looking into a mirror. You see the "me" in reflection. How you see yourself reflects how you are seen by others, how you are treated by them, and how you feel in relation to them. Many persons have been told that they are bad in myriad ways. But you need not be told directly; when you are mistreated, you naturally conclude that you are bad in some way.

The antidote to reflections that damage the "me" is healthier relation-ships and better reflections. But the negative illusions are not easily altered. Affirming attitudes of others may not make a dent; positive comments and praise are often discounted. Why is this? Here's what many patients say: They have learned to conceal their angry feelings. They have been hurt or punished even more severely than usual whenever they protested or showed their natural anger. When others tell them they are friendly, kind, consider-ate, or nice, they protest internally (if not outwardly): "If they really knew how hateful I am inside, they would not think so well of me." "The fact that they like me just *proves* what a phony I am." Such thinking takes the positive regard of others and uses it as fuel to tear yourself down further: "The truth is, I am a phony, a fake." I would counter that the following is also a truth: Such a kind—and angry—person is making a valiant effort to relate posi-tively against great odds created by internal conflict, distrust, and fear. If both of these are legitimate views, which should you choose?

The discrepancy between the friendly and angry aspects of the self also relates to the difference between the public and private self. To have a dis-crepancy between the public and private self is not hypocritical or phony; it is human. It is essential to well-being. Persons whose privacy has been trampled on may not feel entitled to a private self. Recovering from trauma entails shoring up your boundaries, establishing a sense of privacy in your relationships with others, and cultivating and respecting your more private feelings and thoughts.

Persons who have been traumatized in any way, and those who have been abused in particular, have a deep longing for a relationship in which they can feel safe and seek comfort. As discussed in relation to attachment, they seek a "secure base." Establishing secure relationships, however belat-edly, is the cornerstone of healing. But it is good to think not only of the need for such a relationship with others; you need such a relationship *with yourself.*

I pointed out at the beginning of this chapter that two major lines of development are self-development and the development of relatedness to others. I also emphasized that these two aspects of development are inter-dependent: Your relationships with others influence your sense of self and vice versa. Finding relationships in which you are treated with compassion, and allowing yourself to experience and take in that compassion, is a major route to being able to adopt this compassionate attitude toward yourself.

Conversely, the more you are able to be compassionate toward yourself, the more open you will be to compassion from others. The challenge is to get this mutually enhancing cycle going. For those who have experienced trauma in relationships, there are many obstacles to be overcome.

CHAPTER EIGHT

Relationships

Although not all traumas are *caused* by relationships, they may have an *effect* on relationships. Any threat or trauma activates the attachment system: When you are threatened or injured, you feel a need for security and a desire to reestablish your secure base. Even if you were traumatized by something impersonal, you may lose confidence in the protectiveness of your attachments. Perhaps because they disrupt your sense of security, natural disasters and accidents often reawaken past traumas. A car accident can spark memories of child abuse that have been buried for decades.

Trauma embedded in relationships is usually most difficult to bear. Most pernicious is trauma deliberately inflicted in a relationship in which you are in a dependent position—at worst, a parent-child relationship. This chapter focuses on interpersonal trauma, emphasizing trauma embedded in early caregiving relationships. Trauma experienced in earlier relationships is often re-created in subsequent relationships, and this chapter begins by focusing on this ubiquitous, although not immutable, pattern of repetition.

We all develop models of relationships that shape our interactions with others. Our first models evolve from our initial attachments. In this chapter, I explore the phenomenon of "traumatic bonding" that can occur in childhood and adulthood. I then examine a wider array of problematic relationships and interaction patterns, concluding with some thoughts about building healthy relationships.

Repetition of Trauma in Relationships

Perhaps one of the most vexing problems is the seemingly inevitable repetition of earlier traumatic experience in subsequent relationships. It is not uncommon, for example, for a person who has been abused by a parent to choose an abusive mate or to become involved in relationships that carry a high risk for injury or exploitation. Freud called this the "compulsion to repeat" because of the compelling need to repeat the earlier destructive pattern.[1]

Why would anyone compulsively repeat a pattern of behavior that is injurious and painful? There are many reasons why individuals who have been injured by others express their aggression by directing it back onto themselves. But other persons can be enlisted as accomplices in this scenario. You can attack yourself by inducing or permitting others to attack you.

Earlier I described how trauma stirs up severe conflict and painful emotion. The mind does not sit quietly with a terrifying sense of helplessness. Trauma becomes an unsolved problem in the mind, and unsolved problems press for solution. Freud thought that the repetition compulsion might reflect a belated effort at mastery. Traumatized children commonly repeat the trauma in their play, often in relatively undisguised form.[2] Through play, they seem to be attempting to assimilate, digest, and overcome the traumatic experience. Perhaps the same could be said of repetition in adult relationships. A girl who was completely overpowered by an alcoholic father might strive in adulthood to sober up an abusive alcoholic husband. But there is no evidence that repetition of trauma consistently leads to mastery or resolution; on the contrary, it leads to further suffering.[3]

If not for the sake of suffering or mastery, why repeat? I find it helpful to shift the focus from suffering to learning. The *compulsion to repeat* is one form of the *compulsion to relate*. Throughout life, we ceaselessly seek attachments and relationships. We all learn how to relate to others on the basis of our early experience in relationships, and we all generalize patterns we have learned from earlier to later relationships. We *all* repeat what we have learned; we re-create the familiar. We all develop models of relationships, and we are always employing them. When a friend keeps going back to an abusive husband, we think in exasperation, "She'll never learn!" On the contrary, she is merely reenacting what she has learned all too well.

Relationship Models ◆ ◆ ◆ ◆ ◆ ◆ ◆ ◆ ◆

We are great categorizers.[4] We learn patterns. We continually encounter novelty, but we immediately connect whatever confronts us at the moment with what we have experienced in the past. We are always categorizing things in terms of how they relate to our feelings, our needs, and our safety. Before long, we learn to attach labels to categories. This is "good," that is "bad," this is "scary." We do this unconsciously. Just as we categorize the inanimate world (chairs, trees, trains), we categorize relationships with others on the basis of previous patterns—although not with such simple labels.

We all develop *models* of how relationships go. Early in life, we have fewer and simpler models; later in life, we evolve many complex models. The earlier models always serve as a foundation for later relationships. We repeat. Yet we are always modifying and shaping old models to new relationships, developing new patterns of relating that we then generalize into subsequent relationships. We learn.

Your relationship models not only govern your experience of relationships but also govern your behavior toward other people. If you expect others to mistreat you, you keep them at a distance. In this way, your expectations influence how people respond to you. You tend to shape other people's behavior so as to bring them into conformity with your models. Accuse others of having it in for you—and they will! *(You repeat.)* Conversely, others influence you to conform to *their* models. *(They repeat.)* You select partners whose relationship models are compatible or complementary with your own. We all try to work out reasonable matches with each other.

Relationship models have two parts—self and other.[5] The self is distressed, the other comforts; the self yearns, the other neglects; the self is in pain, the other attacks. These two-part models lend an easy flexibility to your relationships. Often you can readily switch parts. Mother comforts child; child comforts mother. In an abusive relationship, both parts are learned with full force: being injured *and* injuring. Those who have suffered abuse may establish subsequent relationships in which they abuse others. Or you can play out these two-part models in the realm of your own mind; you can assault yourself in thought and in action.

Secure attachment is a key relationship model: The infant develops the expectation that contact with a caregiver will be soothing: "When I feel bad, mother holds me, and I feel better." As development proceeds, and opportunities for contact with others expand, this model of secure attachment is generalized to relationships with others—father, sister, brother, grandmother, and teacher. But secure attachment is never the only model. Frustration is a universal model: "Sometimes when I feel bad, mother does no good." Being injured is a universal model: "Sometimes contact with mother hurts."

Bowlby proposed that early attachment patterns influence later relationships by virtue of internal *working models* of the self and the attachment figure.[6] These working models become templates for later relationships: They shape our expectations and behavior toward others. Confidence in the accessibility and responsiveness of the attachment figure hinges on two factors:

> (a) whether or not the attachment figure is judged to be the sort of person who in general responds to calls for support and protection; (b) whether or not the self is judged to be the sort of person towards whom anyone, and the attachment figure in particular, is likely to respond in a helpful way. Logically these variables are independent. In practice they are apt to be confounded. As a result, the model of the attachment figure and the model of the self are likely to develop so as to be complementary and mutually confirming. Thus an unwanted child is likely not only to feel unwanted by his parents but to believe that he is essentially unwantable, namely unwanted by anyone. Conversely, a much-loved child may grow

up to be not only confident of his parents' affection but confident that everyone else will find him lovable too.[7]

Daniel Stern[8] proposed that the fundamental building block of working models is the *interactive moment,* a discrete interaction that takes place within the span of seconds. Examples of interactive moments would be calling to mother, withdrawing from father's frown, taking hold of sister's hand, and returning a smile. Such moments are organized into *scenarios*—sequences of interactive moments such as the following: "(1) infant approaches mother; (2) mother orients and readies her body to receive approach; (3) infant raises arms to be picked up; (4) mother picks up infant; (5) infant nestles head in mother's neck; (6) mother adjusts position appropriately." [9]

You build your working models from such interactive moments and scenarios, and you need to apply a range of models to any complex relationship. Bowlby's term *working model* emphasizes flexibility. Ideally, you can shift and adapt your models from moment to moment. You can expect to be criticized but be open to praise. You can be angry and frustrated, then forgiving and affectionate.

To recapitulate, you accumulate your moment-to-moment interactions with others and categorize them into meaningful sequences and patterns. These patterns become your internal working models of relationships. Those models shape your expectations of relationships and your behavior toward others, and thereby influence how others respond to you.

Bowlby maintained that our attachment models are reasonably accurate reflections of how we have been treated by parents and caregivers.[10] But this does not mean that children play no part in the models that they develop. Children are active interpreters of their caregivers' behavior, constructing models on the basis of their individual perceptions and reactions. A more sensitive child will develop different models from a more obstreperous child. And the child's behavior and temperament will shape the behavior of the caregivers, thus playing a major role in the models that develop.[11] For example, a hyperactive child is likely to evoke criticism. Whatever our environment, we all have models with our own individual stamps. But we can all be overpowered. In the face of severe trauma and malevolent intent on the part of caregivers or others, there is no avoiding pernicious relationship models.

Traustic Bonding   ◆ ◆ ◆ ◆ ◆ ◆ ◆ ◆ ◆

A *New York Times* article described the harsh discipline, deprivation, beatings, and sexual abuse inflicted on children who survived the Branch Davidian cult incident.[12] David Koresh took girls as young as 11 as "wives." Dr. Bruce Perry, chief of psychiatry at Texas Children's Hospital, led a team of therapists that interviewed the children. A shocking finding: "Even after their release, and as they described their treatment by Mr. Koresh, nearly all the children have talked about their love for him. During therapy sessions, several of them drew pictures with hearts, under which they wrote, 'I love David.' "

The Branch Davidian episode is reminiscent of the "Stockholm Syndrome," in which hostages paradoxically become attached to their captors. In August 1973, four employees of the Sveriges Kreditbank in Stockholm, Sweden, were held hostage in a bank vault for 5 days. The hostages developed positive feelings for the robbers, along with antipathy toward the police. When the robbers were finally captured, one woman said, "After it was over, and we were safe and they were in handcuffs, I walked over to them and kissed each one of them and said, 'Thank you for giving me my life back.' " Another referred to the robbers as "great guys." [13]

These astounding episodes are instances of a tragically common phenomenon that has been called *traumatic bonding*. Although it is most dramatically demonstrated in cults and kidnappings and hostage situations, traumatic bonding is far more frequently operative in troubled families. How can a child love and even idolize an abusive parent? How can a battered wife love and protect her abusive husband? In her book *The Battered Woman*, psychologist Lenore Walker has captured the essence of the kind of relationship we need to understand:

> A battered woman is a woman who is repeatedly subjected to any forceful physical or psychological behavior by a man in order to coerce her to do something he wants her to do without any concern for her rights. Battered women include wives or women in any form of intimate relationships with men. Furthermore, in order to be classified as a battered woman, the couple must go through the battering cycle at least twice. Any woman may find herself in an abusive relationship with a man once. If it occurs a second time, and she remains in the situation, she is defined as a battered woman.[14]

◆ A patient in group psychotherapy recounted a childhood in which she was continually frightened by her stepfather's violence toward her mother. Her stepfather was a well-respected union leader, and he was accustomed to having a lot of power. In contrast to his stable image at work, he was intimidating and domineering at home. When he was drinking, he would not only scream at his wife but also slap her, shove her, and push her around. In turn, his wife was verbally abusive toward the children, haranguing them for their shortcomings and misbehavior. The stepfather rarely laid a hand on the children, and he doted on his stepdaughter. He was occasionally intimidating toward her but also loving and attentive.

Partly to get away from home as soon as possible, the patient married immediately after she graduated from high school. Her husband was a kind and gentle man, but he became addicted to drugs and died of an overdose. Heartbroken and feeling abandoned, she quickly married an attractive man she hardly knew. Their relationship rapidly deteriorated. He beat her so frequently and so brutally that she feared for her life. She packed her bags when he was away at work, and she left the state. She resolved never to marry again, but she could not tolerate being alone. She moved in with another man, and this relationship was an improvement. He never physically assaulted her, and he could be loving and affectionate. Yet he was also extremely controlling and intimidating, and she felt as if she continually walked on eggshells. She was reluctant to have children, and she was socially isolated because this man's possessiveness and belligerence kept all prospective friends away. To the consternation of the other group members, her relatives, and even herself, she stayed in this relationship for many years until he left her to marry another woman.

To say that this patient was merely repeating what she had learned from observing her parents' marriage does not do justice to the force of the "repetition compulsion" evident in battering relationships. Common sense dictates that someone who has been repeatedly hurt and mistreated in a relationship would do everything possible to flee or at least to maintain distance. Yet we continually observe the opposite. Individuals become locked into traumatic relationships and cannot let go. The abused person may be beaten and tormented, and may occasionally attempt to break away, but will repeatedly return to the abusive relationship. Common sense and intuition fail us in understanding such behavior.

Hard as it may be to believe, being abused and mistreated can actually *strengthen* the bond in relationships. And this phenomenon is not unique to humans; maltreatment has been shown to accentuate attachment in a range of mammals. Studies show that mistreated animals cling to their caregivers; after reviewing these findings, one researcher concluded that "maintaining social contact and forming attachments is so necessary for life in a social mammal that nothing will interfere with it." [15]

Perhaps it is not so hard to understand why a person would maintain a relationship *despite* abuse; any relationship may be better than none. Moreover, some individuals have a seemingly limitless ability to engage in self-protective denial, ignoring all prior evidence and believing the abuser's claim that he will not do it again. Such denial can be abetted by dissociation and, in the extreme, the person may be amnestic for the episodes of abuse. But how could abuse and maltreatment *increase* attachment? This anomaly is the essence of traumatic bonding: The more one is abused and terrorized, the harder one clings to the abuser.

To understand the paradox of traumatic bonding, we must first learn to appreciate the social context of the abusive relationship. As Walker puts it, "psychosocial factors bind a battered woman to her batterer just as strongly as 'miracle glues' bind inanimate substances." [16] Isolation is one crucial factor. Incest is a common example. Psychologist Denise Gelinas[17] describes the family pattern conducive to incest as beginning with the "parentification" of a child. The parentified child is recruited into an adult role. She is induced to assuming responsibility for tasks and functions in the family that are beyond the usual expectations for her age and development (maintaining the household, being a substitute parent for younger siblings, taking care of her dysfunctional parents). Gelinas observed that mothers of abused children were themselves parentified and are likely to marry immature and dependent men for whom they serve as caregivers. She describes the ensuing pattern as follows: "In incestuous families, the husband has continued to not take responsibility while continuing to make entitled demands on the wife. She, instead of actively dealing with this situation and claiming some legitimate needs of her own, gradually becomes emotionally and relationally avoidant." [18] As time goes on, the wife not only avoids her husband but also avoids her children; "she distances herself, because for her, relationships take and don't give back." [19] Eventually, the father turns to the daughter for affection, and she is catapulted into the parental generation, assuming the role of spouse.

A central component in Gelinas's scenario is the child's social isolation and her exclusive dependence on her father for intimacy. Judith Herman[20] describes this context of traumatic bonding more generally under the rubric of "captivity." For example, "In isolated prisoners . . . where there is no opportunity to bond with peers, pair bonding may occur between victim and perpetrator, and this relationship may come to feel like the 'basic unit of survival.' " She gives another example:

> The same traumatic bonding may occur between a battered woman and her abuser. The repeated experience of terror and reprieve, especially within the isolated context of a love relationship, may result in a feeling of intense, almost worshipful dependence upon an all-powerful, godlike authority. The victim may live in terror of his wrath, but she may also view him as the source of strength, guidance, and life itself. The relationship may take on an extraordinary quality of specialness.[21]

Social isolation is one key contextual factor, and a gross *imbalance of power* in the relationship is another.[22] The person who is continually overpowered feels increasingly incompetent and helpless, ever more reliant on the person in the position of power. Yet the abuser's overt power conceals a sense of weakness and dependency:

> [P]ersons in the high power positions will develop an overgeneralized sense of their own power (just as the low power persons develop an overgeneralized sense of their own powerlessness), and if the symbiotic roles which maintain this sense of power are disturbed, the masked dependency of the high power person on the low power person is suddenly made obvious. One example of this sudden reversal of the power dynamic is the desperate control attempts on the part of the abandoned battering husband to bring his wife back to him through surveillance, intimidation, etc.[23]

The combination of attachment needs, isolation, and the imbalance of power conspires to create a situation conducive to traumatic bonding. The abused or terrorized individual feels *completely dependent on the abuser or terrorist*.[24] Abuse in an exclusive relationship with an attachment figure creates an intolerable conflict: The secure base is a source of danger. Traumatic bonding escalates this conflict: The more the individual is injured and terrorized, the stronger his or her need for protection and comforting.

The alternation of distress and relief cements the traumatic bond. Any shred of affection, comfort, or even respite from injury and terror will tighten the bond. Walker[25] describes a three-phase cycle in battering relationships: 1) a tension-building stage in which there is a gradual escalation of minor battering incidents during which the battered woman makes every effort to appease the batterer; 2) the acute, explosive battering incident; and 3) the loving respite phase during which the batterer is kind, contrite, calm, and giving. Walker[26] points out, "it is during phase three, when the loving-kindness is most intense, that this symbiotic bonding really takes hold."

Intermittent kindness is one key to traumatic bonding, but the bond is also cemented by being spared even more grave harm.[27] Walker found that psychological battering is sustained by the threat of bodily harm; every battered woman "believed the batterer was capable of killing her or himself."[28] Any reprieve from injury and terror and, most important, *the fact of being allowed to live,* evokes enormous gratitude.[29] The terrorist becomes the protector—protector from the terror and injury he *might* inflict. He escalates the need for a secure base and then gratifies the heightened need he has created. As Judith Herman[30] explains, "After several cycles of reprieve from certain death, the victim may come to view the perpetrator, paradoxically, as her savior." The worse the injury, the greater the terror, the stronger the need for security, the tighter the bond.

Problematic Models ◆ ◆ ◆ ◆ ◆ ◆ ◆ ◆ ◆

Traumatic bonding is perhaps the most dramatic way in which trauma shapes relationships. But by the time we assemble countless interactive moments into myriad scenarios and the working models that evolve from them, we have an infinite variety of potential relationships. Stepping back from this infinite variation, I routinely observe several common themes in the relationships of persons who have experienced trauma—isolation, yearning, fearfulness, dependency, vulnerability to harm, extreme needs for control, and internalization of aggressive models. These relationship models are universal. Yet they seem to stand out more starkly in those whose relationships have been marred by trauma.

Isolation

Many abusive relationships entail enforced isolation. Abused children are likely to be isolated from their peers. Even if their isolation is not rigidly enforced by an abusive and domineering parent, it is engendered by secrecy and shame. Secrecy is a barrier to intimacy. If you have been hurt badly by people, it is only natural to stay away from them. Many persons who have been traumatized tend to be withdrawn and isolative. They may prefer solitary activities or find refuge in fantasy.

Yearning

Given the power of attachment needs established by evolution over millennia, isolation is rarely a stable solution. Isolation holds sway by keeping at bay a yearning for closeness, affection, comforting, and protection. A paradox is at work here: The history of trauma abets isolation but also fuels attachment needs. Isolation thus alternates with longing for much-needed caregiving, closeness, and intimacy.

Fearfulness

The inevitable yearning for contact invariably propels traumatized individuals back into relationships. But any closeness or intimacy will be frightening. A slew of working models based on past experience spell all sorts of danger. Distrust may be pervasive. The specific fears will reflect the past traumas. Common fears include those of being physically injured, exploited, dominated, controlled, trapped, intruded upon, smothered, terrorized, humiliated, and degraded.

Dependency

No one who has suffered trauma in relationships is doomed to a life of isolation, yearning, and fearfulness. Many individuals—driven by attachment needs and undaunted by prior injuries—eventually find relationships that provide affection, protection, nurturance, and intimacy. Of course, trust in such relationships is hard won, and achieved only over a long period. It is not surprising that, once found, such relationships grow profoundly important. Seemingly overwhelming needs become focused on the one individual who can meet them within a context of safety. These relationships become safe havens in a world of danger.

Often, however, the long-awaited safe haven or secure base does not turn out to be an unmitigated blessing. Although the fear of being injured gradually gives way, it is likely to be replaced with the fear that the relationship will be lost. Fear of abandonment may engender feelings of resentment and hostility associated with a feeling of being trapped and vulnerable. The long-awaited secure base may not feel so secure after all.

Vulnerability to Harm

The dependency that naturally evolves in any comforting relationship can contribute to a vulnerability to repetition of past trauma. The fear of abandonment may outweigh the pain of further exploitation and injury. At worst, the pattern of traumatic bonding can be reinstated.

The person who repeatedly suffers harm is commonly considered a "victim." We could think of a "victim working model" of relationships. But thinking of yourself as a victim, like thinking of yourself as a "masochist," is rarely helpful. On the contrary, it may be damaging. Accordingly, persons who have been traumatized are often encouraged to think of themselves as *survivors* rather than victims.

Rather than focusing on victimization, Judith Herman[31] emphasizes the *failure of self-protection* in relationships that entail repetitions of abuse. Ironically, the dissociative defenses of detachment and numbing that served to buffer childhood trauma can permit the adult to put up with mistreatment that would otherwise be intolerable.[32]

For persons who have been abused or traumatized by others, self-protection was not possible initially. They may have developed a relationship model that entails helpless victimization, a form of learned helplessness described earlier in connection with depression. Failure of self-protection implies an extension of this early model into subsequent relationships in which self-protection is a possibility. To think that you have been victimized again leads nowhere; to think that you have failed to protect yourself implies a solution. Failure of self-protection points the way from depression to active coping.

Extreme Needs for Control

The worst aspect of traumatic experience is the sense of helplessness it engenders. Trauma entails feeling out of control and at the mercy of others. It is little wonder that control becomes a paramount concern. At one level, you may be extremely averse to any interaction that smacks of being out of control. You may find it extremely difficult to comply, to go along, to follow, or to submit to the desires of another person, even when going along entails no danger or harm. Having your own way may seem absolutely necessary. You may find yourself in power struggles. Avoiding being controlled may not be enough; you may feel secure only when you are able to exert active control over another person. Your sense of security may depend on turning the tables, controlling and dominating others rather than being controlled or dominated by them.

Internalization of Aggressive Models

The tables may be turned even more dramatically when one who has been abused becomes the abuser. This phenomenon has been called "identification with the aggressor," inasmuch as the abuser has been taken as a model for identification. Relationship models have two parts—self and other—and both parts invariably are learned. This applies to the comforter and the comforted as well as to the batterer and the battered. Switching roles is common; we learn to comfort by being comforted. Moreover, the role of aggressor may be appealing because it is associated with a sense of power and it provides an antidote to helplessness and feelings of weakness. Aggression begets aggression: It provides not only a model but also the emotional provocation to go with it—namely, anger. Beating a child for being aggressive is a futile attempt at control: It makes the child angry, and it provides the child with a model for how to behave when angry—aggressively.

Because of the tendency of those who were mistreated as children to mistreat their own children, child abuse is often passed down through generations.[33] This intergenerational transmission of abuse is by no means inevitable, but it is nevertheless common. The figures vary, but a rough estimate is that one-third of abused children will be abusive toward their own children, one-third will not, and one-third will be prone to being abusive, depending on other factors. Abused children who are most likely to become abusive parents are those who deny that they were abused and idealize their abusive parents: "Child victims of maltreatment tend to blame themselves. The single most important modifying factor in intergenerational transmission of child abuse is the capacity of the child victim to grow up with the ability to face the reality of past and present personal relationships." [34]

Problematic Patterns   ◆ ◆ ◆ ◆ ◆ ◆ ◆ ◆ ◆

You build up relationship models from interactive moments and scenarios—that is, sequences of interactions. You may have a wide range of interactions with any given person. The self–other structure of your relationship models is conducive to alternating roles. Ideally, you can nurture, and you can allow yourself to be nurtured. You can depend and be depended upon. But you can also abuse and be abused. You can abandon and be abandoned.

Often, individuals who have been abused by caregivers must endure 180-degree shifts in relationships. Gelinas[35] describes a common pattern in incest in which the abuser is a "regular person" by day and becomes transformed at night: "When the parent becomes that nighttime abuser, he or she 'turns'—that is, becomes someone or something different from who the child has known for so long." As Gelinas says, this "turning" itself is confusing and frightening: "It is one thing to be confronted with something new or strange; it is very different to have something one thought one knew *become* strange." [36]

Such dramatic turnarounds in interactions make for tremendous instability and unpredictability, and it is little wonder that individuals who have been abused frequently have very stormy relationships. Judith Herman paints a vivid portrait:

> The survivor oscillates between intense attachment and terrified withdrawal. She approaches all relationships as though questions of life and death are at stake. She may cling desperately to a person whom she perceives as a rescuer, flee suddenly from a person she suspects to be a perpetrator or accomplice, show great loyalty and devotion to a person she perceives as an ally, and heap

wrath and scorn on a person who appears to be a complacent bystander. The roles she assigns to others may change suddenly, as the result of small lapses or disappointments, for no internal representation of another person is any longer secure.[37]

Our varied relationship models are also conducive to more elaborate sequences. Being harmed can lead us to retreat into isolation, followed by yearning, which leads to a fearful relationship, culminating in self-protective aggression that drives the other person away, leading back to isolation. Herman[38] describes the pattern of "a search for a rescuer" that is commonly seen in the individual who has been abused: "In a quest for rescue, she may seek out powerful authority figures who seem to offer the promise of a special caregiving relationship. By idealizing the person to whom she becomes attached, she attempts to keep at bay the constant fear of being either dominated or betrayed." Understandable as it may be, this quest inevitably has a painful outcome:

> The chosen person fails to live up to her fantastic expectations. When disappointed, she may furiously denigrate the same person whom she so recently adored. Ordinary interpersonal conflicts may provoke intense anxiety, depression, or rage. In the mind of the survivor, even minor slights evoke past experiences of callous neglect, and minor hurts evoke past experiences of deliberate cruelty. . . . Thus the survivor develops a pattern of intense, unstable relationships, repeatedly enacting dramas of rescue, injustice, and betrayal.[39]

Such sequences do not arise de novo in adult relationships; they are repetitions of alternating hope and disillusionment that were part of the "turning" in early traumatic relationships.

Developing New Models ◆ ◆ ◆ ◆ ◆ ◆ ◆ ◆

For many persons who have been abused in caregiving relationships, the experience of secure attachment was short lived; thus, it is likely to be utterly forgotten, perhaps because it occurred only very early in life before the infant or young child was capable of consolidating autobiographical memories that could later be retrieved. Persons who have been traumatized may have no conscious memory of having been protected, nurtured, and comforted. The secure attachment model may be forgotten, but it is there. It is established by evolution and by whatever instances of good experience with caregivers occurred. The secure attachment model is extremely powerful and resilient: The yearning for attachment persists.

Destructive relationship models taught and learned within the context of abusive relationships are generalized to other relationships; trauma is repeated. Here is the challenge for treatment:

> How can we help patients who have been victims of abuse to become sensitive not only to the real tragedy they have suffered at the hands of others, but also to the continuing one that they have become agents of themselves? Helping these patients to grasp how they murder psychic possibilities and foreclose the possibility of meaningful relationship and how violent this process is to internal as well as external life, is essential.[40]

But the very capacity for learning and generalization that perpetuates abusive experience can be the pathway out of destructive relationships. The traumatic models are not dissolved, unlearned, or exorcised. What is learned stays learned. Once a model, always a model. But new models can be learned and generalized, old models supplanted. Although the old traumatic models will forever remain possibilities in relationships, new possibilities can be added.[41] The old models can become unemployed.

How are new models learned? They are learned from and with other people. They are taught, not didactically as in a classroom, but through relating and interacting. For good or for ill, others tend to shape us into the molds of their models. Abusive models are taught in relationships and interactions. So are nurturing models. Models of others as reliable and trustworthy are obviously learned only over a long period of time. One must find good teachers—persons who are kind, trustworthy, and reliable. Abusive relationships set up a vicious cycle: The more you are mistreated, the more you feel devalued and the more mistreatment you tolerate and feel you deserve. Healthy relationships turn the tide, creating a benign cycle: The more you are treated with kindness and respect, the more you feel confident and worthy, and the more you will assert your needs and be treated accordingly.

Nothing is foolproof, and this scenario is not flawless. No one is a perfect judge of character; we are all susceptible to being deceived. Selfprotedion is possible to a degree, but anyone can be overpowered. Rescue is not possible; helpful relationships are. Rescue is an ideal; all helpful relationships are flawed, limited, and disappointing to a degree. Conflicts wax and wane; closeness and distance ebb and flow. This is why Winnicott[42] proposed the concept of the "good enough" mother. We need good-enough friends, good-enough mates, and good-enough therapists.

Although this chapter has focused on several varieties of problematic relationship models, the more benign models also merit some attention. There are many models of secure attachment: comforting, nurturing, protecting, soothing, and caregiving. There are models for making connections: communicating, accepting, affirming, empathizing. There are models for intimacy: loving, being affectionate, and confiding. There are models for cooperation: helping, teaching, supporting, collaborating, sharing, giving, working together, complying. There are models for resolving controversy: confronting, challenging, contesting, and asserting.

The possibilities for benign relationships are limitless and well worth contemplating. It may be a useful exercise to take an inventory of your own relationship models. Which models do you most frequently employ? Which models should you put on unemployment? Which models should you develop and cultivate? What persons in your life go with which models? What are the patterns and sequences of interactions that characterize your relationships? How stable and steady are your interactions? How changeable and stormy?

Self-Dependence ◆ ◆ ◆ ◆ ◆ ◆ ◆ ◆ ◆

Development of the self and development of relationships are intertwined over the life cycle. We must all find a balance between self-development and relatedness, between closeness and distance, between openness and privacy. Each individual must find the optimal blend; there is no ideal suited for everyone.

In thinking about a healthy balance between self-development and relationships with others, the concept of *self-dependence* is useful. Since its inception, American society has placed great value on "independence." But aspiring to independence can be problematic, particularly for individuals who have been traumatized. Independence comes to connote "not needing anyone" and, as such, becomes confused with isolation. Attachment needs are lifelong, and isolation is not viable. Psychoanalyst Joseph Lichtenberg[43] defines self-dependence in a way that balances autonomy and attachment. To be self-dependent requires that you be able to have a sense of continuity in your relationships. You must be able to remember and imagine your relationships with those to whom you are securely attached. Once you develop this capacity, you do not need to be in the continuous presence of the other person to feel secure. In Lichtenberg's[44] words, "To be self-dependent is not to be independent, without reliance on the attachment. Rather, to be self-dependent is to be able to rely on the self to evoke the other in a period of absence, to bridge the gap until reunion or restoration of the attachment." The actual reunion then serves to renew, refuel, and maintain the sense of secure attachment while fostering autonomy and self-development.

PART III

Trauma-Related Psychiatric Disorders

CHAPTER NINE

Posttraumatic Stress Disorder

T he preceding chapters have described
the complex effects of trauma on devel-
opment, attachment, emotion, consciousness, memory, the self, and relationships. The next few chapters examine the effects of traumatic
experience from a somewhat different perspective—through the lens of
psychiatric diagnosis. That is, when the biological, psychological, and social effects of trauma are sufficiently severe as to cause marked distress or
to impair your social and occupational functioning, you are considered to
have a psychiatric disorder. If you are in treatment for trauma-related
problems, I think you should learn what your diagnosis is, and you should
know something about it. A psychiatric diagnosis, like any other medical
diagnosis, is made on the basis of a group of symptoms that tend to cluster

together in a *syndrome*. These syndromes are delineated in the *Diagnostic and Statistical Manual of Mental Disorders,* now in its fourth edition, DSM-IV.[1]

I start this section with posttraumatic stress disorder (PTSD) because this is the psychiatric disorder most directly related to trauma. The PTSD syndrome includes three clusters of symptoms: hyperarousal, reexperiencing the trauma, and avoidance or numbing. As stated in Chapter 1 (Trauma), DSM-IV spells out the traumatic basis of PTSD as follows: "the person experienced, witnessed, or was confronted with an event or events that involved actual or threatened death or serious injury, or a threat to the physical integrity of self or others; the person's response involved intense fear, helplessness, or horror." [2]

A Brief History ◆ ◆ ◆ ◆ ◆ ◆ ◆ ◆ ◆ ◆

Although the scope of "traumatic events" is broad, and the psychological sequelae of trauma have been appreciated for centuries,[3] the modern concept of PTSD has its origins in combat-related trauma. In World War I, the term *shell shock* was employed to implicate subtle brain damage associated with exposure to explosions. In World War II, terms such as *combat fatigue* continued to imply that physical reactions were at the root of the disabling symptoms.

The concept of PTSD was introduced into the diagnostic nomenclature in 1980 after extensive experience in treating Vietnam veterans.[4] By that time, it was possible to formulate the diagnostic criteria on the basis of extensive research. Today, decades later, the devastating psychological effects of the Vietnam War are continuing to come to light. Although the majority of veterans have successfully readjusted, more than one-fourth have had PTSD at some time in their life, and for many, the disorder has become chronic. PTSD is often associated with a host of additional problems, including other psychiatric disorders, adjustment problems, adverse consequences for family members, and extensive need for psychiatric services.[5]

Whereas combat trauma has been in the forefront of PTSD concepts, various kinds of disasters have long been recognized as leading to psychological disturbance. In 1944, psychiatrist Erich Lindemann[6] described "acute grief" reactions stemming from traumatic events, including the disastrous Cocoanut Grove fire in Boston. He observed several characteristic reactions in those who lost loved ones in the fire: waves of physical discomfort triggered by thoughts of the deceased, a sense of unreality and detachment, feelings of guilt and hostility, agitation and restlessness, and social isolation. Lindemann noted that the acute grief reaction may occur immediately after the trauma, or it may be delayed for weeks or even years. He observed that one of the major obstacles to the necessary grief work is "the fact that many patients try to avoid the intense distress connected with the grief experience and to avoid the expression of emotion necessary for it." [7]

In recent years, we have come to appreciate that much psychiatric symptomatology, especially in women, is associated with childhood trauma—sexual abuse in particular.[8] Symptoms formerly diagnosed as depression, anxiety, and personality disorder are now being understood in part as reflecting PTSD. As Lindemann observed, the symptoms of PTSD can be delayed for years, and the traumatic experience itself may be completely forgotten for much of the person's life.

Prevalence ◆ ◆ ◆ ◆ ◆ ◆ ◆ ◆ ◆ ◆ ◆

Trauma is ubiquitous. How common is PTSD? The answer to this question depends in part on the type of trauma experienced and the length of time since it occurred. In addition, as with any other area of psychological research, the figures vary widely from one study to another. The bottom line is that, like trauma, PTSD is a pervasive problem.

Here's a sample of results from different studies. A representative survey of nearly 2,500 persons from the general population in the St. Louis, Missouri, area showed PTSD to be relatively uncommon: Slightly under 1% of the population reported having the disorder at some period in their lifetime (fewer than 0.5% of men and somewhat more than 1% of women).[9] In contrast, a study of 1,000 young adults from a health maintenance organization in the Detroit, Michigan, area found that slightly over 9% of the population had experienced PTSD at some point in time.[10] In a national sample of more than 400,000 women, the lifetime prevalence of PTSD exceeded 12%.[11] Even 1% of the population with a serious psychiatric disorder amounts to a lot of people and a major problem. Nine percent to 12% ranks PTSD among the most common psychiatric disorders.

Naturally, the prevalence of PTSD in populations exposed to trauma will be relatively high. In the Detroit sample, for example, nearly one-fourth of those exposed to trauma had experienced PTSD.[12] The National Vietnam Veterans Readjustment Study[13] found that the lifetime prevalence of PTSD was nearly one-third (30.6%) for men and over one-fourth (26.9%) for women who had served in the Vietnam theater. Moreover, the current prevalence—nearly two decades after the war—is 15.2% for men and 8.5% for women. The current prevalence of PTSD in World War II prisoners of war ranges as high as 50%.[14]

Although war-related PTSD has been most thoroughly studied, varying statistics have been reported for other types of trauma.[15] I will not barrage you with statistics; a few examples will suffice. Among women who have been raped, symptoms of PTSD are evident in more than 90% soon after the rape, and nearly 50% of these women continue to experience PTSD symptoms 3 months afterward.[16] Given the prevalence of rape, rape victims may constitute the largest proportion of persons with PTSD.[17] Lower rates of PTSD are found with robbery, burglary, and nonrape sexual assaults (from 16.7% to 33%), but nearly 60% of persons whose criminal victimization included both injury and threat to life develop PTSD.[18]

Symptoms akin to PTSD have been observed in infants and toddlers who have been exposed to overwhelming experiences.[19] Like adults, infants show symptoms of sleep disturbance, nightmares, hyperarousal, intrusive memories, and personality changes. PTSD is also common among older children exposed to such traumas as war, crime, injury, and accidents; the extent of reported PTSD in sexually abused children ranges from zero to 90%.[20]

The range of traumatic experience is virtually limitless, and there is no doubt that the specific manifestations of PTSD differ according to the type and severity of the trauma. Yet there is also a striking uniformity in responses to severe trauma that justifies the diagnosis of PTSD. These responses fall into three major clusters of symptoms—hyperarousal, reexperiencing, and avoidance/numbing.

Hyperarousal ◆ ◆ ◆ ◆ ◆ ◆ ◆ ◆ ◆ ◆ ◆

DSM-IV lists the following symptoms of increased arousal: difficulty falling or staying asleep; irritability or outbursts of anger; difficulty concentrating; hypervigilance; and exaggerated startle response.[21] These hyper-arousal symptoms are characteristic of anxiety, and PTSD is classified as one of several anxiety disorders (along with panic, generalized anxiety, and phobia, for example).

As is true of anxiety more generally, there are dozens of physiological reactions associated with PTSD in many bodily systems: neuropsychological (e.g., dizziness, blurred vision, altered consciousness), circulatory (pounding heart and irregular or rapid heartbeat), neuromuscular (tremor, various pains, headache, weakness), digestive (nausea, vomiting, abdominal pain, diarrhea, difficulty swallowing), respiratory (breathlessness, irregular breathing, hyperventilation), and others (urge to urinate, perspiration, fever).[22]

Physiological activation is central to the adaptiveness of the fight-or-flight response. As Cannon[23] stated, the bodily changes are "directly serv-iceable in making the organism more effective in the violent display of energy which fear or rage or pain may involve." But trauma, especially when it is prolonged or repeated, may convert this ordinarily adaptive response into a pathological reaction.[24] Consider what it means for a person to be "sensitive," or "hypersensitive." He or she reacts strongly and emotionally to a minor provocation, such as by taking great offense at a minor slight. With so many previous provocations, the latest seems like the "last straw." Earlier experience has *sensitized* the person. So it is with nervous systems. Our neurons can become sensitized. Severe stress can have a long-lasting effect on your nervous system to the extent that you are hyperresponsive to stress and chronically aroused.[25] You may experience relatively constant high levels of tension, anxiety, and irritation. You may react to a relatively minor stress with extreme anxiety, fear, or rage.

Reexperiencing ◆ ◆ ◆ ◆ ◆ ◆ ◆ ◆ ◆ ◆

Hyperarousal characterizes the full range of anxiety disorders, but various forms of reexperiencing the trauma are the hallmark of PTSD.[26] DSM-IV lists the following symptoms: recurrent and intrusive distressful recollec-tions of the event, including images, thoughts, or perceptions; recurrent distressful dreams of the event; acting or feeling as if the traumatic event were recurring, including a sense of reliving the experience, illusions, hallucinations, and dissociative flashback episodes; intense psychological distress at exposure to internal or external cues that symbolize or resemble an aspect of the traumatic event; and physiological reactivity on exposure to internal or external cues that symbolize or resemble an aspect of the traumatic event.[27]

Memories and Flashbacks

Traumatic memories are easily stimulated, and they can be evoked unconsciously, in a fraction of a second. Flashbacks are the most vivid form of reexperiencing. They are not necessarily identical replays, but they correspond to the original experience in varying degrees.[28] Flashbacks typically involve extremely vivid visualization and other sensations, along with a sense that the individual is back in the midst of the traumatic situation.[29] This recurrent sense of reliving gives trauma a quality of timelessness.[30] In addition to visual hallucinatory experiences, there may be distortions or illusions (e.g., loud noises experienced as explosions), smells, and painful bodily sensations associated with the original trauma. Combat veterans may have flashbacks anywhere from daily to annually. Many had flashbacks within a month of the trauma, but others did not have them until 2 or more years afterward.[31]

Psychiatrist Roger Pitman[32] proposed that the reexperiencing symptoms of PTSD result from the activation of complex memory networks associated with strong emotions. These memory networks comprise all components of the initial response to the trauma, including the traumatic situation, the individual's response at the time, and the meaning of the trauma to the individual. Pitman emphasizes that these networks "have become deeply etched into the neural template of the organism" and that "the brain is primed for such etching by the extreme state of arousal brought about by a life-or-death or other traumatic situation." He speculates that the "acid" that "etches" the trauma into the brain may be the "massive and diffuse release of norepinephrine into the cortex" in a process of "superconditioning." [33] Recall from Chapter 6 (Memory), however, that these "superconditioned" memories do not necessarily make any autobiographical sense.

Here's an extremely important point: These long-forgotten but deeply etched memories can be *gradually* primed by escalating stress and accumulating reminders of trauma. With sufficient priming, they break into consciousness in the form of intrusive memories and flashbacks. This gradual priming process, which has been described as *kindling*,[34] may explain the delayed onset of PTSD. Pitman[35] describes a neurophysiological "incubation" process in which stress hormones and memory networks reverberate until clinical PTSD erupts. Here we have another potential vicious circle: "recall of the traumatic event may lead to re-releases of stress hormones that further enhance the strength of the memory trace, leading to a greater likelihood of its intruding again, with yet further releases of stress hormones." [36]

Kindling and incubation provide some insight into how persons who had functioned relatively well for years develop severe PTSD after an accumulation of stressful experiences. The precipitating stressor for PTSD may have been the "last straw" in pushing the emotion–memory network over the threshold. Two examples in the literature[37] are instructive: An aircraft mechanic spent many hours guarding a helicopter crash site while the bodies of several of his acquaintances were removed. He did not experience any symptoms at the time. Eighteen months later, he developed symptoms of PTSD after *hearing about* another helicopter crash. Although he did not witness the second crash, he was involved in the preflight inspection of the craft, and he was to have been one of the passengers. Evidently, the mechanic was sensitized by the first crash, and the second crash was the last straw. An analogous example involved a woman who developed PTSD only after being in the *fourth* of a series of automobile accidents (being struck broadside, being forced off the road, backing into an expensive sports car, and finally being struck from the rear).

The process of sensitization, incubation, and accumulation of stressors often goes back to childhood.

◆ A woman in psychotherapy described a childhood filled with violence, illness, and neglect. Perhaps owing in part to having learned to do battle, she became a successful labor negotiator. Yet the high stress of her job took its toll, continually "kindling" memories of family battles. Against this backdrop of arousal—circulating stress hormones and active memory networks—a new trauma began to incubate. On her way home from work, she was nearly raped but was spared by her combativeness and a police siren that fortuitously sounded in the vicinity. Within a few days of this incident, she had a nightmare in which her grandfather molested her. Then, a couple of days after the nightmare, she began having flashbacks of childhood sexual abuse.

Nightmares and Vicious Circles

Sleep disturbance is a common component of PTSD.[38] Increased arousal precludes relaxation and interferes with sleep. In addition, sleep may be interrupted by anxiety dreams, suddenly awakening in terror, and nightmares. Or the dreams may be relatively straightforward replicas of the trauma—a kind of flashback during sleep. Anticipating such experiences, individuals with PTSD may become afraid to go to sleep.

Sleep disturbance and nightmares can contribute to spiraling emotion in PTSD. As illustrated by the patient whose experience of attempted rape set off a nightmare and flashbacks, the network of traumatic memories is conducive to chain reactions: Activation of any part of the network can activate any other. Heightened arousal primes the entire network, triggering intrusive aspects of PTSD. Anything that makes you anxious or frightened—even if it has *nothing* to do with the original trauma—can prime the whole network of traumatic memories. An automobile accident, for example, could trigger a memory of assault.

The clusters of hyperarousal and reexperiencing of trauma can easily become intertwined in a vicious circle: As a component of the initial traumatic experience, physiological arousal can become a cue that reminds you of earlier trauma. The physiological arousal that triggers this chain reaction need not have anything to do with trauma; it could even begin with physical exertion. Exercise-induced acceleration in heart rate could trigger a memory of a mugging that involved fear-induced acceleration in heart rate. Nausea associated with the flu could trigger memories of disgust associated with sexual abuse. Labored breathing could remind you of feeling smothered. Another vicious circle—as in the case of the patient just described—is flashbacks preceded by nightmares.[39] Dreams could heighten the activation of the PTSD network, increasing the likelihood of intrusive recollections, imagery, and flashbacks.

Reenactments

It is not uncommon for individuals who have undergone trauma to actively re-create it.[40] Sometimes such reenactments are relatively transparent, in the form of the "compulsion to repeat." In other cases, the reenactments are more disguised. For example, somatic reenactments (sometimes called *body memories*) are reactivations of body sensations and pains associated with trauma.[41] A particularly dramatic disguised reenactment is the *unconscious flashback,* in which the individual reenacts a traumatic experience with no awareness of its connection to the original trauma. The individual can be seen to be "carrying out complex integrated actions based on past experiences that are not consciously remembered, with no awareness that he is repeating anything." [42] Consider the case of a surgeon who had struggled with symptoms since his discharge from the army:

> In early 1982 he suddenly walked into a school classroom with a rifle and informed the students and teacher that they were hostages until the Mayor agreed to come and hear his complaints about not being able to obtain treatment for his symptoms. In the ensuing crisis, SWAT team snipers set up posts from which to shoot Dr. N, and officials negotiated with him. The Mayor came and listened to Dr. N's complaints, which were laced with vague references to Vietnam, and Dr. N surrendered after about 5 hours.[43]

Through intensive interviewing, it was discovered that Dr. N had managed to re-create several facets of his traumatic experience in the war, much of which he had blocked by amnesia. For example, the school he invaded resembled a school next to his hospital in Vietnam. In Vietnam he had shot a North Vietnamese prisoner, and in this reenactment, he may have been staging his own punishment by exposing himself to the possibility of being killed by a sniper: "In the school episode Dr. N. was attempting to get himself shot in a war-like situation and thus take the place of the prisoner he himself had shot." [44]

Consider the related case of a woman who was thought to be psychotic because of her bizarre behavior. She had escaped the Cocoanut Grove fire and testified in hearings in 1943; she had not thought about the fire for the next 38 years. Yet she developed numerous psychiatric symptoms that made no sense until they were connected with her memories of persons being trapped in the fire. For example, "On one occasion the patient tried to gather everyone up to leave the hospital. 'We're all moving out today,' she ordered, 'and I'm going to be the last one out, to make sure everyone gets

out. All the doors are coming off today. No more doors!' " On another occasion, "she was brought in by the police for disturbing the peace. Her behavior consisted of pulling fire alarms in numerous buildings and shouting
at people to get out." [45]

Often, however, the reenactments are not so disguised. Some persons
who have been abused end up abusing others; in this fashion, abuse can be
passed on through the generations.[46] We often observe that males are more
likely to repeat the abuse directly, becoming aggressive toward others,
whereas females are more likely to engage in self-destructive behavior, turning their aggression back onto themselves.

Avoidance and Numbing   ◆ ◆ ◆ ◆ ◆ ◆ ◆ ◆

The combination of hyperarousal and intrusive symptoms is an assault on
the mind. In the face of this barrage, the mind quite naturally tries to shut
off the overwhelming stimulation. This self-protective response is the
third component of the diagnostic criteria for PTSD—namely, the persistent avoidance of stimuli associated with the trauma and the numbing
of general responsiveness. DSM-IV includes several specific symptoms:
efforts to avoid thoughts, feelings, or conversations associated with the
trauma; efforts to avoid activities, places, or people that arouse recollec-
tions of the trauma; inability to recall an important aspect of the trauma;
markedly diminished interest or participation in significant activities;
feeling detachment or estrangement from others; a restricted range of affect (e.g., inability to have loving feelings); and a sense of a foreshortened
future (e.g., not expecting to have a career, marriage, children, or a normal life span).[47]

Avoidance

If you have PTSD, you need not understand the ins and outs of neuro-
chemistry to know that you are easily set off by anything reminiscent of
the traumatic experience. You most likely already live in a state of apprehension. You may be fearful of anything that might rekindle the trauma.
You may have learned what to do to avoid triggering a panic or a rage.

If PTSD becomes chronic, your life can become increasingly limited and constricted. Social isolation often results from traumatic relationships. Many persons are traumatized by other persons. If this has been your experience, contact with others can trigger anxiety and intrusive experiences. In addition, you may be afraid to establish close relationships, because the prospect of rejection and abandonment can also be a source of stress that rekindles traumatic memories.

Persons with PTSD often have problems with substance abuse. Substance abuse could be considered one of the avoidance symptoms inasmuch as substances blunt the anxiety and anger associated with PTSD.[48] Little wonder, then, that persons with PTSD often resort to abusing antianxiety medication, alcohol, or drugs such as marijuana—all of these have the effect of blunting arousal.

Numbing

As described earlier, some individuals have the ability to block off traumatic experience by altering their state of consciousness. By means of dissociation, they are able to distance themselves from the state of unbearably intense arousal associated with the trauma. They may maintain a state of extreme detachment, or they may go a step farther, blocking off the memory entirely. PTSD is classified as an anxiety disorder, but the numbing phenomena attest to its overlap with dissociative disorders.

Just as there is a neurochemical basis for arousal, there is also a neurochemical basis for numbing. As described in connection with self-destructive behavior, "stress-induced analgesia" is an internal "narcotic-like" response that blocks pain. The transmitters in this process are the endogenous (internal) opioids. For individuals with PTSD, stress may activate the opioid response and lead to analgesia, contributing to the numbing experience. This phenomenon was recently demonstrated experimentally. When combat veterans with PTSD were exposed to stress, they showed decreased sensitivity to pain.[49]

The combination of hyperarousal and numbing gives an all-or-nothing quality to emotionality in PTSD. Judith Herman[50] has referred to this vacillation as a "dialectic of trauma." Individuals with PTSD may seem emotionally remote, detached, cut off, and unresponsive; then a seemingly minor stressor launches them into a panic or a rage.

Depression is in the background of avoidance and numbing. Indeed, one PTSD criterion—diminished interest in significant activities—is a cardinal symptom of depression. The neurophysiology of prolonged stress can drive an individual into depression. Moreover, it is hardly surprising that depression would become prominent in a syndrome that entails pervasive avoidance, isolation, and pleasurelessness. And depression may be compounded by the use of drugs taken to alleviate anxiety, such as alcohol. No wonder that depression is often a significant complication of PTSD.

Variations in Course ◆ ◆ ◆ ◆ ◆ ◆ ◆ ◆ ◆

The course of an illness, like the course of a voyage, is its trajectory across time. Psychiatric disorders, like other medical illnesses, have a wide variety of courses. As described earlier, PTSD may have a period of incubation. Symptoms of many medical illnesses wax and wane; so do those of PTSD. Diseases may go into periods of remission followed by recurrence; so may PTSD. Any imaginable course is possible: "PTSD may have either an acute or delayed onset and then remit or persist as a chronic form, which in turn may resolve, recur, or fluctuate in intensity." [51] Two of these distinctions are particularly important—immediate versus delayed onset and acute versus chronic course.

Immediate Versus Delayed Onset

It is not uncommon for symptoms of PTSD to emerge immediately in the wake of traumatic experience. The whole complex of hyperarousal, reexperiencing the trauma, and avoidance mechanisms can quickly become evident. For many individuals, however, the syndrome of PTSD emerges only belatedly. The diagnostic criteria specify 6 months as the cutoff point; if the onset of symptoms occurs 6 months or more after the traumatic event, the PTSD is considered to be delayed.

For many individuals, this delay goes far beyond 6 months; it may be years or even decades. Many persons have little or no recollection of severely traumatic childhood experiences until they are well into adulthood. We have much to learn about this capacity to seal off traumatic experience, as well as the process by which such experience becomes unsealed. As described earlier, it seems that virtually any stressor can unlock a history of traumatic experience. The stressor may bear some similarity to the initial trauma, or it may seem incidental. *Anything* that reactivates the feeling of helplessness may be sufficient to reevoke the helplessness associated with the traumatic memory network.

Acute Versus Chronic Course

In DSM-IV, an individual who experiences symptoms for no more than 1 month after the trauma will be diagnosed as having "acute stress disorder." Individuals whose symptoms have lasted more than 1 month but less than 3 months will have a diagnosis of acute PTSD, whereas those whose symptoms continue beyond 3 months will have a diagnosis of chronic PTSD. The 3-month cutoff point is consistent with research studies showing that symptoms enduring past 3 months are likely to persist and to be associated with a relatively chronic course.[52]

Accumulating evidence suggests that PTSD is largely a chronic disorder.[53] As mentioned earlier in this chapter, nearly two decades after Vietnam, a substantial proportion of those who experienced combat show symptoms of PTSD, and many World War II prisoners of war evidence PTSD four decades after captivity. Although the proportion of rape victims with PTSD drops dramatically by the end of 3 months, nearly half of the victims may continue to evidence PTSD at 9 months,[54] and more than 10% may show PTSD after 15 years.[55] Although their symptoms may be delayed for decades, the vast majority of patients we see at The Menninger Clinic with PTSD in relation to prolonged childhood trauma have chronic symptoms. These individuals have a particularly severe form of chronic PTSD, to be discussed next.

Complex PTSD ◆ ◆ ◆ ◆ ◆ ◆ ◆ ◆ ◆ ◆

PTSD is defined on the basis of three main symptom clusters: hyperarousal, reexperiencing, and avoidance/numbing. I have discussed these facets of traumatic responses in terms of emotion, memory, and consciousness. But the effects of trauma—in particular, severe trauma—go beyond these three domains. We have seen that traumatic experience may also have profound effects on attachment, sense of self, and relationships.

Consistent with this broader view, several authors have described trauma syndromes that go beyond the confines of PTSD as defined in DSM-IV.

On the basis of her extensive work with traumatized children, Lenore Terr[56] has described a broad trauma syndrome. Three cardinal symptoms are integral to PTSD: intrusive memories, repetitive behaviors, and trauma-specific fears. But she adds a fourth and very broad effect: changed attitudes about people, aspects of life, and the future. Terr has spelled out a host of more specific effects of severe and repeated trauma, including massive denial and numbing, forgetting whole segments of childhood, reliance on self-hypnosis as an escape mechanism, alternation between rage and extreme passivity, and self-mutilation. These severely traumatized children may be so withdrawn, unresponsive, and numb as to appear robbed of their humanity. Their capacity for attachment is undermined. Terr's description makes plain that severe trauma not only leads to a cluster of symptoms but also affects the *whole personality.*

Psychiatrist Jean Goodwin[57] has used the acronym "FEARS" for symptoms associated with childhood incest. She describes a moderately severe syndrome and an even more severe syndrome. In the moderate syndrome, the symptoms include Fears (hyperalertness and nervousness), Ego constriction (sexual and social inhibitions), Anger dyscontrol (anger and fear of anger), Repetition (flashbacks and nightmares), Sleep disturbance, and Sadness (guilt and depression). Symptoms in the more severe syndrome include Fugues (dissociation and multiple personality disorder), Ego fragmentation (borderline and multiple personality disorders), Antisocial acting out (including drug abuse), Reenactments (e.g., of rape and victimization), Somatization (medical problems) and Suicidality (thoughts and attempts). Other researchers have reported an extremely broad array of symptoms in sexually abused children but have not found evidence for any specific syndrome or single traumatizing process.[58]

Judith Herman[59] has proposed that a new diagnostic category—complex PTSD—is needed to encompass these more severe trauma disorders. She describes the kind of traumatic situation that brings about complex PTSD as follows:

> Captivity, which brings the victim into prolonged contact with the perpetrator, creates a special type of relationship, one of coercive control. This is equally true whether the victim is rendered captive primarily by physical

force (as in the case of prisoners and hostages), or by a combination of physical, economic, social, and psychological means (as in the case of religious cult members, battered women, and abused children). The psychological impact of subordination to coercive control may have many common features, whether that subordination occurs within the public sphere of politics or within the supposedly private (but equally political) sphere of sexual and domestic relations.[60]

Herman delineates the wide range of symptoms associated with complex PTSD, from somatic complaints to dissociative and emotional disturbances, including profound depression. She points out that the sheer multiplicity of symptoms indicates severe trauma. But the effects go beyond specific symptoms to affect profoundly the person's identity and relationships. Herman describes a propensity to expose oneself to repeated victimization, coupled with a pervasive failure of self-protection. Even beyond its effects on self-experience and relationships, the trauma has an existential impact, damaging systems of meaning, altering one's faith, and leading to hopelessness and despair.

The syndrome of complex PTSD delineated by Herman is firmly rooted in the clinical literature, and research was conducted to support the inclusion of the syndrome in DSM-IV under the rubric of "disorders of extreme stress not otherwise specified." [61] But alternative classifications for trauma-related disorders continue to be debated,[62] and—for the time being—complex PTSD has not been included in the official nomenclature. Instead, these complex symptoms are enumerated in DSM-IV as potential "associated features" of PTSD that occur in conjunction with forms of trauma such as abuse, battering, incarceration, and torture.[63]

What Causes PTSD? ◆ ◆ ◆ ◆ ◆ ◆ ◆ ◆ ◆

On the face of it, the question "What causes PTSD?" seems hardly worth asking. The answer is obvious: trauma. But this simplistic answer overlooks two key facts. First, most individuals do not develop PTSD after a traumatic experience. Second, some individuals develop PTSD after stressful experience that falls short of "trauma." [64]

Of course, traumatic experience is the key factor in the etiology of

PTSD, but it is not the *only* factor. There is a well-established dose-response relationship between stress and its effects: The more severe the stress, the more severe the symptoms. Although there are exceptions to this rule,[65] the more severe the trauma, the higher the likelihood of PTSD.[66] At a sufficiently high level of trauma—such as that described by Herman in the etiology of complex PTSD—anyone will succumb. As psychiatrists Roy Grinker and John Spiegel put it in their classic text on war neuroses, "If the stress is severe enough, if it strikes an exposed 'Achilles' heel' and if the exposure to it is sufficiently prolonged, adverse psychological symptoms may develop in anyone." [67] At more moderate levels of trauma, there is room for many other factors to play a role.[68] In this section, I examine genetic and developmental factors that predispose individuals to PTSD, and then review factors subsequent to the trauma that affect the course of PTSD. I conclude with some comments about resilience.

Genetic Factors

I have emphasized the profound role of neurophysiology in trauma throughout this book. As described in the Appendix, genes play a paramount role in the development and ongoing operation of the nervous system. So it should not be surprising that genetic factors play a role in response to trauma. The influence of genetic factors on our physiological responses to stress has long been established in animal research. With a variety of mammals, researchers have been able to breed strains that show differing physiological responsiveness and vulnerability to stress.[69] Although the majority of dogs that are exposed to inescapable shock develop the "learned helplessness" syndrome, one-third of the shock-exposed animals do not.[70]

Animal research has provided ample reason to suspect a genetically based vulnerability to stress, but only recently has research demonstrated a genetic vulnerability to PTSD.[71] A comparison of identical and fraternal male twin pairs among Vietnam veterans demonstrated a significant genetic contribution to the risk of PTSD. There was not only a genetic influence on PTSD in combat veterans but also a genetic influence on PTSD in those who did not serve in Southeast Asia, suggesting that the findings can be generalized beyond combat-related trauma. Surprisingly, genetic factors also contributed to the likelihood of participating in combat. Genetic factors may play a dual role: first, in predisposing some individuals to wind up in traumatic situations, and second, by influencing their responses to trauma.

The genetic factors must be complex if they can influence both our exposure to trauma and our vulnerability to trauma. Yet heredity probably plays a role in PTSD by contributing to vulnerability to stress.[72] Proneness to anxiety is one of the most solidly established temperaments, and PTSD is an anxiety disorder. It stands to reason that the more prone to anxiety you are, the more likely you are to develop an anxiety disorder in the aftermath of a traumatic experience.

Developmental Factors

There is little doubt that personality disturbance occurs in conjunction with PTSD, but it is important also to know whether personality disturbance *predisposes* an individual to PTSD. This question can become a political issue, inasmuch as clinicians are reluctant to "blame the victim" for the disorder.[73] Many patients with chronic PTSD already blame *themselves* ("If I weren't such a wimp . . . ")—and they need no additional encouragement from professionals. But appreciating sources of vulnerability to PTSD can lead to better self-understanding rather than to self-blame. We all have vulnerabilities to a host of disorders and diseases for which we need not be blamed.

I have described how trauma is intertwined with disruptions in attachment, so it should not be surprising that premature separations are a predisposing factor to stress vulnerability in animals[74] and to PTSD in humans.[75] It should also not be surprising that a history of anxiety problems in the individual and/or family contributes to vulnerability to PTSD.[76] Vulnerability to PTSD has also been associated with a wide range of other psychiatric and substance abuse disorders in the family or the individual, as well as with a history of behavioral, conduct, and personality problems.[77] Moreover, responses to trauma may be cumulative; exposure to childhood trauma may increase the risk of PTSD after adult trauma. A recent study of Vietnam veterans found that those with a history of childhood physical and sexual abuse were more likely than those without such a history to develop PTSD after combat exposure.[78]

It is also important to note that developmental factors, like genes, may predispose an individual to being traumatized. For example, whereas participation in—or observation of—atrocities and abusive violence in Vietnam increases the risk of PTSD,[79] the presence of personality and behavioral disturbances before military service predisposes individuals to engage in such behavior while they are in combat.[80] More generally, exposure to trauma has been associated with the same factors that predispose individuals to PTSD, including childhood behavior problems and family history of psychiatric disorder and substance abuse.

Posttrauma Factors

The relationship of PTSD to personality disturbance is bidirectional: Personality disturbance may predispose the individual to traumatic experience and to PTSD. Conversely, as documented throughout this book, traumatic experience can have a deleterious effect on personality functioning. Moreover, chronic PTSD may itself further erode personality functioning.

> Many of the subjects with PTSD have had their image of the fairness or stability of the world so disrupted that they are forced to devote time and energy to adjust to the emotional disturbance this causes. It is this adaptation that probably is responsible for the reported personality changes occurring after the onset of PTSD.[81]

Availability of social support and the capacity to make use of it can protect traumatized persons from developing PTSD. Conversely, lack of social support—or worse, hostile rejection—serves to exacerbate or to maintain PTSD in those who have undergone trauma.[82] But this social isolation can be another vicious circle because, as described earlier, traumatic experience has a deleterious effect on relationships. PTSD may erode your capacity to make use of the social support you need to alleviate the disorder.[83]

Resilience

It stands to reason that factors such as anxiety proneness, psychiatric disorders, and personality characteristics will affect an individual's manner of coping with traumatic experience, as well as his or her ability to deal with its aftermath. As with everything else, there are wide variations among individuals in coping with illness—physical or psychiatric. Looking at the positive side of the ledger, psychiatrist Frederic Flach has discussed the phenomenon of *resilience* in relation to trauma:

> Resilience should provide the tools whereby the extent of the natural disruption that follows is kept within reasonable boundaries, if at all possible. This does not preclude the possibility, however, that if the stressful situations are of sufficient intensity and meaning, the consequent chaos may not assume dramatic proportions. When reintegration takes place, the homeostatic condition that is shaped should be to some degree different from that which existed prior to the events. Moreover, it should represent a higher, more complex, more adaptable level of organization.[84]

In discussing combat stress, Flach[85] proposes: "the real question should not be, Why did some fall apart? but rather, Why on earth didn't they *all* fall apart; not in the middle of the crisis perhaps but why not afterward?" He lists several aspects of psychological resilience: insight into oneself and others, a supple sense of self-esteem, the ability to learn from experience, a high tolerance for distress, a low tolerance for outrageous behavior, open-mindedness, courage, personal discipline, creativity, integrity, a keen sense of humor, a constructive philosophy of life that gives it meaning, and a willingness to dream dreams that can inspire and give genuine hope. He observed that those who coped best with trauma "were those with insight into the emotional impact of what they had just been through and who were able to express their feelings to another immediately following the event." [86]

Reading through Flach's list of resilience factors leaves little doubt that not only innate factors such as temperament but also early life experience contribute to one's vulnerability or resistance to stress. This list also underscores the pernicious impact of prolonged trauma early in life. The consequences of prolonged early trauma are precisely those that are likely to interfere with the development of resilience as Flach defines it.

No wonder that coping with complex PTSD poses such an extraordinary challenge. It is indeed challenging to aspire to a "more adaptable level of organization" in attempting to cope with trauma. Long ago, Karl Menninger[87] proposed the ideal of becoming "weller than well." The illness is the crisis that brings with it the opportunity to develop new ways of coping and more resilience.

Treatment ◆ ◆ ◆ ◆ ◆ ◆ ◆ ◆ ◆ ◆ ◆ ◆

The treatment of trauma will be discussed at length in Part IV, but I want to make a few general points while the details of PTSD are still fresh in your mind. As in the treatment of any other illness, the sooner the intervention, the better. At the first opportunity, the individual should be encouraged to talk about the traumatic experience. This ventilating provides a chance to receive needed support and comforting as well as an opportunity to begin to make sense of the experience.[88] In 1941, in his classic book on war neuroses, psychiatrist Abram Kardiner[89] urged haste in working with combat trauma, remarking, "One can thus come none too abruptly to the question, 'What happened?' " His goals for treatment were straightforward: "No opportunity should be lost to show the patient 1) that these reactions are appropriate defenses, 2) that the world is no longer hostile, and 3) that his powers to master it are growing." [90]

This prompt intervention strategy applies to any traumatic experience or to acute PTSD that can be linked to an identifiable and discussible stressor. But the more severe, complex, and chronic forms of PTSD are often associated with traumatic experiences that were not discussible—for example, because of secrecy in the family. In such instances, intervention cannot occur in the immediate aftermath of the traumatic experience. The opportunity to answer the question "What happened?" may only come years—or even decades—after the fact. And the question may refer to much of childhood, permitting no brief answer. Given the fallibility of memory in conjunction with trauma, the answer to "What happened?" may be extraordinarily difficult to reconstruct.

Kardiner noted that the treatment of war-related trauma requires first and foremost the provision of security and support. In effect, the first message conveyed to the patient must be, "You are safe now." For anyone who has spent most of a lifetime endangered, however, establishing this sense of safety is no mean feat. For many, the feeling "I am safe now" will not be the beginning of treatment but rather the end result. Working on current relationships is crucial. As I will discuss in more detail in Part IV, a sense of safety is best established through healing relationships, often employing some combination of individual and group therapy.

I want to underscore in this context that current reality plays a paramount role in PTSD: "Rearousal of symptoms regularly occurs when the chronic PTSD sufferer is faced with some current interpersonal or physical anxiety provoking situation." [91] To diminish symptoms of PTSD, you must work on two fronts—coming to terms with the past and alleviating stress in the present.

Treatment of PTSD requires not only feeling safe from outside dangers but also feeling safe from assaults from within. PTSD entails high levels of arousal as well as disruptive and often terrifying intrusive experiences (memories, flashbacks, nightmares). Because intrusive experiences such as flashbacks may lead to further sensitization in a vicious circle, it is important to bring such symptoms under control. Medication can be of some benefit in this process (Chapter 12), as can various methods of self-regulation (Chapter 13). Mastering the traumatic experience in therapy and developing a sense of safety in relationships ultimately can make this internal experience manageable.

There is no question about the importance of symptom-oriented treatment in PTSD, as anyone who has experienced the symptoms will attest. But reactions to traumatic experience cannot be reduced to symptoms, especially when the trauma has been prolonged and severe, and when one's "imperfect adaptation" has become chronic. Severely traumatic experience can have profound effects on the self and relationships—and, indeed, on the whole personality. Traumatic experience also has a broader *existential* impact, altering one's relationship with the world and with life. From this perspective, treatment of severe trauma can encompass the full spectrum of therapeutic approaches.

CHAPTER TEN

Dissociative Disorders

Many people who are overwhelmed by traumatic experience learn to cope by altering consciousness. They become extremely detached from the experience when it is happening. They may subsequently remember the events dimly or in fragments—or they may block them from memory more thoroughly by amnesia. Dissociation can feel psychologically life-saving. If you are overpowered and fight or flight is out of the question, dissociation is a way to escape. But dissociation is both a blessing and a curse. You may gain some distance from the trauma temporarily, but it may come back to haunt you later. Also, once you learn to dissociate, you can do it more indiscriminately to deal with a wide range of nontraumatic—but stressful—situations. Then dissociation undermines adaptation by interfering with active coping.

This chapter reviews the broad spectrum of dissociation and the classification of dissociative experiences into various psychiatric disorders. I pay particular attention to the most severe and complex dissociative disorder, dissociative identity disorder (formerly called *multiple personality disorder*).

The Spectrum of Dissociation ◆ ◆ ◆ ◆ ◆ ◆ ◆

Dissociation occurs on a continuum, ranging from relatively mild to very severe.[1] On the mild end are the dissociations of everyday life, such as "highway hypnosis" (driving a distance down a highway and then realizing that you have no recall of having done so), becoming lost in a book or a movie, or being completely absorbed in a daydream during a boring meeting or conversation. These are common and benign forms of "tuning out" or "spacing out."

As described in Chapter 5 (Consciousness), this capacity to tune out or to become completely absorbed in fantasy is a skill. Some individuals are much better at it than others, but almost everyone has some dissociative ability. Perhaps because of its kinship with imagination, children are more prone to dissociation; as you get older, your tendency to dissociate declines somewhat.[2] Yet experiencing trauma fosters this skill.[3] Like any other ability, the more you need it and use it, the better you learn it.

This book focuses on trauma, and dissociation is often a trauma-related symptom. But there is no simple, universal connection between trauma and dissociation.[4] Trauma does not *always* cause dissociation or result in dissociative disorders. And trauma is not the *only* cause of dissociation. Other factors associated with dissociation include childhood loss (death or hospitalization of a family member),[5] as well as neglect and a negative home atmosphere.[6] Moreover, most of the dissociative symptoms to be discussed below—depersonalization, amnesia, fugue, radical personality changes—can be brought on by brain impairment.[7] A wide range of dissociative symptoms are associated with seizures (temporal lobe epilepsy). Sexual abuse itself can be a contributing factor to seizures, and it is important not to misconstrue such seizures (often including sexual feelings and behaviors) as dissociative "pseudoseizures" or flashbacks.[8] Brain-based causes of dissociation also include head trauma, migraine, tumors, and other brain diseases. In addition, dissociative symptoms may result from use of various drugs and medications, including alcohol, barbiturates, antianxiety agents, marijuana, and psychedelics (LSD). As with a wide range of other psychiatric symptoms, potential organic causes should always be ruled out in the course of a diagnostic evaluation.

All forms of dissociation disrupt the continuity of experience to a greater or lesser degree.[9] Dissociation leaves gaps in its wake. The gaps may range from a fuzzy recollection or a sense of unreality about a specific event to complete amnesia for large blocks of time. Some forms of dissociation are far more disruptive than others; some persons are prone to employ dissociation far more frequently than others; and some dissociation-prone persons are compelled by severe trauma to employ dissociation pervasively. Thus, there is a wide range of severity in the dissociative disorders. A psychiatric diagnosis is an attempt to classify the experience in the dissociative gap. Any of the following types of dissociative disorder may range from relatively mild to more severe, although depersonalization tends to be least disruptive and dissociative identity disorder tends to be most disruptive to the continuity of experience.

Depersonalization Disorder ◆ ◆ ◆ ◆ ◆ ◆ ◆

DSM-IV describes *depersonalization* as "a feeling of detachment or estrangement from one's self," often including "a sensation of being an outside observer of one's mental processes, one's body, or parts of one's body." [10] Depersonalization thus involves an altered experience of the self. Individuals who feel depersonalized often describe feeling like a "machine," a "robot," or an "automaton." They may feel as if they are living in a dream or playing a role in a movie. Some individuals describe a strange sensation of feeling as if they are outside their bodies—for example, watching themselves from behind their shoulders or from across the room.[11] A related phenomenon is *derealization*—a sense that other persons or the surrounding environment are unreal (the world is two-dimensional, other people are robots, or everything is dreamlike or veiled in a fog). Although not classified as a psychiatric disorder in its own right, derealization can be a distressing symptom and should be carefully evaluated along with other dissociative symptoms.[12]

Depersonalization and derealization are common feelings, probably felt to some degree by most persons at one time or another. Depersonalization is also a common psychiatric symptom, occurring in conjunction with many other disorders.[13] Depersonalization *disorder* is diagnosed according to DSM-IV when depersonalization itself is persistent or recurrent and when it causes clinically significant distress or impairment in social, occupational, or other important areas of functioning.

Depersonalization and extreme detachment are common responses to traumatic experiences ranging from life-threatening events to prolonged trauma.[14] If you cannot physically get away, you may be able to detach psychologically. You need no teachers to learn to use your imagination, to retreat into fantasy, or to focus your attention away from traumatic experience. As such, depersonalization and derealization are adaptive. But these self-protective mechanisms can take on a life of their own. Any anxiety-provoking situation may trigger depersonalization. At worst, a continuous feeling of unreality can evolve, not only precluding enjoyment and involvement with life but also eroding your capacity to cope with daily tasks and responsibilities. At the same time, pervasive depersonalization leads to a sense of social isolation and alienation.

◆ A young man sought therapy because he felt that his emotions were out of control. Sometimes he felt tense and irritable. At other times he had inexplicable bouts of crying. He connected some of his feelings with being abandoned by his mother at an early age. He felt unprotected, and he had witnessed a number of violent episodes in his family. He was also sexually molested later in childhood. Occasional flashbacks contributed to the anxiety that prompted him to seek psychotherapy. But more problematic was his severe depersonalization. He described a continual feeling of being detached from his feelings and behavior. He did not live his life; he watched it. Even when he appeared to others to be animated and involved, he felt distant and hollow. Apart from bouts of anxiety and tearfulness, he felt emotionally bland. He was starved for closeness but felt incapable of intimacy. He went through periods of compulsively seeking sexual liaisons with women, but he could never feel the warmth for which he longed. He spent hours in solitude, sitting immobile in the woods, as if in a trance. Yet he could not remember what he thought or felt during these periods. He found one escape from detachment: He was a talented actor, and he felt fully alive whenever he performed. Ironically, his capacity for dissociation contributed to his acting talent; when he performed in a play, he was totally absorbed, oblivious to his surroundings and the passage of time.

When we discuss dissociative gaps in my educational group, some patients who experience such pervasive depersonalization exclaim that they *live their lives in the gap.* Such individuals face a long process of giving up detachment and finding a way back to engagement. They must learn gradually to cultivate feelings that they have long avoided.

Dissociative Amnesia and Fugue ◆ ◆ ◆ ◆ ◆ ◆

Some individuals go beyond blunting traumatic experience at the time it is happening to subsequently blocking it from memory. As defined in DSM-IV, *dissociative amnesia* is "an inability to recall important personal information, usually of a traumatic or stressful nature, that is too extensive to be explained by normal forgetfulness." [15] Dissociative amnesia is common after single-blow traumas as well as in relation to more prolonged traumatic experience such as combat or sexual abuse.[16] The gaps in memory may range from minutes to years.

Fugue refers to flight or travel. In DSM-IV, *dissociative fugue* entails "sudden, unexpected travel away from home or one's customary place of daily activities, with inability to recall some or all of one's past," coupled with "confusion about personal identity or even the assumption of a new identity." [17] Fugue, like amnesia, is usually associated with some specific traumatic event or stressor. Fugue goes beyond amnesia, however, by involving physical flight from the stressful situation as well as identity disturbance. In some instances, the individual may develop a new identity (e.g., a previously shy and retiring individual becomes more gregarious and uninhibited). Compared with amnesia, fugue is relatively rare.[18] Yet what might initially appear to be isolated symptoms of amnesia or fugue may turn out to be part of a now-common disorder, *dissociative identity disorder.*

Dissociative Identity Disorder
(formerly *Multiple Personality Disorder*) ◆ ◆ ◆ ◆

◆ I had been Joan's psychotherapist for several months, during her psychiatric hospitalization, never suspecting that dissociation was among her difficulties. The first sign occurred in a psychotherapy session in which Joan—quite out of character—suddenly became angry at me and said, "Goddamn it!" Joan had been extremely reluctant to express anger, and I considered this a breakthrough. Moments later I alluded to what had happened. Joan was totally oblivious to it, denied that it had happened, and accused me of playing a therapeutic game to provoke her anger. As I recounted the events, she began to question her conviction that I was lying, and she became very frightened.

Joan called me the next day to reiterate her confusion and finally accepted that, indeed, she had made this outburst and not remembered it. A few days later she reported that she had started having periods of amnesia. Minutes before Joan's next session, the receptionist told me that the patient had come in, insisting on seeing me immediately. The patient—calling herself Mary—entered in an agitated state, handed me a bag containing whiskey and assorted pills, and implored, "Here, take these quickly and hide them! She's going to kill herself with them." I did as she asked, discussing the situation with her, and—for the moment—acceded to Mary's request that I not tell Joan what had taken place. Then the patient switched states, was completely perplexed and disoriented, and identified the experience as being like her other recent "blackouts." I accompanied her back to the hospital unit and conveyed to her hospital psychiatrist and staff my astonishment at the emergence of multiple personality disorder.

In working with the Mary identity, I learned that she came into being when Joan was about 7, apparently in the midst of a traumatic experience. Mary reemerged in college, in a similarly stressful situation. The pattern of dissociation was then reactivated by stresses in the current hospitalization.

A considerable number of the psychotherapy sessions were devoted to work with Mary, who was able to disclose some painful memories. Occasionally I was impressed by moments during which she would be totally unresponsive. I speculated—incorrectly—that these were transitional states between different identities; but during one of these states she looked at me and, in a childlike voice, said, "Who are you?" I then realized that a *third* identity had emerged, and I explained who I was. In this state, the patient was transported back in time to the age of 7. Her whole experience in this state was that of a 7-year-old child, with the associated capacities, memories, and identity. For example, she had never heard of Burger King, *Sesame Street*, and Sprite. She missed her childhood friends, wanted to return to elementary school, and wondered what she would be when she grew up. It was a challenge to explain to the "child" what was happening—why she was in a grownup body, where she was, and so forth.

There was a layering of identities: When Joan became anxious, she dissociated into Mary; when Mary became anxious, she dissociated into the child state. Each identity employed the same defense. Thus, the child bore the most painful early memories that even Mary could not face. At one point, before she had come to trust me, the child "came out" in a state of terror. She ran out of my office and could only be persuaded to reenter it if I left the door open. Gradually, she felt more secure and could be reassured quite easily that she was safe.

The patient was able to learn relatively quickly to switch back and forth among states. But Mary could not always switch back to Joan at will. One time she came into my office in a panic because she could not switch; together, we concluded that it was because she was so angry—as long as Mary was angry, she could not switch back to Joan because Joan could not tolerate anger. Eventually the patient was able to gain sufficient control of the different identities so that each could negotiate for periods of time to be in control, making the alternations more predictable.[19]

The Trouble With *"Multiple Personality" Disorder*

Ironically, now that multiple personality disorder (MPD) is widely recognized, it is called something else: *dissociative identity disorder.* As befits such a controversial diagnosis, it is itself in the midst of an identity change. The current period of identity confusion is worth tolerating, as there are good reasons for changing the terminology. The change should help patients with the disorder—and the clinicians who treat them—think more clearly about it.

Multiple personality disorder was a misnomer. We ordinarily use the term *personality* as an umbrella term to refer to our whole way of being, whereas the identity shifts typically seen in dissociative identity disorder are restricted to a narrow realm of consciousness, memory, and relationships. In the patient just described, for example, Joan could *not* be angry and Mary could *only* be angry. As psychiatrist George Greaves puts it, "The term 'personality' refers to the collective range of behavior an individual exhibits over time; hence, one logically cannot exhibit more than one collective range of behavior, let alone many." [20] We each have only one personality—extremely complicated, perhaps fragmented, but only one.

Persons with dissociative identity disorder often feel that they do not just have several personalities; they are several *people.* It is not uncommon, for example, for one identity (Betty) to plan to kill another (Carol) by over-dose, convinced that she (Betty) will survive. Psychiatrist Frank Putnam speaks for the whole field in adamantly opposing the tendency to regard such dissociated parts of the self as distinct individuals:

> The implicit and mistaken assumption made by many people is that alter personalities are separate people. This is a serious conceptual error that will lead to therapeutic error. Alter personalities are not separate people! Rather, I think that they are best conceptualized as examples of a fundamental and discrete unit of consciousness, the behavioral state.[21]

Putnam's term *behavioral states* encompasses a coherent set of emotions, memories, thoughts, sense of self, behavior, and relatedness to others. Psychiatrist Mardi Horowitz[22] has used the term *states of mind* in a similar way, and I will use Horowitz's term. I find Horowitz's idea of a "dreaded state of mind"[23] to be a helpful way of thinking about a dissociated "personality" or "alter." If you have dissociative identity disorder, my reference to "states of mind" may not feel right to you. But I believe that it may be the best way to think about your dissociative experience.

As described in Chapter 7 (Self), we all have radically different states of mind. Despite these wide variations, those of us who are not prone to the extremes of dissociation have some continuity in our sense of self. This sense of continuity is a developmental achievement.[24] In infancy, we all go through radical state changes, including crying, alert activity, quiet activity, drowsiness, and sleep. Only gradually do we learn to smooth over these shifts, and we learn that we are the same "self" in the various states: "By age 1, a child may well have added dozens of states and by adulthood may have hundreds of discrete states and is able to make transitions among them almost seamlessly."[25]

Beginning in infancy, emotions are important organizers of changes in state of mind. Over the course of development, our emotional states become more varied and refined. Yet traumatic experience can lead to overwhelming emotions. As a result, you may do everything possible to avoid these dreaded states of mind—and the memories, emotions, and relationships associated with them.[26] If you are able to use dissociation, you can ward off these states of mind to a degree. In the extreme, your experience can become thoroughly compartmentalized in the form of dissociative identity disorder. You may disown certain states of mind as "not me." You may come to think of these dreaded states of mind as "personalities" or separate "people." The idea that the states are separate people is especially appealing because it distances you from the intolerable experience. It is natural to wish that such horrors happened to *someone else*. Dissociative identity disorder is perhaps as close as you can come to realizing this desire.

Popular accounts have contributed favorably to bringing dissociative identity disorder into the open. A recent collection of first-person accounts, *Multiple Personality Disorder From the Inside Out,*[27] eloquently conveys the experience of many individuals. The popular literature has been a mixed blessing. The sometimes dramatic nature of the symptoms can easily lead to misunderstanding, and the disorder is often sensationalized. Unfortunately, dissociative identity disorder is not exotic; it is a common form of dissociative disorder reflecting the desperate coping responses of children overwhelmed by trauma:

> A preoccupation with the arresting phenomena of the personalities has given way to a grim realization that MPD [dissociative identity disorder] is no more than the attempt of a beleaguered youngster, unable to escape or defend against external adversity, to flee inwardly and create alternative selves and alternative constructs of reality that allow the possibility of psychological survival.[28]

The following overview of dissociative identity disorder includes diagnostic criteria, a brief historical perspective, a description of causes and development of the disorder, and its fluctuating course over the life span. I describe the gray areas between dissociative identity disorder and other forms of division of the self. I also address the question of the individual's responsibility for his or her behavior in dissociative states, and I conclude with an overview of the process of integration.

Diagnostic Criteria for Dissociative Identity Disorder

Central to dissociative identity disorder is "the presence of two or more distinct identities or personality states . . . [that] recurrently take control of behavior."[29] In addition, these identity shifts are accompanied by amnesia to a greater or lesser degree. I sometimes think of it this way: Dissociative identity disorder goes beyond dissociative amnesia to include behavior that is distinctly out of character during the amnestic gaps (e.g., a person who is usually shy goes to a party, climbs up on a table, and starts dancing).

Historical Perspective

There are many excellent historical accounts of the evolution of our understanding of dissociative identity disorder.[30] I provide only a brief sketch here, drawing largely on a recent review by psychologist George Greaves.[31]

The first detailed case of dissociative identity disorder was reported in 1791 (a German woman who spoke only French in dissociated states). Authors described a number of cases in the 19th century and, toward the latter part of the century, France was the center of a great deal of interest in dissociation. Pierre Janet, in the late 19th and early 20th centuries, developed both a thoroughly modern understanding of dissociation and an effective treatment approach.[32] Around the turn of the century in the United States, prominent psychologists William James and Morton Prince published case reports, and Janet came to speak at Harvard University—the first transatlantic conference on dissociation.

After this waxing of interest at the turn of the century, the focus on trauma and dissociation waned. Freud turned his attention from external trauma to internal conflict, developed the theory of psychoanalysis, and took psychiatry with him. For much of the 20th century, dissociative identity disorder was considered rare, and publications that dealt with it were few and far between. The publication of *The Three Faces of Eve* in 1957[33] brought the disorder back into public awareness, but Eve was considered an isolated case. Then the case of Sybil was published in the popular press in 1973[34] because publication was shunned by professional journals. During the 1970s, a small group of mental health professionals began seeing a large number of patients with dissociative identity disorder, but overall, the field remained unreceptive. Those who were open to seeing the disorder could not reconcile their experience with the mainstream professional belief that it was rare.

In 1980, however, several publications attesting to the prevalence of dissociative identity disorder appeared in the mainstream psychiatric literature, and the third edition of the psychiatric diagnostic manual, DSM-III,[35] included multiple personality disorder as a diagnosis, albeit described as rare. By the time the diagnostic criteria were revised in DSM-III-R in 1987, the manual noted, "Recent reports suggest that this disorder is not nearly so rare as it has commonly been thought to be." [36] Current estimates of prevalence range from 1% to 10% in psychiatric patients,[37] and psychiatrist Colin Ross and colleagues[38] recently concluded that "5% is a realistic minimum round figure for the frequency of multiple personality disorder on general adult psychiatric inpatient units."

The current burgeoning of interest in dissociation and dissociative identity disorder picks up where French psychiatry left off nearly a century ago. But controversy persists. Despite the wealth of professional literature and a substantial cadre of leaders in the field, some mental health professionals remain skeptical—both of the diagnosis of dissociative identity disorder and of the pervasiveness of childhood trauma as an etiological factor.[39] Skepticism about dissociative identity disorder parallels concerns about false memories, inasmuch as critics consistently argue that therapists inadvertently create dissociative identity disorder by suggesting to patients that they have the disorder.

I have little doubt that some therapists do inadvertently foster patients' misunderstanding. For example, one patient I evaluated frequently entered sadistic states of mind in which she tormented herself by burning her arm with a cigarette. Her therapist, apparently enamored with multiple personality disorder, suggested that she name this sadistic part of herself "Sadie." The patient came for an evaluation somewhat dubious about the diagnosis but stating that she had an alter personality named "Sadie." The therapist's encouragement for her to view herself in this way did not cause her to have dissociative identity disorder, but it added to her confusion about herself. And it is not just therapists who gravitate toward a diagnosis of dissociative identity disorder; some patients also gravitate toward it. I have observed that some patients who have a great deal of confusion about their varied and discordant states of mind lean toward seeing themselves as having dissociative identity disorder to gain a clearer sense of identity. I prefer to be conservative, emphasizing the broad spectrum of dissociation and the gray areas of diagnosis, affirming the diagnosis of dissociative identity disorder only in clear-cut cases. In addition, as many critics note, concern about dissociation and dissociative identity disorder should not blind the patient or the clinician to the other disorders that may contribute to the individual's symptoms.

Causes and Development of Dissociative Identity Disorder

Dissociative identity disorder is the most complex and severe of the dissociative disorders, and specialists believe that it is associated with the most severe traumatic experience.[40] Because dissociative identity disorder is the most elaborate form of dissociative self-protection, it makes sense that it has the most extreme instigation. The trauma is frequent and unpredictable, often sadistic and bizarre. Moreover, the mistreatment often occurs in a relationship with a caregiver, such as a parent, who is alternately loving and abusive.[41] Thus, it is virtually impossible for the child to form a coherent, integrated relationship with the caregiver.

But keep in mind that the causes of dissociative disorders, like those of PTSD, are complex.[42] Trauma is an important factor, but it is not the only one. Those individuals who are most prone to dissociate will probably develop the most elaborate dissociative disorders in coping with trauma. Just as less-severe stress may propel the anxiety-prone person into PTSD, less-severe stress may propel the dissociation-prone person into dissociative identity disorder. Just as extreme trauma is liable to precipitate PTSD in anyone, regardless of predisposition, extreme trauma may precipitate a severe dissociative disorder in anyone with *some* propensity to dissociate. We have a great deal to learn about how dissociative identity disorder develops, and we will be on more solid ground when we have systematic developmental research. I offer here a brief—admittedly speculative—sketch of how separate identities might evolve.

As described in Chapter 5 (Consciousness), dissociation has much in common with trance states. Two well-documented functions of trance are analgesia and posthypnotic amnesia. From the standpoint of self-protection, the ability to control pain and to block traumatic experience from memory would appear to be an ideal adaptation. Trances were not invented by hypnotists; hypnosis is a procedure for evoking this natural ability deliberately. You do not need a hypnotist to learn how to put yourself into a trance state; you may be able to do so spontaneously when you have a dire need.[43]

The first step in developing dissociative identity disorder is the employment of dissociation (or spontaneous self-hypnosis) as a way to block out trauma. Dissociative identity disorder develops by virtue of the *repeated* employment of trancelike states to cope with *repeated* stress or trauma. State-of-mind A, ordinary consciousness, is periodically interrupted by state-of-mind B, the dissociative state evoked to block pain and trauma. As in posthypnotic amnesia, when you return to state-of-mind A, you do not remember state-of-mind B. Using the image I proposed in Chapter 5, picture a defensive moat between the two states of mind.

With repeated alternation, state-of-mind B gradually becomes familiar. Eventually, a sense of continuity evolves, with a set of emotionally related memories and a sense of history. Gradually, this state may evolve a distinct sense of *identity*, including characteristic emotions, a sense of "self," and a way of relating to the abusive person.

An important step for many persons in the development of dissociative identity disorder is giving the altered state of mind and identity a different *name*. This might be a descriptive name ("the scared child"), a characteristic role (the "protector"), or a proper name ("Betty"). Assigning a name to a different state of mind consolidates the process, lending some order to fragmentation. Once consolidated, the dissociative process in dissociative identity disorder can be employed more automatically. Whenever Alice must confront the traumatic situation, Betty takes over to cope with it. Once the event is over, Alice resumes control, with no recollection of what happened. Alice may only know that there is a gap in her experience. She may consider such gaps normal—believing that everyone has them.

But the dissociation rarely stops with two segregated states of mind. With repeated and prolonged traumatic experience, there may be a complex cascading of identities. Once invented, the self-protective creation of identities can be employed again and again. Imagine what happens when Betty encounters a new form of traumatic experience for which she is not prepared. For example, abuse by a father may be followed by assault by a brother. It is only natural for Betty to employ the same defense as Alice; thus, Carol is created to deal with the new traumatic situation. This compartmentalization of experience can be employed over the course of many years to deal with any and all stressors. At the extreme, an individual may develop a complex disorder with hundreds of identities and personality fragments.[44] This compartmentalization of the self, supported by varying degrees of amnesia, is simply an effort to avoid dreaded states of mind—and the associated "black holes" of memory—as much of the time as possible.

Course of Dissociative Identity Disorder

The last decade has witnessed a surge of awareness of dissociative identity disorder in adult psychiatric patients, and now there is a growing awareness of dissociative identity disorder and other dissociative disturbances in children.[45] But it is by no means common for this disorder to become known early in life and to be continuously evident throughout adulthood. On the contrary, one of the hallmarks of the disorder is its hidden quality. Dissociative identity disorder is embedded in a history of secrecy, and several years typically elapse in the course of psychiatric treatment before it is diagnosed.[46]

Psychiatrist Richard Kluft[47] points out that the difficulties in diagnosing dissociative identity disorder stem from a confusing symptom picture and a fluctuating course of illness. Patients with this disorder, like those with PTSD, often present a diagnostic challenge because of the wide array of symptoms and disorders associated with trauma. The presence of an exceptionally large number of symptoms is itself a possible indicator of dissociative identity disorder. The other disorders (anxiety, depression, substance abuse) will be diagnosed, and treatment will focus on prominent symptoms (suicide attempts or self-injurious behavior). The trauma history and dissociative identity disorder may remain hidden. The resilient person spared extreme stress in adulthood may maintain control for years—staying out of dreaded states of mind, suppressing all dissociated identities. Or the dissociated identities may influence the person (e.g., by voices) without taking full control of behavior. The individual who cannot avoid dissociating may nevertheless become adept at concealing his or her dividedness from others:

◆ A patient participating in a diagnostic interview for dissociative symptoms suddenly switched from a rather depressed and guarded state to a highly animated state. She had been gazing at the floor, talking in a monotone. In a moment's time, she looked up at the examiner—alert and animated. She gave no sign of anxiety or apprehension. The examiner began inquiring about her orientation to the situation. For example, he asked her if she knew who he was. With pointed questioning, her effort to conceal her disorientation gave way. She acknowledged that she had no idea who the examiner was. She had no idea where she was. She had come halfway across the country for the evaluation and, as far as she knew, she was still in her home state.

Although the patient's disorientation was striking, it was less dramatic than her seeming lack of anxiety in the situation. She was quite accustomed to suddenly "coming to" in completely unfamiliar situations. She described experiences of suddenly finding herself in a resort with a stranger and of suddenly being confronted by a mugger holding a knife at her throat. She was extremely intelligent, competent, and adept interpersonally. She had always been able to talk herself out of such tight spots, quickly catching on to the demands of whatever situation she found herself in, despite her amnesia for the preceding events.

The severity of dissociation will vary, depending on the level of stress in the individual's life. Dissociative identity disorder may therefore wax and wane, and it may remain hidden or disguised for extended periods. Eventually, unmanageable stress or trauma in later life—or judicious diagnostic efforts—bring the disorder to light.

Gray Areas for Diagnosis

◆ A middle-aged man asked for a consultation regarding dissociation because he wondered if he had multiple personality disorder. He described radical changes in his state of mind and behavior. He described himself as having several personalities with little sense of integration. He was a competent executive at work; sometimes he was highly logical, whereas at other times he could be aggressive and forceful. At home, he was alternately loving and rageful. At other times, he cowered as if he were a frightened child, curling up on a couch and holding a blanket. Most problematic, the slightest provocation could launch him into a tirade. During these tirades, he felt completely out of control of his behavior, as if he were outside of his body and watching himself from a distance. He came to think of this part of himself as "the madman," as if it were another person inside him.

This man was not the first in his family to have problems with explosiveness. He somewhat proudly stated that he was the last in a long line of males with explosive tempers. He had been intimidated and beaten by his father in childhood, as his father had been before him. It is not unlikely that this intergenerational pattern was sustained by temperamental factors as well as by learning and role modeling.

The patient frequently experienced radical changes in his behavior, his feelings, and his sense of identity. He had named some of these various experiences (e.g., "the madman"), perhaps to lend some order to the seeming chaos caused by his shifting states of mind. He did not report amnesia for these personality changes. The examiner explained the continuum of dissociation to him, noting that he fell short of having multiple personality disorder.

As this example illustrates, a sense of self-continuity is difficult to maintain in the face of traumatic experience. With trauma, the state of mind shifts radically. Feelings are extreme. Consciousness changes. Relationships turn 180 degrees. Where do we draw the line between radical changes in state of mind and dissociative identity disorder? The presence of amnesia is one way to draw the line. Many individuals feel as if they are "not themselves" in different states of mind, but they remember these changes. Or they may be amnestic for certain aspects of dissociated experience, but there is no indication that their behavior or experience during these states is out of character. These gray areas are properly considered "dissociation" because the sense of self is to some degree separated from the experience.

Many persons who struggle with dissociation and radical shifts in mood and sense of identity *feel* as if they do not know who they are. Their sense of identity is unclear. The psychiatric classification system has a gray-area category, "dissociative disorder not otherwise specified," for such instances. Sometimes, trying to draw the line can become a matter of semantics or of individual preference. Deciding where to draw the line is not as important as recognizing that the person uses various forms of dissociation to cope with traumatic experience and to blunt or stay out of dreaded states of mind.

Responsibility for Dissociative Behavior ◆ ◆ ◆ ◆ ◆

Who is responsible for actions in dissociative states? This is a psychological question, an ethical question, and a legal question. The question is not unique to dissociative disorders. Is the intoxicated person responsible for injuring someone in a car wreck? Should a person be incarcerated for a crime committed in a psychotic state? More generally, is "mental illness" a legitimate defense? These issues are not new, but they have arisen with particular poignancy in relation to dissociative identity disorder.[48]

Should the individual be held responsible for actions in dissociated states of mind? Yes. To believe otherwise is to make treatment impossible.

Affected individuals often feel that they are punished for their behavior in dissociated states, as if they were being blamed for something someone else did. Certainly, behavior in altered states of mind often results in considerable subsequent suffering. But any person may suffer in one state of mind for actions done in another (e.g., regretting the consequences of angry words or feeling remorse for an injury caused by driving while intoxicated).

Accepting responsibility is a major step toward continuity and integration of experience. At first, you may need to accept responsibility *in principle,* even if you have little sense of control in practice. Commitment to treatment entails some acceptance of responsibility, because it attests to an investment in gaining control. You can learn to exercise some control over the switching process, and you can exercise control over destructive behavior in altered states of mind. But it is not easy.

While advocating responsibility, those who treat patients with dissociative disorders must have compassion for their patients' experience of helplessness, and they must have an understanding of the processes that contribute to the felt lack of control.[49] Psychiatrist Seymour Halleck has addressed this problem with considerable wisdom:

> In assessing responsibility in the clinical setting, we need not invoke the harsh, "all or none" morality required by the criminal justice system. We can acknowledge that many of our patients, particularly those with severe mental disorders, can make socially acceptable choices only at the expense of a certain amount of pain and suffering. This does not, however, mean that they are without choice. It merely means that their choices are hard ones.[50]

Although the idea of accepting responsibility for dissociated behavior is threatening, the prospect of disowning responsibility is even more threatening. Being unable to take responsibility for your behavior—or being told that you are not responsible for your behavior—would promote a profound sense of helplessness and dependency on others. As psychiatrist John Beahrs[51] puts it, "to be absolved of responsibility or treated as special is ironically to be denied basic humanness."

The entire treatment process is aimed toward restoring a sense of control and the sense of responsibility that goes with it. Treating the whole person as responsible for all of his or her actions not only enhances this process; it is a prerequisite for it. As Halleck[52] states, "all schools of therapy are based on the idea that people will behave better and show psychological improvement if they are told they are responsible for their conduct and are held maximally responsible." He concludes that the ideal approach "would emphasize the patient's capacity to behave in a socially acceptable manner from the first day of treatment, while recognizing that it is extremely difficult for him/her to do so." [53] In a similar vein, Beahrs[54] concludes that we should "honor that most precious of all human possessions: basic autonomy, with its fundamental correlate, personal responsibility."

Achieving Continuity and Integration   ◆ ◆ ◆ ◆ ◆

Integration entails being able to experience feelings and to remember life events without the protective mechanism of dissociation. To become more integrated, you need to develop the capacity to enter states of mind (feelings, memories) that you have avoided because they have been overwhelming. Ordinarily, this is a slow and gradual process. You developed self-protective mechanisms for good reasons, and the mere decision to seek treatment is no reason to give them up immediately. You may need to do a lot of groundwork before opening up experiences, memories, and feelings that have been unbearable.[55] Most important, you need a good therapeutic relationship and a solid support network. Then you will be prepared to take the many steps that integration entails.[56] I describe a few of these key steps here.

Making the Diagnosis

For a long period, perhaps years, you may have been treated for a wide range of symptoms while having little awareness and understanding of dissociation. You may have become resigned to feelings of unreality, amnesia, lost time, belongings unaccounted for. You may have viewed such experience as normal. The first step is the awareness that something is wrong, that you have a diagnosable and treatable illness, and that you can find professional help.

Throughout medicine, diagnoses can be confirmed by laboratory tests—blood work, X rays, electrocardiograms, electroencephalograms. Tests are indispensable, but only to diagnosticians familiar with the illness being diagnosed. So it is in the specialty of psychiatry, and so it is in the area of trauma-related disorders. You must find a clinician experienced in the diagnosis and treatment of dissociative disorders. And finding someone who is knowledgeable is not necessarily easy. This relatively new field is producing a rapidly evolving literature. Those who have been in practice for years will have had no training in dissociative disorders, and even those coming into the field now may not receive much specialized training in the area.

There are no laboratory tests for dissociation, but several good diagnostic tools have evolved.[57] I'll give you two examples—one a brief questionnaire and the other an extensive interview. Eve Carlson and Frank Putnam developed the Dissociative Experiences Scale to provide a brief means of detecting dissociative disorders.[58] The Dissociative Experiences Scale is a 28-item questionnaire that most individuals can complete in about 10 minutes. The questionnaire measures three general features of dissociation: tendency to be preoccupied or absorbed in fantasy—in effect, tuned out; depersonalization and derealization; and amnesia and actions in dissociative states.[59] The Dissociative Experiences Scale was not designed to make a firm diagnosis of dissociative disorder; rather, it was intended to alert the diagnosing clinician to the possibility of a dissociative disorder. When the results of the Dissociative Experiences Scale are positive, this indicates the need for a more extensive evaluation.

Psychiatrist Marlene Steinberg developed the most refined method for diagnosing dissociative disorders—the Structured Clinical Interview for DSM-IV Dissociative Disorders.[60] This systematic interview typically ranges in length from 30 minutes to 2 hours, and it covers several aspects of dissociation: amnesia, depersonalization, derealization, identity confusion (inner experience of shifting identity), and identity alteration (the expression of identity shifts in overt behavior). Steinberg designed the interview to yield a specific DSM-IV diagnosis.

Diagnosis is not something to be done to you; it is a process in which you should be an active participant. My mentor, psychologist Paul Pruyser,[61] described the ideal of a "diagnostic partnership" in which the patient becomes "fully engaged in self-diagnosis with the help of a particular expert." Such methods as the Dissociative Experiences Scale and Steinberg's Structured Interview provide an opportunity to engage in such a diagnostic partnership. These methods allow you to articulate your experience and, as you do so, the clinician working with you can begin to educate you about various aspects of dissociation. This process can be highly reassuring, because you will immediately discover that your experience is not utterly unique or foreign; on the contrary, it is widely shared by others who have undergone trauma and coped by dissociating.[62]

Of the various dissociative disorders, the diagnosis of *multiple personality disorder* is often most alarming. Perhaps the new and more accurate term, *dissociative identity disorder,* will be somewhat less so. But being told that you have the disorder is one thing; accepting it is another. Understandably, you are likely to be particularly frightened of having a disorder that has been so sensationalized. Patients often go back and forth between acceptance and denial. Indeed, alternating between acceptance and doubt may go on for months or even years. In the long run, as is the case for any other illness, denial must give way to acceptance for treatment to be viable.

Building Bridges Among Dissociated States

If we think of dissociated states as separated by defensive moats, treatment entails building bridges. You may begin treatment with no direct awareness of altered states; they are blocked by amnesia. Initial awareness may occur by means of "external communication." Other persons, including therapists, may let you know what you have said, felt, and done in altered states. You may consent to audiotaping or videotaping and then listen to the audiotapes or watch the videotapes with your therapist.[63] I have found videotaping to be helpful not only early in the treatment process but also later on. Comparing earlier and later videotapes can underscore the changes that have occurred over the course of treatment.

Another useful form of external communication is "journaling," or keeping a diary—that is, writing down your experiences and actions in different states of mind.[64] In this way, you learn about your behavior in altered states, and you develop some understanding of what takes place during amnestic gaps. Ths external communication builds a greater sense of continuity in experience, filling in the gaps with information. Journaling is especially useful because it enables you to take responsibility for keeping track of your experience, and you can do so without relying exclusively on others.

At some point, you must also establish conscious bridges ("internal communication") by opening your mind to your experiences in altered states.[65] For example, you can be invited to listen for the voice of a dissociated identity, and you can learn to identify that voice. I helped the patient Joan (described earlier) to learn to identify the dissociated state, Mary:

◆ When she was in the Mary state, I asked the patient to think of a phrase she could "say" in her mind to communicate with Joan. Mary came up with the phrase, "The sky is blue." After Mary switched states—back to Joan—I waited as we talked. After a little time had passed, she paused and looked away from me, appearing reflective and somewhat puzzled. I asked her if she had heard a voice, and she nodded. I asked her what she heard and she replied, "The sky is blue." I described how she had planned, in the altered state Mary, to say this phrase. The patient was initially shocked, because identifying the voice with a dissociated state came as a revelation. She had heard this voice for years, and now she could understand its significance. The bridge had been opened.

Such internal communication can evolve into "co-consciousness"; rather than completely tuning out or "going away," you can remain aware (as if observing from the back of the head) when you are in a dissociated state. As one patient described, she could be "semiconscious" instead of unconscious when she became angry. Although she did not feel fully in control, she was able to know what she had done and experienced. In effect, instead of becoming amnestic, she felt depersonalized. After some preparation and some degree of integration, much of the work in therapy sessions is conducted this way, with awareness extending beyond any one facet of the personality.

Conflict Management

Communication among various parts of the self sets the stage for a further step toward integration—namely, cooperation and conflict management.[66] This problem is hardly exclusive to dissociative identity disorder; all of us must reconcile conflicting desires and decide how to allocate our time and resources. Occasionally, we all wage internal battles about the proper course of action at a given moment. We all have competing states of mind. In dissociative identity disorder, these battles occur more frequently and are more polarized. At worst, you may experience a sense of internal pandemonium, being barraged by voices of dissociated parts of yourself vying for control. You are liable to take one course of action at one moment and the opposite course at the next.

Communication among dissociated identities sets the stage for compromise and reconciliation. Agreements must be made about time sharing (what lengths of time you will be in various states of mind) and the allocation of roles and tasks (you may not drive a car or be at work in a childlike state). In this fashion, you can progress toward relative harmony among conflicting goals and wishes. Of course, harmony is only relative for anyone. Integration does not put an end to conflict, it *heightens awareness of conflict.*

Expressing Traumatic Experience

The process of establishing communication and reconciling conflicts among various states of mind is a crucial part of the work with dissociative disorders, but it is not the main agenda. The essence of the work—and the hardest part for patients and therapists—is to gradually remember and express the traumatic experience that initially led to the dissociation and divisions.[67] Dissociated states of mind were created to cope with and contain trauma; these dissociated states must be brought to the fore so that you can come to terms with the feelings and memories.

Opening your mind to the full range of current and past experience permits a sense of history, identity, and continuity of ongoing experience to evolve. In essence, therapy fosters openness to a broader range of feelings, memories, and ideas. In this sense, psychotherapy for dissociative identity disorder resembles exploratory psychotherapy for other disorders. As you accept a broader range of experience, dissociative dividedness diminishes. You no longer live in fear of your own mind, dreading dissociated states. You can shift more flexibly and smoothly from one state of mind to another. As this occurs, you become able to wrestle more freely with unavoidable—and often painful—human conflicts.

Working with traumatic memories in dissociative identity disorder poses the same hazards as it does in PTSD; both are posttraumatic disorders.[68] Most important, the work should be done at a *gradual pace* that enables you to establish control over your feelings rather than being overwhelmed by them.[69] Plunging in too quickly and too deeply can backfire, leading to retraumatization and causing more rather than less dissociation and compartmentalization. Your capacity to function in your daily life should be a guide to the pace of your work on traumatic memories. If intrusive experiences undermine your day-to-day coping, you are probably moving too quickly. Understandably, you may find a slow pace frustrating because of your wish to put the trauma behind you. But keep in mind Kluft's[70] words of wisdom: "The slower you go, the faster you get there."

Integration

On the basis of his extensive experience with patients who have dissociative identity disorder, Kluft[71] makes a compelling case for *integration* as the best outcome of treatment. The process of integration begins with the correct diagnosis and the move toward understanding and accepting it. How far should integration go? Ideally, as far as it goes for anyone— toward a greater sense of wholeness and unity without prominent dissociation. You may be left with hundreds of states of mind, but your consciousness expands so that you don't completely identify yourself with any one of them.[72] You can feel angry at someone and concerned about her feelings at the same time. As you tolerate more conflict, shift more flexibly from one state to another, and develop a more encompassing perspective on yourself, the extremes can become more diluted.

As with all else, this reconciliation of contradictory states of mind is easier said than done. Particularly in the early stages of treatment, many persons with dissociative identity disorder are extremely frightened of integration. It means giving up long-established self-protective strategies. And many patients feel that valued parts of themselves will die or be killed. No sensible person would want to give up self-protection or to destroy parts of the self. Wariness of integration is therefore utterly natural. My own view is that we don't get rid of parts of our selves or lose the capacity to get into various states of mind; rather, *we add new possibilities.*

There are other obstacles to integration. Some persons may not be in a position to undertake the arduous treatment needed for integration. The standard treatment of dissociative identity disorder is long-term, twice-weekly individual psychotherapy, often in combination with hypnosis. This is a costly enterprise, and many patients have long exhausted financial resources for treatment by the time the correct diagnosis is made.[73] But time and expense are not the only obstacles. Some persons may treasure the separateness of dissociated identities and may elect to settle for better harmony and cooperation. For some individuals with dissociative identity disorder, the various dissociated parts of the self become like companions, and the prospect of life without them appears lonely. Of course, the degree of integration to be sought should be decided by the patient, not the therapist.

Although more complete integration may be an unthinkable prospect early in treatment, working on coping with traumatic experience and building bridges among different states of mind lessens the need for dissociation and renders separateness less appealing. The course of therapy may bring about a natural, gradual blending—an opening of all of the mind to realms of previously excluded experience. Expressing traumatic experience and establishing communication may be all that is needed for separateness among identities to recede. Some individuals, however, find special techniques helpful in the final process of merging between dissociated identities.[74] Hypnosis can be used to facilitate such fusion experiences—for example, with images of colors blending or aspects of the self hugging one another and becoming one.

Of course, like any other person, an individual with dissociative identity disorder does not attain a "fusion" of all parts of the personality or a complete sense of "oneness." Owing to our inherent complexity and dividedness—our many brains and the hyperastronomical number of combinations of connections among neurons—we are all forever divided within ourselves to varying degrees.

Other Disorders

Having diabetes does not prevent you from breaking your leg or getting the flu. And hypertension can make you more vulnerable to stroke. So it is with psychiatric disorders; most are not mutually exclusive. A wide range of psychiatric disorders has been observed in conjunction with PTSD,[1] and large-scale population studies have shown that roughly 80% of those with PTSD have at least one additional psychiatric disorder.[2] One group of researchers observed that 95% of all patients with dissociative identity disorder had received one or more psychiatric or neurological diagnoses before the dissociative diagnosis.[3]

Cause and effect is somewhat tricky to discern here. Trauma certainly increases the risk for PTSD; it may or may not increase the risk for other disorders, each of which has its own complex etiology. PTSD may increase the risk for other disorders, such as depression or alcoholism, or other disorders may increase the risk for PTSD.[4] Although trauma is not the exclusive cause of other disorders, it will affect their course and expression.

A review of trauma-related psychiatric disorders could easily become a psychiatry textbook. Lest that happen here, I limit this chapter to a brief review of a small group of disorders commonly seen in conjunction with traumatic experience—namely, anxiety disorders, depressive disorders, substance abuse, somatization disorder, sexual dysfunction, eating disorders, and personality disorders.

Anxiety Disorders ◆ ◆ ◆ ◆ ◆ ◆ ◆ ◆ ◆ ◆

PTSD is one of several anxiety disorders. The "hyperarousal" symptoms of PTSD *are* anxiety symptoms. Because numbing alternates with hyperarousal, PTSD could be classified as a dissociative disorder, but the prominent anxiety symptoms have held sway in its classification with other anxiety disorders.[5]

Anxiety is a prominent emotional reaction to traumatic experience. I would argue that anxiety is *always* the first emotional response, although it may be followed instantly by fear, anger, or shame. Several forms of anxiety disorder may be seen in conjunction with traumatic experience, and they overlap with symptoms of PTSD. For a long while, anxiety may be the tip of the iceberg. The symptoms of hyperarousal may occur without any memory of traumatic experience. When that happens, an anxiety disorder other than PTSD will be the initial diagnosis. PTSD will be diagnosed only when the traumatic origins of the anxiety come to light and intrusive symptoms such as flashbacks occur. Three anxiety disorders besides PTSD may be consequences of trauma: generalized anxiety, panic, and phobia.

Generalized Anxiety

DSM-IV defines *generalized anxiety disorder* as including excessive anxiety and worry along with a number of anxiety symptoms: restlessness or feeling keyed up or on edge; being easily fatigued; having difficulty concentrating or your mind going blank; irritability; muscle tension; and sleep disturbance.[6] Anxiety is *generalized* in the sense that the individual feels anxious in a wide range of situations. This disorder entails a relatively chronic experience of anxiety—that is, with symptoms present more days than not for at least 6 months. Generalized anxiety may be a response to trauma, and generalized anxiety disorder may be diagnosed if intrusive PTSD symptoms are absent.

Panic

DSM-IV defines a *panic attack* as an abrupt onset of intense fear with several cardinal physical symptoms: palpitations, pounding heart, or accelerated heart rate; sweating; trembling or shaking; sensations of shortness of breath or smothering; a feeling of choking; chest pain or discomfort; nausea or abdominal distress; feeling dizzy, unsteady, lightheaded, or faint; derealization or depersonalization; fear of losing control or going crazy; fear of dying; numbness or tingling sensations; and chills or hot flushes.[7] Panic *disorder* is diagnosed when recurrent panic attacks lead to anxiety about the prospect of further attacks.

Extreme bursts of arousal akin to panic attacks may occur in conjunction with flashbacks,[8] in which case PTSD rather than panic disorder would be diagnosed. Emotion may be evoked unconsciously and virtually instantaneously when environmental cues trigger memories associated with trauma. Thus, an individual might feel panicky without any awareness of a link to prior traumatic experience. As long as the traumatic basis of the panic remains obscure, panic disorder may be diagnosed, because there are many other causes of panic besides trauma.

Phobia

Not everyone who is exposed to trauma develops PTSD. It is not uncommon for persons who have had an isolated traumatic experience to develop a phobic reaction to the traumatizing situation. For example, an individual who has been in an automobile accident may develop a driving phobia. Children who have been severely bitten by a dog may develop phobias in relation to dogs or other pets. Such reactions could be construed as posttraumatic simple phobias.[9]

It is also not unusual for persons who have repeated panic attacks to develop a pattern of avoiding the places where they have experienced these attacks. At worst, the individual may become *agoraphobic*—afraid to travel, to be in public places, or even to be out of the home alone. The same process could occur in relation to panic and flashbacks associated with PTSD, as implied by the finding that agoraphobia sometimes occurs in conjunction with PTSD.[10]

Depressive Disorders   ◆ ◆ ◆ ◆ ◆ ◆ ◆ ◆ ◆

Because many of the effects of traumatic experience are depressing, it is little wonder that depression is commonly diagnosed in conjunction with PTSD and dissociative disorders. Traumatic experience is damaging to self-esteem. Self-loathing, shame, and guilt all fuel depression. Imposed helplessness can become *learned* helplessness, contributing to an inclination to give up in the face of stress. A common response to traumatic experience at the hands of other persons is interpersonal isolation. The loneliness and the sense of deprivation and loss associated with isolation are paramount contributors to depression.

In addition to the psychologically depressing effects of traumatic experience, chronic stress contributes to depression on the neurophysiological level.[11] As with a host of psychiatric disorders, genetic predisposition and life experience can interact. Some individuals are more vulnerable to disruptions of their brain biochemistry that render them more susceptible to depressing effects of trauma and stress.

The broad and somewhat fuzzy concept of "depression" covers a wide range of severity, from feeling mildly glum or blue to being incapacitated and unable to get out of bed. Depression may also be short-lived or enduring. DSM-IV distinguishes two main types of depression: major depression (severe and acute) and dysthymic disorder (more mild and long lasting).

Major Depression

Major depressive disorder involves not only the psychological experience of depression but also conspicuous biological signs. Primary symptoms listed in DSM-IV are depressed mood and a markedly diminished interest and pleasure in daily activities. Other symptoms of major depression include feelings of worthlessness or guilt, problems concentrating and making decisions, and recurrent thoughts of death, including suicidal thinking and impulses. In addition, major depression is associated with physiological changes, including weight loss or gain, insomnia (or hyper-somnia, sleeping too much), agitation or retarded motor activity, and fatigue or loss of energy.

Dysthymic Disorder

Thymia refers to mood. *Eu*thymic means good or stable mood; *dys*thymic means disrupted or perturbed mood. Dysthymia is not as severe or incapacitating as major depression, but it is an *enduring* state of depression, diagnosed only after 2 years or more of disturbed mood. The symptoms of dysthymia overlap with those of major depression. They include low self-esteem, low energy, problems with concentration and decision making, feelings of hopelessness, problems with sleep, and low appetite or overeating.[12] Note that these symptoms overlap considerably with the various effects of trauma delineated in Part II of this book. Also, as is obvious from their overlapping symptoms, dysthymia may shade into major depression. Persons who are dysthymic and who also have episodes of more acute depression are sometimes considered to have "double depression."

Substance Abuse   ◆ ◆ ◆ ◆ ◆ ◆ ◆ ◆ ◆

Substance abuse is a frequent problem for persons with a history of traumatic experience and PTSD.[13] The prevalence of substance abuse in Vietnam veterans has been well documented.[14] In addition, several studies have shown a high incidence of substance abuse in persons who were sexually abused.[15]

Substance abuse can be construed as part of the avoidance behavior associated with PTSD.[16] Alcohol is widely used to numb feelings of anxiety and other forms of distress. Opiates (heroin) and marijuana are also used for blunting intolerable emotions. Many professionals view such substance abuse as an attempt to control emotion by "self-medicating." People use drugs because they *work:* They attenuate stress-related arousal in the central nervous system.[17]

Yet addiction becomes counterproductive. Drugs offer short-term relief but contribute to long-term dysfunction. Avoidance behavior is understandable, but it interferes with active coping and resolution. By avoiding, you are temporarily blotting out the problem rather than learning how to solve it. Moreover, these substances further disrupt physiology, leading to medical and psychological complications. Alcohol, for example, counters anxiety and fear because it depresses central nervous system functioning. Depression is a common effect of traumatic experience. Chronic alcohol use can thus make the depression worse. As with the abuse of any substance, you trade one type of problem for another.

Somatization Disorder ◆ ◆ ◆ ◆ ◆ ◆ ◆ ◆ ◆

Many persons who have undergone trauma and its associated physiological disruption develop serious and persistent physical symptoms, albeit often short of diagnosable disease.[18] *Soma* refers to the body; *somatization* refers to the bodily expression of emotions and conflicts. *Somatization disorder* entails a wide range of symptoms in several areas (pain, gastrointestinal, sexual, and neurological) occurring over a span of several years. A DSM-IV diagnosis of somatization disorder requires these symptoms to be unexplainable on the basis of diagnosable medical conditions or diseases (and not attributable to drug abuse or medication).

Somatization disorder does not entail diagnosable disease like that associated with identifiable pathogens or tissue damage. Rather, symptoms of somatization are related to stress. *This does not mean that the illness is only psychological, imaginary, or "all in your head."* On the contrary, these disorders are presumably related to substantial *physiological* disruption associated with traumatic and stressful experience. As described in Chapter 3, attachment provides the comforting and soothing needed to help regulate physiological arousal. Traumatic experience can disrupt attachment and interfere with such physiological self-regulation.

Stress has often been linked to disease. For example, disease may develop in the wake of a significant loss. Despite decades of research, we still have much to learn about the specific mechanisms by which stress eventuates in disease. Stress has dramatic (and complex) effects on hormone secretion and the immune system.[19] The role of stress is indirect, and in various organ systems, stress interacts with may other factors such as genetic vulnerability and subclinical disease. Stress may be a minor player in the equation, or it may be a more major player by tipping the balance.

Fortunately, there is no direct link between traumatic stress and disease; by no means is disease a common outcome of stress. Were it otherwise, our species would not have endured. Yet we have ample reason to believe that stress undermines health, albeit less dramatically and less irreversibly than disease. Psychiatrist Herbert Weiner distinguishes *disease* from *ill health*.[20] Persons in ill health do not feel well. They feel sick, and they go to doctors. They often fear that they have a disease, because they know that their body is out of kilter. Ill health takes many forms and includes a wide variety of physical symptoms: sleep disturbance, hyperventilation, fatigue, nausea, constipation, diarrhea, weight loss, vomiting, irregular heartbeat, fainting, weakness, dizziness, headache, abdominal pain, chest pain, heartburn, joint pain, stiffness, and muscular pain. At worst, although falling short of disease, these physiological symptoms can be incapacitating. The afflicted person may become bedridden and unable to carry out normal functions and responsibilities. Of course, individuals vary widely in their physiological response to stress. Presumably, these individual differences are partly genetic. We each have our own pattern of physiological arousal, and we all seem to have our physiological "weak links." [21]

Something, if not disease, *is* physically wrong. Unfortunately, medicine deals less adeptly with ill health than with disease. Medical interventions may be of some palliative help with respect to some forms of ill health. Specific medical interventions may be targeted at specific symptoms (e.g., analgesics for pain), but it is the whole person who is ill. There is therefore no overall curative medical intervention, because the problems are so complex, and the specific connections between stressful experiences and various forms of ill health have yet to be fully understood. The links are extremely complex because stress perturbs the natural balances among myriad neurotransmitters, hormones, and immune functions, potentially altering communication and interaction among all the body's organ systems.[22]

Although symptom-oriented treatment may be of some benefit, lowering the general level of emotional distress is the best remedy for ill health. To the extent that needed soothing was not provided at the time of the traumatic experience, the individual must learn self-soothing. A number of methods of self-regulation will be described in Chapter 13 (Self-Regulation). As you work on alleviating stress, it is important not to dismiss physical symptoms as being "all in your head" and thereby to fail to obtain proper medical evaluations. It is always important to be attuned to physical symptoms and to rule out diagnosable and treatable medical conditions.

Sexual Dysfunction   ◆ ◆ ◆ ◆ ◆ ◆ ◆ ◆ ◆

As just discussed, traumatic experience may have an impact on all organ systems, and disturbance of sexual functioning may be part of the somatic consequences of trauma. Sexual arousal is mediated by the autonomic (involuntary) nervous system. As noted in the Appendix, the autonomic nervous system is conventionally divided into the sympathetic and the parasympathetic branches. These two branches are somewhat reciprocal; activating one tends to deactivate the other. The sympathetic branch mediates the fight-or-flight response. Sexual responsiveness, on the other hand, depends on parasympathetic activation. Like your mind, your nervous system has a hard time being prepared for fight or flight and being sexually responsive at the same time.

To the degree that sexual responsiveness and fight-or-flight preparedness are incompatible, it is hardly surprising that traumatic experience interferes with sexuality. The hyperarousal that characterizes anxiety and PTSD may interfere with sexuality, even when the trauma was not specifically sexual. To the extent that sexual responsiveness depends on a sense of safety and relaxation, any resurgence of trauma takes its toll. And it is not just the hyperarousal that interferes; so do depression, numbing, and dissociation. Sexual pleasure depends on being actively engaged, tuned in, and fully aware of the here and now. Detachment diminishes the sense of relatedness, as well as the sensory aspects of sexuality.

Sexual responsiveness involves a gradual sequence of arousal that can be interrupted at any point by depression, anxiety, distress, shame, anger, or intrusive experience. Sexual dysfunctions are diagnosed on the basis of the stage of the arousal sequence at which the interruption occurs. At worst, numbing may be associated with a lack of desire or interest in sex (hypoactive sexual desire disorder) or a complete aversion and avoidance of all sexual contact (sexual aversion disorder). Or, even when there is desire and interest, trauma may interfere with sexual excitement—for example, manifested in an inability to attain or maintain lubrication in the female (female sexual arousal disorder) or erection in the male (male erectile disorder). Or the interruption may occur at the final stage in the sequence, such that the individual is able to be sexually excited but unable to achieve orgasm (female or male orgasmic disorder).

Sexual trauma, such as rape or incest, interferes more directly with sexual arousal and pleasure. Because of its similarity to the earlier trauma, sexual contact—or even the *anticipation* of sex—may trigger intrusive memories or flashbacks. At worst, some individuals who have been sexually traumatized may relive the trauma in the context of the sexual relationship. For example, a woman who was sexually abused by her father may see his face instead of her husband's whenever she has intercourse with her husband.

Rape and Sexual Functioning

The potentially traumatizing impact of rape has been amply documented in the literature.[23] Several years before PTSD was added to the psychiatric nomenclature in 1980, Ann Burgess and Lynda Holmstrom[24] delineated the *rape trauma syndrome*. As with any trauma, the anxiety symptoms associated with rape may interfere with sexual functioning. But Burgess and Holmstrom also noted that rape specifically led to a crisis in women's sexual life, with women experiencing fear when they were expected to resume sexual relations. For many women, it was not possible to resume normal sexual activity, and this difficulty was likely to persist well beyond the acute phase of the trauma.

When Judith Becker and her colleagues[25] studied sexual dysfunction associated with rape and incest, they found problems in all phases of sexual arousal: fear of sex, desire dysfunction, and arousal dysfunction (with orgasmic dysfunction less common). Like Burgess and Holmstrom, Becker and her colleagues were struck by the persistence of sexual difficulties. Although the problems may be most severe in the weeks immediately after rape, some women continue to experience difficulty for months and even years.

In light of the potentially detrimental effects of rape, it is important to note that there are effective treatment approaches for rape-related trauma.[26] These cognitive-behavioral techniques include systematic desensitization (imagining the traumatic event while maintaining a state of relaxation), prolonged exposure (imagining the rape scene vividly and describing it out loud, listening to tape recordings of the sessions, and undergoing exposure to feared and avoided situations that instead are safe), and stress inoculation (learning to cope with anxiety by using relaxation, thought stopping, correcting mistaken beliefs, and role playing). With treatment, persistent sexual difficulties need not be inevitable.

Incest and Sexual Functioning

It is hardly surprising that incest may interfere with sexual functioning.[27] Recent research conducted by psychologist Elaine Westerlund[28] found that only a minority of women with a history of incest were free of sexual problems, and that women with such a history report less sexual satisfaction than other women. A key finding is that self-blame (assuming responsibility for the incest) contributes greatly to problems with subsequent sexual adjustment.

Although much research has focused on the relation between incest and sexual *behavior,* there is less understanding of the impact of incest on sexual *experience.* Westerlund conducted research specifically to illuminate women's subjective experience of sexuality. For this reason, her study is worth describing in detail. She used a comprehensive questionnaire combined with in-depth interviews of incest survivors. The effects of incest on sexual functioning vary greatly but share many common themes.

Westerlund discovered several common problem areas associated with a history of incest: negative body perceptions (seeing the body as dirty, bad, out of control; feeling betrayed by the body's arousal), problems with reproduction (apprehension about becoming a parent, reawakening of incest memories and experiences associated with giving birth and nursing); and guilt feelings about sexual fantasy (especially fantasy involving violence, force, humiliation, or pain, as well as fantasy involving the offender). Westerlund found that a majority of women reported difficulties with sexual arousal. For many, sexual arousal and sexual pleasure were followed by shame and guilt. Some reported an absence of sexual desire, associating any desire with shame and guilt. Inability to achieve orgasm was rare, but some women experienced orgasm in the absence of arousal or pleasure. Orgasm was associated with a sense of vulnerability and of being out of control. Westerlund also observed a frequent split between sexual arousal and emotional attachment. A number of women were able to experience sexual arousal only in the absence of intimacy, associating emotional intimacy with vulnerability to reexperiencing the incestuous relationship.

There is no evidence that incest directly affects sexual preference, but Westerlund found confusion over sexual preference to be common. Many women *believe* that their sexual preference is connected to the incest. Like anyone else, women with an incest history may be celibate, lesbian, bisexual, or heterosexual.

Just as there are a variety of sexual preferences, there are also a variety of sexual lifestyles. A minority of Westerlund's subjects had developed a pattern of aversion—that is, revulsion associated with avoidance of sex—fueled by fear and anger. Many reported inhibition, and many had undergone a period of celibacy. Some engaged in compulsive sexual behavior, and a temporary period of promiscuity (in adolescence or early adulthood) was common. Promiscuity occasionally included a period of prostitution. Compulsive sexual behavior was often associated with a desire for power and control, as well as being a vehicle for expressing anger toward the partner and toward the self. Inhibition was more common than compulsion, and it was common for lifestyles to alternate or to change over time.

You should not infer from Westerlund's findings that incest destroys any opportunity for healthy sexual functioning. Notwithstanding the many problems, the majority of sexually active respondents were more satisfied than dissatisfied during sex. Although Westerlund's respondents were somewhat unusual in being members of self-help groups, it was obvious that they were generally struggling—with considerable success—to improve their sexual experience and functioning. Many women in Westerlund's group were able to regain a sense of bodily control through exercise and fitness training.

A range of treatment approaches has been developed to help incest survivors with sexual dysfunction. These treatment approaches build on a substantial history of successful treatment of sexual dysfunction.[29] Current treatment approaches[30] include education as well as individual and group therapy. As in the treatment of sexual dysfunction with other origins, sexual partners are actively involved in the healing process.

Eating Disorders ◆ ◆ ◆ ◆ ◆ ◆ ◆ ◆ ◆ ◆

Another somatic effect of traumatic experience is that it interferes with eating. The eating disturbances may range from mild disruptions to severe disorders. The two common eating disorders are *anorexia,* or weight loss associated with self-starvation, and *bulimia,* or binge eating (often associated with purging by vomiting or laxative use). Both of these disorders may be intertwined with childhood trauma.[31]

Jean Goodwin and Reina Attias[32] noted that symptoms of PTSD "are not conducive to normal enjoyment of food." But they also made it clear that the relation between trauma and eating disturbances may be more direct. Childhood trauma may include starvation, force-feeding, emotional abuse in relation to eating or weight, oral rape, and forced fellatio. Such traumatic experiences not only interfere with normal eating but also may be repeated in a compulsive fashion. For example, a patient who repeatedly binged and purged was found to be reenacting childhood experiences of being forced to eat spoiled food, after which she would vomit.[33] Goodwin and Attias also observed that some abused individuals may mute their feelings by becoming obese, using "encasing layers of fat" as a way to numb themselves.[34] Obesity may also serve to maintain interpersonal distance.

Given that traumatic experience is associated both with eating disorders and with dissociative disorders, it is not surprising that these two disorders often occur together.[35] Psychiatrist Moshe Torem[36] recently reported that disturbed eating behavior was seen in 92% of patients with dissociative identity disorder. Common eating problems included binge eating, excessive dieting, self-induced vomiting, extreme weight fluctuations, laxative abuse, and excessive exercising.

Psychoanalyst Kathryn Zerbe[37] views eating disorders and dissociative disorders as "sister phenomena." She sees anorexia as a "hidden expression of the self, dissociated from other parts," [38] and she views self-starvation as a means of self-expression. When eating disorders are associated with dissociative identity disorder, the bingeing, purging, or starving may be associated with a dissociated part of the self. Zerbe works with eating disorders much as she and other clinicians would work with dissociative disorders, encouraging those aspects of the self associated with eating disturbance to find additional avenues of expression:

> The starving and suffocating selves yearn to find their own voices by an acknowledgment that they exist. The patient begins to see that looking at the fragments of her own personality is not as scary as she once thought. Her

eating disorder will lose its importance as a regressive holding pattern, and she will move toward more full integration of self.[39]

The relationship between eating disorders and sexual abuse is a matter of active investigation. The observation that patients with eating disorders frequently have a history of childhood trauma should not be taken to imply that child abuse—or sexual abuse in particular—*causes* eating disorders. The etiology of eating disorders, like the etiology of most other psychiatric disorders, is extraordinarily complex.[40] An extensive literature review suggested that a reported history of sexual abuse is common among bulimic women but no more so than among many other groups of women without bulimia.[41] A more recent study found that sexual abuse was more common among women with bulimia than among women without any psychiatric disorders but no more common than among women with other psychiatric disorders.[42] The authors concluded that sexual abuse is a risk factor for a variety of psychiatric disorders—bulimia among them.

Even if it is not the sole cause of an eating disturbance, a history of sexual abuse may play an important role in the pattern of eating or the development of eating disorder symptoms, as well as in the overall treatment approach.[43] For any individual struggling with a history of sexual abuse and an eating disorder, it is important to explore the possible psychological links between the two. Recent studies suggest, for example, that purging may be linked to sexual abuse for some women and may serve the function of temporarily reducing tension and self-denigration.[44] Understanding the meaning and origins of such symptoms plays a role in breaking the pattern.

Borderline Personality Disorder ◆ ◆ ◆ ◆ ◆ ◆

DSM-IV defines *personality disorder* as "an enduring pattern of inner experience and behavior that deviates markedly from the expectations of the individual's culture, is pervasive and inflexible, has an onset in adolescence or early adulthood, is stable over time, and leads to distress or impairment." [45] Most personality disorders are exaggerated personality traits. For example, paranoid personality disorder involves pervasive distrust and suspiciousness. Psychiatrist William Meissner[46] has argued that paranoia is part of the human condition. Paranoia is adaptive; it keeps us alert to danger. If you are not sufficiently paranoid, you may be too gullible, naive, easily taken in, and oblivious to risks. But Meissner points out that maltreatment engenders extreme paranoia. Then paranoia becomes maladaptive, because it fosters alienation and precludes closeness.

Let's look at the other extreme: Dependent personality disorder involves an inordinate need for nurturance, submissive and clinging behavior, and fear of being separated or alone. We all have lifelong needs for attachment and a secure base. In this sense, we are *all* dependent over the course of life. But taken to the extreme, dependency interferes with self-reliance and autonomy, as well as leaving us vulnerable to domination and exploitation.

I did not arbitrarily choose the examples of paranoia and dependency; these are two common relationship patterns associated with a history of abuse. Isolation and dependency reflect the poles of abusive experience: The intrusion and injury generate fear and distrust (paranoia) but also heighten the need for protection and comforting (dependency). It is little wonder that people with childhood trauma swing from one pole to the other.

Although a range of personality disorders can be associated with trauma, many researchers have focused on borderline personality disorder (BPD). *Borderline* is a misnomer;[47] the term was originally applied to persons considered on the border between neurosis and psychosis. As currently defined, BPD is common among Vietnam veterans with PTSD,[48] as well as among incest survivors.[49] DSM-IV delineates the cardinal symptoms of BPD as fear of abandonment, unstable and intense relationships, identity disturbance, self-damaging impulsivity, suicidal or self-mutilating behavior, mood instability, feelings of emptiness, intense anger, and stress-related paranoid ideas or dissociative symptoms.[50] The broad array of symptoms listed in DSM-IV illustrates how varied BPD and its etiology may be.[51]

It should not escape the attention of those who read Part II of this book that all symptoms of BPD are also among the potential effects of trauma. Traumatic experience, particularly when it is severe and occurs in the developmentally formative period of childhood, affects the *whole personality*. Moreover, recent research demonstrates considerable overlap between BPD and PTSD at the neurophysiological level.[52] Trauma-related disturbance and BPD overlap considerably, but they are by no means identical.[53]

Trauma does not routinely lead to BPD, and not all individuals with BPD have histories of trauma. Extensive research shows that about 70% of patients diagnosed with BPD report a history of sexual abuse.[54] Sexual abuse may be a particularly important risk factor for BPD,[55] and incest may be the deciding factor for some individuals.[56] But we should not be quick to conclude that sexual abuse is a *primary* cause of BPD. As described in Chapter 1 (Trauma), the forms and effects of sexual abuse are extremely varied. But whatever form abuse takes, extensive trauma and dissociative disturbance are associated with more severe symptoms in individuals with BPD.[57]

Psychiatrist Joel Paris[58] found that 71% of women and 45% of men diagnosed with BPD reported childhood sexual abuse. But most events were single incidents, and most were perpetrated by persons outside the nuclear family. Sexual abuse by caregivers was reported by 26% of the individuals studied, and father-daughter incest was reported by 15%. Severe sexual abuse (involving penetration, multiple perpetrators, force) appeared to play a distinct role in the development of BPD, but such severe abuse occurred in the histories of only a minority of individuals with BPD.

Sexual abuse is not the only form of trauma associated with BPD; Paris found comparable rates of physical abuse, as well as a high prevalence of family violence and verbal abuse. But Paris makes a convincing case that environmental contributions to BPD go far beyond trauma and abuse. Other factors include psychiatric disturbance in parents, neglect and over-control, and lack of family cohesion. Social disintegration in the community also plays a role, because there are no structures outside the family to provide the comfort and containment that might buffer the effects of family dysfunction.

Having pulled together potential environmental contributions to BPD, Paris proposes a *multidimensional* theory of etiology. As discussed in Chapter 4 (Emotion), environment and temperament always interact in the development of personality. Paris postulates that two temperamental factors—affective instability and impulsivity—contribute to vulnerability for BPD. If the affectively reactive and impulsive child has a family and community that provide stability, comfort, and containment, BPD will not develop. If such a child experiences trauma or other detrimental environmental influences, BPD may be the result.

There are numerous pathways to BPD, and the symptoms are highly varied. To summarize: Put problems with attachment at the center.

Many—if not all—forms of trauma may profoundly disrupt attachment. Neglect, loss, and a host of other dysfunctional family patterns can also disrupt attachment. Temperamental and environmental factors also conspire. Persons with BPD are exquisitely sensitive to rejection, separation, and loss. Any event that spells abandonment may evoke intense distress, anxiety, and anger. Impulsive and often destructive behavior relieves tension. The distress and dangerous behavior may also evoke the concern of others, *temporarily* alleviating feelings of abandonment. Yet impulsive behavior is also likely to provoke alarm and rejection, ultimately pushing others away. As others withdraw, fears of abandonment escalate. Relationships become increasingly unstable, and attachment becomes increasingly insecure.

When a history of severe and prolonged trauma is evident, should we call this constellation of symptoms "borderline personality disorder"? As discussed earlier, Judith Herman[59] has proposed the term *complex PTSD* to capture the pervasive effects of severe trauma on psychological functioning. She advocated this new diagnosis in part because calling trauma survivors *borderline* may add insult to injury. There is no question that the term *borderline* has taken on pejorative connotations in some areas of the professional community. For example, *borderline* may imply "attention seeking" or "manipulative." In my view, those who have suffered disrupted attachment need special attention, and they need to learn effective ways of manipulating (influencing) significant others to establish stable relationships that will provide a more enduring sense of security and safety.

Many severely traumatized persons will fit the criteria for BPD as well as PTSD and other trauma-related disorders. Perhaps the best we can do is attempt to cultivate more understanding of the reasons for BPD among the wider professional community. With better understanding may come less stigma, perhaps with more tolerance and compassion.

The Perils of Labeling ◆ ◆ ◆ ◆ ◆ ◆ ◆ ◆ ◆

Decades ago, patients with psychiatric symptoms were often assigned a single label, such as "schizophrenia," "depressive neurosis," or "paranoid personality." This approach to diagnosis raised protests: How can you put a person with complex problems into one narrow box? With DSM-III in

1980, psychiatric diagnoses became far more complicated. The clinician makes all the diagnoses that apply, leaving nothing out. This step is an improvement over the one-box approach, but it often leads to a bewildering array of diagnoses. It is not out of the realm of possibility for one person to have all the diagnoses discussed in Part III of this book (posttraumatic stress disorder, dissociative identity disorder, major depression, alcohol abuse, somatization disorder, anorexia, sexual aversion, and borderline personality disorder). Reading such a list of diagnoses in your medical chart may lead you to wonder, "What's wrong with me, anyway?"

Although the psychiatric diagnostic classification system continues to come in for criticism,[60] careful diagnosis is essential both for proper treatment and for research toward better understanding and treatment. If you are a psychiatric patient, you should know your diagnoses and educate yourself about them. But self-understanding does not come by way of knowing an array of diagnoses or focusing on your symptoms. Self-understanding comes from understanding your development, appreciating how you came to be the person you are. As the mental health profession has learned in recent years, for many people, understanding the complex effects of traumatic experience has helped to make sense of previously bewildering symptoms. The diagnosis of complex PTSD may not be official, but the idea will not disappear. Traumatic experience, intertwined with other detrimental environmental influences and temperamental vulnerabilities, can indeed have complex effects that are being more accurately diagnosed and increasingly understood.

PART IV

Treatment

nd off it" so that *they* do not have to think about it. You may need to press on them the importance of your need for someone to listen. But e listener's feelings of fear and outrage can also interfere with his or her pacity to listen. A woman who has been raped may find that every time e tries to discuss it with her husband, he becomes so embroiled in his wish kill the rapist that he can hardly pay attention to her feelings. In such ases, trying to talk about the trauma can make it worse, not better.

When talking through the trauma with others is not possible, you may eed to turn to a psychotherapist. A psychotherapist not only can provide elp with symptoms but also can help with the process of talking about the rauma. As Judith Herman puts it, the psychotherapist's role is to bear witness. Not that it's easy for the psychotherapist. Psychotherapists can also feel horrified and outraged. But their training, experience, and professional role afford a degree of objectivity that provides a safeguard against their becoming so distressed that they, too, cannot listen.

Psychotherapists are continually challenged to find the right balance between professional detachment and emotional involvement. Empathy for another's feelings requires a delicate blend of emotional sympathy and intellectual understanding. If your psychotherapist goes too far in either direction, you may not feel safe talking about the full extent of your traumatic experience. If your psychotherapist is too detached, you may not feel supported. If your psychotherapist is too emotionally involved, you may feel a need to protect her or him from your feelings. In doing their best to bear witness, psychotherapists inevitably lose the middle ground of empathy to a degree: Sometimes they withdraw into detachment, and at other times they are pulled into distressing emotional involvement. But as long as your psychotherapist spends a good deal of time in the middle range of empathy, you will be able to talk in a way that proves beneficial.

The Therapeutic Alliance

Talking about trauma will go best when you have a good alliance with your psychotherapist. Richard Kluft wrote, in relation to treatment of dissociative identity disorder, that "the cultivation of the therapeutic alliance is the heart and soul of the treatment," [5] and the same could be said of the treatment of trauma more generally. There are many facets to the therapeutic alliance,[6] but the two essential ingredients are a positive relation-

CHAPTER TWELVE

Treatment Approaches

Given the broad array of problems, symptoms, and disorders associated with traumatic experience, it should come as no surprise that virtually all major forms of treatment are applicable. Because of the complexity of trauma-related disturbances, the many forms of trauma, and inherent differences among individuals, treatment must be tailored to each individual's needs and situation. Individual psychotherapy is usually the primary form of treatment for trauma-related problems. But persons who have been severely traumatized and who have chronic symptoms often need a combination of treatment approaches over an extended period of time.

This chapter offers an overview of major treatment approaches, emphasizing issues pertinent to trauma. First, a preliminary matter is addressed: establishing safety. Then, because it is the backbone of treatment, individual psychotherapy is discussed in some detail. Several other commonly employed treatment modalities are discussed more briefly: cognitive-behavior therapy, group psychotherapy, family intervention, medication, hospital treatment, and the continuum of care.

Safety First

Judith Herman[1] rightly declares: "The first task of recovery is to establish the survivor's safety. This task takes precedence over all others, for no other therapeutic work can possibly succeed if safety has not been adequately secured." I reiterate a few of the main points from her chapter on safety in *Trauma and Recovery*—a chapter I consider required reading for all who are in treatment for trauma. A paramount issue in the beginning of treatment, safety remains crucial throughout. Above all, progress in treatment depends on putting an end to ongoing trauma—incest, battering, or any other form of abuse. Safety cannot be predicated on others' declarations that they will no longer inflict harm; rather, "it must be based on the self-protective capability of the victim."[2]

Safety includes not only protection from the maltreatment of others but also protection from self-harm. Many persons who have been severely traumatized continue to feel endangered by their own self-destructive impulses. This vulnerability reaches the extreme in dissociative identity disorder when the individual feels terrorized by dissociated suicidal states. Short of endangerment from abuse at the hands of others or oneself, Herman emphasizes caring for basic needs: finding safe living quarters, eating and sleeping properly, obtaining needed medical care, and providing for financial security. Another crucial component of safety is a social support network—the wider the better. This network may include friends, lovers, trusted family members, self-help groups, and mental health professionals. The process of establishing safety as a foundation for treatment is not easy; Herman likens it to preparing to run a marathon.

Psychiatrist James Chu[3] has proposed the acronym "SAFER" for the ingredients of the early stages of therapy that lay the foundation for remembering and exploring traumatic experience. *Self-care* entails refraining from self-destructive and suicidal behavior by finding better ways of soothing yourself and less destructive ways of coping with stress. *Acknowledgment of trauma* means accepting the role of traumatic experience in your problems

rather than seeing yourself as "crazy" or "bad." *Function* m
need to maintain normal functioning to the extent possi im
means of employment, volunteer jobs, going to school, or p th
tively in treatment programs. *Expression* refers to the neec ca
constructive outlet for expressing feelings, such as art, musi s
tivity, or writing. *Relationships* addresses the need for social t
cluding a therapeutic relationship.

The price of establishing safety can be extremely high. Ma
als face the dilemma of being economically dependent on persc
spouses, or lovers) who continue to inflict trauma. Herman elo
scribes the magnitude of these costs:

> Creating a safe environment required the patient to make major ch
> her life. It entailed difficult choices and sacrifices. This patient discov
> many others have done, that she could not recover until she took ch
> the material circumstances of her life. Without freedom, there can
> safety and no recovery, but freedom is often achieved at great cost. In
> to gain their freedom, survivors may have to give up almost everythin;
> Battered women may lose their homes, their friends, and their livelih
> Survivors of childhood abuse may lose their families. Political refugees
> lose their homes and their homeland. Rarely are the dimensions of this
> rifice fully recognized.[4]

Individual Psychotherapy

The universal prescription for trauma: *Talk about it*. To whom? To
trusted person who will listen—the sooner the better. This universal p
scription works best in conjunction with single-blow traumas, such a
natural disaster, an assault, or a rape. Even then, it is not always easy
"just talk about it." Talking about it may bring back the feelings of terro
or rage engendered by the trauma. Shame may get in the way. As you be
gin to think or speak about it, self-protective dissociation may block the
memory.

It's not always easy for others to listen, even when they are caring and
eager to help. Trauma can be abhorrent. Listening to another person's horrific stories of trauma can itself be traumatizing. It can threaten the listener's sense of safety and security. Friends may urge you to "just get your

ship and a sense of working together with the therapist.[7]

Trust forms the foundation of a positive relationship with a psychotherapist, as does a feeling of being accepted by the therapist.[8] The feeling of trust should be based on your perception that your psychotherapist is trustworthy, reliable, and trying to be helpful. For a good alliance, your psychotherapist must indeed be trustworthy and capable of providing help. Obtaining a referral from a reliable source and checking out your psychotherapist's reputation can help provide a foundation for the alliance. But ultimately you must make a judgment on the basis of your own experience with the psychotherapist. It is important to find a good match; a psychotherapist whom someone else finds helpful may not necessarily be best for you.

A good therapeutic alliance also includes active collaboration. In psychotherapy research at The Menninger Clinic,[9] we have defined the patient's collaborative role as *making active use of the psychotherapy as a resource for constructive change.*[10] You should feel that you and your psychotherapist are working together toward common goals. You should be an active participant in the process. Probably every patient in psychotherapy wishes she or he could just be "cured" by the psychotherapist. Who wouldn't? Psychotherapists I know work very hard. But their patients must work even harder. Your psychotherapist should not be working harder than you are. You are the major contributor to the success of your therapy. Your psychotherapist's job is to provide the guidance and support you need to do your hard work. Talking about trauma is hard work. Coping with trauma is hard work. Like any other hard work, it can't be done continuously. You need breaks; you need rest; you need respite. But the ultimate outcome depends on your persistence—over the long haul, if need be.

Obstacles to the Therapeutic Alliance

Establishing a positive, collaborative relationship with trustworthy persons is easy if you have a history of good relationships. But if you have been traumatized in relationships—especially caregiving relationships—then forming a positive alliance can be a huge challenge. You cannot just plunge into psychotherapy with a good therapeutic alliance.[11] You will bring with you all the problems with attachment and relationships discussed earlier. Three of these problems deserve special emphasis: distrust, dependency, and boundary difficulties.

Distrust. Working productively with your psychotherapist requires trust. If you have been traumatized in intimate relationships or by persons in a caregiving role, trust will not come easily. If you go on the basis of your previous experience—and no one is equipped to do otherwise—distrust is inevitable. You are likely to feel vulnerable to being injured or abandoned—or both, in that order. Here's a catch-22: If you can't trust, you can't do the work of therapy; if you can't do the work, you can't learn to trust. Once in this bind, you will find that developing trust is a gradual process that takes a lot of courage. You may go back and forth. Trust will build slowly; as trust builds, you will be able to do more work; and trust will continue to evolve. And your trust will be challenged from time to time by disappointments and frustrations in response to your therapist's inevitable failings and limitations.

Dependency. It is common for individuals who have been traumatized by other persons to swing from one extreme to another: from distrust to dependency. This alternation should not be surprising: When you finally develop a relationship that meets your needs, you are loath to let go and may rely exclusively on it.

Psychotherapy *requires* a degree of dependency. And psychotherapy can substitute belatedly for the attachment and secure base that was not available at the time of the trauma. In a sense, the psychotherapist takes on the role of the caregiver—mother, father, friend. It is tempting to think of psychotherapy as a kind of "reparenting." But taken much beyond this metaphor, it is sure to lead to disillusionment.[12] Psychotherapists' time, the extent of their caring, and their availability are all limited. Their livelihood depends on payment for their services. Their capacity to be helpful as psychotherapists requires the professional role, without which it would not be possible to provide the essential blend of emotional involvement and professional detachment. Because of the inherent limits on how much you can depend on your therapist, therapy also requires a considerable degree of self-dependence—the capacity to bridge the gap between separation and reunion—from the outset. And it's not easy to be self-dependent when you are struggling with trauma.

Boundary difficulties. Boundaries maintain the integrity of the self. Your boundaries regulate closeness and distance in your relationships. By establishing boundaries, you maintain your privacy and your space. You set limits. Your boundaries shift from one relationship to another—you maintain less distance in intimate relationships. Boundaries need to be flexible, neither too rigid nor too fluid. A cell membrane is a good example of a boundary; it allows connection and interchange with the outside but also regulates what comes in and what goes out.

Trauma always entails intrusion and boundary violation—whether the trauma results from a tornado, from an assault, or from childhood sexual abuse. Persons who have been traumatized repeatedly by other persons, however, are likely to have difficulty with interpersonal boundaries. A girl whose father routinely walked in on her whenever she was in the bathroom has had her boundaries violated. A boy whose mother continually went through his private belongings has had his boundaries violated. A woman whose jealous husband spies on her has had her boundaries violated. A more extreme boundary violation is that of the body—physical or sexual assault. The most extreme boundary violation is that of the mind—brainwashing and totalitarian control, whether in a prison camp or in a home.[13]

Many persons whose boundaries have been violated are exquisitely sensitive to the boundaries of others. They may feel extremely reluctant to intrude on others or to make any demands of them. They keep their distance. They may not call, visit, or ask for help. Still other persons may have experienced such pervasive and severe boundary violations that they have never learned to become aware of interpersonal boundaries. They may lack any sense of privacy. They may intrude on others—using belongings without asking, calling at all hours, making unreasonable demands—and then be surprised or dismayed when rebuffed. Or they may allow themselves to be intruded upon or exploited in this way by others.

Maintaining therapeutic boundaries is essential in the treatment of persons who have been traumatized by caregivers.[14] The relationship must remain thoroughly professional. Psychotherapy is incompatible with business dealings or social contacts. With rare exceptions, such as emergencies, psychotherapy should take place at scheduled times in a professional setting.

The desire to "reparent" goes awry when boundaries are not maintained. Many persons who have been traumatized understandably long for the physical comforting that they should have had. This desire can be extremely powerful. If they had been adequately comforted at the time, the trauma may have been bearable. But within psychotherapy, touch itself is problematic.[15] Psychotherapy is a *verbal* process. The comfort comes from being heard and understood. Many individuals who have been severely hurt and neglected feel that comforting words are a poor substitute for much-needed touch, and the therapy relationship can be frustrating in that respect. Physical comforting is highly desirable, but it should come from *other* relationships. The therapy process can help build the needed trust to make that possible.

Just as we have learned about the alarming prevalence of sexual abuse, we have also become aware of the troubling occurrence of sexual exploitation of patients by psychotherapists.[16] Moreover, it is becoming clear that patients at highest risk for such exploitation are those with a history of sexual abuse.[17] As much as you might crave touch, you are likely to perceive it as a signal that further boundary violations are in the offing. Then your sense of safety is jeopardized, and you lose the fundamental prerequisite for therapy. Thus, the therapist's insistence on maintaining boundaries—which at times may be frustrating to the patient—is an effort to preserve the therapeutic relationship. The same is true of any relationship. If boundaries are seriously violated, the relationship is likely to self-destruct, sooner or later. And the process in psychotherapy can be insidious, involving a *chain* of boundary violations:

> A common sequence involves a transition from last-name to first-name basis; then personal conversation intruding on the clinical work; then some body contact (e.g., pats on the shoulder, massages, progressing to hugs); then trips outside the office; then sessions during lunch, sometimes with alcoholic beverages; then dinner; then movies or other social events; and finally sexual intercourse.[18]

Maintaining a solid therapeutic alliance continually challenges both patient and therapist. Even with patients for whom trauma is not a main focus, the therapeutic alliance is likely to fluctuate considerably over the course of treatment.[19] You might find yourself starting with a relatively positive working relationship, only to find your trust and collaboration plummeting when you get further into the painful work and your relationship with your therapist deepens. Then you will be challenged to grapple with your feelings and conflicts to reestablish the positive relationship. You may find that there are times when your therapy is on the brink of falling apart—perhaps you're infuriated at your therapist or extremely disappointed, and you have some good reason to be. Talk it through. Developing the ability to work through such difficult periods can be the most significant part of the healing process. Serious conflicts are inevitable in *all* close relationships, and resolving them in psychotherapy can be of paramount importance in building your confidence in conflict resolution in other relationships.[20]

Abreaction

A central purpose of establishing a positive therapeutic relationship is to enable you to talk about traumatic experience. Why talk about it? The simple answer—to get rid of the bottled-up feelings. In technical terms, *abreaction* describes this process of reexperiencing the trauma and expressing the strong emotions. In nontechnical terms, this idea of purging blocked emotion can be construed as *catharsis.* Treating symptoms by liberating blocked emotion goes back a century to Freud's early work.[21] This approach to the treatment of trauma is far too simple:

> The clear value of abreaction of childhood trauma in some patients has led to an erroneous belief system that seems widespread among patients and their therapists. This belief system holds that in any clinical situation where childhood abuse is discovered in the history, all efforts should be made to immediately explore and abreact those abusive experiences.[22]

As discussed earlier, the idea of being filled with emotion is an illusion. You are not "filled up" with emotion. Maybe you feel strong emotions much of the time. Maybe you can easily become intensely emotional very quickly. You have a *capacity* to experience intense emotion. You may wish you didn't have this capacity. But just having another episode of extremely intense emotion will not diminish your capacity. You may protest, "I *feel* much better after an emotional outburst!" Releasing tension can lead to temporary relaxation. Like vigorous exercise, it can lower arousal. You may feel calmer after wearing yourself out. But emotional catharsis in itself does not lead to lasting change, and it often poses serious risks, especially for patients with PTSD.[23]

There is ample reason for caution: Abreaction may be retraumatizing rather than helpful. Repeated exposure to traumatic memories may further sensitize you to the slightest reminder of them. Your capacity to function may be increasingly undermined. Especially when dealing with repeated and prolonged trauma, you may find the goal of remembering and abreacting every traumatic experience not only overwhelming but also impossible. At worst, as discussed earlier, you might add insult to injury by constructing inaccurate memories and burdening yourself with additional trauma.

The following scenario commonly precedes extended hospitalization: In the service of "getting it all out," exploring trauma leads to worsening symptoms and self-destructive behavior; the patient becomes increasingly desperate and dependent on the therapist; the therapist makes increasingly heroic efforts to keep the patient going; therapeutic boundaries are eroded by extended sessions, late-night phone calls, and sometimes efforts to provide physical comforting; the therapist becomes overwhelmed, worn out, and starts to withdraw; the patient feels abandoned and becomes distraught; and the patient is finally hospitalized in crisis. At the point of hospitalization, everyone belatedly realizes that the emphasis must shift away from uncovering, exploration, and abreaction to establishing safety and restoring functioning.

The goal of talking about traumatic experience is not to *release* pent-up emotion; instead, it is to gain better *control* over emotion. But the benefits of talking about trauma go beyond emotional control.[24] Previously fragmented and unintelligible experience becomes more meaningful. In the process of talking about the trauma, you come to better understand yourself and your problems. Dissociated experience becomes integrated. Most important, talking about the trauma in an emotional way provides the opportunity to be *heard by someone*. As my colleague, psychologist Mary Jo Peebles-Kleiger, put it,

> The patient's internalization of the presence of the therapist, as well as of the therapist's auxiliary ego-function activities (e.g., perceiving, naming, and regulating), actually restructures the original trauma experience in new, healing ways. Instead of an overwhelming, solitary experience, the patient can weave a new memory trace of an experience tempered by the reassuring, processing presence of another person. In this way, trauma recall is altered and the memory becomes safe.[25]

Desensitization Versus Sensitization

By now, you should see that you and your therapist will confront a dilemma in working with traumatic memories: You need to talk about the
trauma, and you need to do so in an emotionally meaningful way. Yet, in
allowing emotion to come to the fore, you may feel overwhelmed and retraumatized.

Many techniques have been developed to help patients cope with frightening experiences and situations, and all of these techniques require *exposure* to the feared stimulus.[26] If you want to conquer a fear of heights, you
must go to high places. One way or another, you must become *desensitized*
to whatever frightens you. That is, with repeated exposure, your anxiety
gradually decreases, and you respond less strongly to the feared stimulus.
So it is with traumatic memories: By talking about them and integrating
them into your self-understanding, you can become desensitized to them.
If you try to go too fast, however, you can become *sensitized* rather than
desensitized. You may respond *more*—rather than less—strongly to the
memories and images.

The challenge for treatment is to find the right balance. You should not
assume that you must experience extremely intense emotions to benefit
from talking about trauma. In fact, some clinicians have proposed that talking about trauma in a calm state of mind can be therapeutic, and that "what
is essential is the *authenticity* of the experience of trauma-related emotions,
not their intensity." [27] As discussed earlier, two safeguards provide some
assurance that you can talk about the trauma without adding to it: adequate
preparation and pacing the work. Recall Kluft's[28] maxim: "The slower you
go, the faster you get there."

Quality of Life

This brings me to a key conclusion: Some individuals get so caught up
in trying to uncover everything in the service of "getting it all out" that
they completely lose sight of the goal of treatment: improved quality of
life. This point is so obvious that you can breeze right over it without
even thinking about it. So let me emphasize again: *The goal of treatment
is not to uncover memories, not to purge emotion, but to improve the
quality of your life.* At worst, catharsis can become a *way of life* or a

substitute for living. As such, it is not much of a life, and it could be endless.

The Benefits of a Therapeutic Relationship

Psychotherapy is not a cure by love—emotional or physical. Rather than belatedly attempting to provide the level of attachment and mothering that was missing at the time of trauma, your psychotherapist can help you mourn that lack of mothering, comforting, and affection. No amount of psychotherapy can entirely redress that loss.

Although not a cure by love, the relationship established in psychotherapy can be healing and growth promoting. The therapeutic alliance exemplifies the kind of helpful relationship model discussed earlier. Once developed, often by virtue of long and arduous work, this model can be internalized and made a part of yourself.[29]

You may extend the capacity to trust that you establish with your psychotherapist into your relationships with others. You may translate the acceptance provided by your psychotherapist into *self*-acceptance. Your therapist can serve as a model by helping you to think about yourself in a more tolerant and compassionate way. As you become more tolerant and accepting of yourself, you can better confront your problems, conflicts, and limitations. At first, you need your therapist's help; later, you can do these things on your own.

You might think of psychotherapy as a stepping stone to other relationships in which your natural and healthy needs for intimacy and physical comforting can be met. As Bowlby stated, the need for attachments, for a secure base, and for comforting—including touch—is lifelong.[30] Optimally, psychotherapy is but a way station that fosters a capacity to depend on others even more deeply and intimately.

Cognitive-Behavior Therapy   ◆ ◆ ◆ ◆ ◆ ◆ ◆

A century ago, Freud pioneered psychoanalytic treatment of trauma-related problems. Although he shifted focus from external trauma to internal conflict, the insight-oriented approach to psychotherapy that he developed continues to be a mainstay in the field of trauma. Yet now there are hundreds of different psychotherapies,[31] and we can expect many of these competing approaches to be applied to the rapidly evolving field of trauma treatment.

Psychoanalytic psychotherapy has emphasized self-understanding through insight as well as the substantial benefit of a positive therapeutic relationship. Decades ago, behavior therapy took a radically different tack: Rather than promoting insight about the origins of problems, behavior therapists sought means of changing problematic behavior in the present. Then cognitive therapists developed ways to influence patterns of thinking that contributed to painful emotions such as depression and anxiety. Behavior therapy and cognitive therapy are highly compatible in emphasizing active efforts to change present patterns of thought and behavior, and they are typically integrated in what is now called *cognitive-behavior therapy.*

There are many cognitive-behavioral methods, but psychologist Marcia Linehan's[32] approach to the treatment of borderline personality disorder is most pertinent to the agenda of this book—coping with trauma. As described earlier, the effects of trauma and the symptoms of borderline personality disorder overlap considerably. For many individuals, borderline personality disorder could be construed as a complex posttraumatic stress syndrome. Problems with regulation of intense emotion are the focus of Linehan's treatment approach, and she recognizes their common origins in childhood trauma.

The spirit of Linehan's treatment is consonant with that of this book. She cautions that pat answers and simple solutions will not do; the problems are complex, and the work of treatment is arduous. She emphasizes that problematic behavior is an understandable effort to cope with often overwhelming feelings, and her intent is to help individuals find more effective and less self-injurious ways of coping.

The top priority in Linehan's treatment is to decrease suicidal and self-destructive behavior, and careful research has demonstrated considerable success for her approach in this regard.[33] The second priority is to interrupt behavior that interferes with therapy, such as failing to attend treatment sessions, not cooperating in the work required, or not adhering to the therapist's limits. These problematic behaviors, like any others, become the focus of active problem solving. Linehan also gives due attention to aspects of the *therapist's* behavior that might interfere with the process. The third priority is behavior that interferes with the quality of life, such as substance abuse, high-risk or criminal behavior, or financial problems. The next priority is increasing behavioral skills—not only interpersonal skills but also tolerance for distress and techniques for emotional control. Additional treatment agendas include working with posttraumatic stress, increasing self-respect, and achieving individual goals.

The goals Linehan articulates are consistent with those of all other treatment approaches described in this book. Her methods, however, have a somewhat different slant. As in any form of psychotherapy, she places a high value on the development of a positive therapeutic alliance and a collaborative working relationship with the therapist. But cognitive-behavior therapists *actively teach and reinforce adaptive behavior.*

As with other forms of treatment, the therapist works hard, but the patient must work even harder. In cognitive-behavior therapy, the patient is encouraged to be highly active in concrete problem solving—carefully analyzing in step-by-step fashion the chain of events leading to problematic feelings and behaviors, and then identifying new ways of thinking and acting to avert such difficulties in the future. Patients use role playing to practice different ways of handling troublesome situations.

Linehan's method combines individual psychotherapy with group meetings that have a psychoeducational focus. Patients are also encouraged to make use of telephone contact between sessions for on-the-spot consultation regarding hitches in problem solving. Cognitive therapy techniques described in Chapter 4 (Emotion) are incorporated in Linehan's approach, but she also emphasizes the development of many other skills. For example, emotional regulation training[34] involves learning to identify and label emotions, analyzing the functions of emotions, preventing negative emotional states, increasing emotional hardiness, increasing positive emotions, letting go of negative emotions by accepting them and paying attention to them, and changing painful emotions by acting in a manner opposite to the feeling.

As with many other forms of cognitive-behavior therapy, Linehan's approach involves practicing such behavior-change techniques in the therapy sessions as well as in homework assignments. More generally, the whole approach is geared toward fostering a healthier lifestyle. Those who are looking for concrete help with day-to-day coping may find Linehan's approach particularly appealing.

Group Psychotherapy

Attachments form the bedrock of development and well-being, and we develop our first attachments in the context of "dyadic" relationships—twosomes, such as mother and infant. But attachment is gradually extended beyond caregivers and family members to encompass affiliation with groups. As van der Kolk[35] puts it, "the essence of the trauma response is the severance of secure affiliative bonds." Accordingly, he values groups because they provide a sense of safety and comfort, particularly when they are cohesive and stable.

There is tremendous diversity in the kinds of groups that are beneficial to trauma survivors.[36] Many groups are established according to the type of trauma experienced—incest survivors groups, groups for Vietnam veterans, groups for victims of specific natural disasters. Groups are also established for certain purposes or tasks. Judith Herman[37] emphasizes that the type of group should be matched to the stage of recovery. In the first stage, group therapy should focus on safety; in the second, on remembering and talking about traumatic experience; and in the third, on developing sustaining relationships. Moreover, persons who have been traumatized should not begin group therapy until they have achieved initial stability with individual psychotherapy and other social supports. Prematurely entering a group in which traumatic experience is discussed can be overwhelming and retraumatizing—sensitizing rather than desensitizing. It is not uncommon for hospitalized patients just beginning to cope with trauma histories to leave the room abruptly when others describe their own traumatic experiences. Some severely traumatized persons can hardly tolerate hearing words such as *abuse* or even *father*.

But when they are ready, traumatized individuals can benefit enormously from group psychotherapy. Although opinions vary as to the appropriateness of group treatment for patients with dissociative identity disorder,[38] properly conducted group psychotherapy has distinct advantages for such individuals.[39] It is reassuring to learn from a clinician that your dissociative symptoms are not unique and that they can be understood. But it is even more powerful to see with your own eyes that others have had related experiences and have coped in similar ways. Psychiatrists Philip Coons and Karen Bradley[40] found that patients were better able to accept their diagnosis after observing dissociation in other group members. My colleague, psychologist Bonnie Buchele, points out that

> Sitting in a room with others who dissociate is one of the most powerful ways for the multiple personality or dissociative disorder patient to begin winning the battle against the sense of isolation and alienation that accompanies these disorders . . . the notion that "going away" was a creative response to unspeakable traumatization signals the beginning of the attenuation of the fear that has hovered in the patient's mind for years—the fear that he or she really is "crazy." [41]

The universal prescription for trauma—talk about it—applies in particular to groups. It is also challenging, especially if you have felt shackled by secrecy. That's why a group is not the best place to begin and is usually preceded by a period of individual therapy.[42] Establishing trust in a group of individuals with histories of abuse and dissociation is a major challenge.[43] But telling the story and having others bear witness takes on a new dimension within the context of a group. Anyone who has been traumatized has felt helpless, alone, and isolated. But many who have been traumatized have been even more systematically isolated by those who have hurt and abused them and by their own feelings of shame and guilt. Being able to talk in a group helps overcome this sense of isolation, as does learning that others have gone through similar experiences.

Overcoming the sense of isolation and establishing a base of emotional support are probably the most important benefits of group therapy for trauma. Group therapist Irwin Yalom[44] refers to the appreciation that others have struggled with the same problems as "universality." But he also has found that the most common benefit offered by a therapy group is interpersonal learning. Withdrawing from others is a nearly universal response to trauma. Moreover, those who have experienced prolonged childhood trauma often have been systematically isolated from their peers. Therapy groups provide a forum for learning to trust, to manage interpersonal conflicts, and to interact in satisfying ways. Like individual psychotherapy, a group can be a stepping stone to a wider array of relationships and community groups.[45]

Family Intervention ◆ ◆ ◆ ◆ ◆ ◆ ◆ ◆ ◆

Family work in relation to trauma is extremely complex, owing to the diversity of trauma, the multiplicity of family members and their roles, and the many purposes of intervention. Here, as elsewhere, safety is the overriding issue. If family members—spouse, siblings, parents—are involved in ongoing violence or abuse, any treatment effort will be stalemated. Enlisting the support of any family members who *can* be supportive is essential, whether they are in the contemporary family or the family of origin.

Providing Education and Counseling

If mental health professionals have been slow to recognize the impact of trauma and the prevalence of dissociative disorders, what can we expect of families? How well do family members understand PTSD? Flashbacks? Dissociation? Dissociative identity disorder?

A family bewildered and distressed by a member coping with trauma will have difficulty being supportive. Confusion and anxiety may reign. Well-meaning efforts at reassurance or advice ("Just do something to get your mind off it!") may fall on deaf ears. Frustration may ultimately prevail.

Just as the traumatized individual needs to be educated, so, too, does the family.[46] Just clarifying the basis of the traumatized member's difficulties can often prove helpful. But educating family members is no small task, particularly when perplexing dissociative symptoms and dissociative identity disorder are part of the picture. Yet better understanding brings more acceptance and a prospect of calmer interactions. When the family's anxiety abates, the traumatized family member's anxiety also decreases.

When dissociative identity disorder is involved, the process of education and treatment becomes more complex. For those who are married, spouses and children can be appropriately informed about the nature of the disorder and its origins in traumatic experience. Such explanations help enormously to explain previously bewildering experience. The safety of children is a paramount concern in relation to parents' violent or hurtful behavior in dissociated states.[47] In addition, the regular emergence of childlike behavior associated with altered experience can be profoundly disruptive to child rearing. The whole family is likely to need professional guidance in coping with day-to-day challenges of living and supporting the treatment process.[48] Distressed children in the family may benefit from professional evaluation, counseling, or therapy.

How Partners Can Be Supportive

Those to whom we are closest usually bear the brunt of our conflicts. The fears and attachment problems evoked by trauma will have the greatest impact on intimate relationships. Partners who have no awareness of the traumatic basis of intense emotional reactions are bound to convey their exasperation—more or less directly—in the message "Stop acting crazy!" In addition, without adequate understanding of the trauma, a partner may unwittingly trigger traumatic memories.

◆ A woman who had been raped became panicky and rageful when her husband lay on top of her with his face close to hers during sexual intercourse. His weight on her chest interfered with her breathing and triggered memories of feeling suffocated during the rape. This fearful reaction was explained to her husband as being analogous to a Vietnam veteran's flashback on hearing a car backfire. Recognizing this connection enabled the couple to find ways of being sexually intimate without triggering symptoms of PTSD.

No special characteristics are needed to support a traumatized person—just tolerance, patience, understanding, dependability, empathy, compassion, and affection! These characteristics are likely to be needed in considerable measure. I have greatly admired a number of supportive partners, but I have yet to meet a saint. Many persons have these admirable characteristics in large measure, but no one has them in limitless amounts. And support is inevitably intermingled with periods of apprehension, frustration, and discouragement. Patience and tolerance wear thin.

Partners must maintain their own boundaries; they must know their limits and set them. Partners who overextend themselves will not be able to sustain their support and are likely to withdraw or break off the relationship. Partners can be helpful in fostering other supportive relationships and in encouraging involvement in whatever form of treatment may be needed.

Partners who are willing to bear witness to the trauma may find themselves traumatized vicariously. Exposure to another person's trauma can be traumatizing, especially when you are emotionally close to that person. Partners may experience painful emotions, have nightmares, or be aware of intrusive thoughts about the trauma. Short of vicarious trauma, they may feel strained and taxed by emotional turbulence in the relationship. To be supportive, partners need to be supported. They must take care of themselves to be able to be caregivers. They also need supportive relationships, and they may find it helpful to participate in treatment with the traumatized person or to find their own treatment.

Disclosure and Confrontation

Seeking support requires you to let others know something about the trauma you've undergone. This openness may not be so difficult if the trauma was an accident or a criminal assault. But much traumatic experience—rape, child abuse, incest—is associated with a great deal of shame. In such cases, disclosure is no easy matter. Children who disclose sexual abuse often experience adverse consequences (not believed, not supported, blamed for ensuing family problems). Such negative outcomes of disclosure are associated with more severe symptoms in adulthood.[49]

If the traumatic experience involved abuse within your family of origin, then disclosing the trauma within the family will prove particularly challenging. On the basis of their extensive experience with such disclosures, Emily Schatzow and Judith Herman recommend that you make a list of family members and friends of family, then begin telling persons who are most likely to be receptive or who may be able to provide validation by offering additional information. Such planning makes disclosure a thoughtful, step-by-step process. In the case of father-daughter incest, disclosure to the mother "provides an opportunity to heal the mother-daughter bond," which can be particularly crucial: "For many survivors, forgiveness for their mothers is inextricably linked to forgiveness for themselves."[50]

At various points, disclosure shades into confrontation. For example, when incest is revealed to unknowing family members (siblings, mother), resentment or outrage at their failure to protect or their complicity may also come to the fore. Some individuals may even decide to confront those who abused them as the final step in bringing the traumatic experience to light.

Preparation

Disclosure and confrontation are likely to have a powerful impact, for better or for worse. To ensure a better chance of their being therapeutic instead of destructive, careful preparation is essential. Schatzow and Herman recommend that disclosure and confrontation be done—*if at all*—in the later stages of treatment rather than at the beginning. It is particularly important to resist being pressured into premature disclosure by an outraged friend, family member, or survivors' group.

Progress in therapy can be a gauge for your readiness to disclose the trauma outside of therapy. Readiness for disclosure is marked by being able to talk about the trauma without becoming emotionally overwhelmed or dissociating. Disclosure and confrontation require that you be comfortable with expressing anger and experiencing the sense of power that goes with it. The motto "safety first" applies to this situation as it does elsewhere. You should have built up a reliable support network and trustworthy allies—in the family or outside it. The process of disclosure can be extremely stressful and will necessitate additional support. Also, you should be at a point where you feel in control of any self-destructive inclinations and can ensure your self-protection. Finally, some individuals may use the help of a therapist or consultant in the disclosure process.[51]

Setting realistic goals helps pave the way for disclosure and confrontation. Schatzow and Herman emphasize the sense of empowerment that disclosure can bring, in part because unburdening yourself can facilitate giving up secrecy, shame, guilt, and a feeling of responsibility for the trauma. Disclosure may also bring forth validating information, bolstering your sense of reality. Ideally, disclosure and confrontation can open up communication within the family and provide an opportunity to establish more healthy adult relationships.

Some goals are understandable but counterproductive. Revenge is a likely motive for confrontation. The desire for revenge may be more or less conscious, but it is probably always present to some degree. If vengeance is in the forefront, an explosive situation may be in the offing, which heightens the potential for retraumatization. A related goal may be to have an emotional catharsis—in effect, "If I could just let him have it, I would feel better." But the idea of a cure by catharsis is just as dubious in the context of family work as it is in individual or group therapy.

No matter how extensive your preparation, you cannot be assured that disclosure and confrontation will lead to any particular outcome—or even a good outcome. At best, the result is likely to involve a mixture of satisfaction and disappointment.[52] It is best to keep in mind that you cannot control others; you can only control what *you* do. If your well-being depends on a certain outcome, such as being believed or hearing expressions of remorse, you could be risking additional traumatic experience. If you can settle for being satisfied with having spoken out and told the truth, regardless of the consequences, then you will have more control over the whole process.

The Possibility of Family Healing

Families can be torn apart—figuratively and literally—by disclosure of incest. When abuse is ongoing, the child or parent may be removed from the home as a result of legal intervention.

Given the level of dysfunction characteristic of families in which incest occurs,[53] it is reasonable to have limited expectations for change. Yet it would be unduly pessimistic to assume that significant healing is always out of the question. Families vary so widely that there can be no universal prescriptions. Psychologist Denise Gelinas—exceptional in her optimism—emphasizes family strengths and resources that can be mobilized in the healing process. She believes that the father's need for relatedness can provide powerful motivation to establish more appropriate relationships and that, with support, the mother can mobilize her caregiving ability:

> Seen as expressions of filial loyalty, the father's needs for relationship, the mother's felt obligation to care for her family, and the possibility of establishing a coordinated therapeutic network around a family with an entrenched problem provides the therapist with therapeutic approaches that are very different from the "problem" orientation. The family's capacity for caring, and thus change, is mobilized; individual and family needs can be better addressed; and the family structures and incest, with its consequences, can be treated. The very process of discovery or disclosure contributes to this and functions as a hidden resource; it can provide therapeutic opportunities not available in other stuck family and marital situations.[54]

Emancipation and Connection in Adulthood

Extricating yourself from traumatic relationships is not easy. At worst, traumatic bonding may be like emotional Super Glue. Many adult children who felt abused by their parents remain highly dependent on them yet angry and resentful toward them—the adult counterpart of ambivalent attachment. They encounter extreme frustration and disillusionment as they continue to hope—despite much ongoing evidence to the contrary—that family relationships will be more fulfilling. It is not easy to gauge how much change is possible and how much energy to devote to it. Persistence is admirable, but it can be carried too far.

Often, adults struggling with ambivalent attachments to their parents go from one extreme to another. Feeling frustrated and hurt, they are tempted to break their ties completely and cut themselves off from the family. In some cases, a period of distance may be needed to maintain safety and to prevent retraumatization. In the long run, however, family cutoffs are incompatible with lifelong needs for attachment. Becoming more self-dependent does not mean becoming completely independent. In some instances, family therapy may help adult children strike a better balance, becoming more separate and autonomous so as to remain emotionally connected in a more stable and satisfying way.

Medication   ◆ ◆ ◆ ◆ ◆ ◆ ◆ ◆ ◆ ◆ ◆

There are antianxiety medications. There are antidepressants, antipsychotics, and anticonvulsants. There are no antidissociative drugs and no anti-PTSDs. But many medications initially developed for other psychiatric disorders have proven of benefit for trauma-related symptoms. Drug classifications should not be taken too seriously. The brain seems to have "a mind of its own"; it has no respect for our labels. Regardless of the name we assign a drug, it is the brain that determines what to do with it. *Antidepressants,* for example, have turned out to be highly effective in preventing panic attacks—a form of anxiety disorder.

Psychopharmacology (treatment of psychological symptoms with medication) is evolving at a frenetic pace. New drugs are flooding the market, and older drugs are being tried in new ways. To date, most of the research on the effectiveness of drugs for the treatment of PTSD has been limited to male combat veterans. There is little completed research—but considerable clinical experience—in using these drugs with other populations, such as adults experiencing the residual effects of child abuse.

This section describes the extensions of the major classes of psychiatric drugs to the treatment of PTSD and dissociation. I present this material not to imply that you should be taking any specific medications; that's between you and your psychiatrist. Although I include some details here for your reference, I'm primarily interested in getting across a few general points. First, an awareness of drug treatment will underscore the significance of biological factors in trauma-related problems. Second, there are lots of possible avenues of help with medication. Third, you should appreciate the complexity of treating trauma-related symptoms with medication. As with the rest of treatment, you may need substantial doses of patience and persistence.

Antianxiety Drugs

Antianxiety drugs are obviously pertinent to PTSD, which is one type of anxiety disorder. The most common antianxiety agents are the benzodiazepines, such as diazepam (Valium), alprazolam (Xanax), and lorazepam (Ativan). A number of authors have also attested to the potential benefits of the benzodiazepine clonazepam (Klonopin) in the treatment of PTSD.[55] The benzodiazepines can help reduce general anxiety levels, and they have been effective in treating panic, nightmares, flashbacks, and insomnia. Benzodiazepines may also reduce dissociative switching triggered by high levels of anxiety.

The benzodiazepines resemble alcohol in their neurophysiological effects, and they can also be addictive. You can develop a "tolerance" to them so that you need higher and higher doses to get the same effect. In addition, abrupt withdrawal can be dangerous—for example, leading to seizures and "rebound" anxiety. The benzodiazepines must therefore be carefully prescribed and tapered, and they are particularly problematic for individuals prone to addiction. In addition, two potentially adverse side effects for persons coping with trauma are depression and decreased ability to inhibit violent impulses.[56]

Antidepressants

Depression is a common result of trauma. Many persons with severe traumatic histories have major depression, dysthymia, or both. Depression that occurs in conjunction with dissociation or PTSD can be treated with standard antidepressant medications,[57] although depression in the context of PTSD may be particularly difficult to treat.[58] The antidepressant drugs include tricyclics such as amitriptyline (Elavil), desipramine (Norpramin), and clomipramine (Anafranil), as well as monoamine oxidase inhibitors such as phenelzine (Nardil). Failing to stay within the bounds of their labels, these antidepressants have also been shown to be of some benefit in treating PTSD symptoms such as reexperiencing of trauma.[59]

Another class of antidepressants, the selective serotonin reuptake inhibitors (SSRIs), has become quite popular in the treatment of PTSD. These drugs include fluoxetine (Prozac), sertraline (Zoloft), and paroxetine (Paxil). Serotonergic drugs increase the availability of the neurotransmitter *serotonin* in the brain (by inhibiting the reuptake that terminates its action). Serotonin is believed to have a broad modulating and regulating role in the nervous system.[60] In addition to serving as antidepressants, these serotonergic drugs can help control hyperarousal, and they also appear to help with behavioral control. Thus, SSRIs may play a useful role in treating symptoms such as self-directed aggression, explosiveness, and behavioral reenactment of trauma.[61] They also may be of benefit with respect to the avoidance behavior common in PTSD.[62]

Mood Stabilizers

Some agents employed as antiseizure medications (anticonvulsants) also appear to be of benefit in stabilizing mood. Certain PTSD symptoms are *analogous* to seizures in the sense that a hypersensitivity develops in the brain with repeated stimulation. Repeated trauma, including flashbacks, sensitizes the neurons so that they need less and less stimulation to fire. This phenomenon has been called *kindling*.[63] As with a true seizure, the sensitized neurons might then start firing spontaneously *without* the traumatic stimulus, triggering hyperarousal, reexperiencing, and the fight-or-flight response. Carbamazepine (Tegretol) is one stabilizing drug that has been used in controlling seizure disorders. It has also been found helpful in the treatment of the PTSD symptoms of hyperarousal, flashbacks, nightmares, impulsive behavior, self-destructive behavior, and explosiveness.[64] Divalproex sodium (Depakote) is another such drug; it has also been used in the treatment of hyperarousal, impulsivity, and explosiveness.[65]

Lithium carbonate (Eskalith) has a long history of use as an antimanic agent; it is helpful in preventing manic episodes for persons with bipolar (manic-depressive) disorder. But lithium also can serve more generally as a mood stabilizer. Lithium has been of some benefit with impulsivity, rage, and self-injurious behavior associated with PTSD.[66]

Antipsychotic Drugs

"Psychotic" symptoms reflect a loss of contact with reality. Common psychotic symptoms include hallucinations (hearing voices), delusions (extremely unrealistic beliefs, such as believing one's food to be poisoned), and severely disorganized thinking. Persons in the throes of severe traumatic reexperiencing may have dissociative symptoms analogous to psychotic hallucinations and delusions. For example, I worked with a woman in the hospital whose PTSD was linked to prolonged childhood sexual abuse. The man who abused her had died many years before her hospitalization. Yet she still had flashbacks in which she heard his voice and saw him coming after her. She saw and heard her abuser instead of me, even when I was looking her straight in the eye and talking to her. When she was not having flashbacks, she was utterly convinced that her abuser was nearby and would attack her for having disclosed the abuse.

Such dissociative symptoms should not be confused with hallucinations and delusions in primary psychotic disorders such as schizophrenia and bipolar disorder.[67] Nevertheless, these severe PTSD symptoms may respond to low doses of antipsychotic *(neuroleptic)* medications such as haloperidol (Haldol).[68] The patient just described required antipsychotic medication to remain stable throughout her long course of treatment. Antipsychotic medication may also be helpful in controlling extreme agitation (sometimes with assaultiveness) associated with PTSD. These neuroleptic drugs may have serious side effects, and their indications in the treatment of PTSD are not clear cut.[69] Thus, they are typically used only after other medications (antianxiety agents and antidepressants) have failed to control the symptoms.

Blocking the Fight-or-Flight Response

As noted repeatedly throughout this book, the basic response to trauma is fight or flight, which entails sympathetic nervous system arousal. The link between posttraumatic stress and the sympathetic nervous system has been recognized since World War I.[70] The hyperarousal characteristic of PTSD is a result of chronic sympathetic arousal. Two drugs used primarily to treat hypertension (high blood pressure) have been enlisted in the treatment of PTSD because of their dampening effects on sympathetic arousal.[71] Clonidine (Catapres) and propranolol (Inderal) block physiological arousal, thereby potentially decreasing subjective distress and removing the physiological triggers for panic attacks. As with benzodiazepines, these drugs can decrease anxiety levels and thereby may also reduce uncontrolled dissociative switching.[72] Like other psychiatric medication, these antihypertensive drugs may have serious side effects and thus should be carefully prescribed and monitored.

Individual Differences

There are already lots of potentially helpful drugs, and lots more will undoubtedly come on the market. Not only are there many individual drugs to choose from, but these are also frequently used in combination. The huge number of possible drugs, combinations, dosages, and lengths of treatment makes choosing the optimal drug treatment extremely complex.

The particular treatment must be matched to the individual's symptoms. There has been more research on drug treatment of PTSD than on drug treatment of dissociative disorders, and there is no medication specifically for treating dissociation.[73] Drugs have played a relatively limited role in treating dissociative identity disorder, which is the most complex of the trauma-related disorders.[74] As one psychiatrist with extensive experience put it, patients with dissociative identity disorder "need supportive and sympathetic education about our current lack of pharmacological anodynes for their distress. At the same time, we must do what we can with or without medications to relieve suffering."[75] Symptoms that consistently pervade the whole personality may be more amenable to drug treatment than the specific phenomena of dissociative states; of course, drugs that help with PTSD symptoms will have a general stabilizing effect.[76]

In addition to having different symptom patterns, individuals will differ widely in how they respond to specific drugs. What works for someone else may not work for you, even if your symptoms are similar. These individual differences are undoubtedly related to constitutional factors such as genetic makeup and metabolism. Because of the genetic contribution, a family history of drug response may be a useful guide. If a parent or sibling benefited from a particular medication, you may also respond well to it. But drug treatment invariably involves some trial and error to find the optimal drugs, as well as some tinkering to find the best combinations and dosages. In addition, various drugs should receive an adequate trial; for some drugs, as much as 8 weeks to several months may be needed to achieve the optimal benefit.[77]

Integrated Treatment

It is utterly natural to wish for a "cure" by drugs—or by anything else, for that matter. Anyone would. For severe PTSD and dissociative disorders, however, the current drugs are only moderately effective, at best. And drugs are only part of more comprehensive treatment. Drug treatment is not an alternative to psychotherapy and other forms of psychological treatment; instead, psychological and pharmacological treatment work best together, because they enhance each other.[78] If your symptoms are severe and you feel completely out of control, working productively in psychotherapy may be out of the question. Drug treatment may be essential to provide the stability for psychotherapy to be feasible. Moreover, psychotherapy may entail exploring traumatic memories, and this exploration can temporarily heighten anxiety and arousal. Drug treatment may be needed to keep arousal within bounds. And it works both ways: Psychotherapy, by fostering self-understanding and self-control, may help control arousal so that the medication will be most effective. At best, from a psychosomatic perspective, psychotherapy and pharmacotherapy work synergistically: Mind stabilizes brain and brain stabilizes mind.

One final point about medication: It won't work if you don't take it. This obvious point is worth addressing, because patient compliance with any kind of medical treatment is notoriously poor. Yet it is crucial not only to take the medication as prescribed but also to keep track of its benefits and side effects and report them to your psychiatrist. Making optimal use of medication therefore requires a high level of collaboration between patient and physician. Your psychiatrist will have no way to judge the potential effectiveness of the medication without your collaboration and feedback. Without active collaboration, the nearly inevitable trial-and-error process will entail a lot more trial and a lot more error.

Problems with dissociation, however, can make collaboration and compliance even more challenging. If dissociation leads to gaps in memory, you may not remember what medication you have taken, and you may have more difficulty evaluating its benefits. Persons with dissociative identity disorder may have conflicts about medication played out among dissociated identities. When such problems significantly interfere with medication compliance, treatment in a structured setting, such as an inpatient unit or day hospital, may be needed so that regular observation is possible. Otherwise, it's another catch-22 situation: You need to be taking the medication for the symptoms that interfere with your taking the medication.

Hospital Treatment   ◆ ◆ ◆ ◆ ◆ ◆ ◆ ◆ ◆

Many persons can cope with trauma without any treatment. For others, individual psychotherapy may suffice. But those with more severe symptoms and trauma histories may require multiple forms of treatment—individual, group, and pharmacotherapy—and hospitalization also may be needed during periods of crisis. By far the most common precipitant for hospitalization is self-destructive behavior such as a suicide attempt. Hospitalization may also be necessary to prevent violence toward others. Ideally, the individual in crisis can be hospitalized during periods of high risk *before* acting on destructive impulses.

Although typically prompted by the prospect of destructive behavior, hospitalization may also be indicated for episodes of severe dissociation.[79] Recurrent flashbacks, uncontrolled switching among dissociative states, and continual interruption of ongoing experience by amnesia can make it virtually impossible to cope with the demands of daily life. Beset by dissociation, you may not be able to take care of your own basic needs, much less hold down a job or run a household.

There are several common precipitants for crises associated with destructive behavior or increased problems with dissociation. The initial un-covering of traumatic experience can be profoundly disruptive. An individual who has gone for years or even decades with no thought of childhood trauma may have this past brought to awareness by some stressor in adult-hood such as an accident, an assault, a loss, or a divorce. The mind may be flooded by visual images and painful body sensations. Childhood feelings of terror and shame may be evoked. Confusion, panic, and feelings of guilt can fuel destructive and self-destructive urges. This initial period of crisis may therefore require hospitalization to provide a sense of safety and sup-port while the person begins to come to terms with the trauma. Sub-sequently, individuals who have a history of multiple traumas may go through additional crises as different aspects of traumatic experience come into awareness. These subsequent crises may also require additional treat-ment support or hospitalization.

In addition to the initial emergence of traumatic experience, the erup-tion of dissociative symptoms can result in a crisis. Many individuals with dissociative identity disorder will have been able to manage, contain, and conceal their dissociative symptoms. But over time, their dissociative de-fenses may escalate, as evidenced in uncontrolled switching and the emer-gence of aggressive and self-destructive behavior. Hospitalization may be of benefit not only to help prevent harmful behavior but also to provide con-tinuous observation so that the correct diagnosis can be made, the patient and family can learn about the disorder, and the appropriate treatment can begin.

The principle of "safety first" applies as much to hospitalization as it does to any other form of treatment. Initially, however, the individual will be confronted with an unfamiliar environment, many strangers, and a number of restrictions. It is not uncommon for people to want to leave the hospital soon after they arrive. But during a crisis, it can become a needed haven of safety. The main function of hospital treatment is to protect the patient from self-harm and to enhance his or her self-control over destruc-tive impulses.[80] But hospitalization also serves a variety of other functions by providing protection from intruders, a structured day with constructive activities, an opportunity for 24-hour observation to monitor dissociation and switching, a healthy daily cycle of sleep and wakefulness, and medica-tion and medical care. Hospital treatment also encourages the individual to reach out and make contact with others rather than remaining isolated. The latter function is especially important: The hospital environment ensures that the individual will be involved in relationships, which ultimately hold the key to healing.

Not uncommonly, patients enter the hospital with the hope of delving into memories of trauma in a safe environment. There is no question that a hospital can be a safe place to do painful therapeutic work. Yet hospitalization for that purpose alone is questionable. If hospitalization is needed because of the likelihood that you would become emotionally overwhelmed or at risk for destructive behavior, that is an indication that the balance has tipped too far away from adaptive functioning in favor of painful remembering. In the background of such goals may be the illusion of the curative catharsis. Recently proposed standards for the treatment of dissociative identity disorder caution as follows: "In general, inpatient treatment with the goal of 'getting out all of the memories' and achieving a rapid fusion of personalities is inappropriate, and does not produce a positive outcome." [81]

The vast bulk of treatment, even for those with dissociative identity disorder, will be carried out on an outpatient basis.[82] With the correct diagnosis and proper treatment, patients need a minimal hospital stay. In general, hospitalizations for crises will be brief. Some individuals, however, may need longer hospitalizations.[83] Factors that may necessitate longer hospital stays in the treatment of trauma-related disorders are similar to those that make for extended hospitalization in the treatment of other psychiatric disorders.[84] These factors include protracted destructive or self-destructive behavior, complex dissociative symptoms that do not allow for a rapid restoration of continuity, other severe symptoms that do not respond to outpatient treatment (such as severe depression or eating disorders), family problems that preclude discharge to a safe environment, or complications in establishing appropriate posthospital treatment. Adequate discharge planning is crucial; without a good posthospital treatment plan, hospitalization may be prolonged, and any stability attained in the hospital may be jeopardized.

Most individuals will be hospitalized for brief stays on general psychiatric units,[85] but hospital treatment of dissociative identity disorder poses particular challenges.[86] Given these challenges, there are now specialty psychiatric units for treatment of trauma-related disorders all over the country. These units provide a number of advantages: staff members with special interest and expertise in trauma-related disorders, specific treatment programs designed for trauma-related problems, and an opportunity to relate to other patients with similar problems and backgrounds.

Continuum of Care ◆ ◆ ◆ ◆ ◆ ◆ ◆ ◆ ◆

In psychiatry, as in the rest of medicine, the need for cost containment has produced pressure to discharge patients rapidly from hospitals. Many individuals have extremely limited financial coverage for hospital treatment. Longer hospital stays for complex and protracted problems may be desirable but not possible. Many persons who formerly would have been treated in hospitals are now being discharged to outpatient treatment.

To ease the cost of treatment, the mental health field is moving toward providing a broader spectrum of services. Hospitalization can be shortened if adequate support systems outside the hospital can be put in place. Ideally, treatment programs would provide a continuum of care, including inpatient treatment, day-hospital programs, residential treatment, halfway and quarterway houses, activity and vocational programs, medication clinics, and social work services, as well as individual and group psychotherapy.[87] In such programs, you could have whatever level of support you need during a given period of treatment. Optimally, you would continue to work with a psychotherapist or core treatment team when you move from one level of care to another, such as from inpatient to partial hospital to outpatient treatment.

CHAPTER THIRTEEN

Self-Regulation

Helplessness is at the core of trauma. If you have PTSD, the sense of help-lessness and lack of control does not end when the traumatizing situation is over. Having withstood the assault from without, you may later feel assaulted from within—by physiological arousal or by intrusive memories, flashbacks, and nightmares. Even your attempts to block such assaults by numbing and detachment can take on a life of their own, adding to the feeling of being out of control. At worst, to cope with unbearably painful feelings, some individuals resort to self-destructive ways of reducing tension—alcohol, drugs, eating binges, self-starvation, self-injury, and violence.[1] This chapter is devoted to self-enhancing ways of regulating and reducing tension.

Control is the antidote to helplessness. Control over the initial trauma was not possible. But some control over the subsequent effects of trauma is possible. Coping with the internal aftermath of trauma entails *self*-control.

267

The term *self-control,* however, may have negative connotations. The admonition "Control yourself!" may add insult to injury. *Self-regulation,* a term used in much of the psychological literature, is more neutral. Regulation implies being ordered, within limits, and predictable. The ultimate goal is not to squelch yourself but rather to experience an enhanced sense of self-awareness, self-mastery, volition, and freedom of choice.[2]

This chapter reviews several commonly used methods of self-regulation: sleep, exercise, relaxation, imagery, meditation, hypnosis, and biofeedback. It would be misleading to present these techniques as easy solutions to PTSD and dissociation. That would be like saying, "Control yourself!" or "Think positive!" Traumatic experience makes doing this difficult. I start with the difficulties. Then I focus on one goal of these techniques—to create positive emotional experiences. Having a clear idea of where you are going emotionally may make it easier for you to use these techniques to get there.

Simple but Difficult ◆ ◆ ◆ ◆ ◆ ◆ ◆ ◆ ◆

Trauma and stress are not new. Techniques of self-regulation are ancient. You may not have studied them, but you have used them. Most methods of self-regulation, such as exercise and relaxation, are simple. In relation to meditation, Jon Kabat-Zinn uses the phrase "simple but not easy." [3] For persons struggling with PTSD and dissociation, I have been putting it more strongly: *simple but difficult.* If they were not difficult, you'd already be using them successfully rather than reading this chapter. Three sources of this difficulty are worth thinking about: Methods of self-regulation require practice; they can be fraught with complications for persons with a history of trauma; and they require caring for yourself.

Practice

Learning to regulate your emotions and physiology is like any other skill—it requires practice.[4] It's like learning to play the piano. To become proficient requires determination and commitment. Such a major effort is no short-term project. If you are dealing with chronic PTSD, you are facing an indefinite need for self-regulation. You are in for the long haul. And these techniques do work, as long as you use them regularly. To some degree, they may become so natural that you employ them unconsciously; then regular practice is less necessary. But if you are struggling with a disorder that is distressing at best and incapacitating at worst, daily practice of self-regulation techniques is well worth the effort—perhaps even an hour or more a day as needed. As Kabat-Zinn says about meditation, "Try it for a few years and see what happens." [5]

Complications

The second source of difficulty: Problems associated with PTSD and dissociation can complicate the use of these techniques. Techniques designed to enhance self-control may instead trigger anxiety, flashbacks, or dissociation. Persons with a trauma history can easily be demoralized when the very things offered as helpful prove instead to be unusable or retraumatizing. Fortunately, there is such a wide range of techniques that there is bound to be something for everyone. But finding what works for you may be difficult. It may take time and effort. You may be in for a period of trial and error.

The ubiquity of complications in the techniques to be discussed here should be taken as a word of caution. These techniques have been studied extensively and demonstrated to be helpful and effective in relation to one symptom of PTSD—anxiety—as well as having a range of other benefits, depending on the technique. But they have only begun to be studied specifically in relation to PTSD, and the research results are not yet in.

Caring for Yourself

The third and often most serious difficulty: Techniques of self-regulation-are intended to help you feel better—to even feel *good*. This means taking care of yourself. How can this be a seemingly insurmountable obstacle? Taking care of yourself implies *valuing* yourself. To the degree that the aftermath of trauma entails self-blame or self-hatred, taking care of yourself will go against the grain. "Why should I do anything good for myself when I don't deserve it?" Your self-concept has a steering function, and this train of thought can lead to a self-perpetuating stalemate. If you hate yourself, you won't take care of yourself, then you'll feel bad, hate yourself, ad infinitum.

Consider this argument: You must feel better about yourself first, then you will be able to use these techniques to take care of yourself. Logical, but maybe self-defeating. A good way to start feeling better about yourself is to take better care of yourself. Working on self-regulation could come first. It's difficult, but some of the rewards start occurring right away, and they can enhance your motivation to continue.

Methods of self-regulation are self-enhancing and freeing. They are designed to help you nourish yourself and build yourself up. The compass can be reset: There is no avoiding pain and suffering, but it helps to make a conscious decision to steer toward more positive emotional experience. Perhaps you could view self-regulation like a prescription: Positive emotional experience is like good medicine for PTSD. Take it several times daily. Granted, it may be difficult to swallow, at least at first.

Positive Emotions ◆ ◆ ◆ ◆ ◆ ◆ ◆ ◆ ◆ ◆

Fortunately, while legions of psychologists and others have studied the various forms of distress that befall us, a few have worked to understand positive emotion. We should be devoting at least as much energy to learning about feeling good as we do to learning about feeling bad.

It is easy to appreciate the biological significance of "negative emotions" like fear and anger. Fight and flight can save our skins. But positive emotion is just as biologically necessary. While pain and negative emotions tell us what to steer clear of, positive feelings tell us what to head for. Positive feelings go with activities that satisfy our basic needs, such as hunger, thirst, and sex. Positive feelings go with activities that lead to growth, development, mastery, and accomplishment. Positive feelings also accompany the healthy forms of relatedness. Neurophysiologist Jean-Didier Vincent puts it plainly: "This choice [between pleasure and pain] helps the species to adapt. What is good for it causes pleasure and what is bad causes displeasure." [6] Our brains come with billions of possible connections, and we have to hook them up on the basis of our experience. Good feelings are a guide: Hook this up! Do it again!

Unless you know what it feels like to feel good, you don't know how to get there. As a start, you must learn to identify your positive feelings. Look for them. Notice them. Pay attention to them. Then you can use various methods to cultivate them. Make them a more prominent part of your experience. Make good experience a habit, a daily routine. Ultimately, you can gain a sense of choice and freedom about your feelings. You can learn to change unnecessary distress—to bring it within more tolerable bounds and to shift into more positive experience. Beware, however, that you cannot necessarily change quickly from negative to positive feelings. Anxiety, fear, and anger create a blast of transmitters that remain in circulation—in the brain and in the rest of the body—sometimes for a long while. The switch can be turned on in an instant but it can be turned off only gradually.

We are quite accustomed to dividing up aversive emotions into anxiety, fear, anger, shame, depression, and the like. How do we divide up the positive emotions? Here the divisions are less clear-cut. I divide the pie somewhat arbitrarily into several slices—pleasure, interest and excitement, flow, enjoyment and joy, contentment, and pride.

Pleasure

Pleasure is probably the closest we have to a generic term for positive emotional experience. Somewhat fortuitously in the early 1950s, James Olds and Peter Milner[7] discovered what seemed to be a "pleasure center" in the brain. Put a microelectrode in the correct spot of a rat's brain, and the rat will forget about everything else in its life and keep stimulating it. The rat's attitude: Forget sex, food, and water, just let me stimulate these neurons! One rat in the original study[8] pressed a bar at the rate of 1,920 times an hour to keep the stimulation going; later studies showed response rates as high as 7,000 per hour.[9] Not just rats but all vertebrates seem to possess these little pockets of neurons that we like to have stimulated. The idea of a "pleasure center" has fallen out of vogue, and the circuitry for the brain reward system is turning out to be more complex than was originally supposed.[10] As Lewis Thomas[11] says, "it is precisely because of the existence of loose-minded people like me that the neurobiologists have gone carefully with this problem." But he concludes that "there is such a thing as pure pleasure, and there is a mechanism for mediating it alive in our brains. And not just our superior, world-class super-primate human brains, but perhaps in all kinds of brains."[12] What do these neural circuits signify? Thomas: "It must be something important, signifying something we need to have signified for our satisfaction in life."[13] He boils it down to the pleasure in the feeling of being alive—pleasure in life itself. I wonder if these circuits are turned on when we are in the midst of desirable activity, perhaps contributing something of the pleasurable inner coloring to the experience—a good brew of "transmitter soup" to match the consumption of a delectable meal.

Pleasure is closely linked to appetites—not just to eating a great meal but also to quenching thirst and having sex. Pleasure—with its close cousin pain—is intimately tied to bodily experience. We learn about pleasure through the body—nursing, being held and stroked. Pleasure comes through the appetites, the body, and the senses. Think of pleasurable sights, sounds, tastes, smells, and touch. Extending sensory pleasure a bit, think of aesthetic pleasure—wrapping your consciousness around something beautiful.

Intimate relationships provide a powerful source of pleasure. Early attachments provide the foundation for pleasure in contact and closeness, and later relationships afford an opportunity for intense physical pleasure. Joseph Lichtenberg[14] distinguishes between sexual and sensual pleasure. Sensual pleasure, evident from infancy onward, comes from being touched, held, stroked, and soothed. Sensual pleasure may spark sexual excitement, but not necessarily. Sensual pleasure can stand on its own. Many persons who have been traumatized find massage to be pleasurable and soothing when they are able to find a masseuse with whom they feel safe.

For those who have been sexually traumatized—raped or sexually abused—the pleasure that normally goes with sexuality has often become linked with negative emotions. Among the most confusing aspects of sexual trauma is the intermingling of sexual pleasure with fear, pain, shame, and guilt. Even in the midst of horrifying experience, the body and brain can respond sexually with excitement and orgasm—the circuits have been established over millions of years of evolution to respond to certain stimuli, and they work.

Sexual trauma can undermine sexual pleasure, because sexual arousal and excitement can become associated with danger, pain, and a host of negative emotions. But sexual trauma can also undermine *sensual* pleasure. Because sensual and sexual pleasure are often linked, sensual pleasure may be avoided. Yet touch is a vital need,[15] and trauma-related aversion to touch can result in severe deprivation.

Alternatively, if you have been sexually traumatized, you may desire sensual pleasure without sexual involvement. Some individuals put up with sex only for the purpose of obtaining some sensual pleasure in the process. Being held, touched, and stroked is soothing and may rekindle a sense of having a secure base. Many persons who have been injured sexually are content to forgo sexual pleasure entirely, remaining satisfied with being held and cuddled. Others stay tuned in to the physical contact preceding sex and then dissociate as soon as the interaction becomes sexual.

Interest and Excitement

We come wired to experience pleasure in our active engagement with the world.[16] This biologically based pleasure is on a spectrum ranging from interest (milder) to excitement (more intense). A capacity for interest and excitement is evident in infancy. These emotions are associated with a gradual and pleasurable rise in arousal. As Donald Nathanson[17] puts it, "Whatever causes an optimal increase in the intensity and rate of activity of anything going on in the brain will trigger the affect interest." Excitement gives life sparkle and zest. Interest and excitement bolster curiosity and novelty seeking. They fuel enthusiasm and involvement. They spark growth and development, motivating a wide range of activity and learning.

Relationships are a main arena for interest and excitement and a foremost source of positive emotions.[18] We also come wired with curiosity about other persons. Others are a continual source of novelty. Robert Emde[19] took the smiling baby as the model of positive emotion. Babies smile at other persons. Smiling is borne of mutual interest and sharing of excitement.

Excitement and fear have a common denominator—arousal. But the arousal in fear is more abrupt and severe. Novelty can be interesting and exciting or frightening and anxiety provoking. Because of this overlap, however, excitement and anxiety have only a fine line between them. Even our language blurs the distinction: We say we're "anxious" to do something when, in actuality, we're eager to do it—excited about it. PTSD can erode our sense of excitement, because any arousal can quickly trigger anxiety. The arousal does not stay within bounds. In turn, anxiety can trigger dissociation. Numbing, detachment, and avoidance can interfere with interest and involvement in a host of potentially pleasurable activities. Disengagement cuts you off from pleasure and points you toward depression. It is therefore crucial to become aware of the distinction between excitement and anxiety so as to enhance your capacity for pleasure.

Flow

Here's a new one: Psychologist Mihaly Csikszentmihalyi[20] has devoted his career to the study of optimal experience. His question: What is human experience at its best? This is something we should all know about. Csikszentmihalyi has been interested in *"the quality of subjective experience that made a behavior intrinsically rewarding."* [21] This is the behavior that we will keep doing for its own sake. Csikszentmihalyi captured it in the word *flow*. Positive engagement with the world is the wellspring of pleasure, and flow epitomizes optimal engagement.

Examples of flow abound. Csikszentmihalyi found them by asking hundreds of individuals about their optimal experiences. He and his colleagues also monitored persons throughout the day, periodically interrupting them to find out how often they were in flow and, if so, what they were doing at the time. At its most intense, flow involves a high level of challenging activity—mountain climbing, sailing, skiing, racing. In these instances, flow stands out clearly. It entails a high level of involvement and concentration. When you are in flow, you are completely absorbed in an activity; you are keenly conscious but not self-conscious.

Don't leap to the conclusion that flow is out of the question because you're not climbing Mount Everest. You can experience flow in less risky and dramatic activities. Flow is conspicuous in intellectually challenging endeavors—games like chess, writing, lively conversation or repartee, or any sort of problem solving. You can be in flow during quiet activities like reading or meditating. You can experience flow in routine activities of daily living. Many persons experience flow in the course of their work. Contrary to what you may think, you are more likely to be in flow at work than in leisure, especially if you have a challenging occupation. Watching TV is usually a low-flow activity.

After studying thousands of flow experiences, Csikszentmihalyi boiled it down to a simple formula: To be in flow, you must balance the challenge of the activity with your level of skill. You're in flow when you're doing something challenging *and* you have the ability to pull it off. Flow is self-enhancing and growth promoting: As you continue doing the activity, your skills increase; then you need to increase the level of challenge to stay in flow. It doesn't matter whether it's a sport, an intellectual discipline, or a craft.

Being in flow is like walking a tightrope. The balance tips, and you're into something else. If your skills fall below the level of challenge, you're in trouble: you become anxious—or worse, if your flow is in mountain climbing. Anxiety is the antithesis of flow: Anxiety goes with being immobilized, stuck, unable to move forward. Flow is the opposite of "behavioral inhibition." But anxiety is not the only alternative to flow. If the challenge is way below your level of skill, you become bored. If the activity involves neither challenge nor skill, you become apathetic.

The range of potential flow activities is endless. Flow is not in the activity; it's in your consciousness. Flow does not require a high level of skill; it entails finding the right level of challenge. Flow is intrinsic to human consciousness—and probably not unique to humans. But it is also partly a personality trait—some individuals are able to find opportunities for flow in the bleakest of situations. Csikszentmihalyi describes individuals in concentration camps who sustained themselves by dreaming up imaginative intellectual challenges. The environment need not be an obstacle to enjoyment: "The Eskimos in their bleak, inhospitable lands learned to sing, dance, joke, carve beautiful objects, and create an elaborate mythology to give order and sense to their experiences." [22] Others can spend megabucks on yachts, electronics, and sporting gear, only to remain bored and apathetic.

Finding your way from anxiety or detachment to flow may not be easy. A history of trauma and preoccupation with emotional survival is hardly conducive to flow. And exciting activities conducive to flow can trigger excessive arousal and anxiety. But flow is captivating and self-perpetuating; it feeds on itself. Once you hit on something, you want to repeat it for its own sake. Here is Csikszentmihalyi's summary of what goes into flow:

> First, the experience usually occurs when we confront tasks we have a chance of completing. Second, we must be able to concentrate on what we are doing. Third and fourth, the concentration is usually possible because the task undertaken has clear goals and provides immediate feedback. Fifth, one acts with a deep but effortless involvement that removes from awareness the worries and frustrations of everyday life. Sixth, enjoyable experiences allow per-

sons to exercise a sense of control over their actions. Seventh, concern for the self disappears, yet paradoxically the sense of self emerges stronger after the flow experience is over. Finally, the sense of the duration of time is altered; hours pass by in minutes, and minutes can stretch out to seem like hours. The combination of all these elements causes a sense of deep enjoyment that is so rewarding people feel that expending a great deal of energy is worthwhile simply to be able to feel it.[23]

Enjoyment and Joy

If interest and excitement are in the anticipation, enjoyment and joy are in the consummation. Nathanson[24] contends that, just as interest and excitement are associated with a pleasurable rise in arousal, enjoyment and joy are associated with a pleasurable decrease: "anything capable of causing a decrease in the rate and intensity of neuronal firing in the brain of infant or adult will trigger the response of a smile." Ahhhh—satisfaction! After great exertion, success! Relief! I put flow between excitement and enjoyment because I think it captures the experience of using your skills to transform challenge to success.

Contentment

Nathanson extends the enjoyment-joy curve down to the state of "contentment," where the arousal of excitement followed by enjoyment has largely subsided. I think it is worth highlighting this end of the curve, whether we call it contentment, tranquillity, peace, relaxation, calm, stillness, or quiet. A model of contentment is the calm after orgasm—assuming freedom from traumatic sexual experience. Another example is relief after distress: "observe the infant and note that every time distress is relieved, the baby smiles and becomes calm. No matter what the source of distress, relief produces contentment." [25] The goal of relaxation exercises is the feeling of contentment.

Pride

Emde's[26] studies of smiling babies led him to appreciate the pleasure in "getting it right." This marvelous phrase captures the pleasure in learning, understanding, and reaching a goal. Getting it right leads to a feeling of competence, control, efficacy. The pleasure in getting it right is the flip side of helplessness.

Nathanson thinks of pride and shame as being polar opposites. Shame involves a plummeting of pleasure associated with deflation. Pride follows the enjoyment of success. He spells out three conditions necessary for pride:

> (1) A purposeful, goal-directed, intentional activity is undertaken while under the influence of the affect interest—excitement; (2) this activity must be successful in achieving its goal; following which (3) the achievement of the goal suddenly releases the individual from the preceding effort and the affect that accompanies and amplifies it, thus triggering enjoyment—joy.[27]

This captures much of what Csikszentmihalyi puts into flow. Think of pride as the afterglow of flow.

Pride, like shame, is a social emotion. When you feel proud, you want to be noticed and admired. You want to share your accomplishments. Shame is the opposite: When you feel ashamed, you are inclined to withdraw, to hide your face. Traumatic experience can interfere with pride the same way it interferes with all other emotions. Just as pleasure can become connected to shame, the pleasure in pride can also be connected to shame. Self-doubt, self-criticism, and self-hatred are incompatible with pride. With a history of trauma, pride may be extremely hard to come by. It's well worth cultivating this source of pleasure as an antidote to shame.

The Elusiveness of Pleasure

How often have you thought at a moment of peak pleasure, "I wish I could preserve this moment forever!" or "I wish I could keep this going!" You couldn't. The moment you start thinking about how great something feels, you become self-conscious, and the pleasure is liable to start evaporating.

Consciousness does not hold still. A pleasurable cycle involves excitement, enjoyment, contentment. The first morsel delights; with succeeding bites, the intensity of the pleasure fades. Psychologists have a name for it: "habituation." The effect wears off. We respond similarly to many drugs. Stronger doses become necessary to get the same pleasurable effect. A destructive cycle involves pleasure, then painful addiction.

Nor is constant contentment and relaxation a possibility. Just try it. With years of practice, meditators can sit still for prolonged periods of time. Without such dedication, stillness leads to boredom and apathy. Constant pleasure, constant relaxation, are both impossible. Emotions are in flux. Hedonism—the pursuit of pleasure—is futile. Pleasure turns into frustration. Contentment follows exertion and achievement. No pain, no gain. No challenge, no flow.

Under the best of circumstances, there is no such thing as a life of unmitigated pleasure. But life can be filled—to varying degrees—with *moments* of pleasure, excitement, flow, enjoyment, contentment, and pride. The pleasurable moments cannot be sought for their own sake; they are by-products of absorption and involvement in rewarding activities and relationships.

Anyone who has experienced the extraordinary pain of trauma would do well to take advantage of every opportunity available for healthy doses of pleasure. Emde points out that positive emotion is a good buffer against stress.[28] Good medicine. The more positive experiences you can have, the more resilient you will be. Developing a better sense of choice and control—an enhanced capacity for self-regulation—can be a major source of pleasure and pride.

Go Slow With Pleasure

Before turning to the tried-and-true methods of generating positive emotions, I want to issue a warning: You may need to *take pleasure in small doses*. Build up your tolerance to pleasure gradually. You may have little difficulty understanding your need to accustom yourself slowly to feeling and expressing anger. You may find it odd to think of pleasure in similar ways. But for many persons who have been through trauma, pleasure has been associated with pain. Pleasurable feelings can become a danger signal. I have talked to patients who have felt suicidal after experiencing intense pleasure, because their positive feelings triggered fear, shame, and guilt. You may need to go slowly with pleasure, gradually desensitizing yourself to it, learning over time to suppress the connection between pleasure and the painful emotions associated with it in the past.

Methods of Self-Regulation ◆ ◆ ◆ ◆ ◆ ◆ ◆

Many fine books have been devoted to methods of self-regulation. You would do well to read them, since I can give only a brief overview here. If you've had traumatic experience, you have a head start. To the extent that you have felt out of control, you have doubtlessly devoted thought and effort to regaining control. As you read through many of these methods, you may find yourself thinking, "That's what I've been trying to do." People have been trying to achieve more self-control for millennia. The professional and academic contribution has been to refine what people have done naturally throughout the ages. But before considering the more refined methods, the most basic form of physiological self-regulation—sleep—deserves attention.

Sleep

The chronic stress associated with posttraumatic symptoms is wearing. I often hear, "I didn't do anything all day—Why am I so exhausted?" Even if you have not run a marathon, your sympathetic nervous system may have been in high gear throughout the day. Anxiety, irritation, and other distressing emotions are tiring. Depression is enervating. Sleep is the best medicine: In his recent book, *The Chemistry of Conscious States,* Harvard psychiatrist and neurophysiologist Allan Hobson[29] contends: "Of all the practices known to be associated with good health, sleep is the most fundamental." Sleep not only restores the balance of key neurotransmitters essential for daytime alertness but also enhances immune function.

Hobson's prescription: You need "to figure out how much sleep you need and to see that you get it." [30] There are wide individual differences—partly genetic—in need for sleep. Although 7.5 hours is a useful average, some persons function well with a few hours, whereas others may need 9 or 10. Hobson recommends keeping track of quantity and quality of sleep in conjunction with daytime activities and mood. Doing this for a month may reveal the length of sleep conducive to daily well-being. Hobson's advice if you need more sleep: "Go to bed earlier." [31]

Hobson's recommendations are *simple but difficult* if you're struggling with trauma-related problems. Anxiety and depression often follow trauma, and they are notorious for depriving people of sleep. In addition, persons prone to traumatic nightmares may become phobic about sleeping and then may avoid sleeping. Or those whose traumatic experience has occurred at night may only be able to sleep during daylight hours, disrupting their sleep-wake cycle. Here we have more vicious circles: Symptoms interfere with sleep, and disrupted sleep intensifies symptoms.

Depression is especially challenging, because it alters the balance of neurotransmitters and disrupts the organization of sleep, leading to excess dreaming (rapid eye movement, or *REM*) sleep and loss of deep, nondreaming sleep. In the context of depression, more sleep is *not* restorative. Hobson proposes regular exercise to correct the disruptive imbalance of neurotransmitters. But depressed persons will quickly recognize the catch-22: You need sleep to have the energy to exercise, and you need exercise to get proper sleep.

Fortunately, antidepressant medications can assist in restoring the balance of regulatory neurotransmitters. Depending on the source of interference, not only antidepressants but also a wide range of other psychiatric medications may be helpful in restoring sleep. But Hobson emphasizes the downside of drugs, viewing them as a last resort best used on a short-term basis. He advocates changes in lifestyle: "The brain knows best. It knows what it needs, it knows how to get it, and it knows what to do once its needs are met. Sleep is of the brain, by the brain, for the brain. And it benefits the body as well. But the naturally beneficial effects of sleep can occur only if we let them occur." [32]

Although the difficulties in getting needed sleep are not easily overcome, the first step is to *take seriously* your feelings of exhaustion and your need for sleep. Sleeping might become your highest priority, the best way to take care of yourself, day after day. But getting adequate sleep may not be easy. Like other means of self-regulation, it can be a long-term project. Pressure to sleep will just keep you awake.

Exercise

The benefits of exercise have been widely touted, and they need little reiteration here. Cooper's book *Aerobics*[33] conveys the enthusiasm and provides the prescriptions. Beyond its value as a global elixir, exercise has much to offer persons coping with trauma.

Although not specific to PTSD, a substantial amount of research has shown that exercise can decrease anxiety and depression.[34] Westerlund[35] also observed that many incest survivors find exercise to be one of the best ways to regain a sense of control over their bodies. Despite the widespread enthusiasm for the psychological benefits of exercise, we await a convincing physiological explanation for the effects of exercise on mood.[36] Moreover, as in virtually all areas of psychological research, there are many contradictory findings, and it is difficult to generalize from one individual to another.[37] Exercise may or may not work for you.

It may seem ironic that exercise can be anxiety reducing, because it requires a high level of activation. But chronic anxiety entails an activated fight-or-flight response that has no outlet in vigorous activity. Exercise such as running is a natural way to defuse that tension and arousal. Nevertheless, some persons find that exercise *increases* anxiety, probably because of its initially arousing effects.

I have worked with persons who have been afraid to exercise because they were catapulted into panic attacks by it. Others have had flashbacks triggered by exercise. Some begin to dissociate and then become confused and disoriented. Arousal is likely to be the culprit. Rapid heartbeat or labored breathing, for example, is often a response to traumatic experience. Anything that increases heart rate or makes a person gasp for breath—even if it has nothing to do with trauma—can evoke traumatic memories and bring back the whole constellation of traumatic experience.

The possibility that exercise can increase anxiety or evoke intrusive memories should be taken as a caution; hard exercise may not work for you. The risk of increased anxiety is also an indication that exercise should be approached gradually—not a bad idea for many reasons. You don't have to run; you can walk. A manageable routine for exercise can provide a sense of predictability, control, and accomplishment. Success is just doing it regularly—at whatever level. This is where the need for commitment and determination comes in.

Relaxation

Relaxation is the simplest of the simple techniques. You may want to read Herbert Benson's book, *The Relaxation Response.*[38] Benson spells out four components to relaxation: 1) a quiet environment with few distractions; 2) a mental focus on a particular sound, word, phrase, or object; 3) a passive, "let it happen" attitude, free of concern about how well you are do-ing; and 4) a comfortable position to minimize muscle tension. You may add deep, regular breathing, but you shouldn't force it. Diaphragmatic breathing is best: Breathe into your belly, not your chest. Some individu-als like to use progressive muscle relaxation: Tense and relax the muscles in various parts of your body, just to highlight the difference between ten-sion and relaxation. Begin at your feet or your forehead; work your way up or down.

The relaxation response is the innate counterpart to the fight-or-flight response. To facilitate vigorous action, the fight-or-flight response depends on heightened sympathetic nervous system activation. Metabolism is at its peak. The relaxation response is a state of rest that slows metabolism. Heart rate, oxygen consumption, and respiration are lowered—the physiology of contentment.

This technique can be simple but difficult: With a house full of children and a ringing telephone, finding a quiet spot and uninterrupted time might be more challenging than mountain climbing. But all is not lost: It takes only minutes to relax. Benson recommends 10 to 20. As with exercise, a routine for relaxation is essential. Succeeding merely involves doing it regu-larly. Relaxation is like exercise: As long as you keep doing it, it works. Stop, and the benefits stop—unless you've managed to weave it into your daily routine.

It's hard to imagine anything more innocuous than relaxation. But re-laxation can be problematic for persons who have been traumatized. This paradoxical response has been observed frequently enough to have a name—*relaxation-induced anxiety.*[39] You may associate relaxation with let-ting your guard down. In a relaxed state, you may feel vulnerable to attack. So you may need to be alert at all times. Before letting yourself relax, you may need to do whatever is necessary to assure yourself that you are in a safe place, protected from any intrusion.

Relaxation entails focusing inward, on your breathing and on your muscles. Your attention is directed away from outer reality onto your body. When you let go of focus on outer reality, you may be prone to dissociate.[40] Rather than feeling relaxed, you might begin to feel spaced out or unreal. Dissociation is the opposite of feeling grounded in outer reality. Relaxation exercises tend to remove this sensory scaffolding.

Ideally, you can learn to become grounded in the physical reality of your

body—for example, by focusing on your breathing. Yet if you have had your bodily integrity violated, you may often work hard to avoid any awareness of your body. Some individuals feel as if they do not exist from the neck down. If this is your experience, standard relaxation exercises may be intolerable.

Fortunately, it is not necessary to do body awareness exercises to relax. Sitting quietly may be enough. Quiet activities like reading or handicrafts can be relaxing for many persons. Routinely setting aside time for quiet activities may be a way to ease into more formal relaxation practice.

Imagery

Picture a field of wildflowers. Hear the sound of a waterfall. You have been using imagery all your life. For most persons, visual imagery is especially vivid and powerful. Imagery is essential to memory, particularly autobiographical memory.

Imagery is tied to memory and to emotion. Intrusive images of traumatic experience are common symptoms of PTSD. Sights, sounds, smells, tastes, and body sensations can all be associated with reexperiencing trauma. No one knows the power of imagery better than someone who has struggled with PTSD.

Think of yourself as having a library of images. Picture a section of the library devoted to traumatic images—but don't open any of the books in that section now! You have a section for imagery associated with positive experiences—pleasure, excitement, enjoyment, contentment, and pride. This is a section worth browsing in. Spend lots of time there. You may not have checked out some of the volumes for a long time. Put them back in circulation. Check them out regularly in your spare moments.

You can use imagery flexibly and creatively. You can piece together images from memory to imagine something that you have not actually experienced, like floating on a cloud. Much of your anxiety and worry revolves around imagery—anticipating the worst. Your images are also accompanied by changes in your physiological state, so anticipating the worst tends to promote it. But you can create library shelves devoted to imagined scenes that are pleasurable and calming.

Many therapies use *guided* imagery,[41] which simply means that you are provided with suggestions for images that will evoke certain ideas and emotions. You may be told to picture yourself lying on a beach on a beautiful sunny day, watching puffy clouds float by, hearing the sound of waves gently lapping at the shore, feeling the warmth of sand against your skin. Although such imagery may initially be suggested by a therapist, ultimately developing your own images is better than using someone else's. For months, I suggested to a woman that she picture herself sinking into relaxation by slowing descending a staircase; eventually, she confessed that she had all the while been picturing herself floating down a river on a raft! To each her own. Given the choice, I suppose I'd opt for the raft, too.

For plants, territoriality is a done deal. We animals have to work at it. Yet we each need a safe place—preferably many safe places. Deep relaxation should be practiced in a safe place. But imagery can also be used to bolster a sense of safety. Imagined safe places, tailored to your own experience and preferences, can be comforting. Many persons can enhance their feeling of safety by imagining themselves in secluded and protected places.

In coping with stress, anxiety, and trauma, we use imagery in a virtually instinctive way. As discussed in relation to consciousness and dissociative disorders, many traumatized individuals use imagery in the service of mental escape. Some persons in the midst of traumatic experience can dissociate themselves from the trauma by imaging themselves to be elsewhere—outside in the garden among beautiful flowers, wrapped up in a sleeping bag, or traveling through the outer reaches of the galaxy.

But comforting imagery developed in situations of desperation may be problematic. Some soothing images will be so closely linked to traumatic experience that bringing them to mind will also tend to reevoke the traumatic memories. These well-worn images may be haunted by trauma. This section of your imagery library may be adjacent to the traumatic images section. You might be better off moving to a new area and creating new volumes of fresh imagery.

Because imagery is so closely linked to dissociation for many persons, the process of evoking positive images may lead to dissociative states. You might find that you become so absorbed in imagery that you lose track of time, lose touch with your surroundings, or feel somewhat spacey or unreal. Or images that start off benign may lead down a path of associations to more disturbing images—into the black hole.[42] Working with a therapist can help you learn to use imagery in a way that helps you stay grounded and also leads away from traumatic memories rather than back into them.

Meditation

Of all the techniques described here, meditation probably has the most venerable history.[43] Meditation practice is ancient, having evolved in the context of early Eastern religions. Meditation and prayer have much in common, and for many, the spiritual dimension forms the foundation of meditation. But meditation can also be separated from religion and spirituality. Meditation can enhance consciousness. Meditation has much in common with relaxation. Herbert Benson's[44] methods of eliciting the relaxation response combine relaxation instruction and techniques from transcendental meditation.

What is the essence of meditation? Definitions vary, as do meditative practices. Dean Shapiro[45] defines *meditation* as "a family of techniques which have in common a conscious attempt to focus attention in a nonanalytical way and an attempt not to dwell on discursive, ruminating thought." *Ruminating thought* includes dwelling on the past and worrying about the future.

I think *mindfulness* is the single most useful idea in meditation. Buddhist teacher Thich Nhat Hanh[46] defines mindfulness as "keeping one's consciousness alive to the present reality." Mindfulness is consciousness without self-consciousness—flow. But shutting out self-consciousness is no easy matter. We are the beneficiaries of an evolutionary history that has endowed us with self-awareness and has enabled us to transcend the present by bridging from past to future. This grand evolutionary achievement can also ruin our conscious lives by continually dragging us out of the present:

> Even the simplest or most pleasurable of daily activities—walking, eating, conversing, driving, reading, waiting, thinking, making love, planning, gardening, drinking, remembering, going to a therapist, writing, dozing, emoting, sight-seeing—all pass rapidly in a blur of abstract commentary as the mind hastens to its next mental occupation.[47]

Coping with trauma entails separating the past from the present, not being unduly apprehensive about the dangers of the future, and seeing the present for what it is. Alan Watts[48] put it pithily: "There is never anything but the present, and if one cannot live there, one cannot live anywhere." There is no better term for this ideal than *mindfulness*.

Mindfulness meditation is probably the best example of a technique that is simple but difficult. Like all other forms of self-regulation, it requires practice.[49] Just sit in a chair and pay attention to your breath, nothing else. Be aware of your belly expanding and contracting. Concentrate on the sensations of the air passing through your nostrils. How many seconds go by before you are thinking about something else? Not many:

> The body is sitting, but the mind is seized constantly by thoughts, feelings, inner conversations, daydreams, fantasies, sleepiness, opinions, theories, judgments about thoughts and feelings, judgments about judgments—a never-ending torrent of disconnected mental events that the meditators do not even realize are occurring except at those brief instants when they remember what they are doing.[50]

Meditation practice assumes that your attention will be wandering continually. Before you know it, you are worrying. You are planning. You are rehashing the past. No matter how long you practice meditation, you will drift away from the present. It's inevitable, and criticizing yourself for it runs counter to meditation practice. Chalk it up to evolution. Just gently bring your attention back to the present focus, for example, on your breathing.

Mindfulness can be the antithesis of dissociation—the opposite end of the spectrum. Dissociation is associated with a sense of unreality; mindfulness is a state of being highly aware of reality, not spaced out but tuned in. This is why meditation may be helpful in relation to dissociation. Mindfulness could enhance "grounding" techniques that focus attention on current sensory experience.

Another cornerstone of meditation is the attitude of *equanimity*.[51] Equanimity entails a degree of detachment, but not to the extreme of dissociation. Equanimity involves an attitude of acceptance toward your experience, whatever it may be. Benson[52] calls it a "passive attitude." It is a noncritical stance: If your mind wanders, so be it. If you feel tension or discomfort, so be it. If you feel anxious or angry, so be it. Mindfulness and equanimity are a good pair. They foster awareness and acceptance of current experience—a sense of ease regarding whatever state of mind you're in. Throw in compassion for yourself, no matter what you feel, and you will be in good shape.

In principle, meditation, like relaxation, can be done anywhere. Mindfulness and equanimity are beneficial attitudes at just about any time. People commonly learn to meditate, however, by sitting in a quiet place, the goal being "to simplify the situation to the bare minimum."[53] Meditation, like relaxation, can be done lying down; with both, you may be prone to falling asleep. Falling asleep may not be a bad thing, but the point is to learn to regulate waking consciousness. Some persons like to sit in the lotus position or to use paraphernalia like meditation cushions or tailor-made benches. Some take on the challenge of sitting motionless for long periods. Like anything else, this whole thing should not be carried to extremes: "a certain amount of 'sitting just to sit' might well be the best thing in the world for the jittery minds and agitated bodies of Europeans and Americans—provided they do not use it as a method for turning themselves into Buddhas."[54]

Meditation is an ancient practice, but a host of scientific research now attests to its beneficial effects.[55] In his highly readable books, *Full Catastrophe Living*[56] and *Wherever You Go, There You Are*,[57] Jon Kabat-Zinn has described in detail the meditation procedures that he and his colleagues have used in stress-reduction programs. He has done an admirable job of translating Eastern meditation practice into Western concepts and language. Recently, he and his colleagues have shown that a meditation-based stress reduction program was highly effective in the treatment of anxiety disorders,[58] although PTSD was not included. The meditation training was also helpful in reducing depression.

Like every other technique of self-regulation, meditation is not without risks.[59] Meditation can be used as an escape from living.[60] Sitting motionless for prolonged periods can have a trance-inducing effect. For persons who are prone to dissociation, meditation can lead to a sense of loss of control rather than to enhanced control. Meditation is conducive to opening up the inner world of thoughts and feelings. For this reason, it can evoke anxiety, painful memories, or distressing images and ideas. Although the *intent* may be to foster your ability to concentrate on one thing (your breathing), the actual *effect* may be that you get stuck in painful experience. If you become emotionally overwhelmed, you may not *be able* to gently bring your attention back to the focus of awareness.

Picking up a book on meditation and starting to practice might be like trying self-hypnosis without adequate preparation—unwise. Like hypnosis, meditation can be learned as part of a therapy process. Or meditation can be practiced with the support of a teacher or a group. However, for persons coping with trauma, meditation—like any other technique—should be started gradually and cautiously.

Hypnosis

Hypnosis is a procedure to help a person enter a trance state. The idea of one person "hypnotizing" another is misleading. A therapist can *help* someone who wishes to do so enter a hypnotic state. As stated earlier, some individuals are more "hypnotizable" than others: They are more adept at entering a trance state, they need less help to do so, they can enter a deeper state, they can do it more quickly, and they may be able to do it spontaneously (without help).[61]

Trance induction.   Helping a willing and able subject to enter a trance state is not difficult. There are probably as many methods of doing so as there are therapists who use hypnosis. Many therapists use relaxation techniques and guided imagery, coupled with suggestions that the individual will sink deep into a trance or hypnotic sleep. The trance can be deepened gradually by counting—for example, "As I count from one to ten, I want you to enter a pleasant hypnotic sleep—1, 2, 3 . . . deeper . . . 4, 5, etc." The therapist provides the suggestions, and it's up to you to find a way to enter the trance state, given the opportunity.

The trance state.   What is a hypnotic trance? This is not an easy question to answer. The trance state is complex, having many facets that work to-gether.[62] A common element is *relaxation,* and relaxation instructions are often part of the hypnotic induction. The trance state also entails a shift in *attention.* Ordinarily, your attention is all over the place, open to any kind of input, like a wide-angle camera lens. But a trance state is more like a telephoto lens, zooming in on a narrow band, shutting out the rest. The trance also makes use of *dissociation.* In the trance state, attention is focused inward, dissociated from the outer environment. The therapist may suggest that you close your eyes and ignore all sounds but that of her voice. Other dissociations can be suggested—for example, that your arm lifts as if pulled up by a helium balloon, without a sense that you are doing it voluntarily.

Finally, the trance state entails heightened *suggestibility,* an openness to the ideas and guidance of the therapist and a willingness to follow instructions. Many persons have misconceptions about suggestibility. It is not as if a "hypnotist" takes over your mind. You remain in control over what you say and do, and you do not follow suggestions that go against your moral beliefs. Hypnosis does not require you to *give up* control; it enhances your control.[63]

Therapeutic uses of the trance state.   It is easy to help a hypnotizable person get into a trance state—the challenge is in what to do next. Being in a trance state is not in itself therapeutic. But the trance state can be used to facilitate or enhance many therapeutic techniques and interventions. The work to be done in trance should be carefully planned, and the patient and therapist should have a clear understanding and agreement about this plan so as to be able to work together productively.

The narrowed field of attention and heightened concentration provide much of the power of hypnosis. The trance state can highlight and amplify whatever you are attending to. Images become so vivid that they seem real. Vivid imagery can facilitate relaxation or sense of safety.[64] You can have the illusion that you really *are* on that peaceful beach or in that protected forest sanctuary. You can fully immerse your mind in an image or idea, planting it more firmly than you could do otherwise. The power of words is magnified. You can really hear and take in suggestions that build self-esteem and confidence, concentrating on your positive qualities and accomplishments, amplifying your positive feelings, and reinforcing your sense of self-control.

The enhanced focus afforded by the trance state can also be used to explore memories—with the caveat that there is no assurance of the historical accuracy of memories reconstructed in this way. The trance helps to clear away distractions. Traumatic memories are often intruding in bits and pieces, in the form of isolated images that make little sense. These may be fleeting images that stir up fear and anxiety so that you try to get them out of your mind rather than concentrating on them. In trance, it is possible to hold the images in mind and slowly explore their connections to a traumatic scene. Because emotions and memories are packaged, it is also possible to use feelings as a bridge to memories.[65] For example, you can concentrate on feeling angry, and go back in time from one memory to another connected with that angry feeling. In the process, the traumatic experiences composed of images and feelings can be put into words and communicated to the therapist. The story can be told.

It is also possible to use trance to regulate the intensity of emotion, a particularly important part of working with traumatic memories.[66] Techniques to regulate emotion are limited only by the imagination of you and your therapist. For example, using imagery related to videotape can be helpful.[67] You can imagine memories stored on videotapes; you can play the tape at a rate—speeded up or slowed down—that makes the emotion manageable. You can imagine that the memory is being played on a TV or movie screen that is distant or very small. You can picture a dial to turn up and down the intensity of your feelings. You may agree in advance on a signal, such as raising a finger, to convey to the therapist that your feelings are beginning to become too strong, and then you can back off and concentrate on relaxing imagery.

David Spiegel[68] gives an example of the "split screen" technique in working with traumatic experiences. Patients are instructed to maintain a pleasant sense of floating relaxation in their body, and to picture in their mind an imaginary screen. They are asked to picture two images side by side on this screen. The first is drawn from memories of the traumatic experience. They are taught to balance this image with one representing what they did to protect themselves: in combat, what efforts were made to save a buddy's life, even at the risk of their own; in the case of the loss of a friend in combat, remembering those experiences of joy that were shared together and will remain even though the friend is gone; in the case of rape, the efforts that the victim made to defend herself or protect her life. The split screen is, metaphorically, a way of helping patients put the traumas into perspective by seeing it as a part but not all of themselves.

You may also use trance states to reinforce images of containing strong feelings or memories.[69] For example, you can put the film or videotape away when you have remembered enough. You can put it on a shelf or in a vault. You can put the feelings behind a concrete dam or bury them in a well-sealed trunk. Such ideas and images may not be as powerful if you try them in an ordinary waking state; it takes experimentation and practice to have voluntary control with imagery. In a trance state, however, images can have an immediate and powerful effect.

Just as the trance state can be used to focus on images, ideas, and memories, it can also be used to better control the process of dissociation. Indeed, hypnosis is controlled dissociation. In the face of trauma, dissociation becomes an automatic, reflexive defense. You may do it spontaneously without wanting to. With the aid of hypnosis, you can develop a sense of control over the process of dissociation.[70] Just going in and out of a trance state deliberately can enable you to develop a sense of voluntary control over the process. In the trance state, the sense of reality fades; as you come back out of the trance, the sense of reality returns. In the process of going back and forth, you can begin to establish a sense of control over your feeling of connection to reality.

You can also use the trance state to bring to mind dissociated states,[71] such as dissociated traumatic memories or otherwise inaccessible states of mind in dissociative identity disorder. For example, you can imagine that you are on a stage, and different parts of you can be invited to come out to the front of the stage and speak. Through this process, you can gain a sense of control over the dissociative switching between different states of mind. What previously happened automatically or was blocked from memory can be done deliberately under the added mental control afforded by the trance state. Hypnosis can also facilitate the final process of unification in dissociative identity disorder.[72]

Potential problems.   Trust is essential in any therapeutic relationship, and problems with trust are often brought to the fore when hypnosis is part of the treatment. You might erroneously conclude that you cannot be "hypnotized," because you have been unable to enter a trance with a particular therapist. You may have been perfectly capable of entering a trance state, but you did not feel safe with that therapist. Feeling safe and having confidence in your therapist are prerequisites for hypnosis. Distrust is a self-protective safeguard. To enter a deep trance, you will need to trust, and your feeling of trust must be based on the therapist's being trustworthy and adequately trained in the use of hypnosis.

Having a trustworthy therapist is essential, but it may not be enough. Persons who have been injured by caregivers will have substantial difficulty trusting. This will be highlighted when it comes to hypnosis, which entails letting down your guard and going along with suggestions while in an altered state of mind. Merely closing your eyes in the presence of a therapist may intensify your feelings of vulnerability. Problems with trust are always prime material for discussion in any therapeutic relationship, and some patients find that they can begin to use hypnosis only after a substantial period of building trust in the therapist and the therapy process. For some patients, developing the ability to overcome the distrust associated with hypnosis proves to be therapeutic in itself.[73]

The trance state evoked by hypnosis is therapeutic to the extent that the experience is controlled and regulated.[74] But this may be easier said than done. Because hypnosis makes images and memories so vivid, the emotions can spiral to an overwhelming level. The techniques for emotional regulation come into play here. In addition, your experience of dissociation is likely to be associated with trauma. That is, just as certain feelings and images are connected with traumatic memories, so, too, is the protective mechanism of dissociation. Being in a state of dissociation may therefore remind you of the traumatic experience that initially prompted it. The feeling of being in a trance state can itself trigger traumatic memories and painful emotions. For this reason, if you have been having difficulty with PTSD and dissociation, the initial trance work may be largely devoted to feeling calm and safe and developing a sense of control over different states of consciousness.

Self-hypnosis.   If you have coped with trauma by dissociating, you have been using a kind of "self-hypnosis." [75] That is, you automatically do something to put yourself into a trance state. You may stare at a spot or concentrate on fantasies or images that evoke a trance state. Psychologist Shirley Sanders[76] thinks that it is misleading to call such techniques *self-hypnosis*. She calls this instinctual, survival-oriented trance state *archetypal self-hypnosis* to distinguish it from *clinical self-hypnosis*, which is learned in the course of a therapy process.

Clinical self-hypnosis is an extension of clinical hypnosis. It is analogous to homework. You can practice the skills learned in therapy at home on your own, increasing your mastery and making them more a part of your daily life. Once having worked with a therapist and having learned to use the trance state in a deliberate and controlled way, you can learn to do it without the therapist's immediate presence. This is best done gradually. For example, the therapist will use a certain induction technique, such as counting or employing certain images or cues, to help you enter a trance. You could also begin self-hypnosis by doing it all in your own head with the therapist present. The therapist would be there to help as needed. Eventually, with practice, you could use self-hypnosis to enter a trance state when you are by yourself—for example, to enhance imagery and deepen relaxation. Or you may tape-record the therapist's induction and play it back to help you enter a trance state when you are by yourself.

For persons with a history of trauma, PTSD, and dissociative disorders, clinical self-hypnosis should be approached with considerable caution. Obviously, it would not make sense to use self-hypnosis to try to uncover traumatic memories or to do anything else that would have a risk of leading to unmanageably strong emotions. Instead, it is helpful to use self-hypnosis to bolster a sense of control and mastery—for example, to enhance relaxation or a feeling of being in a safe place.

Biofeedback and Psychophysiological Self-Regulation

Compared with most of the age-old methods of self-regulation described here, biofeedback is a recent innovation—only about three decades old. And, unlike the rest, biofeedback requires some technology.

Psychophysiological self-regulation is a mouthful, but the basic idea behind biofeedback is really not that complicated. You can change what goes on in your body by your behavior and by what you imagine and think about. Sit down, breathe deeply, imagine being in a pleasant spot, and you will relax—your heart rate will slow, and your muscles will relax. Start imagining your traumatic experience or anything else frightening, and your level of physiological arousal will zoom back up. This capacity to use thought and imagery to influence emotion reflects the influence of your rational brain (neocortex) on your emotional brain (limbic system).

To some degree, you can tell how physiologically aroused you are by paying attention to your body; your emotional brain is in tune with your physiology and provides your rational brain with information about it. Also, partly for neurophysiological reasons, individuals differ in sensitivity to physiology;[77] some are relatively insensitive to internal changes, whereas others are *hyper*sensitive. To one degree or another, you can feel your heart pound, you can feel your respiration quicken, and you can feel your muscles tense. The more in tune you are with your body, the more you will be able to regulate your physiological arousal. If your body has been violated, however, you may have difficulty being aware of your physiological state. You may have learned to tune out your body.

But you don't have to rely on your own inner bodily sensations. Here's where biofeedback comes in: Biofeedback is "the feedback of biological information to a person." [78] Feedback is essential to learning any skill.[79] In learning to talk, you rely on the sound of your voice to make the needed adjustments in your vocalization. With the aid of biofeedback technology, you can now rely on external feedback such as meters or tones to help you make adjustments in your physiological state. Biofeedback is not in itself a means of self-regulation; it provides feedback about physiological responses that can facilitate your use of other techniques such as relaxation, visualization, or meditation. The proper term is *biofeedback-assisted self-regulation*.[80] By means of biofeedback, you can gradually learn to broaden your sphere of conscious, voluntary control over any physiological activity you can monitor. With the aid of technology, you give your rational brain an added edge in influencing your emotional brain. In the process, you are not training your body; you are training your brain.[81]

A lot of gear has been developed to measure physiological arousal precisely. You can hook yourself up to a heart-rate monitor and observe exactly how fast your heart is beating from moment to moment. With such equipment, you can detect subtle cardiovascular changes that you might not normally be aware of. You can also become aware of the influence of your own thought processes on your heart rate. With increasing awareness, you can use your thoughts and visual imagery deliberately to exert more exact control over what goes on in your body. This is biofeedback. Instruments provide you with feedback about your "bio" processes. What you do with it is in your hands (or head).

Fortunately, there is a simple and inexpensive window into the physiology of one important aspect of the relaxation response—a little thermometer that measures finger temperature. Finger temperature is a sensitive gauge of autonomic nervous system arousal. With sympathetic nervous system arousal, blood flow is diverted into the large muscles in preparation for vigorous action. With parasympathetic activation, blood flows into the periphery—the tips of your fingers and toes. When you're nervous, your hands get cold; when you can warm your hands, you become calm. You can tape a little thermometer designed for that purpose to a finger and have an excellent barometer of autonomic nervous system activity. If you can get your finger temperature above 95°F and hold it there for several minutes, you can rest assured that you have lowered your sympathetic nerv-

ous system arousal, resulting in a pleasant, emotionally relaxed state. Here's
the physiological account:

> Warmth in the periphery relates to emotional quietness because hand and
> foot warming depend largely on increased blood flow, which depends on
> vasodilation, which in turn depends on "turn-off" (decrease) of firing in the
> peripheral vascular section of the sympathetic nervous system and control
> thereby of the behavior of smooth muscles in blood vessel walls (peripheral
> vasodilation). And when this voluntary turn-down of sympathetic firing is
> established through biofeedback-aided visualization training, which seems
> to mean that the limbic brain is involved in making appropriate changes in
> hypothalamic circuits, the psychological result, or cause, or correlate, is emo-
> tional quietness.[82]

Once you become aware of how this relaxed state feels, and you have discovered how to get yourself there, you can do it without the little thermometer. You can do it anywhere in the midst of any activity, to remain
or restore calm. Although we often think of relaxation in connection with
slowing down and resting, it is possible to be relaxed and active, and biofeedback can also be employed to increase skills and enhance performance.[83]

Hand warming is likely to be a good way to start, but there are many
other physiological responses that can be monitored and deliberately regulated. Muscle tension, for example, which can be monitored in the forehead,
is often regulated with biofeedback. You can use a device that alters the pitch
of a tone in response to slight changes in muscle tension—a higher pitch
when you're tense, a lower pitch when your muscles are more relaxed. This
provides not only a direct measure of tension but also an extremely sensitive
monitoring of subtle changes in tension.

With even more elaborate equipment, you can be provided with feedback about your brain's activity.[84] The electroencephalogram (EEG), which
has long been used to measure brain activity, has been an important diagnostic tool in detecting seizure disorders such as epilepsy. Resting EEG activity, however, can also be used to measure states of mind. A high
prevalence of alpha frequencies, for example, indicates mental relaxation
and an inner sense of comfort and well-being. A high prevalence of theta
frequencies is associated with vivid imagery and openness to inner feelings

and thoughts that are ordinarily unconscious. Thus, theta training can be used to enhance imagery and access memory in the same way as hypnosis, by fostering an integration of conscious and unconscious processes.[85] Notably, recent research has shown promising leads in the use of brain-wave training to moderate symptoms of PTSD in Vietnam veterans.[86]

Like exercise and relaxation, biofeedback is something you could conceivably use on your own. You don't need EEG equipment; you could buy a little thermometer and learn to warm your hands. But it is best to begin by working with a trained biofeedback therapist who can teach you about physiological self-regulation in more depth and who can guide you in the use of the technology. Hand warming will suffice for many persons, but the optimal technique will depend on the specific problematic pattern of physiological arousal.

Like any other technique that enhances relaxation, biofeedback can backfire. It can contribute to a sense of vulnerability as you release tension and let down your guard. And the inward focus may also open up traumatic memories and imagery. This openness to inner experience can be productive and healing in the presence of a competent therapist, but it can potentially lead to overwhelming emotion and retraumatization. When carefully prescribed and monitored, biofeedback has the specific advantages of bolstering awareness of the body and providing a sense of control and mastery. Feedback is ideal for providing tangible evidence of self-regulation and mastery.

Putting It All Together ◆ ◆ ◆ ◆ ◆ ◆ ◆ ◆ ◆

I have covered only a sample of techniques evolved for enhancing experience. These are all tried-and-true methods, and they have all been amply researched. But there are problems to be aware of and to solve with each of them, particularly for persons who have been traumatized and who are prone to dissociate. Each of these methods has its adherents—those who proclaim it to be the best. The general tenor of research is that these methods are all effective, but it is hard to show that any one is generally better than any other.[87] My own view is that they are all good, they all have problems, and you have to find what works for you. It may take time, and it may not be easy. You may have to experiment. When you find a helpful technique, you may want to make it part of your life.

It should also be obvious that these techniques are not mutually exclusive. They can work well together. This is the spirit of contemporary "eclectic therapy," which is based on the premise that there are many equally effective forms of therapy. The challenge is not to show that any one form is better than any other, but rather to draw from a number of methods to choose whatever works best for a given individual. Benson[88] combines relaxation with meditation. You can use exercise and relaxation. Imagery plays an important role in relaxation, hypnosis, and meditation.

Psychologists Steve Fahrion and Patricia Norris[89] have proposed a model approach of eclectic treatment that includes biofeedback-assisted self-regulation. To foster psychophysiological self-regulation, they employ a combination of relaxation techniques, breathing exercises, and imagery, coupled with various forms of biofeedback. There are two facets to their strategy. First, the various techniques are integrated to help the patient master self-regulation skills in the office. Second, the patient applies the techniques to achieve self-regulation throughout the course of daily life. The real challenge is to use the methods to achieve the state of calm in the midst of a stressful situation: "There are many ways to relax muscles other than progressive muscle relaxation: hot baths, massages, or good naps. Yet relaxed muscles per se may not ameliorate anxiety as well as does the confidence that relaxation can be purposively accomplished in the face of the tensions of everyday life." [90] To reiterate, the key is not to be in any particular state of mind; the key is to develop a sense of voluntary control, freedom, choice, and a sense of ease about your state of mind.

In the context of PTSD and dissociation, the ultimate challenge is to use techniques of self-regulation to head off intrusive experiences and overwhelming emotions. Developing this capacity for self-control has a beneficial ripple effect: It enhances self-esteem while improving the quality of life. These methods are proven in the treatment of anxiety apart from trauma. We might hope that future research will home in on their optimal integration in the treatment of PTSD and dissociative disorders.

CHAPTER FOURTEEN

Conclusions

Before you close the covers of this book for the last time, I want to make sure that I've conveyed my main points. This chapter summarizes the key ideas from each of the preceding chapters and takes up one new matter.

Trauma Happens ◆ ◆ ◆ ◆ ◆ ◆ ◆ ◆ ◆

The ubiquity of trauma and its potentially severe psychological consequences motivated me to write this book. Recognizing the pervasive role of trauma in symptoms, psychiatry has shifted course in the past decade. The modern formulation of posttraumatic stress disorder in the context of the Vietnam war provided a conceptual framework for the broader spectrum of trauma—not the least of which is child abuse. This is not a new direction for the mental health field; it is a century-old direction. It's about time we returned to it: With the escalation of violence in our society and brutal wars around the globe, trauma theory will become more—not less—important in years to come.

In seeking to help you understand your symptoms and problems, I have cautioned you against making assumptions: Not all symptoms come from trauma; not all trauma leads to symptoms; and no particular type of trauma has priority. Specifically, sexual abuse is not the only form of trauma that counts. Sexual trauma, such as incest and rape, can be particularly pernicious in its effects. But trauma is trauma. As a small child, you can fear for your life in the face of a raging parent, even if you are never touched. And it is often unclear what facet of any complex experience is most detrimental. In the long run, the neglect or lack of comforting may be more harmful than the traumatic threat or injury.

Trauma Is One Factor Among Many

To be traumatized is to be overpowered, and trauma can powerfully affect the course of development. But development is always a conjoint product of nature and nurture—or lack of nurture. Individual constitution and environmental factors always interact dynamically, not only from the time of birth but even from the moment of conception.

Your genetic makeup, temperament, and personality will influence how you cope with trauma. You may be more or less fearful, angry, or depressed. You may be more or less capable of dissociating or taking refuge in fantasy. You may be more inclined to blame yourself and retreat or to blame others and fight back. Trauma will be one shaping force in your personality development, and your personality may in turn influence your exposure to subsequent trauma.

Trauma will interact not only with your constitution and temperament but also with other environmental factors. Just as there is longitudinal consistency in the child's temperament and abilities, so, too, there is longitudinal consistency in the child's environment—for better or for worse.[1] Child abuse does not occur in an environmental vacuum. Sexual abuse, for example, often intertwines with a broad pattern of family dysfunction.[2] By adulthood, disentangling the effects of sexual abuse from hostility, tirades, beatings, boundary violations, social isolation, neglect, illnesses, injuries, accidents, and a host of other potential insults may be virtually impossible. But fortunately, trauma is not the only environmental factor. The course of development will be influenced profoundly by supportive relationships. For some individuals, a single good relationship may have an overriding effect.

Seeing yourself as an active survivor of trauma rather than a passive victim is consistent with contemporary developmental theory: Development reflects the ongoing interaction between an active child and an active environment.[3] Your survivorship will have the stamp of your individuality and coping skills as you interact with a host of environmental influences—traumatic and supportive. If you have been severely traumatized, particularly over a prolonged period, being a survivor may always remain a prominent part of your identity. But trauma is only one factor among many in development, and survivorship should be only one facet of your identity.

Understand Your Brain and Be Gentle on Your Mind ◆ ◆ ◆ ◆ ◆ ◆ ◆ ◆

To a significant degree, your individual constitution will affect how your nervous system responds to trauma. But the basic stress response has been wired in by 180 million years of mammalian evolution. Your nervous system was not constructed to withstand prolonged, severe trauma. The fight-or-flight response evolved to cope with adaptive emergencies, not protracted human malevolence. Prolonged stress may lead to long-term adaptations of your nervous system that can render you more vulnerable to anxiety, irritability, and depression—as well as to the intrusive symptoms of PTSD. And your nervous system is connected to all other organ systems in your body, so prolonged stress may eventuate in ill health.

If you berate yourself for your nervous system's natural response to trauma, you will compound your nervous system's problems by piling on more stress—in addition to needlessly pummeling your self-esteem. You can exert some influence over your nervous system, but you should adopt an attitude of humility. Manipulating a hundred billion neurons with ten trillion connections is not easy. Be patient with yourself.

Safety Rests on a Secure Base

Let me reiterate what I believe is the single most important concept for trauma theory, the "secure base from which a child or an adolescent can make sorties into the outside world and to which he can return knowing for sure that he will be welcomed when he gets there, nourished physically and emotionally, comforted if distressed, reassured if frightened." [4] The need for attachments and a secure base is a core mammalian characteristic, and it is a lifelong need. The secure base buffers us from the pernicious effects of traumatic experience, and the lack of a secure base at the time of trauma doubtlessly makes trauma more traumatic. Consequently, establishing a secure base, however belatedly, becomes the first priority in coping with trauma.

Emotions Are Adaptive

If you have been traumatized, emotions may be your nemesis. Your feelings may seem like tidal waves or a churning sea. Many "symptoms" of trauma—substance abuse, self-injurious behavior, dissociation—are efforts to escape from overwhelming emotions.

Coping with trauma requires making peace with emotions, perhaps one by one, little by little. We respond emotionally for a reason: Emotions are adaptive. They guide us. Each one serves a purpose: Anxiety stops us in our tracks when something goes wrong and prompts us to search for an appropriate course of action. Fear energizes flight. Anger powers confrontation and self-defense. Shame and guilt feelings spur self-appraisal and constructive change. Pleasure provides incentive to satisfy vital needs. Pride and joy sustain development and growth. Depression is a tough one—perhaps we shut down before we completely burn ourselves up.

Your emotions, like your attachment needs, are rooted in your old mammalian brain. You need your newer rational brain to temper emotion with reason. But you cannot live on reason alone. You also need feeling and intuition. Cultivating feelings rather than blocking them is a key to coping with trauma. By becoming more aware of your feelings, you can learn to use their guidance and to regulate them before they escalate beyond the point of no return.

Dissociation Is a Blessing and a Curse ◆ ◆ ◆ ◆ ◆

By definition, trauma is inescapable. If you could have escaped, you would have, and you would not be reading this book. If you could not fight or flee, you may have coped by altering your consciousness—tuning out, taking refuge in fantasy, or keeping some realms of experience segregated from others. You may have blocked some of the traumatic experience with amnesia. Dissociation is a skill—and, in the face of prolonged trauma, it may seem to be a blessing.

But dissociation may put you at higher risk for posttraumatic problems. Also, once honed, the skill of dissociation can be used to deal with any and all stress. Then dissociation can become a curse. Dissociation is a defense for dire emergencies; it is not an adaptive way to deal with daily hassles or the continual press of worries and anxiety. Dissociation undermines adaptation; without continuity in your experience, you cannot function. And dissociation precludes active coping and mastery; you cannot solve a problem you have blotted out.

Even if dissociation has become a curse, it is not a skill you should relinquish entirely. You just need to use it more selectively. You need to be able to ground yourself in reality. But who would want to remain completely grounded in reality? What would your life be like without your capacity to be absorbed in fantasy? Moderation in all things.

Your Autobiography Is a Continual Construction ◆ ◆

Many traumatized individuals have no reason to be concerned about the accuracy of autobiographical memory. They have never forgotten their traumatic experience, and they have no reason to question their memories. For others, matters are far murkier—for example, if the traumatic experience occurred during the period of normal childhood amnesia, if it was shrouded in dissociation, or if it was denied by others.

Your autobiography is not lodged in your brain just waiting to be discovered. It is a continually evolving self-portrait, shaped by your self-concept at every moment of reconstruction. It is likely to comprise both fact and fiction, gaps filled in with plausible details—the whole of it encompassing memories ranging from totally accurate to totally inaccurate with everything in between. You need not be defensive about false memories—we all have them. If you have been traumatized, you may have more than your share. Keep in mind that there is a false-memory problem of unknown proportions and a trauma problem of huge known proportions.

Your identity requires an autobiography, and your identity is shaped by the contents of that autobiography. If you have a patchy autobiography, with many pages or whole chapters missing, you must undertake the task of reconstruction. You may need a supportive relationship to engage in this process. The greater the trauma, the greater the dissociation, the greater your proneness to fantasy, the greater the denial, the harder the reconstruction. You may be filled with doubt, and you may need to tolerate a great deal of ambiguity and uncertainty, some of which may never be fully resolved. You may want to do some investigation and some detective work.

Your autobiography is never written once and for all. You will keep working on it for the rest of your life, not only adding to it but also revising and reorganizing it. Consider it always a working draft.

Your Self-Concept Is a Compass

The helplessness of trauma—sometimes compounded by deliberate degradation—erodes self-efficacy, self-confidence, and self-esteem. At worst, the result is self-hatred. Damaged self-esteem can have a profound effect on the course of development: How you think about yourself influences how you feel, how you act, and who you are. A positive self-concept steers you in the direction of healthy relationships and success; a negative self-concept can lead you into destructive relationships, self-injurious behavior, and failure.

If your self-concept has been significantly damaged by trauma, you know that injunctions to "think positive thoughts" about yourself do not do the trick. They may even make you feel worse if you can't do this. Positive thoughts about yourself may not sink in. You certainly cannot go from self-hatred to self-appreciation in one grand leap. As with everything else, you need to go slowly. Just pause over an occasional positive thought about yourself or a brief feeling of accomplishment. If the power of positive thinking is more than you can tolerate, how about the power of less negative thinking? Maybe this will put you within reach of neutrality. Once you're there, a more positive attitude may be more thinkable. One gradation at a time.

I have written this book as an invitation to work on understanding yourself, perhaps steering you toward more neutral territory. If I have been successful, the self-understanding you've gained may be fertile ground for more self-acceptance, self-tolerance, and even self-compassion.

Outdated Relationship Models
Can Be Put on Unemployment

We begin building working models of relationships as soon as we are born. We learn, we remember, and we categorize every new experience accordingly. Our prior experience will always shape our future experience. We not only apply our old models to new relationships, we actively shape others to conform to our working models of them. Relationships entail continual negotiation as we try to nudge each other into our various models. As we do so, we manage to repeat our prior experience, sometimes with the destructive force of the "repetition compulsion."

But repetition is only one part of the story. Just as we are continually applying what we have learned, we are also continually learning. We always have the capacity for new learning, and we can always reshape our old models and develop new ones. Like any new learning, learning new ways of relating can be discomfiting at first. Novelty is a prime source of anxiety. But anxiety can bridge into excitement, pleasure, and satisfaction.

Profoundly traumatic relationships will not be forgotten, and they will always fit your current experience to some degree. Any close and enduring relationship will entail frustration and disappointment. But the fit of your old models to your new relationships may be relatively poor. Then the traumatic models can be put on unemployment. When you no longer apply the traumatic models to your relationships, you'll no longer be nudging others into them, and others may treat you better. You'll move from vicious circles to benign circles: better models, better relationships, better models.

Avoid Retraumatization

To relive trauma is to be retraumatized. Being retraumatized is bad enough in itself, but there is another danger: You can become sensitized.

Each intrusive experience—nightmares, flashbacks, emotional upheav-als—may lower your threshold for the next. You can become mired in a vicious circle: Episodes beget episodes.[5]

You cannot avoid retraumatization entirely. To be able to do so would be tantamount to rubbing out PTSD—something we've obviously been un-able to do. But you can lower the likelihood of such reexperiencing by taking care of yourself—for example, by emphasizing safety and a secure base, by refraining from self-destructive behavior, and by avoiding traumatic rela-tionships.

Here we encounter the perennial dilemma in the treatment of trauma. You need to remember and talk about trauma, but doing so may be retrau-matizing—making matters worse rather than better. In trying to find the right balance, I am inclined to err on the side of caution. Here's Kluft's[6] maxim for the third (and last) time: "The slower you go, the faster you get there."

Dissociation Diminishes With Self-Expansion

Dissociative identity disorder has been sensationalized, but we now recog-nize that it is a relatively common way of coping with severe, prolonged traumatic experience in childhood—for those highly predisposed to dis-sociation.

There is clear consensus that the mainstay of treatment for dissociative identity disorder is psychodynamic psychotherapy[7]—a venerable form of treatment, hardly unique to dissociative disorders. Dynamic psychotherapy provides an opportunity to explore and to become more accepting of your thoughts, feelings, and fantasies—and to understand their origins in early experience. So it is with dissociative disorders. *Gradually,* you may open your mind to dissociated feelings and memories. As your openness to pre-viously dissociated experience increases, your sense of self becomes more encompassing, more complex, and more flexible. Extremes are tempered. Formerly dissociated states of mind meld into a richer identity.

Dynamic psychotherapy is not only an opportunity for self-exploration but also a source of support.[8] Establishing a therapeutic alliance in a reliable psychotherapy relationship—perhaps augmented by group therapy and other treatment supports—can be a cornerstone of your secure base. In addition, therapeutic relationships can provide a forum for reshaping working models that you can generalize to other supportive relationships.

Focus on Trauma Should
Not Obscure Other Problems ◆ ◆ ◆ ◆ ◆ ◆ ◆

The psychological and neurophysiological effects of trauma are complex, and so is the range of associated psychiatric disorders. Proper treatment requires a comprehensive evaluation that addresses the full range of potential medical, psychological, and social problems, as well as including a specialized evaluation of posttraumatic and dissociative symptoms. Complex problems often make for complex treatment. You may need a combination of individual and group therapy, medication, and intermittent hospitalization or partial hospital treatment. In the face of multifaceted problems, it is no small feat to set priorities and to establish a focus for treatment. "Safety first" is a helpful point of orientation; that accomplished, the rest may follow.

The Goal of Treatment Is to
Improve the Quality of Life ◆ ◆ ◆ ◆ ◆ ◆ ◆

You must come to terms with trauma by thinking about it and talking about it. But the temptation to uncover and abreact traumatic memories is fraught with risk. If you push too hard and too fast, you may become sensitized rather than desensitized. Symptoms of PTSD and dissociation may escalate. At worst, you may be so intent on recovering memories that you lose sight of the whole purpose of therapy while your functioning goes downhill. You must always balance exploration with support. It might not be a bad idea to think of good functioning as a precondition for deeper exploration. The autobiography can always wait; it's a lifelong project.

Care for Yourself and Your Nervous System ◆ ◆ ◆ ◆

If you are struggling with chronic PTSD and dissociation, you need to take care of your nervous system as well as your self. Your nervous system, like your mind, has been traumatized. It is hyperactive and hyperreactive and prone to taking a dive into depression. All standard forms of psychiatric and psychological treatment are potentially helpful but may not be enough.

Several methods of self-regulation, from ancient to more modern, provide direct pathways to regaining a sense of control—the antidote to trauma and stress. The standard smorgasbord includes exercise, relaxation, guided imagery, meditation, and hypnosis. Given the inevitable physiological disruption of trauma, the addition of biofeedback to foster psychophysiological self-regulation is particularly appealing. All methods of self-regulation have risks and problems for persons who have been traumatized. It may take trial and error, and you may need to go slowly. Yet I think anyone who has been coping with trauma would do well to find some of these techniques that work and to use them over the long haul. It's really no different in principle from using appropriate preventive measures for any other chronic illness.

Beyond Fight or Flight ◆ ◆ ◆ ◆ ◆ ◆ ◆ ◆ ◆

There are no treatments for the existential impact of trauma. Traumatic experience strikes at the heart of our ultimate concerns—death, freedom, isolation, and meaninglessness.[9]

Our belief systems provide some sense of predictability and thereby serve as a buffer against stress.[10] But trauma challenges basic assumptions, engenders a sense of meaninglessness, and fuels helplessness. Psychologist Ronnie Janoff-Bulman, in her book *Shattered Assumptions,*[11] identified three core assumptions rooted in our culture: the world is benevolent, the world is meaningful, and the self is worthy. Trauma undermines these assumptions. Compared with those who have not been traumatized, trauma survivors hold more negative assumptions about themselves and the world—especially when the trauma was deliberately inflicted by other persons. Children who have undergone trauma at the hands of those they trusted and depended on may never develop sturdy positive assumptions. Either the experience of new trauma or the emergence of intrusive symptoms of PTSD will profoundly disrupt the equilibrium of adulthood. As Janoff-Bulman states, "recovery," in the sense of returning to your state of mind before the eruption of trauma, is not a possibility:

> Trauma survivors do not simply get over their experience. It is permanently encoded in their assumptive world; the legacy of traumatic life events is some degree of disillusionment. From the perspective of their inner worlds, victims recover not when they return to their prior assumptive world but when they reestablish an integrated, comfortable assumptive world that incorporates their traumatic experience.[12]

Establishing a workable "assumptive world" is perhaps one of the greatest challenges in coping with trauma. There are no road maps. For many, the challenges are not only psychological and existential, they are also spiritual. Thus, many persons find pastoral counseling essential in their recovery.

Janoff-Bulman[13] proposes that three factors auger well for the process of reconstructing meaning: the capacity to tolerate distressing emotions, the ability to reappraise creatively the disruptive information about the world and the self, and the support of others. She also observes that many survivors find meaning in helping others. In a similar vein, Judith Herman[14] describes a survivor mission: "These survivors recognize a political or religious dimension in their misfortune and discover that they can transform the meaning of their personal tragedy by making it the basis for social action. While there is no way to compensate for an atrocity, there is a way to transcend it, by making it a gift to others."

Finding your way out of meaninglessness is a major step, but there is another—finding hope. My mentor, Paul Pruyser,[15] saw early attachments as the wellspring of hope: "hoping is based on a belief that there is *some benevolent disposition toward oneself somewhere in the universe, conveyed by a caring person.*" He must have been right; hopelessness is a glaring result of trauma in relationships with caregivers. But the search for benevolent attachment is rarely squelched, even in those who have suffered dire childhood trauma. The quest for secure attachment and hope thus conjointly lay the foundation for coping with trauma:

I suggest that hoping may be a third basic type of response that does not have the vehement aggressivity of fighting nor the limp abdication of fleeing. If hoping is developmentally based on having experienced the mutuality of trust and having received some benevolent care, a person may be prepared by such experiences for meeting adverse circumstances with quiet courage rather than in a competitive fighting posture or in meek retreat. The fight and the flight responses are reflex actions programmed in the limbic system; hoping is a much more thoughtful response that presupposes consciousness, freedom, and choosing, and is surely organized at cortical levels of brain action.[16]

Beyond fight or flight, there is hope.

The Biology of Trauma

Your biology is as important to self-understanding as your psychology. Your mind and your brain are inextricable, and your nervous system may be profoundly affected by trauma. You may erroneously attribute common neurophysiological consequences of trauma to your psychological "hang-ups" and personal failings. In doing so, you compound your struggles by needlessly flogging yourself.

Being informed about the effects of trauma on your nervous system may afford some relief from self-criticism, but the fact that trauma may have detrimental neurophysiological effects is hardly welcome news. The effects of trauma may be not only acute but also persistent, contributing to chronic posttraumatic symptoms. This is why you need to think of caring not only for your *self* but also for your *nervous system*.

This Appendix expands on several topics introduced in Chapter 2 (Development) and reiterated throughout the book. I begin with our newly emerging appreciation of the role of genetic factors in trauma-related disorders. Then I present some more detail about the fluid brain—the transmitters. In Chapter 2, I contrasted the "rational" neocortex with the "emotional" limbic system. Here I round out this picture by describing Paul MacLean's evolutionary conception of the *triune* (three-part) brain. I conclude by amplifying the neurophysiology of the acute traumatic response—fight or flight.

Gene Doings ◆ ◆ ◆ ◆ ◆ ◆ ◆ ◆ ◆ ◆ ◆

Many psychiatric disorders have a genetic basis. For example, heredity contributes to a heightened risk for schizophrenia and bipolar (manic-depressive) disorder. Posttraumatic stress disorder would seem to be the *least* likely candidate for an inherited condition. It is one of few psychiatric disorders with a distinct environmental cause—trauma. But a genetic contribution to risk for posttraumatic stress disorder has recently been discovered. How do genes contribute to disorders?

Genes are the units of heredity. Evolution takes place by means of genetic change. Genetic variation determines differences both among species and among individuals within species. The more we learn, the more we appreciate the hereditary basis of a wide range of human behavior. Consider this astounding example of identical twins, two individuals with the same genes, who were separated 4 weeks after their birth in 1940:

> They grew up 45 miles apart in Ohio. After they were reunited in 1979, they discovered they had some eerie similarities: both chain-smoked Salems, both drove the same-model blue Chevrolet, both chewed their fingernails, and both had dogs named Toy. Further, they had both vacationed in the same neighborhood in Florida. When tested for such personality traits as sociability and self-control, they responded almost identically.[1]

We humans have 46 chromosomes, 22 pairs of *autosomes,* and a pair of sex chromosomes. The largest chromosome (#1) is about six times the size of the smallest (#21). The number of genes per chromosome ranges from about 1,500 to 10,000[2]; the whole human genome has about 100,000. That's an astronomical number of possible combinations and allows for a staggering amount of individual variation—the engine of evolution.

How do we get from genes to personality? The short answer: Genes build brains. It's no small matter to manufacture a hundred billion neurons (nerve cells) and then hook them up. Once the egg is fertilized, the cells start dividing at a frenetic pace. They differentiate into separate kinds of cells to make specific tissues (nerve, muscle, bone, skin). The genes are signaling each other all along the way. Each cell in an individual starts with the same genes. The difference between one kind of tissue and another is that different genes are operative; some are turned off while others remain on. There's no precise blueprint for brain production. The brain starts working when the cells are being made, and the embryonic "experience" of the neurons partly determines how they all get hooked up. Survival of the fittest also works at the cellular level; in some parts of the brain, up to 70% of the neurons may die along the way.[3]

But genes don't just oversee brain construction; they also supervise brain operation once assembly is complete. Genes don't just sit there in the cells—they are subject to myriad influences that affect their *expression*. That is, they are continually being turned on and off during the life of the neuron. They're like reference works in a technical library,[4] providing instructions for manufacturing what the cell needs to function. Of most interest to psychiatry and trauma theory, genes specify the production of neurotransmitters—proteins that neurons use to signal (excite or inhibit) one another. Transmitter production can go into overtime, particularly when given the added incentive of trauma.

The Biochemical Brain ◆ ◆ ◆ ◆ ◆ ◆ ◆ ◆

The nervous system has been likened to a telephone switchboard. But you cannot understand the role of neurotransmitters in trauma with only the switchboard-brain half of the story. Jean-Didier Vincent,[5] a French neurophysiologist, aptly calls the telephone-switchboard brain the "cabled brain." But to explain the emotions, he adds the concept of a "vague brain" or "hazy brain" that is superimposed on the cabled brain. I think of it as the "fluid brain." Neurons are densely packed and ceaselessly signaling their immediate neighbors, but they're all awash in circulating transmitters. Vincent points out that some neurons "spray their messengers over a large area" in the brain.[6] The composition of the fluid changes, and our emotional states change along with it.

There is a little bundle of neurons in the brain stem called the locus coeruleus. The locus coeruleus has been dubbed the "trauma center" of the brain.[7] This little protein factory manufactures norepinephrine (adrenaline), one of the major ingredients in the neurotransmitter fluid. When the locus coeruleus is activated (by an alarming stimulus), it sends a blast of norepinephrine into many areas of the brain. Norepinephrine has an activating effect. Your level of arousal goes up, and you become anxious. Your sympathetic nervous system is prepared for action.

The locus coeruleus is one of the manufacturing centers. The genes in its neurons contain the manufacturing instructions. Your genes may encode for high productivity of norepinephrine, an inclination passed down through generations of management. Your fluid-brain biochemistry tends to be heavy on norepinephrine. You tend to be an anxious person. You may be more susceptible to posttraumatic stress disorder. If your fluid-brain biochemistry is characteristically light on norepinephrine, you may tend to be more placid—or perhaps more depressed.

Beware that this picture is drastically oversimplified. There are many compounds that function as neurotransmitters, and new ones continue to be discovered. They seem to be proliferating like subatomic particles. Psychiatry is focusing on a few major neurotransmitters, such as norepinephrine, serotonin, and dopamine. They all interact. The level of one may affect the levels of the others. These three neurotransmitters are sometimes called neuromodulators or neuroregulators because of their broad effects on the running of the cabled brain. For example, norepinephrine and dopamine are activators; they may function like amplifiers, turning up or down the gain in the overall cabled-brain system.

This is where medication comes in. Medicine changes the composition of the biochemical fluid, increasing or decreasing the proportions of various constituents. By working on the fluid brain, medication can produce broad changes in brain activity. Medication can increase or decrease the general level of activation in various parts of the brain, or it can assist with regulation, control, and inhibition. Many medications exert their long-range effects by changing the characteristic pattern of gene expression in various neural circuits.[8] The drugs change the way the genes run the neurons, perhaps compensating for changes wrought by trauma.

Another complication: The line between neurotransmitters and neuromodulators is difficult enough to draw. But matters are even hazier than that. The line between a neurotransmitter and a hormone is also difficult to draw. We think of the neurotransmitters as providing neuron-to-neuron signals as they cross the synaptic gaps between neurons. We think of "hormones" as substances secreted by endocrine glands; once secreted, hormones are transported in the bloodstream to various organ systems. Neurotransmitters act locally; hormones act at a distance. But the same substance, such as norepinephrine, can function as a neurotransmitter in the brain and as a hormone in another part of the body. Even in the brain, some neurotransmitters act at a distance; they are sprayed from the brain stem up into other parts of the brain. Calling them neuromodulators or neuroregulators places them somewhere between neurotransmitters and hormones. To put the icing on this complicated cake, the brain itself is an endocrine gland. In coping with trauma, the brain secretes hormones that produce arousal.

Now that we've allowed hormones into the picture, we have another important constituent to consider—endorphins. These are peptides secreted in the body (the gut) as well as in the brain. Endorphins are like opiates; they are the body's own narcotic supply. Endorphins are secreted in response to painful stimuli; they appear to be part of the body's defense system against pain. You've heard how injured football players go on playing without feeling pain. It doesn't hurt until later because the endorphins act as analgesics or painkillers. This stress-related endorphin response has been called *stress-induced analgesia*.[9] Some persons who have been traumatized attempt to control their distress by evoking stress-induced analgesia. Self-cutting or self-burning, for example, may appear to others as self-*injury;* owing to endorphin release, however, these behaviors may induce a relatively *pain-free* state.

The Triune Brain   ◆ ◆ ◆ ◆ ◆ ◆ ◆ ◆ ◆

Now the hardware: We attribute our status as the "highest" animals primarily to our brains. But the human brain has not been perfectly constructed in evolution. I emphasize "imperfect adaptation" because our human capacity to reason misleads us. We are prone to believing that we should be able to respond consistently in logical, effective ways. But we are upstarts. In evolutionary time, we are a brand-new species. Picture the time line of evolution as the length of a football field. The earth formed on the 90-yard line. Single-celled organisms began on the 70-yard line. We *(Homo sapiens)* came onto the scene less than a tenth of an inch from the goal line. We are latecomers in a long line, yet we have a long tradition of believing that we are a world apart. In fact, we share a goodly proportion of our genetic material with bacteria, and we share nearly 99% of it with chimpanzees.[10] What a difference a percent makes! But maybe not as much as we are inclined to think.

Evolution is a tinkerer; it takes what's on hand, refashioning and adding to it. Nothing is built from scratch according to some sensible design. The brain is an amalgam of different structures superimposed on one another over the course of evolution:

> The designers of the first jet engine started with a clean drawing board. Imagine what they would have produced if they had been constrained to "evolve" the first jet engine from an existing propeller engine, changing one component at a time, nut by nut, screw by screw, rivet by rivet. A jet engine so assembled would be a weird contraption indeed. It is hard to imagine that an aeroplane designed in that evolutionary way would ever get off the ground. Yet in order to complete the biological analogy we have to add yet another constraint. Not only must the end product get off the ground; so must every intermediate along the way, and each intermediate must be superior to its predecessor. When looked at in this light, far from expecting animals to be perfect we may wonder that anything about them works at all.[11]

Paul MacLean has been making sense of the brain for about half a century. He's been fascinated by all kinds of brains and the behavior that goes with them—from lizards to rats to monkeys to humans. His understanding of evolution, comparative psychology, and neurobiology enabled him to figure out how our human brains are cobbled together. In the process, he has explained why our thoughts and feelings don't always coalesce. In short, thoughts and feelings "are products of different cerebral mechanisms." [12]

The brain has evolved in concentric circles, like the rings of a tree. We'll ignore what MacLean calls the *neural chassis*—the brain stem and spinal cord—and concentrate instead on what's grown on top of it. We advanced mammals have three brains—a *triune* brain. Although these three brains are richly interconnected, they operate somewhat independently. The contradiction between what we think and what we feel has been a preoccupation of psychology throughout its history.[13] The triune brain is the basis of the disparities:

> By itself, the neural chassis might be likened to a vehicle without a driver. Significantly, in the more advanced vertebrates the evolutionary process has provided the neural chassis not with a single guiding operator, but rather a combination of three, each markedly different in its evolutionary age and development, and each radically different in structure, chemistry, and organization.[14]

Brain 1 is the reptilian brain, the lowest level above the brain stem, the first concentric ring. Dinosaurs had reptilian brains, current reptiles have them, and we mammals also have them. Evolution did not get rid of reptilian brains; it just packed more brains on top of them. Our reptilian brains may do for us much of what they've always done for reptiles. They govern our basic habits, our daily routines, our allegiance to territory, and some of the basic expressions for social communication. We nod our heads in a passing greeting; so do lizards. We'll just nod to our reptilian brains in passing here.

Brain 2, the limbic system, is the paleomammalian (ancient mammal) brain. It's fair to think of the limbic system as the emotional brain. The limbic system is a complex set of structures, and it serves many functions, all of which are central to trauma. Brain 2 is the lead player in this book. It is the seat of emotions. It is linked directly to our vital needs. It monitors our internal (bodily) world. In sum, the limbic system provides the emotional guidance "for self-preservation and preservation of the species."[15]

Brain 2 subserves several other psychological functions besides emotion that are crucial to understanding trauma. The limbic system is the seat of memory. Memory and emotion are closely tied. They need to be: We need to remember what feels good and what feels bad. The limbic system also lends a sense of reality to our perceptions of the outer and inner worlds. And, not least, the limbic brain enables what is dearest to the hearts of mammals: caregiving. As MacLean puts it, "the history of the evolution of the limbic system is the history of the evolution of mammals, while the history of the evolution of mammals is the history of the evolution of the family." [16] Without their limbic systems, mammals would be incapable of nursing; separated offspring would not have the equipment to emit the distress cry that reunites them with their mothers; and none would engage in play. Mammalian life without the limbic system would be dull—and short.

Brain 3 is the neocortex, the outer covering of the brain, the third concentric ring. In MacLean's scheme, this brain is the neomammalian (new mammal) brain. This brain is most extensively developed in the recent mammals, us primates. It is our high-tech, sophisticated, "rational" brain. The limbic brain is directly tuned to the internal milieu of the fluid brain. The neocortex is in the bath with the limbic brain, but it is also tuned to the outer world. It is the seat of "intelligence," including perception, language ability, abstract reasoning, and complex problem-solving. Brain 3 enables us to anticipate the future and to organize, plan, and regulate our behavior accordingly. Because it helps us anticipate the future, brain 3 enables us to feel anxiety. But, as MacLean contends, our problem-solving intelligence is not the only thing about brain 3 that makes us distinctly human (or primate). We can project into our futures, and we can project ourselves into others, identifying with their feelings. Brain 3 thus endows us with empathy, altruism, and conscience.

Like evolution, I keep piling complication on top of complication. MacLean's idea of the *triune brain* may be new to you. But you've probably heard something about the "right brain" versus the "left brain." Some educators are fond of schemes for training the "right brain." This can start sounding as if the right brain were in Chicago and the left brain in New York. The right and left cerebral hemispheres are indeed split right down the middle, but they are connected point-to-point by a huge bundle of nerve fibers, the corpus callosum. They work in tandem, not necessarily in opposition. But the right and left hemispheres do serve different (coordinated) functions, perhaps compounding the rational versus emotional differences between brain 2 and brain 3. In most individuals, the left hemisphere is expert in language and logical analysis, whereas the right hemisphere is more specialized for the perception and expression of emotion.[17]

Plainly, it is quite a feat to get all of the parts of our brains to work together. We have lizard, rat, and monkey brains; we have cabled and fluid brains; we have left and right brains; and this doesn't even begin to touch on the complexity of what has rightly been called "the most complicated material object in the known universe." [18] Taking charge of it with the human mind calls for an attitude of humility.

The Neurophysiology of the
Fight-or-Flight Response ◆ ◆ ◆ ◆ ◆ ◆ ◆ ◆

Ranking among the fittest for now, we have survived innumerable threats for millennia by means of an exquisite device—the fight-or-flight response. The fight-or-flight response is mediated by the sympathetic nervous system. Here's the general layout: The nervous system is divided into the central nervous system (the brain and spinal cord) and the peripheral nervous system (the nerves extending from the spinal cord to the sensory receptors, internal organs, and muscles). The peripheral nervous system is divided into the somatic (sensory and motor) nervous system and the autonomic nervous system. There are two branches of the autonomic nervous system: the sympathetic and the parasympathetic. The autonomic nervous system supervises the internal organs and is ordinarily not under voluntary control.

The locus coeruleus–norepinephrine circuit operates in concert with the hypothalamic-pituitary-adrenal axis to produce sympathetic activation. [19] Here's the chain: The hypothalamus, at the center of the "emotional brain," secretes CRF (corticotropin-releasing factor), activating the pituitary, which secretes ACTH (adrenocorticotropic hormone), in turn activating the adrenals, which secrete steroid hormones that mediate the stress response. The cabled brain and the fluid brain work in concert: The cabled brain stimulates the adrenal medulla, and the fluid brain provides hormones to stimulate the adrenal cortex. In turn, the adrenal glands secrete hormones (epinephrine, norepinephrine, corticosteroids) that activate organ systems in the body needed for the fight-or-flight response. For example, sympathetic arousal oxygenates the blood, increases blood flow, diverts blood to large muscles, and makes glucose available for needed energy. [20]

While we're in the autonomic nervous system, we need to spend a moment on the parasympathetic branch. The sympathetic and parasympathetic branches are somewhat reciprocal; when one is more activated, the other tends to be more *de*activated. The parasympathetic branch is restorative and regulates the digestive and eliminative functions as well as sexual responses. As Vincent puts it, the sympathetic system "spends, while the parasympathetic saves." [21] My colleague, psychologist Patricia Norris, explains it this way: If the sympathetic branch is akin to the accelerator, the parasympathetic branch would be the brakes. This reciprocity between the sympathetic and parasympathetic branches makes it difficult to be pleasurably aroused sexually when you're frightened or angry. But the two systems are not entirely reciprocal—at worst, we can have one foot on the accelerator and the other foot on the brake. [22]

Perhaps the analogy to the car is the plainest way to appreciate the persistent effects of trauma on the nervous system. Trauma—especially when prolonged or repeated—can result in a hyperresponsive or hyperexcitable sympathetic nervous system. [23] Trauma can also interfere with the self-limiting mechanisms in the sympathetic nervous system response. [24] It's not as if you have the accelerator floored constantly. Rather, you are liable to step on it frequently in response to alarm. The locus coeruleus "trauma center" described earlier in this Appendix is a key part of the brain's circuitry for maintaining vigilance. [25] If you have a history of trauma, you may be *hyper*vigilant—always alert to danger. Your sympathetic nervous system responds to the slightest provocation. It is as if you are on the run, always hearing police sirens, and tromping on the accelerator time after time. Moreover, the neurophysiological brakes may be worn. The key to coping with trauma is keeping your foot off the accelerator when there is no current danger. For that, you need your neocortex—perhaps with the aid of medication to serve as a governor.

Concluding Biological Reflections   ◆ ◆ ◆ ◆ ◆ ◆

Throughout this book, I have attempted to cultivate a biological perspective. Trauma-related disorders are psychosomatic—not in the sense of physical symptoms being "all in your head" but rather in the sense that traumatic experience has a profound effect on the nervous system and other major organ systems. And traumatic effects are also somatopsychic: The physiological effects reverberate in consciousness. Moreover, the basic capacity for traumatic experience is not just human, it is mammalian. We humans, however, can use our unique conscious creativity to exert some influence over this biological heritage. The greater challenge will be to use our humanity to transcend our uniquely human penchant for inflicting trauma.

Notes

Chapter 1.   Trauma

1. Webster's New Twentieth Century Dictionary 1983
2. American Psychiatric Association 1994a, pp. 427–428
3. Breslau et al. 1991
4. Resnick et al. 1993
5. Terr 1991
6. B. L. Green 1993
7. Bolin 1993
8. Bolin 1993
9. Kilpatrick and Resnick 1993
10. Gelinas 1993
11. Gelinas 1993, p. 2
12. Brende 1983
13. Agger 1989; Basoglu et al. 1994; Herman 1992b; Realmuto et al. 1992
14. Glodich 1993
15. Kilpatrick and Resnick 1993
16. Turns and Blumenreich 1993
17. Foa and Riggs 1993
18. Crime Victims Research and Treatment Center 1992
19. Kilpatrick and Resnick 1993
20. Russell 1986
21. Koss 1993
22. Rose 1993, p. 465
23. Browne 1993
24. Biden 1993, p. 1059
25. Menninger 1983, p. 329
26. B. D. Perry 1994, p. 235
27. Putnam 1993, p. 222
28. Herman 1981
29. Russell 1986
30. Finkelhor et al. 1990
31. Herman 1981
32. Finkelhor 1984

33. Finkelhor et al. 1990
34. Kinsey et al. 1953
35. Feldman et al. 1991
36. Nash et al. 1993
37. Kendall-Tackett et al. 1993
38. Brown and Finkelhor 1986
39. Kendall-Tackett et al. 1993
40. Wolfner and Gelles 1993
41. Malinosky-Rummell and Hansen 1993
42. Eth and Pynoos 1994
43. Herman 1992a, 1992b
44. Sackheim and Devine 1992
45. Goodwin 1993a, 1993b
46. March 1993; Weiner 1992
47. J. Goldberg et al. 1990
48. March 1993
49. S. Perry et al. 1992
50. March 1993, p. 46
51. McNally 1993b

Chapter 2.   Development

1. Scarr 1992, p. 5
2. Mayr 1991, p. 2
3. Mayr 1988
4. Leakey 1992
5. Gazzaniga 1992
6. Scarr 1992, p. 5
7. Epstein 1994
8. Weiner 1992, p. 155
9. Weiner 1992
10. Weiner 1992
11. Cannon 1953, pp. 377–378
12. Searle 1992
13. Reiser 1984
14. Churchland 1986, pp. 83–84
15. Thomas 1992, p. 113
16. Edelman 1992

Chapter 3.   Attachment

1. Bowlby 1982, p. xi
2. Bowlby 1973, 1982, 1988
3. MacLean 1985
4. Bowlby 1982
5. Eccles 1989
6. Bowlby 1988, p. 11
7. Erikson 1963
8. Bowlby 1988, p. 62
9. Bowlby 1973
10. Slade and Aber 1992
11. Slade and Aber 1992
12. V. Carlson et al. 1989; Crittenden and Ainsworth 1989; S. Goldberg 1991; Main et al. 1985
13. Winnicott 1950/1958
14. V. Carlson et al. 1989; Main and Solomon 1990
15. Main et al. 1985; Slade and Aber 1992
16. V. Carlson et al. 1989
17. Main and Solomon 1990
18. S. Goldberg 1991
19. V. Carlson et al. 1989; Main and Solomon 1990; Main et al. 1985; Slade and Aber 1992
20. Main and Hesse 1990
21. V. Carlson et al. 1989; Main and Hesse 1990; Main and Solomon 1990; Slade and Aber 1992
22. Main and Solomon 1990
23. Main and Hesse 1990
24. Scarr 1992; Slade and Aber 1992
25. Kagan 1989b
26. Main et al. 1985
27. Ainsworth 1989; Main et al. 1985
28. S. Goldberg 1991; Slade and Aber 1992
29. S. Goldberg 1991

30. Ainsworth 1989
31. Bowlby 1982, p. 208
32. Bowlby 1973
33. Bowlby 1982
34. Lichtenberg 1989
35. Ainsworth 1989; Lichtenberg 1989
36. Main et al. 1985; Slade and Aber 1992
37. Field 1985; Field and Reite 1985; Hofer 1984; G. J. Taylor 1992; van der Kolk 1987c; van der Kolk and Fisler 1994
38. Bowlby 1973
39. Field and Reite 1985, p. 474
40. Lichtenberg 1989, p. 103
41. Scott 1987
42. MacLean 1990
43. Bowlby 1973, p. 146
44. Searles 1960

Chapter 4. Emotion

1. Darwin 1965; Nathanson 1992
2. Lichtenberg 1989
3. Levinson 1994
4. Allen 1980; Frijda 1994; Glore 1994
5. Gray 1982, 1988, 1991a, 1991b
6. Gray 1991b, p. 110
7. Barlow 1991
8. Barlow 1991
9. Dawkins 1989
10. Herman 1992b
11. Falsetti et al. 1995
12. Ovsiew and Yudofsky 1993; Piacente 1986
13. D. O. Lewis 1992
14. Carmen and Rieker 1989
15. Lerner 1985, p. 1
16. M. Lewis 1993
17. Lerner 1985; Lichtenberg 1989; Parens 1992, 1993

18. Parens 1992, p. 82
19. D. O. Lewis 1992, p. 384
20. Parens 1992
21. Fromm 1973
22. de Waal 1989, p. 16
23. Gould 1993, pp. 280–281
24. De Waal 1989
25. Briere and Runtz 1991
26. Solomon 1980
27. Nathanson 1992
28. Nathanson 1992, p. 30
29. Nathanson 1992, pp. 340–341
30. Nathanson 1992, p. 341
31. M. Lewis 1993, p. 159
32. M. Lewis 1993, pp. 162–163
33. Rapee and Barlow 1991
34. Clark et al. 1994; Watson and Clark, in press
35. Hyman and Nestler 1993; Whybrow 1994
36. Seligman 1975
37. Seligman 1975, p. 93
38. Schmale 1972
39. Clark and Watson 1994
40. Seligman 1975, p. 93
41. Kagan 1994
42. Bates and Wachs 1994; Kagan and Snidman 1992
43. Buss 1992
44. Akiskal 1991; Buss 1992; Clark et al. 1994; Klein et al. 1993; Ovsiew and Yudofsky 1993; Plomin et al. 1990; Rutter 1987
45. Allen 1994; Bates and Wachs 1994; Costa and Widiger 1994; Watson et al. 1994
46. Kagan 1989a, 1989b, 1992, 1994; Kagan and Snidman 1992
47. Kagan 1994, p. 261
48. Kagan 1989a, 1994
49. Kagan 1989a
50. Kagan 1994
51. van der Kolk 1987a; Weiner 1992

52. Beck 1991; Burns 1980; Thase and Beck 1993
53. Novaco 1975, 1978
54. Novaco 1978
55. Lerner 1985
56. Novaco 1978, p. 150
57. Meichenbaum and Novaco 1985
58. Allen 1995; Segrin and Abramson 1994

Chapter 5.   Consciousness

1. Lynn and Rhue 1994
2. Cardeña 1994
3. Frankel 1994b
4. Young 1988, p. 35
5. Kluft 1992, p. 143
6. Searle 1992
7. Edelman 1992
8. Edelman 1992; Griffin 1992
9. Baars 1988
10. Baars 1988
11. Kihlstrom 1984
12. Searle 1992
13. Singer and Bonanno 1990, p. 420
14. Kihlstrom 1984, 1987; Kihlstrom and Hoyt 1990
15. D. Spiegel 1990
16. Bowers 1994a
17. Braun and Sachs 1985; Kluft 1984
18. E. B. Carlson 1994; E. B. Carlson and Putnam 1992; Irwin 1994; B. Sanders et al. 1989; S. Sanders and Giolas 1991; Waldinger et al. 1994
19. Lynn and Rhue 1988; Wilson and Barber 1983
20. Wilson and Barber 1983, p. 347
21. Levey 1971, p. 9
22. Bowers 1992; Hilgard 1986; D. Spiegel 1990

23. Hilgard 1965; H. Spiegel 1974
24. Lynn and Rhue 1988; Wilson and Barber 1983
25. Hilgard 1965
26. Kihlstrom et al. 1994
27. Bremner et al. 1995; Koopman et al. 1994; Marmar et al. 1994
28. Singer and Bonanno 1990, p. 424
29. Singer 1993
30. Koopman et al. 1994
31. Braun 1988a, 1988b
32. Allen 1993
33. Putnam 1988, 1994
34. Braun 1988a
35. Putnam 1994
36. Allen 1993
37. Torem 1989

Chapter 6.   Memory

1. van der Kolk 1989
2. Edelman 1989
3. Allen 1993; Bower 1981; Lang 1985; Matthysse 1991; Reiser 1990
4. Kihlstrom 1984
5. Cowan 1988
6. Matthysse 1991
7. Burstein 1985; Mellman and Davis 1985
8. Frankel 1994a; Reisberg and Heuer 1995
9. Burstein 1985
10. Pitman and Orr 1990, p. 469
11. Wegner and Erber 1992
12. van der Kolk 1994
13. Torem 1989
14. S. E. Taylor 1989
15. Matthysse 1991, p. 221
16. Freud 1896/1962, p. 208
17. Freud 1896/1962, p. 203

18. Freud 1896/1962, p. 217
19. Freud 1896/1962, p. 204
20. Freud 1887–1902/1954, p. 215
21. Freud 1887–1902/1954,
    pp. 215–216
22. Freud 1896/1962, p. 207
23. Freud 1933/1964, p. 120
24. Davis 1993; Ellenberger 1970; Gay
    1988
25. Grinker and Spiegel 1945; Kardiner
    1941; Watkins 1949
26. American Psychiatric Association
    1980
27. Ferenczi 1949
28. Sinnett 1993
29. Bowlby 1988, p. 78
30. Bowlby 1988, p. 77
31. Bowlby 1973, p. 202, italics mine
32. Bowlby 1988, p. 149
33. Herman 1992b
34. Herman 1992b
35. Appelbaum 1992; Gutheil 1993;
    Loftus 1993a; Loftus and
    Rosenwald 1993; Terr 1994a;
    Wakefield and Underwager 1992;
    Wylie 1993
36. Loftus 1993a
37. Loftus and Rosenwald 1993
38. Summit 1992
39. Wylie 1993
40. Kihlstrom 1993, p. 10
41. Carstensen et al. 1993
42. Loftus 1993a, p. 533
43. Kihlstrom 1987; Kihlstrom and
    Barnhardt 1993; Schacter 1989a,
    1989b; D. Spiegel et al. 1993;
    Tulving 1972
44. Brewer 1986; Nelson 1993
45. Howe and Courage 1993
46. Loftus and Loftus 1980
47. Minsky 1980, 1986
48. Brewer 1986; Loftus and Loftus
    1980

49. Neisser 1986
50. Kihlstrom 1994
51. Bartlett 1932, p. 213
52. Barclay 1986; Barclay and Wellman
    1986; Rubin 1982
53. Brewer 1986; Neisser 1988; Nelson
    1993
54. Loftus 1993a, p. 530
55. Garry and Loftus 1994
56. Neisser 1986, p. 77
57. Kihlstrom 1994, p. 341
58. Sanitioso et al. 1990
59. Barclay 1986
60. Marmer 1991
61. Squire 1987
62. Squire 1987, p. 77
63. Brewer 1986; Reisberg and Heuer
    1995
64. Barclay and Wellman 1986
65. Christianson 1992; Heuer and
    Reisberg 1992; Terr 1994a
66. Reisberg and Heuer 1995
67. Barclay 1986, p. 97
68. Neisser 1988
69. Brewer 1986; R. Brown and Kulik
    1977; Craik 1989
70. Gold 1995; Pitman and Orr 1995
71. McGaugh 1992; Thompson 1993
72. Pitman 1989; Squire 1987; van der
    Kolk 1994
73. Garry and Loftus 1994; Loftus
    1993a; Schwarz et al. 1993
74. van der Kolk 1989, 1994; van der
    Kolk and van der Hart 1991
75. Braun 1988a
76. Erdelyi 1994a; van der Kolk 1994
77. Charney et al. 1993; LeDoux et al.
    1989; Southwick et al. 1993a
78. Terr 1988, p. 103
79. Charney et al. 1993, p. 294
80. Le Doux 1994; van der Kolk 1993,
    1994
81. Allen, in press

82. Ganaway 1989
83. Neisser 1988; Nelson 1993
84. Pillemer and White 1989
85. Nelson 1993
86. Loftus and Kaufman 1992
87. Spence 1994
88. Saunders and Arnold 1993
89. Ferenczi 1949; Modell 1991
90. Rieker and Carmen 1986, p. 363
91. Summit 1983, p. 181
92. Carmen and Rieker 1989; Rieker and Carmen 1986
93. Modell 1991, p. 237
94. Allen, in press
95. Appelbaum 1992; Gutheil 1993; Loftus 1993a; Wakefield and Underwager 1992
96. Terr 1988
97. Nelson 1993
98. Wetzler and Sweeney 1986
99. Schacter and Kihlstrom 1989
100. Howe and Courage 1993
101. Pillemer and White 1989; Usher and Neisser 1993
102. Nelson 1993; Wilson and Barber 1983
103. Usher and Neisser 1993
104. Howe and Courage 1993
105. Terr 1988
106. Loewenstein 1991a, p. 191
107. Loewenstein 1991a; Schacter and Kihlstrom 1989; D. Spiegel et al. 1993
108. Loftus 1993a
109. Herman and Schatzow 1987
110. Binder et al. 1994; Briere and Conte 1993; Feldman-Summers and Pope 1994; Loftus et al. 1994b
111. Loftus et al. 1994b
112. Briere and Conte 1993
113. Feldman-Summers and Pope 1994
114. L. M. Williams 1994
115. Loftus et al. 1994a, p. 1177
116. Pope and Hudson 1995
117. Ganaway 1989; Goodwin 1993a, 1993b; Putnam 1991b; Sackheim and Devine 1992; Young et al. 1991
118. Schouten 1994; Torem 1993b
119. Wylie 1993
120. Kosko 1993
121. Gabbard 1994; Kluft 1984b; Laub and Auerhahn 1993; Terr 1994b
122. Gutheil 1993, p. 528
123. Allen, in press
124. Terr 1988
125. Terr 1988
126. Ganaway 1989
127. Garry and Loftus 1994; Loftus 1993a
128. Kosslyn 1994
129. Terr 1988
130. Herman and Harvey 1993
131. Esman 1994; Loftus 1993a; Loftus and Rosenwald 1993
132. Laurence and Perry 1983; Weekes et al. 1992
133. Terr 1988
134. Terr 1994b
135. D. Spiegel and Scheflin 1994
136. Herman and Schatzow 1987
137. Herman and Schatzow 1987, p. 11
138. Coons 1994; Coons and Milstein 1986
139. Feldman-Summers and Pope 1994
140. Della Femina et al. 1990, p. 231
141. Oliver 1993
142. Herman and Harvey 1993; Loftus 1993b
143. Frankel 1993; Kihlstrom, in press; Loftus 1993a; Pope and Hudson 1995; Rich 1990; Wakefield and Underwager 1992

144. American Psychiatric Association 1994b; Garry and Loftus 1994; Kihlstrom 1994; Slovenko 1993; D. Spiegel and Scheflin 1994
145. Herman and Harvey 1993
146. Loftus 1993a
147. Briere 1990
148. Kluft 1993c, p. 7, italics mine
149. Spence 1982
150. Barach 1993; Briere 1990; Calof 1993; Gabbard 1994
151. American Psychiatric Association 1994b, p. 263, italics mine
152. American Psychiatric Association 1994b, p. 264
153. Chu 1992; Herman 1992b
154. Horevitz 1993
155. Ganaway 1989, p. 216
156. Kihlstrom and Barnhardt 1993; Loftus 1993a; Loftus and Loftus 1980; M. C. Smith 1983
157. Erdelyi 1994b
158. Kihlstrom, in press
159. Laurence and Perry 1983; Laurence et al. 1986
160. Labelle et al. 1990
161. Laurence et al. 1986
162. Garry and Loftus 1994; Weekes et al. 1992
163. Council on Scientific Affairs 1985, p. 1922
164. Council on Scientific Affairs 1985, p. 1922
165. Kluft 1982
166. Allen and Smith 1993, p. 340
167. van der Kolk 1989
168. Janoff-Bulman 1992
169. D. P. Brown and Fromm 1986; Gabbard 1994; Peebles 1989b; D. Spiegel 1988; van der Hart and Brown 1992

170. D. P. Brown and Fromm 1986; Fine 1991; Grame 1993; Kluft 1982, 1988a, 1989, 1991c; Peebles 1989a, 1989b; W. H. Smith 1993a, 1993b
171. van der Kolk 1994
172. Herman 1992b
173. Thomas 1983, pp. 141–142

Chapter 7. Self

1. Herman 1992a, p. 385
2. Blatt and Blass 1992
3. Sartre 1957
4. Blatt and Blass 1990
5. Dennett 1991; Minsky 1986; Varela et al. 1991
6. Modell 1992, p. 3
7. Modell 1992, p. 3
8. Modell 1992, p. 5
9. Horowitz 1991; Lichtenberg and Schonbar 1992; Mitchell 1991; Stern 1985
10. Dennett 1991; Varela et al. 1991
11. Wolff 1987
12. D. Spiegel 1991b
13. Kagan 1992
14. Freud 1923/1961
15. Ehrenberg 1992
16. Ehrenberg 1992, p. 160
17. Ehrenberg 1992, p. 162
18. Braun 1988b
19. Herman 1992b, p. 106
20. Stern 1985, 1990
21. Stern 1985, p. 71
22. D. Spiegel 1988, p. 19
23. Herman 1992b
24. Modell 1992, p. 9
25. Edelman 1992

26. Stern 1989; Zeanah et al. 1989
27. S. E. Taylor 1989
28. Kabat-Zinn 1990, p. 2
29. Janoff-Bulman 1992
30. Carmen and Rieker 1989; Rieker and Carmen 1986; Summit 1983
31. Herman 1992b, p. 103
32. Herman 1992b, p. 54
33. Herman 1992b
34. McNally 1993a
35. van der Kolk 1989
36. Favazza and Rosenthal 1993, p. 134
37. Favazza and Rosenthal 1993; Walsh and Rosen 1988
38. Favazza and Rosenthal 1993; L. J. Kaplan 1991; van der Kolk et al. 1991; Walsh and Rosen 1988
39. Favazza and Rosenthal 1993
40. Favazza 1987
41. Favazza 1987, pp. 45–46
42. Favazza 1987, p. 51
43. Favazza 1987, p. 51
44. L. J. Kaplan 1991
45. Favazza 1987
46. Favazza and Rosenthal 1993; Walsh and Rosen 1988
47. Charney et al. 1993; Pitman et al. 1990; van der Kolk and Saporta 1991; van der Kolk et al. 1989
48. Favazza and Rosenthal 1993; Walsh and Rosen 1988
49. L. J. Kaplan 1991
50. Walsh and Rosen 1988
51. Schetky 1990
52. Blumenthal 1990
53. van der Kolk et al. 1991
54. van der Kolk et al. 1991, p. 1669
55. S. E. Taylor 1989

Chapter 8.   Relationships

1. Freud 1920/1964
2. Terr 1988
3. van der Kolk 1989
4. Edelman 1989
5. Allen 1977
6. Bowlby 1973, 1982
7. Bowlby 1973, pp. 204–205
8. Stern 1989
9. Stern 1989, p. 63
10. Bowlby 1973
11. Slade and Aber 1992
12. Rimer and Verhovek 1993
13. Strentz 1982, p. 156
14. Walker 1979, p. xv
15. Scott 1987, p. 46
16. Walker 1979, p. xvi
17. Gelinas 1993
18. Gelinas 1993, p. 16
19. Gelinas 1993, p. 17
20. Herman 1992b, p. 92
21. Herman 1992b, p. 92
22. Walker 1979
23. Dutton and Painter 1981, pp. 147–148
24. Symonds 1982
25. Walker 1979
26. Walker 1979, p. 68
27. Strentz 1982
28. Walker 1979, p. xv
29. Graham et al. 1988; Strentz 1982; Symonds 1982
30. Herman 1992b, p. 77
31. Herman 1992b
32. Ehrenberg 1992
33. D. O. Lewis 1992; Oliver 1993
34. Oliver 1993, p. 1322
35. Gelinas 1993, p. 5
36. Gelinas 1993, p. 6
37. Herman 1992b, p. 93
38. Herman 1992b, p. 111

39. Herman 1992b, p. 111
40. Ehrenberg 1992, p. 166
41. Horowitz 1992
42. Winnicott 1950/1958
43. Lichtenberg 1989
44. Lichtenberg 1989, p. 104

Chapter 9.   Posttraumatic Stress Disorder

1.   American Psychiatric Association 1994a
2.   American Psychiatric Association 1994a, pp. 427–428
3.   Trimble 1985
4.   American Psychiatric Association 1980
5.   Kulka et al. 1990
6.   Lindemann 1944
7.   Lindemann 1944, p. 143
8.   Browne and Finkelhor 1986; Kluft 1990b
9.   Helzer et al. 1987
10. Breslau et al. 1991
11. Resnick et al. 1993
12. Breslau et al. 1991
13. Kulka et al. 1990
14. Blank 1993
15. J. R. T. Davidson and Fairbank 1993
16. Rothbaum and Foa 1993
17. Foa and Riggs 1993
18. Kilpatrick and Resnick 1993
19. Drell et al. 1993
20. McNally 1993b
21. American Psychiatric Association 1994a, p. 428
22. de Loos 1990
23. Cannon 1953, p. 226
24. Bremner et al. 1993b; Chrousos and Gold 1992

25. Charney et al. 1993; Chrousos and Gold 1992; Kolb 1987, 1993; Krystal et al. 1989; Simson and Weiss 1994; Southwick et al. 1993a; Veith and Marburg 1994
26. Pitman 1989
27. American Psychiatric Association 1994a, p. 428
28. Frankel 1994a; Reisberg and Heuer 1995
29. Burstein 1985; Kline and Rausch 1985; Mellman and Davis 1985
30. Pitman and Orr 1995
31. Mellman and Davis 1985
32. Pitman 1988
33. Pitman 1988, p. 187
34. Lipper 1990
35. Pitman 1989
36. Pitman and Orr 1995, p. 81
37. McCaffrey and Fairbank 1985
38. R. J. Ross et al. 1989
39. Burstein 1985
40. Chu 1991; van der Kolk 1989
41. Lindy et al. 1992
42. Blank 1985, p. 297
43. Blank 1985, p. 298
44. Blank 1985, p. 300
45. van der Kolk and Kadish 1987, p. 176
46. Oliver 1993
47. American Psychiatric Association 1994a, p. 428
48. Friedman 1990
49. Pitman et al. 1990
50. Herman 1992b
51. Blank 1993, p. 9
52. Rothbaum and Foa 1993
53. J. R. T. Davidson and Fairbank 1993
54. Rothbaum and Foa 1993
55. Kilpatrick and Resnick 1993
56. Terr 1991
57. Goodwin 1990

58. Kendall-Tackett et al. 1993
59. Herman 1992a, 1992b, 1993
60. Herman 1992a, p. 378
61. Herman 1993
62. Brett 1993; J. R. T. Davidson 1993; J. R. T. Davidson and Foa 1991, 1993
63. American Psychiatric Association 1994a
64. Foy et al. 1987; March 1993
65. S. Perry et al. 1992
66. J. R. T. Davidson and Fairbank 1993; March 1993
67. Grinker and Spiegel 1945, p. 54
68. J. R. T. Davidson 1993; J. R. T. Davidson and Foa 1993; Foy et al. 1987; McFarlane 1990
69. Weiner 1992
70. Seligman 1975
71. True et al. 1993
72. van der Kolk 1987a
73. Reich 1990
74. Weiner 1992
75. Breslau et al. 1991
76. Breslau et al. 1991; Reich 1990
77. Breslau et al. 1991; J. R. T. Davidson 1993; Foy et al. 1987; Helzer et al. 1987; Kulka et al. 1990
78. Bremner et al. 1993a
79. Foy et al. 1987
80. Boman 1990
81. Reich 1990, p. 71
82. Foy et al. 1987; B. L. Green et al. 1985; S. Perry et al. 1992
83. Boman 1990; Reich 1990
84. Flach 1990, p. 40
85. Flach 1990, p. 41
86. Flach 1990, p. 42
87. Menninger 1963, p. 406
88. Marmar et al. 1993
89. Kardiner 1941, p. 220
90. Kardiner 1941, p. 221
91. Kolb 1993, p. 298

Chapter 10. Dissociative Disorders

1. Bernstein and Putnam 1986; Braun 1988a; Putnam 1991a; Steinberg 1991
2. E. B. Carlson and Putnam 1992
3. E. B. Carlson 1994; E. B. Carlson and Putnam 1992; B. Sanders et al. 1989
4. Tillman et al. 1994
5. Irwin 1994
6. S. Sanders and Giolas 1991
7. Good 1993
8. Grieg and Betts 1992
9. Allen 1993
10. American Psychiatric Association 1994a, p. 488
11. Gabbard and Twemlow 1984
12. Steinberg 1994; Steinberg et al. 1993
13. Steinberg 1991
14. Gabbard 1994; D. Spiegel 1991a; Steinberg 1991
15. American Psychiatric Association 1994a, p. 478
16. Loewenstein 1991a
17. American Psychiatric Association 1994a, p. 481
18. Loewenstein 1991a
19. adapted from J. Davidson et al. 1987
20. Greaves 1993, p. 372
21. Putnam 1992, p. 96
22. Horowitz 1991
23. Horowitz 1992, p. 494
24. D. Spiegel 1991b, 1993
25. Putnam 1994, pp. 288–289

26. Horowitz 1992
27. Cohen et al. 1991
28. Kluft and Fine 1993, p. xviii
29. American Psychiatric Association 1994a, p. 484
30. Bliss 1986; Ellenberger 1970; Kluft 1991c; Putnam 1989
31. Greaves 1993
32. Janet 1907; van der Hart and Friedman 1989
33. Thigpen and Cleckley 1957
34. Schreiber 1973
35. American Psychiatric Association 1980
36. American Psychiatric Association 1987, p. 271
37. Steinberg et al. 1993
38. C. A. Ross et al. 1991b, p. 1719
39. Fahy 1988; Frankel 1993; Freeland et al. 1993; Merskey 1992; Piper 1994; Tillman et al. 1994; van Praag 1993; Weissberg 1993
40. Braun and Sachs 1985; Kluft 1984b; Putnam 1989
41. Braun 1988b
42. Braun and Sachs 1985; Kluft 1984b
43. Bliss 1986
44. Kluft 1988b
45. Kluft 1984a; McMahon and Fagan 1993; Putnam 1994
46. Putnam et al. 1986
47. Kluft 1991b
48. Slovenko 1991; Steinberg et al. 1993
49. Kluft 1993a
50. Halleck 1990, p. 303
51. Beahrs 1994, p. 95
52. Halleck 1990, p. 307
53. Halleck 1990, pp. 311–312
54. Beahrs 1994, p. 95
55. Herman 1992a
56. Greaves 1989; Kluft 1993b

57. Allen and Smith 1993
58. Bernstein and Putnam 1986; E. B. Carlson 1994; E. B. Carlson et al. 1993
59. E. B. Carlson 1994; C. A. Ross et al. 1991a
60. Steinberg 1994, 1995; Steinberg et al. 1990, 1991
61. Pruyser 1979, pp. 255–256
62. Allen and Smith 1993
63. Caul 1984
64. de Vito 1993; Kluft 1993b
65. Greaves 1989; Kluft 1993b
66. Greaves 1989; Kluft 1993b
67. Putnam 1989
68. D. Spiegel 1993
69. Fine 1991, 1993; Kluft 1982, 1988a, 1989, 1991a
70. Kluft 1993a, p. 42
71. Kluft 1993b
72. Bowers 1994b
73. Putnam and Loewenstein 1993
74. Kluft 1993b

Chapter 11.   Other Disorders

1. J. R. T. Davidson and Fairbank 1993
2. Breslau et al. 1991; Helzer et al. 1987
3. Putnam et al. 1986
4. J. R. T. Davidson and Fairbank 1993
5. Brett 1993; J. R. T. Davidson and Foa 1991
6. American Psychiatric Association 1994a, p. 436
7. American Psychiatric Association 1994a, p. 395
8. Pitman 1993
9. McNally and Saigh 1993
10. Breslau et al. 1991; J. R. T. Davidson and Fairbank 1993

11. Chrousos and Gold 1992; Hyman and Nestler 1993
12. American Psychiatric Association 1994a, p. 349
13. Breslau et al. 1991; J. R. T. Davidson and Fairbank 1993; Helzer et al. 1987
14. Kulka et al. 1990
15. Schetky 1990
16. Friedman 1990
17. Charney et al. 1993
18. de Loos 1990; Golding 1994; Loewenstein 1990; Saxe et al. 1994
19. Carson and Butcher 1992; Norris 1989a; Weiner 1992
20. Weiner 1992
21. Carson and Butcher 1992
22. Weiner 1992
23. Foa and Riggs 1993
24. Burgess and Holmstrom 1974
25. Becker et al. 1982
26. Foa et al. 1991; Foa and Riggs 1993
27. Becker et al. 1982; Bolen 1993; Browne and Finkelhor 1986; Stevens-Simon and Reichert 1994
28. Westerlund 1992
29. H. S. Kaplan 1974
30. Bolen 1993
31. Zerbe 1993a
32. Goodwin and Attias 1993, p. 333
33. Torem 1990
34. Goodwin and Attias 1993, p. 337
35. Putnam et al. 1986
36. Torem 1993a
37. Zerbe 1993b, p. 324
38. Zerbe 1993b, p. 322
39. Zerbe 1993b, p. 325
40. Zerbe 1993a
41. Pope and Hudson 1992
42. Welch and Fairburn 1994
43. Torem 1990, 1993a; Goodwin and Attias 1993; Waller 1991; Zerbe 1993a
44. Waller et al. 1993a, 1993b
45. American Psychiatric Association 1994a, p. 629
46. Meissner 1978
47. Paris 1994
48. Southwick et al. 1993b
49. Stone 1990
50. American Psychiatric Association 1994a, p. 654
51. Horwitz et al., in press
52. Silk 1994
53. Kroll 1993
54. Paris 1994
55. Weaver and Clum 1993
56. Stone 1990
57. Shearer 1994
58. Paris 1994
59. Herman 1992a, 1992b, 1993
60. van Praag 1993

Chapter 12. Treatment Approaches

1. Herman 1992b, p. 159
2. Herman 1992b, p. 169
3. Chu 1992
4. Herman 1992b p. 172
5. Kluft 1992, p. 152
6. Allen et al. 1984; Colson et al. 1988; Frieswyk et al. 1984; Horwitz 1974
7. Luborsky 1976; Luborsky et al. 1983
8. Allen et al. 1984
9. Horwitz et al., in press
10. Frieswyk et al. 1984
11. Chu 1992
12. Chu 1992
13. Herman 1992b

14. Barach 1993; Chu 1992; Gutheil and Gabbard 1993; Herman 1992a
15. Barach 1993; Carmen and Rieker 1989; Chu 1992; Gutheil and Gabbard 1993
16. Gabbard 1989
17. Kluft 1990a
18. Gutheil and Gabbard 1993, p. 188
19. Horwitz et al., in press
20. Chu 1992; Peebles-Kleiger 1989
21. van der Hart and Brown 1992
22. Chu 1992, p. 353
23. D. P. Brown and Fromm 1986; Peebles 1989; D. Spiegel 1988; van der Hart and Brown 1992
24. D. P. Brown and Fromm 1986; Peebles 1989; D. Spiegel 1988; van der Hart and Spiegel 1993
25. Peebles-Kleiger 1989, p. 198
26. Carson and Butcher 1992
27. van der Hart and Spiegel 1993, p. 203, italics mine
28. Kluft 1993a, p. 42
29. Horwitz 1974
30. Bowlby 1988
31. Herink 1980
32. Linehan 1987, 1993a, 1993b
33. Linehan et al. 1991
34. Linehan 1993b
35. van der Kolk 1987b, p. 153
36. van der Kolk 1987b
37. Herman 1992b
38. Barach 1993
39. Buchele 1993; Caul 1984; Caul et al. 1986; Coons and Bradley 1985; Hogan 1992
40. Coons and Bradley 1985
41. Buchele 1993, p. 363
42. Caul 1984
43. Caul et al. 1986; Coons and Bradley 1985
44. Yalom 1970

45. van der Kolk 1987b
46. Porter et al. 1993; Sachs et al. 1988; M. B. Williams 1991
47. Kluft 1993b; Porter et al. 1993; Sachs et al. 1988
48. Sachs et al. 1988
49. Roesler 1994
50. Schatzow and Herman 1989, p. 338
51. Schatzow and Herman 1989
52. Schatzow and Herman 1989
53. Briere and Elliott 1993; Carmen and Rieker 1989; Hulsey et al. 1992; Kroll 1993; Nash et al. 1993; Rose 1993; Weaver and Clum 1993
54. Gelinas 1986, p. 357
55. J. R. T. Davidson 1992; Loewenstein et al. 1988; Saporta and Case 1993
56. J. R. T. Davidson 1992
57. J. R. T. Davidson 1992
58. Saporta and Case 1993; Southwick et al. 1994
59. J. R. T. Davidson 1992; J. R. T. Davidson et al. 1993; Friedman 1990; Krystal et al. 1989; Southwick et al. 1992, 1994
60. Aghajanian 1987; Saporta and Case 1993
61. Saporta and Case 1993
62. J. R. T. Davidson 1992
63. Lipper 1990
64. J. R. T. Davidson 1992; Fichtner et al. 1990; Saporta and Case 1993
65. Saporta and Case 1993
66. J. R. T. Davidson 1992; Saporta and Case 1993
67. J. R. T. Davidson 1992
68. Marmar et al. 1993; Saporta and Case 1993
69. J. R. T. Davidson 1992
70. Kolb 1987; Krystal et al. 1989

71. Braun 1990; J. R. T. Davidson 1992; Gilman et al. 1990; Krystal et al. 1989
72. Braun 1990
73. Saporta and Case 1993
74. Loewenstein 1991b; Loewenstein et al. 1988
75. Loewenstein 1991b, p. 738
76. Loewenstein 1991b
77. J. R. T. Davidson 1992
78. Marmar et al. 1993
79. Kluft 1991b
80. Pawlicki and Gaumer 1993
81. Barach 1993, p. 16
82. Braun 1993; Kluft 1991b; Putnam 1989; Putnam and Loewenstein 1993
83. Braun 1993; Kluft 1991b
84. Allen et al. 1987, 1990
85. Braun 1993
86. J. Davidson et al. 1987; Kluft 1991b; Lewin 1991; C. A. Ross 1987; Steinmeyer 1991
87. Kelly 1993

Chapter 13.   Self-Regulation

1. Briere and Runtz 1991
2. Norris 1986
3. Kabat-Zinn 1994, p. 8
4. Norris 1986
5. Kabat-Zinn 1994, p. 104
6. Vincent 1986/1990, p. 142
7. Olds 1956, 1958; Olds and Milner 1954
8. Olds and Milner 1954
9. Olds 1958
10. Thompson 1993
11. Thomas 1992, p. 33
12. Thomas 1992, p. 34
13. Thomas 1992, p. 35
14. Lichtenberg 1989
15. Brazelton 1990
16. Watson and Clark, in press
17. Nathanson 1992, p. 73
18. Watson and Clark, in press
19. Emde 1992
20. Csikszentmihalyi 1990
21. Csikszentmihalyi 1988, p. 7
22. Csikszentmihalyi 1990, p. 85
23. Csikszentmihalyi 1990, p. 49
24. Nathanson 1992, p. 79
25. Nathanson 1992, p. 79
26. Emde 1992
27. Nathanson 1992, p. 83
28. Emde 1992
29. Hobson 1994, p. 226
30. Hobson 1994, p. 226
31. Hobson 1994, p. 235
32. Hobson 1994, p. 241
33. Cooper 1968
34. Sime 1984
35. Westerlund 1992
36. Dunn and Dishman 1991
37. Seraganian 1993
38. Benson 1975
39. Fahrion and Norris 1990, p. 225
40. Fitzgerald and Gonzales 1994
41. D. P. Brown and Fromm 1986; E. E. Green and Green 1986; Horowitz 1970
42. Pitman and Orr 1990
43. Watts 1957
44. Benson 1975
45. Shapiro 1982, p. 268
46. Hanh 1987, p. 11
47. Varela et al. 1991, p. 25
48. Watts 1957, p. 124
49. Hanh 1987, 1991
50. Varela et al. 1991, p. 25
51. Shapiro 1982
52. Benson 1975
53. Varela et al. 1991, p. 24
54. Watts 1957, p. 112

55. Levy and Levy 1991; Murphy and Donovan 1988; Shapiro 1982; Shapiro and Walsh 1984
56. Kabat-Zinn 1990
57. Kabat-Zinn 1994
58. Kabat-Zinn et al. 1992
59. Lazarus 1984
60. Hanh 1991
61. Hilgard 1965; H. Spiegel 1974
62. Baker 1992; D. P. Brown and Fromm 1986
63. W. H. Smith 1990, 1993a
64. D. P. Brown and Fromm 1986; W. H. Smith 1993a
65. D. P. Brown and Fromm 1986; Watkins 1971
66. Kluft 1988b, 1989
67. D. P. Brown and Fromm 1986; Peebles 1989; W. H. Smith 1993a
68. D. Spiegel 1988, pp. 27–28
69. Grame 1993
70. W. H. Smith 1993b
71. Allen and Smith 1993; Kluft 1982; W. H. Smith 1993b
72. Kluft 1982, 1993b
73. Kluft 1982
74. Kluft 1982
75. Bliss 1986
76. S. Sanders 1991
77. Kagan 1994
78. E. E. Green and Green 1986
79. Norris 1986
80. Norris 1989b, p. 274
81. E. E. Green and Green 1986; Norris 1986, 1989b
82. E. E. Green and Green 1986, p. 571
83. Norris 1986
84. E. E. Green and Green 1986
85. Norris 1989b
86. Peniston and Kulkosky 1991
87. Fahrion and Norris 1990
88. Benson 1975
89. Fahrion and Norris 1990
90. Fahrion and Norris 1990, p. 222

Chapter 14. Conclusions

1. Sameroff 1993
2. Briere and Elliott 1993; Hulsey et al. 1992; Kroll 1993; Nash et al. 1993; Rose 1993; Weaver and Clum 1993
3. Sameroff 1993; Scarr 1992
4. Bowlby 1988, p. 11
5. Post 1992
6. Kluft 1993a, p. 42
7. Kluft 1993a; Putnam and Loewenstein 1993
8. Horwitz 1974; Horwitz et al., in press; Rockland 1989
9. Yalom 1980
10. Thompson 1993
11. Janoff-Bulman 1992
12. Janoff-Bulman 1992, p. 171
13. Janoff-Bulman 1992
14. Herman 1992b, p. 207
15. Pruyser 1987, p. 467
16. Pruyser 1987, p. 472

Appendix: The Biology of Trauma

1. Carson and Butcher 1992, p. 59
2. Wills 1991
3. Edelman 1988
4. Wills 1991
5. Vincent 1986/1990
6. Vincent 1986/1990, p. 70
7. Krystal et al. 1989
8. Hyman and Nestler 1993
9. Pitman 1993; van der Kolk et al. 1989

10. Leakey 1992; Wills 1991
11. Dawkins 1982, pp. 38–39
12. MacLean 1990, p. 12
13. Epstein 1994
14. MacLean 1990, p. 23
15. MacLean 1990, p. 452
16. MacLean 1990, p. 247
17. Beaton 1985; Borod 1992
18. Edelman 1992, p. 17
19. Bremner et al. 1993b; Charney et al. 1993; Chrousos and Gold 1992; Hyman and Nestler 1993
20. Campbell 1990
21. Vincent 1986/1990, p. 100
22. P. A. Norris, personal communication, November 1993
23. Simson and Weiss 1994; Veith and Marburg 1994
24. Simson and Weiss 1994
25. Aston-Jones et al. 1994

References

Agger I: Sexual torture of political prisoners: an overview. Journal of Traumatic Stress 2:305–318, 1989

Aghajanian GK: Serotonin, in Encyclopedia of Neuroscience, Vol 2. Edited by Adelman G. Boston, MA, Birkhäuser, 1987, pp 1082–1083

Ainsworth MDS: Attachments beyond infancy. Am Psychol 44:709–716, 1989

Akiskal HS: An integrative perspective on recurrent mood disorders: the mediating role of personality, in Psychosocial Aspects of Depression. Edited by Becker J, Kleinman A. Hillsdale, NJ, Lawrence Erlbaum, 1990, pp 215–235

Allen JG: Ego states and object relations. Bull Menninger Clin 41:522–538, 1977

Allen JG: Adaptive effects of affect and their implications for therapy. Psychoanal Rev 67:217–230, 1980

Allen JG: Dissociative processes: theoretical underpinnings of a working model for clinician and patient. Bull Menninger Clin 57:287–308, 1993

Allen JG: Temperament: the biological shaper of personality. Menninger Letter 2:4–5, 1994

Allen JG: Depression causes vicious circles in relationships. Menninger Letter 3:6, 1995

Allen JG: The spectrum of accuracy in memories of childhood trauma. Harvard Review of Psychiatry, in press

Allen JG, Smith WH: Diagnosing dissociative disorders. Bull Menninger Clin 57:328–343, 1993

Allen JG, Newsom G, Gabbard GO, et al: Scales to assess the therapeutic alliance from a psychoanalytic perspective. Bull Menninger Clin 48:383–400, 1984

Allen JG, Coyne L, Beasley C, et al: A conceptual model for research on required length of psychiatric hospital stay. Compr Psychiatry 28:131–140, 1987

Allen JG, Coyne L, Logue AM: Do clinicians agree about who needs extended psychiatric hospitalization? Compr Psychiatry 31:355–362, 1990

American Psychiatric Association: Diagnostic and Statistical Manual of Mental Disorders, 3rd Edition. Washington, DC, American Psychiatric Association, 1980

American Psychiatric Association: Diagnostic and Statistical Manual of Mental Disorders, 3rd Edition, Revised. Washington, DC, American Psychiatric Association, 1987

American Psychiatric Association: Diagnostic and Statistical Manual of Mental Disorders, 4th Edition. Washington, DC, American Psychiatric Association, 1994a

American Psychiatric Association: Statement on memories of sexual abuse. Int J Clin Exp Hypn 42:261–264, 1994b

Appelbaum PS: Memories and murder. Hosp Community Psychiatry 43:679–680, 1992

Aston-Jones G, Valentino RJ, Van Bockstaele EJ, et al: Locus coeruleus, stress, and PTSD: neurobiological and clinical parallels, in Catecholamine Function in Posttraumatic Stress Disorder: Emerging Concepts. Edited by Marburg MM. Washington, DC, American Psychiatric Press, 1994, pp 17–62

Baars BJ: A Cognitive Theory of Consciousness. New York, Cambridge University Press, 1988

Baker E: Advanced Hypnosis (Continuing Education Workshop). The Menninger Clinic, Topeka, KS, May 7, 1992

Barach PM: Draft of "Recommendations for treating dissociative identity disorder." ISSMP & D (International Society for the Study of Multiple Personality and Dissociation) News, October 1993, pp 14–19

Barclay CR: Schematization of autobiographical memory, in Autobiographical Memory. Edited by Rubin DC. New York, Cambridge University Press, 1986, pp 82–99

Barclay CR, Wellman HM: Accuracies and inaccuracies in autobiographical memories. Journal of Memory and Language 25:93–103, 1986

Barlow DH: The nature of anxiety: anxiety, depression, and emotional disorders, in Chronic Anxiety: Generalized Anxiety Disorder and Mixed Anxiety-Depression. Edited by Rapee RM, Barlow DH. New York, Guilford, 1991, pp 1–28

Bartlett FC: Remembering: A Study in Experimental and Social Psychology. New York, Cambridge University Press, 1932

Basoglu M, Paker M, Paker O, et al: Psychological effects of torture: a comparison of tortured with nontortured political activists in Turkey. Am J Psychiatry 151:76–81, 1994

Bates JE, Wachs TD (eds): Temperament: Individual Differences at the Interface of Biology and Behavior. Washington, DC, American Psychological Association, 1994

Beahrs JO: Why dissociative disordered patients are fundamentally responsible: a master class commentary. Int J Clin Exp Hypn 42:93–96, 1994

Beaton A: Left Side, Right Side: A Review of Laterality Research. New Haven, CT, Yale University Press, 1985

Beck AT: Cognitive therapy: a 30-year retrospective. Am Psychol 46:368–375, 1991

Becker JV, Skinner LJ, Abel GG, et al: Incidence and types of sexual dysfunctions in rape and incest victims. Journal of Sex and Marital Therapy 8:65–74, 1982

Benson H: The Relaxation Response. New York, Avon Books, 1975

Bernstein EM, Putnam FW: Development, reliability, and validity of a dissociation scale. J Nerv Ment Dis 174:727–735, 1986

Biden JR: Violence against women: the congressional response. Am Psychol 48:1059–1061, 1993

Binder RL, McNiel DE, Goldstone RL: Patterns of recall of childhood sexual abuse as described by adult survivors. Bull Am Acad Psychiatry Law 22:357–366, 1994

Blank AS Jr: The unconscious flashback to the war in Vietnam veterans: clinical mystery, legal defense, and community problem, in The Trauma of War: Stress and Recovery in Vietnam Veterans. Edited by Sonnenberg SM, Blank AS Jr, Talbott JA. Washington, DC, American Psychiatric Press, 1985, pp 293–308

Blank AS Jr: The longitudinal course of posttraumatic stress disorder, in Posttraumatic Stress Disorder: DSM-IV and Beyond. Edited by Davidson JRT, Foa EB. Washington, DC, American Psychiatric Press, 1993, pp 3–22

Blatt SJ, Blass RB: Attachment and separateness: a dialectic model of the products and processes of development throughout the life cycle. Psychoanal Study Child 45:107–127, 1990

Blatt SJ, Blass RB: Relatedness and self-definition: two primary dimensions in personality development, psychopathology, and psychotherapy, in Interface of Psychoanalysis and Psychology. Edited by Barron JW, Eagle MN, Wolitzky DL. Washington, DC, American Psychological Association, 1992, pp 399–428

Bliss EL: Multiple Personality, Allied Disorders and Hypnosis. New York, Oxford University Press, 1986

Blumenthal SJ: An overview and synopsis of risk factors, assessment, and treatment of suicidal patients over the life cycle, in Suicide Over the Life Cycle: Risk Factors, Assessment, and Treatment of Suicidal Patients. Edited by Blumenthal SJ, Kupfer DJ. Washington, DC, American Psychiatric Press, 1990, pp 685–733

Bolen JD: Sexuality-focused treatment with survivors and their partners, in Treatment of Adult Survivors of Incest. Edited by Paddison PL. Washington, DC, American Psychiatric Press, 1993, pp 55–75

Bolin R: Natural and technological disasters: evidence of psychopathology, in Environment and Psychopathology. Edited by Ghadirian AA, Lehmann HE. New York, Springer, 1993, pp 121–140

Boman B: Are all Vietnam veterans like John Rambo? in Posttraumatic Stress Disorder: Etiology, Phenomenology, and Treatment. Edited by Wolf ME, Mosnaim AD. Washington, DC, American Psychiatric Press, 1990, pp 80–93

Borod JC: Interhemispheric and intrahemispheric control of emotion: a focus on unilateral brain damage. J Consult Clin Psychol 60:339–348, 1992

Bower GH: Mood and memory. Am Psychol 36:129–148, 1981

Bowers KS: Imagination and dissociation in hypnotic responding. Int J Clin Exp Hypn 4:253–275, 1992

Bowers KS: Dissociated control, imagination, and the phenomenology of dissociation, in Dissociation: Culture, Mind, and Body. Edited by Spiegel D. Washington, DC, American Psychiatric Press, 1994a, pp 21–38

Bowers KS: Three levels of consciousness: implications for dissociation, in Psychological Concepts and Dissociative Disorders. Edited by Klein RM, Doane BK. Hillsdale, NJ, Lawrence Erlbaum, 1994b, pp 155–186

Bowlby J: Attachment and Loss, Vol 2: Separation. New York, Basic Books, 1973

Bowlby J: Attachment and Loss, 2nd Edition, Vol 1: Attachment. New York, Basic Books, 1982

Bowlby J: A Secure Base: Parent-Child Attachment and Healthy Human Development. New York, Basic Books, 1988

Braun BG: The BASK model of dissociation. Dissociation 1:4–23, 1988a

Braun BG: The BASK model of dissociation, II: treatment. Dissociation 1:16–23, 1988b

Braun BG: Unusual medication regimens in the treatment of dissociative disorder patients, I: noradrenergic agents. Dissociation 3:144–150, 1990

Braun BG: Aids to the treatment of multiple personality disorder on a general psychiatric inpatient unit, in Clinical Perspectives on Multiple Personality Disorder. Edited by Kluft RP, Fine CG. Washington, DC, American Psychiatric Press, 1993, pp 155–175

Braun BG, Sachs RG: The development of multiple personality disorder: predisposing, precipitating, and perpetuating factors, in Childhood Antecedents of Multiple Personality. Edited by Kluft RP. Washington, DC, American Psychiatric Press, 1985, pp 37–64

Brazelton TB: Touch as touchstone: summary of the round table, in Touch: The Foundation of Experience. Edited by Barnard KE, Brazelton TB. Madison, CT, International Universities Press, 1990, pp 561–566

Bremner JD, Southwick SM, Johnson DR, et al: Childhood physical abuse and combat-related posttraumatic stress disorder in Vietnam veterans. Am J Psychiatry 150:235–239, 1993a

Bremner JD, Davis M, Southwick SM, et al: Neurobiology of posttraumatic stress disorder, in American Psychiatric Press Review of Psychiatry, Vol 12. Edited by Oldham JM, Riba MB, Tasman A. Washington, DC, American Psychiatric Press, 1993b, pp 183–204

Bremner JD, Southwick SM, Charney DS: Etiological factors in the development of posttraumatic stress disorder, in Does Stress Cause Psychiatric Illness? Edited by CM Mazure. Washington, DC, American Psychiatric Press, 1994, pp 149–185

Brende J: A psychodynamic view of character pathology in Vietnam combat veterans. Bull Menninger Clin 47:193–216, 1983

Breslau N, Davis GC, Andreski P, et al: Traumatic events and posttraumatic stress disorder in an urban population of young adults. Arch Gen Psychiatry 48:216–222, 1991

Brett EA: Classifications of posttraumatic stress disorder in DSM-IV: anxiety disorder, dissociative disorder, or stress disorder? in Posttraumatic Stress Disorder: DSM-IV and Beyond. Edited by Davidson JRT, Foa EB. Washington, DC, American Psychiatric Press, 1993, pp 191–204

Brewer WF: What is autobiographical memory? in Autobiographical Memory. Edited by Rubin DC. New York, Cambridge University Press, 1986, pp 25–49

Briere J: Dr. Briere replies (letter). Am J Psychiatry 147:1389–1390, 1990

Briere J, Conte J: Self-reported amnesia for abuse in adults molested as children. Journal of Traumatic Stress 6:21–31, 1993

Briere J, Elliott DM: Sexual abuse, family environment, and psychological symptoms: on the validity of statistical control. J Consult Clin Psychol 61:284–288, 1993

Briere J, Runtz M: The long-term effects of sexual abuse: a review and synthesis, in Treating Victims of Child Sexual Abuse. Edited by Briere J. San Francisco, CA, Jossey-Bass, 1991, pp 3–13

Brown DP, Fromm E: Hypnotherapy and Hypnoanalysis. Hillsdale, NJ, Lawrence Erlbaum, 1986

Brown R, Kulik J: Flashbulb memories. Cognition 5:73–99, 1977

Browne A: Violence against women by male partners: prevalence, outcomes, and policy implications. Am Psychol 48:1077–1087, 1993

Browne A, Finkelhor D: Impact of child sexual abuse: a review of the research. Psychol Bull 99:66–77, 1986

Buchele BJ: Group psychotherapy for persons with multiple personality and dissociative disorders. Bull Menninger Clin 57:362–370, 1993

Burgess AW, Holmstrom LL: Rape trauma syndrome. Am J Psychiatry 131:981–986, 1974

Burns DD: Feeling Good: The New Mood Therapy. New York, William Morrow, 1980

Burstein A: Posttraumatic flashbacks, dream disturbances, and mental imagery. J Clin Psychiatry 46:374–378, 1985

Buss AH: Personality: primate heritage and human distinctiveness, in Personality Structure in the Life Course: Essays on Personology in the Murray Tradition. Edited by Zucker RA, Rabin AI, Aronoff J, et al. New York, Springer, 1992, pp 57–100

Calof D: Facing the truth about false memory. Family Therapy Networker, September/October 1993, pp 39–45

Campbell NA: Biology, 2nd Edition. Redwood City, CA, Benjamin/Cummings, 1990

Cannon WB: Bodily Changes in Pain, Hunger, Fear and Rage, 2nd Edition. Boston, MA, Charles T. Branford, 1953

Cardeña E: The domain of dissociation, in Dissociation: Clinical and Theoretical Perspectives. Edited by Lynn SJ, Rhue JW. New York, Guilford, 1994, pp 15–31

Carlson EB: Studying the interaction between physical and psychological states with the Dissociative Experiences Scale, in Dissociation: Culture, Mind, and Body. Edited by Spiegel D. Washington, DC, American Psychiatric Press, 1994, pp 41–58

Carlson EB, Putnam FW, Ross CA, et al: Validity of the Dissociative Experiences Scale in screening for multiple personality disorder: a multicenter study. Am J Psychiatry 150:1030–1036, 1993

Carlson V, Cicchetti D, Barnett D, et al: Finding order in disorganization: lessons from research on maltreated infants' attachments to their caregivers, in Child Maltreatment: Theory and Research on the Causes and Consequences of Child Abuse and Neglect. Edited by Cicchetti D, Carlson V. New York, Cambridge University Press, 1989, pp 494–528

Carmen E, Rieker PP: A psychosocial model of the victim-to-patient process: implications for treatment. Psychiatr Clin North Am 12:431–443, 1989

Carson RC, Butcher JN: Abnormal Psychology and Modern Life, 9th Edition. New York, Harper Collins, 1992

Carstensen LL, Gabrieli J, Shepard R, et al: Repressed objectivity (letter). American Psychological Society Observer, March 1993, p 2

Caul D: Group and videotape techniques for multiple personality disorder. Psychiatric Annals 14:43, 47, 49–50, 1984

Caul D, Sachs RG, Braun BG: Group therapy in the treatment of multiple personality disorder, in Treatment of Multiple Personality Disorder. Edited by Braun BG. Washington, DC, American Psychiatric Press, 1986, pp 143–156

Charney DS, Deutch AY, Krystal JH, et al: Psychobiologic mechanisms of posttraumatic stress disorder. Arch Gen Psychiatry 50:294–305, 1993

Christianson S: Remembering emotional events: potential mechanisms, in The Handbook of Emotion and Memory: Research and Theory. Edited by Christianson S. Hillsdale, NJ, Lawrence Erlbaum, 1992, pp 307–340

Chrousos GP, Gold PW: The concepts of stress and stress system disorders: overview of physical and behavioral homeostasis. JAMA 267:1244–1252, 1992

Chu JA: The repetition compulsion revisited: reliving dissociated trauma. Psychotherapy 28:327–332, 1991

Chu JA: The therapeutic roller coaster: dilemmas in the treatment of childhood abuse survivors. Journal of Psychotherapy Practice and Research 1:351–370, 1992

Churchland PS: Neurophilosophy: Toward a Unified Science of the Mind-Brain. Cambridge, MA, MIT Press, 1986

Clark LA, Watson D: Distinguishing functional from dysfunctional affective responses, in The Nature of Emotion: Fundamental Questions. Edited by Ekman P, Davidson RJ. New York, Oxford University Press, 1994, pp 131–136

Clark LA, Watson D, Mineka S: Temperament, personality, and the mood and anxiety disorders. J Abnorm Psychol 103:103–116, 1994

Cohen BM, Giller EL Jr, "W Lynn" [an anonymous patient] (eds): Multiple Personality Disorder From the Inside Out. Baltimore, MD, Sidran Press, 1991

Colson DB, Horwitz L, Allen JG, et al: Patient collaboration as a criterion for the therapeutic alliance. Psychoanalytic Psychology 5:259–268, 1988

Coons PM: Confirmation of childhood abuse in child and adolescent cases of multiple personality disorder and dissociative disorder not otherwise specified. J Nerv Ment Dis 182:461–464, 1994

Coons PM, Bradley K: Group psychotherapy with multiple personality patients. J Nerv Ment Dis 173:515–521, 1985

Coons PM, Milstein V: Psychosexual disturbances in multiple personality: characteristics, etiology, and treatment. J Clin Psychiatry 47:106–110, 1986

Cooper K: Aerobics. New York, Evans, 1968

Costa PT Jr, Widiger TA (eds): Personality Disorders and the Five-Factor Model of Personality. Washington, DC, American Psychological Association, 1994

Council on Scientific Affairs, American Medical Association: Scientific status of refreshing recollection by the use of hypnosis. JAMA 253:1918–1923, 1985

Cowan N: Evolving conceptions of memory storage, selective attention, and their mutual constraints within the human information-processing system. Psychol Bull 104:163–191, 1988

Craik FIM: On the making of episodes, in Varieties of Memory and Consciousness: Essays in Honour of Endel Tulving. Edited by Roediger HL III, Craik FIM. Hillsdale, NJ, Lawrence Erlbaum, 1989, pp 43–57

Crime Victims Research and Treatment Center: Rape in America: A Report to the Nation. Charleston, SC, Department of Psychiatry and Behavioral Sciences, Medical University of South Carolina, 1992

Crittenden PM, Ainsworth MDS: Child maltreatment and attachment theory, in Child Maltreatment: Theory and Research on the Causes and Consequences of Child Abuse and Neglect. Edited by Cicchetti D, Carlson V. New York, Cambridge University Press, 1989, pp 432–463

Csikszentmihalyi M: Introduction, in Optimal Experience: Psychological Studies of Flow in Consciousness. Edited by Csikszentmihalyi M, Csikszentmihalyi IS. New York, Cambridge University Press, 1988, pp 3–14

Csikszentmihalyi M: Flow: The Psychology of Optimal Experience. New York, Harper Collins, 1990

Darwin C: The Expression of the Emotions in Man and Animals. Chicago, IL, University of Chicago Press, 1965

Davidson J, Allen JG, Smith WH: Complexities in the hospital treatment of a patient with multiple personality disorder. Bull Menninger Clin 51:561–568, 1987

Davidson JRT: Drug therapy of post-traumatic stress disorder. Br J Psychiatry 160:309–314, 1992

Davidson JRT: Issues in the diagnosis of posttraumatic stress disorder, in American Psychiatric Press Review of Psychiatry, Vol 12. Edited by Oldham JM, Riba MB, Tasman A. Washington, DC, American Psychiatric Press, 1993, pp 141–155

Davidson JRT, Fairbank JA: The epidemiology of posttraumatic stress disorder, in Posttraumatic Stress Disorder: DSM-IV and Beyond. Edited by Davidson JRT, Foa EB. Washington, DC, American Psychiatric Press, 1993, pp 147–169

Davidson JRT, Foa EB: Diagnostic issues in posttraumatic stress disorder: considerations for the DSM-IV. J Abnorm Psychol 100:346–355, 1991

Davidson JRT, Foa EB (eds): Posttraumatic Stress Disorder: DSM-IV and Beyond. Washington, DC, American Psychiatric Press, 1993

Davidson JRT, Kudler HS, Saunders WB, et al: Predicting response to amitriptyline in posttraumatic stress disorder. Am J Psychiatry 150:1024–1029, 1993

Davis RH: Freud's Concept of Passivity. Madison, CT, International Universities Press, 1993

Dawkins R: The Extended Phenotype. New York, Oxford University Press, 1982

Dawkins R: The Selfish Gene, New Edition. New York, Oxford University Press, 1989

Della Femina D, Yeager CA, Lewis DO: Child abuse: adolescent records vs. adult recall. Child Abuse Negl 14:227–231, 1990

de Loos WS: Psychosomatic manifestations of chronic posttraumatic stress disorder, in Posttraumatic Stress Disorder: Etiology, Phenomenology, and Treatment. Edited by Wolf ME, Mosnaim AD. Washington, DC, American Psychiatric Press, 1990, pp 94–104

Dennett DC: Consciousness Explained. Boston, Little, Brown, 1991

de Vito RA: The use of amytal interviews in the treatment of an exceptionally complex case of multiple personality disorder, in Clinical Perspectives on Multiple Personality Disorder. Edited by Kluft RP, Fine CG. Washington, DC, American Psychiatric Press, 1993, pp 227–240

de Waal F: Peacemaking Among Primates. Cambridge, MA, Harvard University Press, 1989

Drell MJ, Siegel CH, Gaensbauer TJ: Post-traumatic stress disorder, in Handbook of Infant Mental Health. Edited by Zeanah CH. New York, Guilford, 1993, pp 291–304

Dunn AL, Dishman RK: Exercise and the neurobiology of depression, in Exercise and Sports Science Reviews, Vol 19. Edited by Holloszy JO. Baltimore, MD, Williams & Wilkins, 1991, pp 41–98

Dutton D, Painter SL: Traumatic bonding: the development of emotional attachments in battered women and other relationships of intermittent abuse. Victimology 6:139–155, 1981

Eccles JC: Evolution of the Brain: Creation of the Self. New York, Routledge & Kegan Paul, 1989

Edelman GM: Topobiology: An Introduction to Molecular Embryology. New York, Basic Books, 1988

Edelman GM: The Remembered Present: A Biological Theory of Consciousness. New York, Basic Books, 1989

Edelman GM: Bright Air, Brilliant Fire: On the Matter of the Mind. New York, Basic Books, 1992

Ehrenberg DB: The Intimate Edge: Extending the Reach of Psychoanalytic Interaction. New York, WW Norton, 1992

Ellenberger HF: The Discovery of the Unconscious: The History and Evolution of Dynamic Psychiatry. New York, Basic Books, 1970

Emde RN: Positive emotions for psychoanalytic theory: surprises from infancy research and new directions, in Affect: Psychoanalytic Perspectives. Edited by Shapiro T, Emde RN. Madison, CT, International Universities Press, 1992, pp 5–44

Epstein S: Integration of the cognitive and the psychodynamic unconscious. Am Psychol 49:709–724, 1994

Erdelyi MH: Dissociation, defense, and the unconscious, in Dissociation: Culture, Mind, and Body. Edited by Spiegel D. Washington, DC, American Psychiatric Press, 1994a, pp 3–20

Erdelyi MH: Hypnotic hypermnesia: the empty set of hypermnesia. Int J Clin Exp Hypn 42:379–390, 1994b

Erikson EH: Childhood and Society, 2nd Edition. New York, WW Norton, 1963

Esman AH: Child abuse and multiple personality disorder (letter). Am J Psychiatry 151:948, 1994

Eth S, Pynoos RS: Children who witness the homicide of a parent. Psychiatry 57:287–306, 1994

Fahrion SL, Norris PA: Self-regulation of anxiety. Bull Menninger Clin 54:217–231, 1990

Fahy TA: The diagnosis of multiple personality disorder: a critical review. Br J Psychiatry 153:597–606, 1988

Falsetti SA, Resnick HS, Dansky BS, et al: The relationship of stress to panic disorder: cause or effect?, in Does Stress Cause Psychiatric Illness? Edited by Mazure CM. Washington, DC, American Psychiatric Press, 1995, pp 111–147

Favazza AR: Bodies Under Siege: Self-Mutilation in Culture and Psychiatry. Baltimore, MD, Johns Hopkins University Press, 1987

Favazza AR, Rosenthal RJ: Diagnostic issues in self-mutilation. Hosp Community Psychiatry 44:134–140, 1993

Feldman W, Feldman E, Goodman JT, et al: Is childhood sexual abuse really increasing in prevalence? an analysis of the evidence. Pediatrics 88:29–33, 1991

Feldman-Summers S, Pope KS: The experience of "forgetting" childhood abuse: a national survey of psychologists. J Consult Clin Psychol 62:636–639, 1994

Ferenczi S: Confusion of tongues between the adult and the child. Int J Psychoanal 30:225–230, 1949

Fichtner CG, Kuhlman DT, Gruenfeld MJ, et al: Decreased episodic violence and increased control of dissociation in a carbamazepine-treated case of multiple personality. Biol Psychiatry 27:1045–1052, 1990

Field T: Attachment as psychobiological attunement: being on the same wavelength, in The Psychobiology of Attachment and Separation. Edited by Reite M, Field T. New York, Academic Press, 1985, pp 415–454

Field T, Reite M: The psychobiology of attachment and separation: a summary, in The Psychobiology of Attachment and Separation. Edited by Reite M, Field T. New York, Academic Press, 1985, pp 455–479

Fine CG: Treatment stabilization and crisis prevention: pacing the therapy of the multiple personality disorder patient. Psychiatr Clin North Am 14:661–675, 1991

Fine CG: A tactical integrationalist perspective on the treatment of multiple personality disorder, in Clinical Perspectives on Multiple Personality Disorder. Edited by Kluft RP, Fine CG. Washington, DC, American Psychiatric Press, 1993, pp 135–153

Finkelhor D: Child Sexual Abuse: New Theory and Research. New York, Free Press, 1984

Finkelhor D, Hotaling G, Lewis IA, et al: Sexual abuse in a national survey of adult men and women: prevalence, characteristics, and risk factors. Child Abuse Negl 14:19–28, 1990

Fitzgerald SG, Gonzalez E: Dissociative states induced by relaxation training in a PTSD combat veteran: failure to identify trigger mechanisms. Journal of Traumatic Stress 7:111–115, 1994

Flach F: The resilience hypothesis and posttraumatic stress disorder, in Posttraumatic Stress Disorder: Etiology, Phenomenology, and Treatment. Edited by Wolf ME, Mosnaim AD. Washington, DC, American Psychiatric Press, 1990, pp 36–45

Foa EB, Riggs DS: Posttraumatic stress disorder and rape, in American Psychiatric Press Review of Psychiatry, Vol 12. Edited by Oldham JM, Riba MB, Tasman A. Washington, DC, American Psychiatric Press, 1993, pp 273–303

Foa EB, Rothbaum BO, Riggs DS, et al: Treatment of posttraumatic stress disorder in rape victims: a comparison between cognitive-behavioral procedures and counseling. J Consult Clin Psychol 59:715–723, 1991

Foy DW, Resnick HS, Sipprelle RC, et al: Premilitary, military, and postmilitary factors in the development of combat-related posttraumatic stress disorder. Behavior Therapist 10:3–9, 1987

Frankel FH: Adult reconstruction of childhood events in the multiple personality literature. Am J Psychiatry 150:954–958, 1993

Frankel FH: The concept of flashbacks in historical perspective. Int J Clin Exp Hypn 42:321–336, 1994a

Frankel FH: Dissociation in hysteria and hypnosis: a concept aggrandized, in Dissociation: Clinical and Theoretical Perspectives. Edited by Lynn SJ, Rhue JW. New York, Guilford, 1994b, pp 80–93

Freeland A, Manchanda R, Chiu S, et al: Four cases of supposed multiple personality disorder: evidence of unjustified diagnosis. Can J Psychiatry 38:245–247, 1993

Freud S: The aetiology of hysteria (1896), in The Standard Edition of the Complete Psychological Works of Sigmund Freud, Vol 3. Translated and edited by Strachey J. London, Hogarth Press, 1962, pp 187–221

Freud S: Beyond the pleasure principle (1920), in The Standard Edition of the Complete Psychological Works of Sigmund Freud, Vol 18. Translated and edited by Strachey J. London, Hogarth Press, 1964, pp 1–64

Freud S: The ego and the id (1923), in The Standard Edition of the Complete Psychological Works of Sigmund Freud, Vol 19. Translated and edited by Strachey J. London, Hogarth Press, 1961, pp 1–66

Freud S: New introductory lectures on psycho-analysis (1933), in The Standard Edition of the Complete Psychological Works of Sigmund Freud, Vol 22. Translated and edited by Strachey J. London, Hogarth Press, 1964, pp 1–182

Freud S: The Origins of Psycho-Analysis: Letters to Wilhelm Fliess, Drafts and Notes: 1887–1902. Edited by Bonaparte M, Freud A, Kris E. New York, Basic Books, 1954

Friedman MJ: Interrelationships between biological mechanisms and pharmacotherapy of posttraumatic stress disorder, in Posttraumatic Stress Disorder: Etiology, Phenomenology, and Treatment. Edited by Wolf ME, Mosnaim AD. Washington, DC, American Psychiatric Press, 1990, pp 205–225

Frieswyk SH, Colson DB, Allen JG: Conceptualizing the therapeutic alliance from a psychoanalytic perspective. Psychotherapy 21:460–464, 1984

Frijda NH: Emotions are functional, most of the time, in The Nature of Emotion: Fundamental Questions. Edited by Ekman P, Davidson RJ. New York, Oxford University Press, 1994, pp 112–122

Fromm E: The Anatomy of Human Destructiveness. New York, Holt, Rinehart, & Winston, 1973

Gabbard GO (ed): Sexual Exploitation in Professional Relationships. Washington, DC, American Psychiatric Press, 1989

Gabbard GO: Psychodynamic Psychiatry in Clinical Practice: The DSM-IV Edition. Washington, DC, American Psychiatric Press, 1994

Gabbard GO, Twemlow SW: With the Eyes of the Mind: An Empirical Analysis of Out-of-Body States. New York, Praeger, 1984

Ganaway GK: Historical versus narrative truth: clarifying the role of exogenous trauma in the etiology of MPD and its variants. Dissociation 2:205–220, 1989

Garry M, Loftus EF: Pseudomemories without hypnosis. Int J Clin Exp Hypn 42:363–378, 1994

Gay P: Freud: A Life for Our Time. New York, WW Norton, 1988

Gazzaniga MS: Nature's Mind: The Biological Roots of Thinking, Emotions, Sexuality, Language, and Intelligence. New York, Basic Books, 1992

Gelinas DJ: Unexpected resources in treating incest families, in Family Resources: The Hidden Partner in Family Therapy. Edited by Karpel MA. New York, Guilford, 1986, pp 327–358

Gelinas DJ: Relational patterns in incestuous families, malevolent variations, and specific interventions with the adult survivor, in Treatment of Adult Survivors of Incest. Edited by Paddison PL. Washington, DC, American Psychiatric Press, 1993, pp 1–34

Gilman AG, Rall TW, Nies AS, et al: Goodman and Gilman's The Pharmacological Basis of Therapeutics, 8th Edition. New York, Pergamon, 1990

Glodich A: Oral testimony: healing the psychological destruction of torture. Master's thesis, Smith College School for Social Work, Northampton, MA, 1993

Glore GC: Why emotions are felt, in The Nature of Emotion: Fundamental Questions. Edited by Ekman P, Davidson RJ. New York, Oxford University Press, 1994, pp 103–111

Gold PE: Modulation of emotional and nonemotional memories: same pharmacological systems, different neuroanatomical systems, in Brain and Memory: Modulation and Mediation of Neuroplasticity. Edited by McGaugh JL, Weinberger NM, Lynch G. New York, Oxford University Press, 1995, pp 41–74

Goldberg J, True WR, Eisen SA, et al: A twin study of the effects of the Vietnam war on posttraumatic stress disorder. JAMA 263:1227–1232, 1990

Goldberg S: Recent developments in attachment theory and research. Can J Psychiatry 36:393–400, 1991

Golding JM: Sexual assault history and physical health in randomly selected Los Angeles women. Health Psychology 13:130–138, 1994

Good MI: The concept of an organic dissociative syndrome: what is the evidence? Harvard Review of Psychiatry 1:145–157, 1993

Goodwin JM: Applying to adult incest victims what we have learned from victimized children, in Incest-Related Syndromes of Adult Psychopathology. Edited by Kluft RP. Washington, DC, American Psychiatric Press, 1990, pp 55–74

Goodwin JM: Human vectors of trauma: illustrations from the Marquis de Sade, in Rediscovering Childhood Trauma: Historical Casebook and Clinical Applications. Edited by Goodwin JM. Washington, DC, American Psychiatric Press, 1993a, pp 95–111

Goodwin JM: Sadistic abuse: definition, recognition, and treatment. Dissociation 6:181–187, 1993b

Goodwin JM, Attias R: Eating disorders in survivors of multimodal childhood abuse, in Clinical Perspectives on Multiple Personality Disorder. Edited by Kluft RP, Fine CG. Washington, DC, American Psychiatric Press, 1993, pp 327–341

Gould SJ: Eight Little Piggies: Reflections in Natural History. New York, WW Norton, 1993

Graham DLR, Rawlings E, Rimini N: Survivors of terror: battered women, hostages, and the Stockholm Syndrome, in Feminist Perspectives on Wife Abuse. Edited by Yllö K, Bograd M. Newbury Park, CA, Sage, 1988, pp 217–233

Grame CJ: Internal containment in the treatment of patients with dissociative disorders. Bull Menninger Clin 57:355–361, 1993

Gray JA: The Neuropsychology of Anxiety: An Enquiry Into the Functions of the Septo-Hippocampal System. New York, Oxford University Press, 1982

Gray JA: The neuropsychological basis of anxiety, in Handbook of Anxiety Disorders. Edited by Last CG, Hersen M. New York, Pergamon, 1988, pp 10–37

Gray JA: Neural systems, emotion and personality, in Neurobiology of Learning, Emotion and Affect. Edited by Madden J IV. New York, Raven, 1991a, pp 273–306

Gray JA: The neuropsychology of temperament, in Explorations in Temperament. Edited by Strelau J, Angleitner A. New York, Plenum, 1991b, pp 105–128

Greaves GB: Precursors of integration in the treatment of multiple personality disorder: clinical reflections. Dissociation 2:224–233, 1989

Greaves GB: A history of multiple personality disorder, in Clinical Perspectives on Multiple Personality Disorder. Edited by Kluft RP, Fine CG. Washington, DC, American Psychiatric Press, 1993, pp 355–380

Green BL: Disasters and posttraumatic stress disorder, in Posttraumatic Stress Disorder: DSM-IV and Beyond. Edited by Davidson JRT, Foa EB. Washington, DC, American Psychiatric Press, 1993, pp 75–97

Green BL, Wilson JP, Lindy JD: Conceptualizing post-traumatic stress disorder: a psychosocial framework, in Trauma and Its Wake: The Study and Treatment of Post-Traumatic Stress Disorder. Edited by Figley CR. New York, Brunner/Mazel, 1985, pp 53–69

Green EE, Green AM: Biofeedback and states of consciousness, in Handbook of States of Consciousness. Edited by Wolman BB, Ullman M. New York, Van Nostrand, 1986, pp 553–589

352   *Coping With Trauma: A Guide to Self-Understanding*

Greig E, Betts T: Epileptic seizures induced by sexual abuse: pathogenic and pathoplastic factors. Seizure 1:269–274, 1992

Griffin DR: Animal Minds. Chicago, IL, University of Chicago Press, 1992

Grinker RR, Spiegel JP: Men Under Stress. Philadelphia, PA, Blakiston, 1945

Gutheil TG: True or false memories of sexual abuse? a forensic psychiatric view. Psychiatric Annals 23:527–531, 1993

Gutheil TG, Gabbard GO: The concept of boundaries in clinical practice: theoretical and risk-management dimensions. Am J Psychiatry 150:188–196, 1993

Halleck SL: Dissociative phenomena and the question of responsibility. Int J Clin Exp Hypn 38:298–314, 1990

Hanh TN: The Miracle of Mindfulness: A Manual on Meditation, 2nd Edition. Translated by Ho M. Boston, MA, Beacon Press, 1987

Hanh TN: Peace Is Every Step: The Path of Mindfulness in Everyday Life. Edited by Kotler A. New York, Bantam, 1991

Helzer JE, Robins LN, McEvoy L: Post-traumatic stress disorder in the general population: findings of the Epidemiologic Catchment Area survey. N Engl J Med 317:1630–1634, 1987

Herink R: The Psychotherapy Handbook. New York, New American Library, 1980

Herman JL: Father-Daughter Incest. Cambridge, MA, Harvard University Press, 1981

Herman JL: Complex PTSD: a syndrome in survivors of prolonged and repeated trauma. Journal of Traumatic Stress 5:377–391, 1992a

Herman JL: Trauma and Recovery. New York, Basic Books, 1992b

Herman JL: Sequelae of prolonged and repeated trauma: evidence for a complex posttraumatic syndrome (DESNOS), in Posttraumatic Stress Disorder: DSM-IV and Beyond. Edited by Davidson JRT, Foa EB. Washington, DC, American Psychiatric Press, 1993, pp 213–228

Herman JL, Harvey MR: The false memory debate: social science or social backlash? Harvard Mental Health Letter 9:4–6, 1993

Herman JL, Schatzow E: Recovery and verification of memories of childhood sexual trauma. Psychoanalytic Psychology 4:1–14, 1987

Heuer F, Reisberg D: Emotion, arousal, and memory for detail, in The Handbook of Emotion and Memory: Research and Theory. Edited by Christianson S. Hillsdale, NJ, Lawrence Erlbaum, 1992, pp 151–180

Hilgard ER: Hypnotic Susceptibility. New York, Harcourt, Brace & World, 1965

Hilgard ER: Divided Consciousness: Multiple Controls in Human Thought and Action, Expanded Edition. New York, Wiley, 1986

Hobson JA: The Chemistry of Conscious States: How the Brain Changes its Mind. New York, Little, Brown, 1994

Hofer MA: Relationships as regulators: a psychobiologic perspective on bereavement. Psychosom Med 46:183–197, 1984

Hogan LC: Managing persons with multiple personality disorder in a heterogeneous inpatient group. Group 16:247–256, 1992

Horevitz R: Hypnosis in the treatment of multiple personality disorder, in Handbook of Clinical Hypnosis. Edited by Rhue JW, Lynn SJ, Kirsch I. Washington, DC, American Psychological Association, 1993, pp 395–424

Horowitz MJ: Image formation and cognition. New York, Appleton-Century-Crofts, 1970

Horowitz MJ: Person schemas, in Person Schemas and Maladaptive Interpersonal Patterns. Edited by Horowitz MJ. Chicago, IL, University of Chicago Press, 1991, pp 13–31

Horowitz MJ: The effects of psychic trauma on mind: structure and processing of meaning, in Interface of Psychoanalysis and Psychology. Edited by Barron JW, Eagle MN, Wolitzky DL. Washington, DC, American Psychological Association, 1992, pp 489–500

Horwitz L: Clinical Prediction in Psychotherapy. New York, Jason Aronson, 1974

Horwitz L, Gabbard GO, Allen JG, et al: Borderline Personality Disorder: Tailoring the Therapy to the Patient. Washington, DC, American Psychiatric Press, in press

Howe ML, Courage ML: On resolving the enigma of infantile amnesia. Psychol Bull 113:305–326, 1993

Hulsey TL, Sexton MC, Nash MR: Perceptions of family functioning and the occurrence of childhood sexual abuse. Bull Menninger Clin 56:438–450, 1992

Hyman SE, Nestler EJ: The Molecular Foundations of Psychiatry. Washington, DC, American Psychiatric Press, 1993

Irwin HJ: Proneness to dissociation and traumatic childhood events. J Nerv Ment Dis 182:456–460, 1994

Janet P: The Major Symptoms of Hysteria: Fifteen Lectures Given in the Medical School of Harvard University. New York, Macmillan, 1907

Janoff-Bulman R: Shattered Assumptions: Towards a New Psychology of Trauma. New York, Free Press, 1992

Kabat-Zinn J: Full Catastrophe Living: Using the Wisdom of Your Body and Mind to Face Stress, Pain, and Illness. New York, Bantam Doubleday, 1990

Kabat-Zinn J: Wherever You Go, There You Are. New York, Hyperion, 1994

Kabat-Zinn J, Massion AO, Kristeller J, et al: Effectiveness of a meditation-based stress reduction program in the treatment of anxiety disorders. Am J Psychiatry 149:936–943, 1992

Kagan J: The concept of behavioral inhibition to the unfamiliar, in Perspectives on Behavioral Inhibition. Edited by Reznick JS. Chicago, IL, University of Chicago Press, 1989a, pp 1–23

Kagan J: Unstable Ideas: Temperament, Cognition, and Self. Cambridge, MA, Harvard University Press, 1989b

Kagan J: A conceptual analysis of the affects, in Affect: Psychoanalytic Perspectives. Edited by Shapiro T, Emde RN. Madison, CT, International Universities Press, 1992, pp 109–129

Kagan J: Galen's Prophecy: Temperament in Human Nature. New York, Basic Books, 1994

Kagan J, Snidman N: Infant predictors of inhibited and uninhibited children, in Future Directions in Infant Development Research. Edited by Suci GJ, Robertson SS. New York, Springer-Verlag, 1992, pp 71–88

Kaplan HS: The New Sex Therapy: Active Treatment of Sexual Dysfunctions. New York, Brunner/Mazel, 1974

Kaplan LJ: Female Perversions: The Temptations of Emma Bovary. New York, Doubleday, 1991

Kardiner A: The Traumatic Neuroses of War. Washington, DC, National Research Council, 1941

Kelly KA: Multiple personality disorders: Treatment coordination in a partial hospital setting. Bull Menninger Clin 57:390–398, 1993

Kendall-Tackett KA, Williams LM, Finkelhor D: Impact of sexual abuse on children: a review and synthesis. Psychol Bull 113:164–180, 1993

Kihlstrom JF: Conscious, subconscious, unconscious: a cognitive perspective, in The Unconscious Reconsidered. Edited by Bowers KS, Meichenbaum D. New York, Wiley, 1984, pp 149–211

Kihlstrom JF: The cognitive unconscious. Science 237:1445–1452, 1987

Kihlstrom JF: The recovery of memory in the laboratory and clinic. Paper presented at the joint convention of the Rocky Mountain Psychological Association and the Western Psychological Association, Phoenix, AZ, April 1993

Kihlstrom JF: Hypnosis, delayed recall, and the principles of memory. Int J Clin Exp Hypn 42:337–345, 1994

Kihlstrom JF: Exhumed memory, in Truth in Memory. Edited by Lynn SJ, Spanos NP. New York, Guilford, in press

Kihlstrom JF, Barnhardt TM: The self-regulation of memory: for better and for worse, with and without hypnosis, in Handbook of Mental Control. Edited by Wegner DM, Pennebaker JW. Englewood Cliffs, NJ, 1993, pp 88–125

Kihlstrom JF, Hoyt IP: Repression, dissociation, and hypnosis, in Repression and Dissociation: Implications for Personality Theory, Psychopathology, and Health. Edited by Singer JL. Chicago, IL, University of Chicago Press, 1990, pp 181–208

Kihlstrom JF, Glisky ML, Angiulo MJ: Dissociative tendencies and dissociative disorders. J Abnorm Psychol 103:117–124, 1994

Kilpatrick DG, Resnick HS: Posttraumatic stress disorder associated with exposure to criminal victimization in clinical and community populations, in Posttraumatic Stress Disorder: DSM-IV and Beyond. Edited by Davidson JRT, Foa EB. Washington, DC, American Psychiatric Press, 1993, pp 113–143

Kinsey AC, Pomeroy WB, Martin CE, et al: Sexual Behavior in the Human Female. Philadelphia, PA, WB Saunders, 1953

Klein MH, Wonderlich S, Shea MT: Models of relationships between personality and depression: toward a framework for theory and research, in Personality and Depression: A Current View. Edited by Klein MH, Kupfer DJ, Shea MT. New York, Guilford, 1993, pp 1–54

Kline NA, Rausch JL: Olfactory precipitants of flashbacks in posttraumatic stress disorder: case reports. J Clin Psychiatry 46:383–384, 1985

Kluft RP: Varieties of hypnotic interventions in the treatment of multiple personality. American Journal of Clinical Hypnosis 24:230–240, 1982

Kluft RP: Multiple personality in childhood. Psychiatr Clin North Am 7:121–134, 1984a

Kluft RP: Treatment of multiple personality disorder: a study of 33 cases. Psychiatr Clin North Am 7:9–29, 1984b

Kluft RP: On treating the older patient with multiple personality disorder: "race against time" or "make haste slowly"? American Journal of Clinical Hypnosis 30:257–266, 1988a

Kluft RP: The phenomenology and treatment of extremely complex multiple personality disorder. Dissociation 1:47–58, 1988b

Kluft RP: Playing for time: temporizing techniques in the treatment of multiple personality disorder. American Journal of Clinical Hypnosis 32:90–98, 1989

Kluft RP: Incest and subsequent revictimization: the case of therapist-patient sexual exploitation, with a description of the sitting duck syndrome, in Incest-Related Syndromes of Adult Psychopathology. Edited by Kluft RP. Washington, DC, American Psychiatric Press, 1990a, pp 263–287

Kluft RP (ed): Incest-Related Syndromes of Adult Psychopathology. Washington, DC, American Psychiatric Press, 1990b

Kluft RP: Clinical presentations of multiple personality disorder. Psychiatr Clin North Am 14:605–629, 1991a

Kluft RP: Hospital treatment of multiple personality disorder: an overview. Psychiatr Clin North Am 14:695–719, 1991b

Kluft RP: Multiple personality disorder, in American Psychiatric Press Review of Psychiatry, Vol 10. Edited by Tasman A, Goldfinger SM. Washington, DC, American Psychiatric Press, 1991c, pp 161–188

Kluft RP: Discussion: a specialist's perspective on multiple personality disorder. Psychoanalytic Inquiry 12:139–171, 1992

Kluft RP: Basic principles in conducting the psychotherapy of multiple personality disorder, in Clinical Perspectives on Multiple Personality Disorder. Edited by Kluft RP, Fine CG. Washington, DC, American Psychiatric Press, 1993a, pp 19–50

Kluft RP: Clinical approaches to the integration of personalities, in Clinical Perspectives on Multiple Personality Disorder. Edited by Kluft RP, Fine CG. Washington, DC, American Psychiatric Press, 1993b, pp 101–133

Kluft RP: Multiple personality disorder: a contemporary perspective. Harvard Mental Health Letter 10:5–7, 1993c

Kluft RP, Fine CG (eds): Clinical Perspectives on Multiple Personality Disorder. Washington, DC, American Psychiatric Press, 1993

Kolb LC: A neuropsychological hypothesis explaining posttraumatic stress disorders. Am J Psychiatry 144:989–995, 1987

Kolb LC: The psychobiology of PTSD: perspectives and reflections on the past, present, and future. Journal of Traumatic Stress 6:293–304, 1993

Koopman C, Classen C, Spiegel D: Predictors of posttraumatic stress symptoms among survivors of the Oakland/Berkeley, California, firestorm. Am J Psychiatry 151:888–894, 1994

Kosko B: Fuzzy Thinking: The New Science of Fuzzy Logic. New York, Hyperion, 1993

Koss MP: Rape: scope, impact, interventions, and public policy responses. Am Psychol 48:1062–1069, 1993

Kosslyn SM: Image and Brain: The Resolution of the Imagery Debate. Cambridge, MA, MIT Press, 1994

Kroll J: PTSD/Borderlines in Therapy: Finding the Balance. New York, WW Norton, 1993

Krystal JH, Kosten TR, Southwick S, et al: Neurobiological aspects of PTSD: review of clinical and preclinical studies. Behavior Therapy 20:177–198, 1989

Kulka RA, Schlenger WE, Fairbank JA, et al: Trauma and the Vietnam War Generation: Report of Findings from the National Vietnam Veterans Readjustment Study. New York, Brunner/Mazel, 1990

Labelle L, Laurence JR, Nadon R, et al: Hypnotizability, preference for an imagic cognitive style, and memory creation in hypnosis. J Abnorm Psychol 99:222–228, 1990

Lang PJ: The cognitive psychophysiology of emotion: fear and anxiety, in Anxiety and the Anxiety Disorders. Edited by Tuma AH, Maser J. Hillsdale, NJ, Lawrence Erlbaum, 1985, pp 131–170

Laub D, Auerhahn NC: Knowing and not knowing massive psychic trauma: forms of traumatic memory. Int J Psychoanal 74:287–302, 1993

Laurence JR, Perry C: Hypnotically created memory among highly hypnotizable subjects. Science 222:523–524, 1983

Laurence JR, Nadon R, Nogrady H, et al: Duality, dissociation, and memory creation in highly hypnotizable subjects. Int J Clin Exp Hypn 34:295–310, 1986

Lazarus AA: Meditation: the problems of any unimodal technique, in Meditation: Classic and Contemporary Perspectives. Edited by Shapiro DH Jr, Walsh RN. New York, Aldine, 1984, p 691

Leakey R: Origins Reconsidered: In Search of What Makes Us Human. New York, Doubleday, 1992

LeDoux JE: Memory versus emotional memory in the brain, in The Nature of Emotion: Fundamental Questions. Edited by Ekman P, Davidson RJ. New York, Oxford University Press, 1994, pp 311–312

LeDoux JE, Romanski L, Xagoraris A: Indelibility of subcortical emotional memories. Journal of Cognitive Neuroscience 1:238–243, 1989

Lerner HG: The Dance of Anger: A Woman's Guide to Changing the Patterns of Intimate Relationships. New York, Harper & Row, 1985

Levenson RW: Emotional control: variation and consequences, in The Nature of Emotion: Fundamental Questions. Edited by Ekman P, Davidson RJ. New York, Oxford University Press, 1994, pp 273–279

Levey M: The Life and Death of Mozart. New York, Stein & Day, 1971

Levy J, Levy M: Quality of Mind: Tools for Self-Mastery and Enhanced Performance. Boston, MA, Wisdom Publications, 1991

Lewin RA: Preliminary thoughts on milieu treatment of patients with multiple personality disorder. The Psychiatric Hospital 22:161–163, 1991

Lewis DO: From abuse to violence: psychophysiological consequences of maltreatment. J Am Acad Child Adolesc Psychiatry 31:383–391, 1992

Lewis M: The development of anger and rage, in Rage, Power, and Aggression. Edited by Glick RA, Roose SP. New Haven, CT, Yale University Press, 1993, pp 148–168

Lichtenberg JD: Psychoanalysis and Motivation. Hillsdale, NJ, Analytic Press, 1989

Lichtenberg JD, Schonbar RA: Motivation in psychology and psychoanalysis, in Interface of Psychoanalysis and Psychology. Edited by Barron JW, Eagle, MN, Wolitzky DL. Washington, DC, American Psychological Association, 1992, pp 11–36

Lindemann E: Symptomatology and management of acute grief. Am J Psychiatry 101:141–148, 1944

Lindy JD, Green BL, Grace M: Somatic reenactment in the treatment of posttraumatic stress disorder. Psychother Psychosom 57:180–186, 1992

Linehan MM: Dialectical behavior therapy for borderline personality disorder: theory and method. Bull Menninger Clin 51:261–276, 1987

Linehan MM: Cognitive-Behavioral Treatment of Borderline Personality Disorder. New York, Guilford, 1993a

Linehan MM: Skills Training Manual for Treating Borderline Personality Disorder. New York, Guilford, 1993b

Linehan MM, Armstrong HE, Suarez A, et al: Cognitive-behavioral treatment of chronically parasuicidal borderline patients. Arch Gen Psychiatry 48:1060–1064, 1991

Lipper S: Carbamazepine in the treatment of posttraumatic stress disorder: implications for the kindling hypothesis, in Posttraumatic Stress Disorder: Etiology, Phenomenology, and Treatment. Edited by Wolf ME, Mosnaim AD. Washington, DC, American Psychiatric Press, 1990, pp 185–203

Loewenstein RJ: Somatoform disorders in victims of incest and child abuse, in Incest-Related Syndromes of Adult Psychopathology. Edited by Kluft RP. Washington, DC, American Psychiatric Press, 1990, pp 75–111

Loewenstein RJ: Psychogenic amnesia and psychogenic fugue: a comprehensive review, in American Psychiatric Press Review of Psychiatry, Vol 10. Edited by Tasman A, Goldfinger SM. Washington, DC, American Psychiatric Press, 1991a,
pp 189–221

Loewenstein RJ: Rational psychopharmacology in the treatment of multiple personality disorder. Psychiatr Clin North Am 14:721–740, 1991b

Loewenstein RJ, Hornstein N, Farber B: Open trial of clonazepam in the treatment
of posttraumatic stress symptoms in MPD. Dissociation 1:3–12, 1988

Loftus EF: The reality of repressed memories. Am Psychol 48:518–537, 1993a

Loftus EF: Repressed memories of childhood trauma: are they genuine? Harvard
Mental Health Letter 9:4–5, 1993b

Loftus EF, Kaufman L: Why do traumatic experiences sometimes produce good
memory (flashbulbs) and sometimes no memory (repression)? in Affect and
Accuracy in Recall: The Problem of "Flashbulb" Memories. Edited by Winograd
E, Neisser U. New York, Cambridge University Press, 1992, pp 212–223

Loftus EF, Loftus GR: On the permanence of stored information in the human
brain. Am Psychol 35:409–420, 1980

Loftus EF, Rosenwald LA: Buried memories, shattered lives. American Bar Association Journal 79:70–73, 1993

Loftus EF, Garry M, Feldman J: Forgetting sexual trauma: what does it mean when
38% forget? J Consult Clin Psychol 62:1177–1181, 1994a

Loftus EF, Polonsky S, Fullilove MT: Memories of childhood sexual abuse: remembering and repressing. Psychology of Women Quarterly 18:67–84, 1994b

Luborsky L: Helping alliances in psychotherapy, in Successful Psychotherapy. Edited by Claghorn JL. New York, Brunner/Mazel, 1976, pp 92–116

Luborsky L, Crits-Cristoph P, Alexander L, et al: Two helping alliance methods for
predicting outcomes of psychotherapy: a counting signs versus a global rating
method. J Nerv Ment Dis 171:480–491, 1983

Lynn SJ, Rhue JW: Fantasy proneness: hypnosis, developmental antecedents, and
psychopathology. Am Psychol 43:35–44, 1988

Lynn SJ, Rhue JW (eds): Dissociation: Clinical and Theoretical Perspectives. New
York, Guilford, 1994

MacLean PD: Brain evolution relating to family, play, and the separation call. Arch
Gen Psychiatry 42:405–417, 1985

MacLean PD: The Triune Brain in Evolution: Role in Paleocerebral Functions. New
York, Plenum, 1990

Main M, Hesse E: Parents' unresolved traumatic experiences are related to infant
disorganized attachment status: is frightened and/or frightening parental behavior the linking mechanism? in Attachment in the Preschool Years: Theory,
Research, and Intervention. Edited by Greenberg MT, Cicchetti D, Cummings
EM. Chicago, IL, University of Chicago Press, 1990, pp 161–182

References 359

Main M, Solomon J: Procedures for identifying infants as disorganized/disoriented during the Ainsworth Strange Situation, in Attachment in the Preschool Years: Theory, Research, and Intervention. Edited by Greenberg MT, Cicchetti D, Cummings EM. Chicago, IL, University of Chicago Press, 1990, pp 121–160

Main M, Kaplan N, Cassidy J: Security in infancy, childhood, and adulthood: a move to the level of representation, in Growing Points of Attachment Theory and Research (Monographs of the Society for Research in Child Development, Vol 50, 1–2, Serial No. 209). Edited by Bretherton I, Waters E. Chicago, IL, University of Chicago Press, 1985, pp 66–104

Malinosky-Rummell R, Hansen DJ: Long-term consequences of childhood physical abuse. Psychol Bull 114:68–79, 1993

March JS: What constitutes a stressor? the "Criterion A" issue, in Posttraumatic Stress Disorder: DSM-IV and Beyond. Edited by Davidson JRT, Foa EB. Washington, DC, American Psychiatric Press, 1993, pp 37–54

Marmar CR, Foy D, Kagan B, et al: An integrated approach for treating posttraumatic stress, in American Psychiatric Press Review of Psychiatry, Vol 12. Edited by Oldham JM, Riba MB, Tasman A. Washington, DC, American Psychiatric Press, 1993, pp 239–272

Marmar CR, Weiss DS, Schlenger WE et al: Peritraumatic dissociation and posttraumatic stress in male Vietnam theater veterans. Am J Psychiatry 151:902–907, 1994

Marmer SS: Multiple personality disorder: a psychoanalytic perspective. Psychiatr Clin North Am 14:677–693, 1991

Matthysse S: Mood disorders and the dynamic stability of the system of memories, in Neurobiology of Learning, Emotion and Affect. Edited by Madden J IV. New York, Raven, 1991, pp 215–228

Mayr E: Toward a New Philosophy of Biology: Observations of an Evolutionist. Cambridge, MA, Harvard University Press, 1988

Mayr E: One Long Argument: Charles Darwin and the Genesis of Modern Evolutionary Thought. Cambridge, MA, Harvard University Press, 1991

McCaffrey RJ, Fairbank JA: Behavioral assessment and treatment of accident-related posttraumatic stress disorder: two case studies. Behavior Therapy 16:406–416, 1985

McFarlane AC: Vulnerability to posttraumatic stress disorder, in Posttraumatic Stress Disorder: Etiology, Phenomenology, and Treatment. Edited by Wolf ME, Mosnaim AD. Washington, DC, American Psychiatric Press, 1990, pp 2–20

McGaugh JL: Affect, neuromodulatory systems, and memory storage, in The Handbook of Emotion and Memory: Research and Theory. Edited by Christianson S. Hillsdale, NJ, Lawrence Erlbaum, 1992, pp 245–268

McMahon PP, Fagan J: Play therapy with children with multiple personality disorder, in Clinical Perspectives on Multiple Personality Disorder. Edited by Kluft RP, Fine CG. Washington, DC, American Psychiatric Press, 1993, pp 253–276

McNally RJ: Self-representation in posttraumatic stress disorder: a cognitive perspective, in The Self in Emotional Distress: Cognitive and Psychodynamic Perspectives. Edited by Segal ZV, Blatt SJ. New York, Guilford, 1993a, pp 71–91

McNally RJ: Stressors that produce post-traumatic stress disorder in children, in Posttraumatic Stress Disorder: DSM-IV and Beyond. Edited by Davidson JRT, Foa EB. Washington, DC, American Psychiatric Press, 1993b, pp 57–74

McNally RJ, Saigh PA: On the distinction between traumatic simple phobia and posttraumatic stress disorder, in Posttraumatic Stress Disorder: DSM-IV and Beyond. Edited by Davidson JRT, Foa EB. Washington, DC, American Psychiatric Press, 1993, pp 207–212

Meichenbaum D, Novaco R: Stress inoculation: a preventative approach. Issues in Mental Health Nursing 7:419–435, 1985

Meissner WW: The Paranoid Process. New York, Jason Aronson, 1978

Mellman TA, Davis GC: Combat-related flashbacks in posttraumatic stress disorder: phenomenology and similarity to panic attacks. J Clin Psychiatry 46:379–382, 1985

Menninger KA: The Vital Balance. New York, Viking, 1963

Menninger KA: The suicidal intention of nuclear armament. Bull Menninger Clin 47:325–353, 1983

Merskey H: The manufacture of personalities: the production of multiple personality disorder. Br J Psychiatry 160:327–340, 1992

Minsky M: K-lines: a theory of memory. Cognitive Science 4:117–133, 1980

Minsky M: The Society of Mind. New York, Simon & Schuster, 1986

Mitchell SA: Contemporary perspectives on self: toward an integration. Psychoanalytic Dialogues 1:121–147, 1991

Modell AH: A confusion of tongues or whose reality is it? Psychoanal Q 60:227–244, 1991

Modell AH: The private self and private space. The Annual of Psychoanalysis, Vol 20. Hillsdale, NJ, Analytic Press, 1992, pp 1–14

Murphy M, Donovan S: The Physical and Psychological Effects of Meditation: A Review of Contemporary Meditation Research with a Comprehensive Bibliography, 1931–1988. San Rafael, CA, Esalen Institute, 1988

Nash MR, Hulsey TL, Sexton MC, et al: Long-term sequelae of childhood sexual abuse: perceived family environment, psychopathology, and dissociation. J Consult Clin Psychol 61:276–283, 1993

Nathanson DL: Shame and Pride: Affect, Sex, and the Birth of the Self. New York, WW Norton, 1992

Neisser U: Nested structure in autobiographical memory, in Autobiographical Memory. Edited by Rubin DC. New York, Cambridge University Press, 1986, pp 71–81

Neisser U: Time present and time past, in Practical Aspects of Memory: Current Research and Issues. Edited by Gruneberg MM, Morris PE, Sykes RN. New York, Wiley, 1988, pp 545–560

Nelson K: The psychological and social origins of autobiographical memory. Psychological Science 4:7–14, 1993

Norris PA: Biofeedback: voluntary control, and human potential. Biofeedback and Self Regulation 11:1–20, 1986

Norris PA: Clinical psychoneuroimmunology: strategies for self-regulation of immune system responding, in Biofeedback: Principles and Practice for Clinicians, 3rd Edition. Edited by Basmajian JV. Baltimore, MD, Williams & Wilkins, 1989a, pp 57–66

Norris PA: Current conceptual trends in biofeedback and self-regulation, in Eastern and Western Approaches to Healing: Ancient Wisdom and Modern Knowledge. Edited by Sheikh AA, Sheikh KS. New York, Wiley, 1989b, pp 264–295

Novaco RW: Anger Control: The Development and Evaluation of an Experimental Treatment. Lexington, MA, DC Heath, 1975

Novaco RW: Anger and coping with stress: cognitive behavioral interventions, in Cognitive Behavior Therapy: Research and Application. Edited by Foreyt JP, Rathjen DP. New York, Plenum, 1978, pp 135–173

Olds J: Pleasure centers in the brain. Scientific American 195:105–116, 1956

Olds J: Self simulation of the brain: its use to study local effects of hunger, sex, and drugs. Science 127:315–324, 1958

Olds J, Milner P: Positive reinforcement produced by electrical stimulation of septal area and other regions of rat brain. J Comp Physiol Psychol 47:419–427, 1954

Oliver JE: Intergenerational transmission of child abuse: rates, research, and clinical implications. Am J Psychiatry 150:1315–1324, 1993

Ovsiew F, Yudofsky S: Aggression: a neuropsychiatric perspective, in Rage, Power, and Aggression. Edited by Glick RA, Roose SP. New Haven, CT, Yale University Press, 1993, pp 213–230

Parens H: A view of the development of hostility in early life, in Affect: Psychoanalytic Perspectives. Edited by Shapiro T, Emde RN. Madison, CT, International Universities Press, 1992, pp 75–108

Parens H: Rage toward self and others in early childhood, in Rage, Power, and Aggression. Edited by Glick RA, Roose SP. New Haven, CT, Yale University Press, 1993, pp 123–147

Paris J: Borderline Personality Disorder: A Multidimensional Approach. Washington, DC, American Psychiatric Press, 1994

Pawlicki CM, Gaumer C: Nursing care of the self-mutilating patient. Bull Menninger Clin 57:380–389, 1993

Peebles MJ: Through a glass darkly: the psychoanalytic use of hypnosis with posttraumatic stress disorder. Int J Clin Exp Hypn 37:192–206, 1989

Peebles-Kleiger MJ: Using countertransference in the hypnosis of trauma victims: a model for turning hazard into healing. Am J Psychother 43:518–530, 1989

Peniston EG, Kulkosky PJ: Alpha-theta brainwave neuro-feedback therapy for Vietnam veterans with combat-related post-traumatic stress disorder. Medical Psychotherapy 4:47–60, 1991

Perry BD: Neurobiological sequelae of childhood trauma: PTSD in children, in Catecholamine Function in Posttraumatic Stress Disorder: Emerging Concepts. Edited by Marburg MM. Washington, DC, American Psychiatric Press, 1994, pp 233–255

Perry S, Difede J, Musngi G, et al: Predictors of posttraumatic stress disorder after burn injury. Am J Psychiatry 149:931–935, 1992

Piacente GJ: Aggression. Psychiatr Clin North Am 9:329–339, 1986

Pillemer DB, White SH: Childhood events recalled by children and adults, in Advances in Child Development and Behavior, Vol 21. Edited by Reese HW. New York, Academic Press, 1989, pp 297–340

Piper A Jr: Multiple personality disorder. Br J Psychiatry 164:600–612, 1994

Pitman RK: Post-traumatic stress disorder, conditioning, and network theory. Psychiatric Annals 18:182–184, 187–189, 1988

Pitman RK: Post-traumatic stress disorder, hormones, and memory. Biol Psychiatry 26:221–223, 1989

Pitman RK: Biological findings in posttraumatic stress disorder: implications for DSM-IV classification, in Posttraumatic Stress Disorder: DSM-IV and Beyond. Edited by Davidson JRT, Foa EB. Washington, DC, American Psychiatric Press, 1993, pp 173–189

Pitman RK, Orr SP: The black hole of trauma. Biol Psychiatry 27:469–471, 1990

Pitman RK, Orr SP: Psychophysiology of emotional memory networks in posttraumatic stress disorder, in Brain and Memory: Modulation and Mediation of Neuroplasticity. Edited by McGaugh JL, Weinberger NM, Lynch G. New York, Oxford University Press, 1995, pp 75–83

Pitman RK, Orr SP, van der Kolk BA, et al: Analgesia: a new dependent variable for the biological study of posttraumatic stress disorder, in Posttraumatic Stress Disorder: Etiology, Phenomenology, and Treatment. Washington, DC, American Psychiatric Press, 1990, pp 141–147

Plomin R, Chipuer HM, Loehlin JC: Behavioral genetics and personality, in Handbook of Personality: Theory and Research. Edited by Pervin LA. New York, Guilford, 1990, pp 225–243

Pope HG, Hudson JI: Is childhood sexual abuse a risk factor for bulimia nervosa? Am J Psychiatry 149:455–463, 1992

Pope HG, Hudson JI: Can memories of childhood sexual abuse be repressed? Psychol Med 25:121–126, 1995

Porter S, Kelly KA, Grame CJ: Family treatment of spouses and children of patients with multiple personality disorder. Bull Menninger Clin 57:371–379, 1993

Post RM: Transduction of psychosocial stress into the neurobiology of recurrent affective disorder. Am J Psychiatry 149:999–1010, 1992

Pruyser PW: The diagnostic process: touchstone of medicine's values, in Nourishing the Humanistic in Medicine: Interactions With the Social Sciences. Edited by Rogers WR, Barnard D. Pittsburgh, PA, University of Pittsburgh Press, 1979, pp 245–261

Pruyser PW: Maintaining hope in adversity. Bull Menninger Clin 51:463–474, 1987

Putnam FW: The switch process in multiple personality disorder and other state-change disorders. Dissociation 1:24–32, 1988

Putnam FW: Diagnosis and Treatment of Multiple Personality Disorder. New York, Guilford, 1989

Putnam FW: Dissociative phenomena, in American Psychiatric Press Review of Psychiatry, Vol 10. Edited by Tasman A, Goldfinger SM. Washington, DC, American Psychiatric Press, 1991a, pp 145–160

Putnam FW: The satanic ritual abuse controversy. Child Abuse Negl 15:175–179, 1991b

Putnam FW: Discussion: are alter personalities fragments or figments? Psychoanalytic Inquiry 12:95–111, 1992

Putnam FW: Commentary on Fenton. Psychiatry 56:222–227, 1993

Putnam FW: Dissociative disorders in children and adolescents, in Dissociation: Clinical and Theoretical Perspectives. Edited by Lynn SJ, Rhue JW. New York, Guilford, 1994a, pp 175–189

Putnam FW: The switch process in multiple personality disorder and other state-change disorders, in Psychological Concepts and Dissociative Disorders. Edited by Klein RM, Doane BK. Hillsdale, NJ, Lawrence Erlbaum, 1994b, pp 283–304

Putnam FW, Loewenstein RJ: Treatment of multiple personality disorder: a survey of current practices. Am J Psychiatry 150:1048–1052, 1993

Putnam FW, Guroff JJ, Silberman EK, et al: The clinical phenomenology of multiple personality disorder: review of 100 recent cases. J Clin Psychiatry 47:285–293, 1986

Rapee RM, Barlow DH (eds): Chronic Anxiety: Generalized Anxiety Disorder and Mixed Anxiety–Depression. New York, Guilford, 1991

Realmuto GM, Masten A, Carole LF, et al: Adolescent survivors of massive childhood trauma in Cambodia: life events and current symptoms. Journal of Traumatic Stress 5:589–599, 1992

Reich JH: Personality disorders and posttraumatic stress disorder, in Posttraumatic Stress Disorder: Etiology, Phenomenology, and Treatment. Edited by Wolf ME, Mosnaim AD. Washington, DC, American Psychiatric Press, 1990, pp 64–79

Reisberg D, Heuer R: Emotion's multiple effects on memory, in Brain and Memory: Modulation and Mediation of Neuroplasticity. Edited by McGaugh JL, Weinberger NM, Lynch G. New York, Oxford University Press, 1995, pp 84–92

Reiser MF: Mind, Brain, Body: Toward a Convergence of Psychoanalysis and Neurobiology. New York, Basic Books, 1984

Reiser MF: Memory in Mind and Brain: What Dream Imagery Reveals. New York, Basic Books, 1990

Resnick HS, Kilpatrick DG, Dansky BS, et al: Prevalence of civilian trauma and posttraumatic stress disorder in a representative national sample of women. J Consult Clin Psychol 61:984–991, 1993

Rich CL: Accuracy of adults' reports of abuse in childhood (letter). Am J Psychiatry 147:1389, 1990

Rieker PP, Carmen E: The victim-to-patient process: the disconfirmation and transformation of abuse. Am J Orthopsychiatry 56:360–370, 1986

Rimer S, Verhovek SH: Youngsters tell of growing up under Koresh. New York Times, Tuesday, May 4, 1993, pp. A1, A13

Rockland LH: Supportive Therapy: A Psychodynamic Approach. New York, Basic Books, 1989

Roesler TA: Reactions to disclosure of childhood sexual abuse: the effect on adult symptoms. J Nerv Ment Dis 182:618–624, 1994

Rose DS: Sexual assault, domestic violence, and incest, in Psychological Aspects of Women's Health Care: The Interface Between Psychiatry and Obstetrics and Gynecology. Edited by Stewart DE, Stotland NL. Washington, DC, American Psychiatric Press, 1993, pp 447–483

Ross CA: Inpatient treatment of multiple personality disorder. Can J Psychiatry 32:779–781, 1987

Ross CA, Joshi S, Currie R: Dissociative experiences in the general population: a factor analysis. Hosp Community Psychiatry 42:297–301, 1991a

Ross CA, Anderson G, Fleisher WP, et al: The frequency of multiple personality disorder among psychiatric inpatients. Am J Psychiatry 148:1717–1720, 1991b

Ross RJ, Ball WA, Sullivan KA, et al: Sleep disturbance as the hallmark of posttraumatic stress disorder. Am J Psychiatry 146:697–707, 1989

Rothbaum BO, Foa EB: Subtypes of posttraumatic stress disorder and duration of symptoms, in Posttraumatic Stress Disorder: DSM-IV and Beyond. Edited by Davidson JRT, Foa EB. Washington, DC, American Psychiatric Press, 1993, pp 23–35

Rubin DC: On the retention function for autobiographical memory. Journal of Verbal Learning and Verbal Behavior 21:21–38, 1982

Russell DEH: The Secret Trauma: Incest in the Lives of Girls and Women. New York, Basic Books, 1986

Rutter M: Temperament, personality and personality disorder. Br J Psychiatry 150:443–458, 1987

Sachs RG, Frischholz EJ, Wood JI: Marital and family therapy in the treatment of multiple personality disorder. Journal of Marital and Family Therapy 14:249–259, 1988

Sakheim DK, Devine SE: Out of Darkness: Exploring Satanism and Ritual Abuse. New York, Macmillan, 1992

Sameroff AJ: Models of development and developmental risk, in Handbook of Infant Mental Health. Edited by Zeanah CH. New York, Guilford, 1993, pp 3–13

Sanders B, McRoberts G, Tollefson C: Childhood stress and dissociation in a college population. Dissociation 2:17–23, 1989

Sanders S: Clinical Self-Hypnosis: The Power of Words and Images. New York, Guilford, 1991

Sanders S, Giolas MH: Dissociation and childhood trauma in psychologically disturbed adolescents. Am J Psychiatry 148:50–54, 1991

Sanitioso R, Kunda Z, Fong GT: Motivated recruitment of autobiographical memories. J Pers Soc Psychol 59:229–241, 1990

Saporta JA Jr, Case J: The role of medications in treating adult survivors of childhood trauma, in Treatment of Adult Survivors of Incest. Edited by Paddison PL. Washington, DC, American Psychiatric Press, 1993, pp 101–134

Sartre JP: The Transcendence of the Ego: An Existentialist Theory of Consciousness (1936). Translated by Williams F, Kirkpatrick R. New York, Farrar, Straus & Giroux, 1957

Saunders EA, Arnold F: A critique of conceptual and treatment approaches to borderline psychopathology in light of findings about childhood abuse. Psychiatry 56:188–203, 1993

Saxe GN, Chinman G, Berkowitz R, et al: Somatization in patients with dissociative disorders. Am J Psychiatry 151:1329–1334, 1994

Scarr S: Developmental theories for the 1990s: development and individual differences. Child Development 63:1–19, 1992

Schacter DL: Memory, in Foundations of Cognitive Science. Edited by Posner MI. Cambridge, MA, MIT Press, 1989a, pp 683–725

Schacter DL: On the relation between memory and consciousness: dissociable interactions and conscious experience, in Varieties of Memory and Consciousness: Essays in Honour of Endel Tulving. Edited by Roediger HL III, Craik FIM. Hillsdale, NJ, Lawrence Erlbaum, 1989b, pp 355–389

Schacter DL, Kihlstrom JF: Functional amnesia, in Handbook of Neuropsychology, Vol 3. Edited by Boller F, Grafman J. New York, Elsevier, 1989, pp 209–231

Schatzow E, Herman JL: Breaking secrecy: adult survivors disclose to their families. Psychiatr Clin North Am 12:337–349, 1989

Schetky DH: A review of the literature on the long-term effects of childhood sexual abuse, in Incest-Related Syndromes of Adult Psychopathology. Edited by Kluft RP. Washington, DC, American Psychiatric Press, 1990, pp 35–54

Schmale AH: Depression as affect, character style, and symptom formation, in Psychoanalysis and Contemporary Science, Vol 1. Edited by Holt RR, Peterfreund E. New York, Macmillan, 1972, pp 327–351

Schouten R: Allegations of sexual abuse: a new area of liability risk. Harvard Review of Psychiatry 1:350–352, 1994

Schreiber FR: Sybil. Chicago, IL, Regnery, 1973

Schwarz ED, Kowalski JM, McNally RJ: Malignant memories: post-traumatic changes in memory in adults after a school shooting. Journal of Traumatic Stress 6:545–553, 1993

Scott JP: The emotional basis of attachment and separation, in Attachment and the Therapeutic Process: Essays in Honor of Otto Allen Will, Jr., M.D. Edited by Sacksteder JL, Schwartz DP, Akabane Y. Madison, CT, International Universities Press, 1987, pp 43–62

Searle JR: The Rediscovery of the Mind. Cambridge, MA, MIT Press, 1992

Searles HF: The Nonhuman Environment, in Normal Development and in Schizophrenia. New York, International Universities Press, 1960

Segrin C, Abramson LY: Negative reactions to depressive behaviors: a communication theories analysis. J Abnorm Psychol 103:655–668, 1994

Seligman MEP: Helplessness: On Depression, Development, and Death. San Francisco, CA, Freeman, 1975

Seraganian P (ed): Exercise Physiology: The Influence of Physical Exercise on Psychological Processes. New York, Wiley, 1993

Shapiro DH Jr: Overview: clinical and physiological comparison of meditation with other self-control strategies. Am J Psychiatry 139:267–274, 1982

Shapiro DH Jr, Walsh RN (eds): Meditation: Classic and Contemporary Perspectives. New York, Aldine, 1984

Shearer SL: Dissociative phenomena in women with borderline personality disorder. Am J Psychiatry 151:1324–1328, 1994

Silk KR (ed): Biological and Neurobehavioral Studies of Borderline Personality Disorder. Washington, DC, American Psychiatric Press, 1994

Sime WE: Psychological benefits of exercise training in the healthy individual, in Behavioral Health: A Handbook of Health Enhancement and Disease Prevention. Edited by Matarazzo JD, Weiss SM, Herd JA, et al. New York, Wiley, 1984, pp 488–508

Simson PE, Weiss JM: Altered electrophysiology of the locus coeruleus following uncontrollable stress: relationship to anxiety and anxiolytic action, in Catecholamine Function in Posttraumatic Stress Disorder: Emerging Concepts. Edited by Marburg MM. Washington, DC, American Psychiatric Press, 1994, pp 63–86

Singer JL: Experimental studies of ongoing conscious experience, in Experimental and Theoretical Studies of Consciousness (Ciba Foundation Symposium 174). Edited by Bock GR, Marsh J. New York, Wiley, 1993, pp 100–122

Singer JL, Bonanno GA: Personality and private experience: individual variations in consciousness and in attention to subjective phenomena, in Handbook of Personality: Theory and Research. Edited by Pervin LA. New York, Guilford, 1990, pp 419–444

Sinnett KK: Foreword. Bull Menninger Clin 57:281–284, 1993

Slade A, Aber JL: Attachments, drives, and development: conflicts and convergences in theory, in Interface of Psychoanalysis and Psychology. Edited by Barron JW, Eagle MN, Wolitsky DL. Washington, DC, American Psychological Association, 1992, pp 154–185

Slovenko R: How criminal law has responded in multiple personality cases. Psychiatric Times, November 1991, pp 22, 25–26

Slovenko R: The "revival of memory" of childhood sexual abuse: is the tolling of the statute of limitations justified? Journal of Psychiatry and Law 21:7–34, 1993

Smith MC: Hypnotic memory enhancement of witnesses: does it work? Psychol Bull 94:387–407, 1983

Smith WH: Hypnosis in the treatment of anxiety. Bull Menninger Clin 54:209–216, 1990

Smith WH: Hypnotherapy with rape victims, in Handbook of Clinical Hypnosis. Edited by Rhue JW, Lynn SJ, Kirsch I. Washington, DC, American Psychological Association, 1993a, pp 479–491

Smith WH: Incorporating hypnosis into the psychotherapy of patients with multiple personality disorder. Bull Menninger Clin 57:344–354, 1993b

Solomon RL: The opponent-process theory of acquired motivation: the costs of pleasure and the benefits of pain. Am Psychol 35:691–712, 1980

Southwick SM, Krystal JH, Johnson DR, et al: Neurobiology of posttraumatic stress disorder, in American Psychiatric Press Review of Psychiatry, Vol 11. Edited by Tasman A, Riba MB. Washington, DC, American Psychiatric Press, 1992, pp 347–367

Southwick SM, Krystal JH, Morgan A, et al: Abnormal noradrenergic function in posttraumatic stress disorder. Arch Gen Psychiatry 50:266–274, 1993a

Southwick SM, Yehuda R, Giller EL Jr: Personality disorders in treatment-seeking combat veterans with posttraumatic stress disorder. Am J Psychiatry 150:1020–1023, 1993b

Southwick SM, Yehuda R, Giller EL Jr, et al: Use of tricyclics and monoamine oxidase inhibitors in the treatment of PTSD: a quantitative review, in Catecholamine Function in Posttraumatic Stress Disorder: Emerging Concepts. Edited by Murburg MM. Washington, DC, American Psychiatric Press, 1994, pp 293–305

Spence DP: Narrative Truth and Historical Truth: Meaning and Interpretation in Psychoanalysis. New York, WW Norton, 1982

Spence DP: Narrative truth and putative child abuse. Int J Clin Exp Hypn 42:289–303, 1994

Spiegel D: Dissociation and hypnosis in post-traumatic stress disorders. Journal of Traumatic Stress 1:17–33, 1988

Spiegel D: Hypnosis, dissociation, and trauma: hidden and overt observers, in Repression and Dissociation: Implications for Personality Theory, Psychopathology, and Health. Edited by Singer JL. Chicago, IL, University of Chicago Press, 1990, pp 121–142

Spiegel D: Dissociation and trauma, in American Psychiatric Press Review of Psychiatry, Vol 10. Edited by Tasman A, Goldfinger SM. Washington, DC, American Psychiatric Press, 1991a, pp 261–275

Spiegel D: Foreword, in American Psychiatric Press Review of Psychiatry, Vol 10. Edited by Tasman A, Goldfinger SM. Washington, DC, American Psychiatric Press, 1991b, pp 143–144

Spiegel D: Multiple posttraumatic personality disorder, in Clinical Perspectives on Multiple Personality Disorder. Edited by Kluft RP, Fine CG. Washington, DC, American Psychiatric Press, 1993, pp 87–99

Spiegel D, Scheflin AW: Dissociated or fabricated? psychiatric aspects of repressed memory in criminal and civil cases. Int J Clin Exp Hypn 42:411–432, 1994

Spiegel D, Frischholz EJ, Spira J: Functional disorders of memory, in American Psychiatric Press Review of Psychiatry, Vol 12. Edited by Oldham JM, Riba MB, Tasman A. Washington, DC, American Psychiatric Press, 1993, pp 747–782

Spiegel H: The grade 5 syndrome: the highly hypnotizable person. Int J Clin Exp Hypn 22:303–319, 1974

Squire LR: Memory and Brain. New York, Oxford University Press, 1987

Steinberg M: The spectrum of depersonalization: assessment and treatment, in American Psychiatric Press Review of Psychiatry, Vol 10. Edited by Tasman A, Goldfinger SM. Washington, DC, American Psychiatric Press, 1991, pp 223–247

Steinberg M: Interviewer's Guide to the Structured Clinical Interview for DSM-IV Dissociative Disorders (SCID-D), Revised. Washington, DC, American Psychiatric Press, 1994

Steinberg M: Handbook for the Assessment of Dissociation: A Clinical Guide. Washington, DC, American Psychiatric Press, 1995

Steinberg M, Rounsaville B, Cicchetti DV: The Structured Clinical Interview for DSM-III-R Dissociative Disorders: preliminary report on a new diagnostic instrument. Am J Psychiatry 147:76–82, 1990

Steinberg M, Rounsaville B, Cicchetti DV: Detection of dissociative disorders in psychiatric patients by a screening instrument and a structured diagnostic interview. Am J Psychiatry 148:1050–1054, 1991

Steinberg M, Bancroft J, Buchanan J: Multiple personality disorder in criminal law. Bull Am Acad Psychiatry Law 21:345–356, 1993

Steinmeyer SM: Some hard-learned lessons in milieu management of multiple personality disorder. The Psychiatric Hospital 22:1–4, 1991

Stern DN: The Interpersonal World of the Infant: A View From Psychoanalysis and Developmental Psychology. New York, Basic Books, 1985

Stern DN: The representation of relational patterns: developmental considerations, in Relationship Disturbances in Early Childhood: A Developmental Approach. Edited by Sameroff AJ, Emde RN. New York, Basic Books, 1989, pp 52–69

Stern DN: Diary of a Baby. New York, Basic Books, 1990

Stevens-Simon C, Reichert S: Sexual abuse, adolescent pregnancy, and child abuse: a developmental approach to an intergenerational cycle. Arch Pediatr Adolesc Med 148:23–27, 1994

Stone MH: Incest in the borderline patient, in Incest-Related Syndromes of Adult Psychopathology. Edited by Kluft RP. Washington, DC, American Psychiatric Press, 1990, pp 183–204

Strentz T: The Stockholm Syndrome: law enforcement policy and hostage behavior, in Victims of Terrorism. Edited by Ochberg FM, Soskis DA. Boulder, CO, Westview Press, 1982, pp 149–163

Summit RC: The child sexual abuse accommodation syndrome. Child Abuse Negl 7:177–193, 1983

Summit RC: Abuse of the child sexual abuse accommodation syndrome. Journal of Child Sexual Abuse 1:153–163, 1992

Symonds M: Victim responses to terror: understanding and treatment, in Victims of Terrorism. Edited by Ochberg FM, Soskis DA. Boulder, CO, Westview Press, 1982, pp 95–103

Taylor GJ: Psychosomatics and self-regulation, in Interface of Psychoanalysis and Psychology. Edited by Barron JW, Eagle MN, Wolitsky DL. Washington, DC, American Psychological Association, 1992, pp 464–488

Taylor SE: Positive Illusions: Creative Self-Deception and the Healthy Mind. New York, Basic Books, 1989

Terr L: What happens to early memories of trauma? a study of twenty children under age five at the time of documented traumatic events. J Am Acad Child Adolesc Psychiatry 27:96–104, 1988

Terr L: Childhood traumas: an outline and overview. Am J Psychiatry 148:10–20, 1991

Terr L: True memories of childhood trauma: quirks, absences, and returns. Paper presented at the 102nd Annual Convention of the American Psychological Association, Los Angeles, CA, 1994a

Terr L: Unchained Memories: True Stories of Traumatic Memories, Lost and Found. New York, Basic Books, 1994b

Thase ME, Beck AT: An overview of cognitive therapy, in Cognitive Therapy With Inpatients: Developing a Cognitive Milieu. Edited by Wright JH, Thase ME, Beck AT, et al. New York, Guilford, 1993, pp 3–34

Thigpen C, Cleckley H: The Three Faces of Eve. New York, McGraw-Hill, 1957

Thomas L: Late Night Thoughts on Listening to Mahler's Ninth Symphony. New York, Viking, 1983

Thomas L: The Fragile Species. New York, Macmillan, 1992

Thompson RF: The Brain: A Neuroscience Primer, 2nd Edition. New York, Freeman, 1993

Tillman JG, Nash MR, Lerner PM: Does trauma cause dissociative pathology?, in Dissociation: Clinical and Theoretical Perspectives. Edited by Lynn SJ, Rhue JW. New York, Guilford, 1994, pp 395–414

Torem MS: Recognition and management of dissociative regressions. Hypnos 16:197–213, 1989

Torem MS: Covert multiple personality underlying eating disorders. Am J Psychother 44:357–368, 1990

Torem MS: Eating disorders in patients with multiple personality disorder, in Clinical Perspectives on Multiple Personality Disorder. Edited by Kluft RP, Fine CG. Washington, DC, American Psychiatric Press, 1993a, pp 343–353

Torem MS: The perils of extremism and the wisdom of moderation. ISSMP & D News, June 1993b, pp 1–2

Trimble MR: Post-traumatic stress disorder: history of a concept, in Trauma and Its Wake: The Study and Treatment of Post-Traumatic Stress Disorder. Edited by Figley CR. New York, Brunner/Mazel, 1985, pp 5–14

True WR, Rice J, Eisen SA, et al: A twin study of genetic and environmental contributions to liability for posttraumatic stress symptoms. Arch Gen Psychiatry 50:257–264, 1993

Tulving E: Episodic and semantic memory, in Organization of Memory. Edited by Tulving E, Donaldson W. New York, Academic Press, 1972, pp 381–403

Turns DM, Blumenreich PE: Epidemiology, in Managing the Violent Patient: A Clinician's Guide. Edited by Blumenreich PE, Lewis S. New York, Brunner/Mazel, 1993, pp 5–20

Usher JA, Neisser U: Childhood amnesia and the beginnings of memory for four early life events. Journal of Experimental Psychology: General 122:155–165, 1993

van der Hart O, Brown P: Abreaction re-evaluated. Dissociation 5:127–140, 1992

van der Hart O, Friedman B: A reader's guide to Pierre Janet on dissociation: a neglected intellectual heritage. Dissociation 2:3–16, 1989

van der Hart O, Spiegel D: Hypnotic assessment and treatment of trauma-induced psychoses: the early psychotherapy of H. Bruekink and modern views. Int J Clin Exp Hypn 41:191–209, 1993

van der Kolk BA: The psychological consequences of overwhelming life experiences, in Psychological Trauma. Edited by van der Kolk BA. Washington, DC, American Psychiatric Press, 1987a, pp 1–30

van der Kolk BA: The role of the group in the origin and resolution of the trauma response, in Psychological Trauma. Edited by van der Kolk BA. Washington, DC, American Psychiatric Press, 1987b, pp 153–171

van der Kolk BA: The separation cry and the trauma response: developmental issues in the psychobiology of attachment and separation, in Psychological Trauma. Edited by van der Kolk BA. Washington, DC, American Psychiatric Press, 1987c, pp 31–62

van der Kolk BA: The compulsion to repeat the trauma: re-enactment, revictimization, and masochism. Psychiatr Clin North Am 12:389–411, 1989

van der Kolk BA: Biological considerations about emotions, trauma, memory, and the brain, in Human Feelings: Explorations in Affect Development and Meaning. Edited by Ablon SL, Brown D, Khantzian EJ, et al. Hillsdale, NJ, Analytic Press, 1993, pp 221–240

van der Kolk BA: The body keeps the score: memory and the evolving psychobiology of post traumatic stress. Harvard Review of Psychiatry 1:253–265, 1994

van der Kolk BA, Fisler RE: Childhood abuse and neglect and loss of self-regulation. Bull Menninger Clin 58:145–168, 1994

van der Kolk BA, Kadish W: Amnesia, dissociation, and the return of the repressed, in Psychological Trauma. Edited by van der Kolk BA. Washington, DC, American Psychiatric Press, 1987, pp 173–190 van der Kolk BA, Saporta J: The biological response to psychic trauma: mechanisms and treatment of intrusion and numbing. Anxiety Research 4:199–212, 1991

van der Kolk BA, van der Hart O: The intrusive past: the flexibility of memory and the engraving of trauma. American Imago 48:425–454, 1991

van der Kolk BA, Greenberg MS, Orr SP, et al: Endogenous opioids, stress induced analgesia, and posttraumatic stress disorder. Psychopharmacology Bulletin 25:417–421, 1989

van der Kolk BA, Perry JC, Herman JL: Childhood origins of self-destructive behavior. Am J Psychiatry 148:1666–1671, 1991

van Praag HM: "Make-Believes" in Psychiatry, or The Perils of Progress. New York, Brunner/Mazel, 1993

Varela FJ, Thompson E, Rosch E: The Embodied Mind: Cognitive Science and Human Experience. Cambridge, MA, MIT Press, 1991

Veith RC, Marburg MM: Assessment of sympathetic nervous system function in PTSD: a critique of methodology, in Catecholamine Function in Posttraumatic Stress Disorder: Emerging Concepts. Edited by Marburg MM. Washington, DC, American Psychiatric Press, 1994, pp 309–333

Vincent J-D: The Biology of Emotions (1986). Translated by Hughes J. Cambridge, MA, Basil Blackwell, 1990

Wakefield H, Underwager R: Recovered memories of alleged sexual abuse: lawsuits against parents. Behavioral Sciences and the Law 10:483–507, 1992

Waldinger RJ, Swett C Jr., Frank A, et al: Levels of dissociation and histories of reported abuse among women outpatients. J Nerv Ment Dis 182:625–630, 1994

Walker LE: The Battered Woman. New York, Harper & Row, 1979

Waller G: Sexual abuse as a factor in eating disorders. Br J Psychiatry 159:664–671, 1991

Waller G, Halek C, Crisp AH: Sexual abuse as a factor in anorexia nervosa: evidence from two separate case series. J Psychosom Res 37:873–879, 1993a

Waller G, Ruddock A, Pitts C: When is sexual abuse relevant to bulimic disorders? the validity of clinical judgments. European Eating Disorders Review 1:143–151, 1993b

Walsh BW, Rosen PM: Self-Mutilation: Theory, Research, and Treatment. New York, Guilford, 1988

Watkins JG: Hypnotherapy of War Neuroses: A Clinical Psychologist's Casebook. New York, Ronald Press, 1949

Watkins JG: The affect bridge: a hypnoanalytic technique. Int J Clin Exp Hypn 19:21–27, 1971

Watson D, Clark LA: Extraversion and its positive emotional core, in Handbook of Personality Psychology. Edited by Hogan R, Johnson J, Briggs S. San Diego, CA, Academic Press, in press

Watson D, Clark LA, Harkness AR: Structures of personality and their relevance to psychopathology. J Abnorm Psychol 103:18–31, 1994

Watts AW: The Way of Zen. New York, Random House, 1957

Weaver TL, Clum GA: Early family environments and traumatic experiences associated with borderline personality disorder. J Consult Clin Psychol 61:1068–1075, 1993

Webster's New Twentieth Century Dictionary of the English Language, Unabridged, 2nd Edition. New York, Simon & Schuster, 1983

Weekes JR, Lynn SJ, Green JP, et al: Pseudomemory in hypnotized and task-motivated subjects. J Abnorm Psychol 101:356–360, 1992

Wegner DM, Erber R: The hyperaccessibility of suppressed thoughts. J Pers Soc Psychol 63:903–912, 1992

Weiner H: Perturbing the Organism: The Biology of Stressful Experience. Chicago, IL, University of Chicago Press, 1992

Weissberg M: Multiple personality disorder and iatrogenesis: the cautionary tale of Anna O. Int J Clin Exp Hypn 41:15–34, 1993

Welch SL, Fairburn CG: Sexual abuse and bulimia nervosa: three integrated case control comparisons. Am J Psychiatry 151:402–407, 1994

Westerlund E: Women's Sexuality After Childhood Incest. New York, WW Norton, 1992

Wetzler SE, Sweeney JA: Childhood amnesia: an empirical demonstration, in Autobiographical Memory. Edited by Rubin DC. New York, Cambridge University Press, 1986, pp 191–201

Whybrow PC: Neuroendocrinology, in Biological Bases of Brain Function and Disease. Edited by Frazer A, Molinoff PB, Winokur A. New York, Raven, 1994, pp 143–162

Williams LM: Recall of childhood trauma: a prospective study of women's memories of child sexual abuse. Paper presented at the Annual Meeting of the American Society of Criminology, Phoenix, AZ, October 27, 1993

Williams MB: Clinical work with families of MPD patients: assessment and issues for practice. Dissociation 4:92–98, 1991

Wills C: Exons, Introns, and Talking Genes: The Science Behind the Human Genome Project. New York, Basic Books, 1991

Wilson SC, Barber TX: The fantasy-prone personality: implications for understanding imagery, hypnosis, and parapsychological phenomena, in Imagery: Current Theory, Research, and Application. Edited by Sheikh AA. New York, Wiley, 1983, pp 340–387

Winnicott DW: Aggression in relation to emotional development (1950), in Collected Papers: Through Paediatrics to Psycho-Analysis. London, Tavistock, 1958, pp 204–218

Wolff PH: The Development of Behavioral States and the Expression of Emotions in Early Infancy: New Proposals for Investigation. Chicago, IL, University of Chicago Press, 1987

Wolfner GD, Gelles RJ: A profile of violence toward children: a national study. Child Abuse Negl 17:197–212, 1993

Wylie MS: The shadow of a doubt. Family Therapy Networker September/October 1993, pp 18–29, 70, 73

Yalom ID: The Theory and Practice of Group Psychotherapy. New York, Basic Books, 1970

Yalom ID: Existential Psychotherapy. New York, Basic Books, 1980

Young WC: Psychodynamics and dissociation: all that switches is not split. Dissociation 1:33–38, 1988

Young WC, Sachs RG, Braun BG, et al: Patients reporting ritual abuse in childhood: a clinical syndrome: report of 37 cases. Child Abuse Negl 15:181–189, 1991

Zeanah CH, Anders TF, Seifer R, et al: Implications of research on infant development for psychodynamic theory and practice. J Am Acad Child Adolesc Psychiatry 28:657–668, 1989

Zerbe KJ: The Body Betrayed: Women, Eating Disorders, and Treatment. Washington, DC, American Psychiatric Press, 1993a

Zerbe KJ: Selves that starve and suffocate: the continuum of eating disorders and dissociative phenomena. Bull Menninger Clin 57:319–327, 1993b

Index

*Page numbers in **boldface** type refer to figures or tables.*

Anger *(continued)*
shame and, 61
shame-rage spiral and, 61
Anxiety, 69–70
behavioral inhibition and, 51
case example of, 94–95
exercise and, 280–281
relaxation induced, 69–70
self-regulation and, 275
Anxiety disorders, 216–218
generalized anxiety, 216–217
panic and, 217
phobia and, 217–218
PTSD and, 216–271, 217–218
Attachment, 35–48
arousal and, 46–47
child development and, 36–37
disruption of, 44–45
experiences of, 43–44
pattern of, 43
reciprocity and, 42–43
restoration of security and,
47–48
secure base and, 37–38
strange situation and, 38–39, 40,
41
support system and, 35–36
theory of, 36
types of
disorganized, 41–42
insecure, 39–40
secure, 39, 43–44, 47–48
vicious circles and, 42–43
Attias, Reina, 226
Autobiographical memory,
100–103, 103, 104–105, 106,
107, 303–304

Avoidance, 178–179, 305–306
PTSD and, 178–179
Bartlett, Sir Frederic, 101
Beahrs, John, 207–208
Becker, Judith, 223
Behavioral inhibition, 51, 65–66
Benson, Herbert, 281–282
Biochemistry of the brain, 313–315
Biofeedback, 293–296
Borderline personality disorder,
227–230
etiology of, 229–230
PTSD and, 228–229
sexual abuse and, 229
symptoms of, 228
Bowlby, John, 36–37, 37–38, 44, 47,
98, 152–153
Brain, 315–319
biochemistry of, 313–315
mind and, 30–31, 301
Braun, Bennet, 86–87
Buchele, Bonnie, 250
Burgess, Ann, 223
Cannon, Walter, 29
Carlson, Eve, 209
Case example, 18–19, 19–20,
20–21, 24, 26–27, 51, 59,
61–62, 73–74, 77, 89–90,
93–94, 94–95, 118–119, 122,
127, 134, 139, 142, 155,
175–176, 177–178, 194,
195–197, 204–205, 205–206,
211, 252
Catharsis, 123
abreaction and, 243–244
Chu, James, 236–237
Cognitive therapy, 67–69

Self-regulation *(continued)*
overcoming difficulties with,
268–270
positive emotions and, 270–278
practice and, 268–269
self-concept and, 269–270
self-control and, 267–268
Self-understanding, 123–124
Seligman, Martin, 62–63, 63–64
Sensitization, 245
Separation, 28
Sexual abuse, 10–11
amnesia and, 108–109
borderline personality disorder
and, 229
in childhood, 10–11, 108–109
eating disorders and, 227
memory and, 117
Sexual dysfunction, 222–225
incest and, 224–225
rape and, 223–224
Shame, 59–60, 61
Shame-rage spiral, 61
Smith, William H., 121–122
Somatization disorder, 220–222
diagnosis of, 220
ill health and, 221–222
stress and, 220–221
symptoms of, 221
Spectrum of accuracy, 110–111
Steinberg, Marlene, 209–210
Stern, Daniel, 133–134, 153
Structured Clinical Interview,
209–210
Substance abuse, 219–220
avoidance behavior and,
219–220

PTSD and, 219
Suicide, 141–143
etiology of, 142
self-destructiveness and,
141–143
self-mutilation and, 141–142
Taylor, Shelley, 136–137
Temperament, 64–66
behavioral inhibition and, 65–66
dimensions of, 64–65, 66
personality and, 64–66
Terr, Lenore, 182
Therapeutic alliance, 238–239,
239–242
individual psychotherapy and,
238–239, 239–242
obstacles to, 239–242
boundary difficulties, 240–242
dependency, 240
distrust, 240
Thomas, Lewis, 124–125, 271–272
Trauma, 3–16
attachment and, 35–48
avoidance and, 3
biology of, 311–321
conclusions about, 299–310
consciousness and, 73–88
definition of, 4
development and, 17–31
dissociative disorders and,
191–214
emotion and, 49–71
environmental factors and,
300–301
examples of, 5–6
genetic factors and, 312–313
memory and, 89–125